TEXAS
ITS LAND AND ITS PEOPLE

JAMES KILLORAN

STUART ZIMMER

MARK JARRETT

JARRETT PUBLISHING COMPANY

East Coast Office
19 Cross Street
Lake Ronkonkoma, NY 11779
516-981-4248

Texas Office
15643 Pebble Lake Drive
Houston, TX 77095
713-463-8357

West Coast Office
10 Folin Lane
Lafayette, CA 94549
510-906-9742

1-800-859-7679 ★ Fax: 516-588-4722

ACKNOWLEDGMENTS

The authors wish to acknowledge the help of **Dr. Joel Fischer,** who provided ideas for some of the activities and many suggestions on improving the manuscript. The authors also wish to thank **Vernon Cannamore,** Coordinator of Social Studies, Galena Park I.S.D., for his suggestions and advice regarding the needs of Texas educators. Several teachers from Texas also reviewed this book. Their comments, suggestions and recommendations proved invaluable. These teachers are:

- **Laura Bridges:** Tice Elementary School, Galena Park I.S.D.
- **Irma Ponce Herández:** Coldwell Elementary-Middle School, El Paso I.S.D.
- **Lyn Ann Baker-Orduna:** Fiest Elementary School, Cypress-Fairbanks I.S.D.
- **Sherry Sanders:** Central Elementary School, Duncanville I.S.D.
- **Jim Wilkerson:** Glenoaks Elementary, Northside I.S.D.

In addition, we would like thank **Dr. Neil Foley,** Assistant Professor of History at the University of Texas at Austin and **Dr. Gary McKenzie,** Associate Professor of Education at the University of Texas at Austin. Both of them reviewed the manuscript and offered important suggestions. Dr. McKenzie suggested the mnemonic devices on page 5, and the ABC's of Culture on page 52. We would also like to thank **Anne Cooke** at the Texas Department of Transportation and **Diane Bruce** at the University of Texas, Texas Institute of Cultures. Both contributed to the visual elements in this book. Finally, the authors would like to thank Julie Fleck and Hanna Kisiel for their many suggestions and insightful comments on the manuscript.

Cover design by Burmar Technical Corporation, Albertson, N.Y.
Illustrations by Ronald Scott Zimmer.
Maps and graphics by C.F. Enterprises and Burmar Technical Corporation.
Layout and typesetting: Burmar Technical Corporation, Albertson, N.Y.

This book is dedicated to ...

my wife Donna, and my children Christian, Carrie, and Jesse. .... *James Killoran*
my wife Joan, and my children Todd and Ronald. .... *Stuart Zimmer*
my wife Goska, and my children Alexander and Julia. .... *Mark Jarrett*

ISBN 1-882422-20-1

Printed in the United States of America
First Edition

ABOUT THE AUTHORS

James Killoran, a retired Assistant Principal in New York City, has written *Ohio: Its Land and Its People; Ohio: Its Neighbors, Near and Far; Mastering Ohio's 9th Grade Citizenship Test;* and *Mastering Ohio's 12th Grade Citizenship Test.* In addition, he has written *Mastering Global Studies; Mastering U.S. History and Government; Government and You; Economics and You; The Key To Understanding Global Studies; The Key To Understanding U.S. History and Government; Nuestro Mundo: Su Historia, Sus Culturas; Los Estados Unidos: Su Historia, Su Gobierno; Principios De Economía;* and *Historia Y Gobierno De Los Estados Unidos.* Mr. Killoran has extensive experience in test writing for the New York State Board of Regents in Social Studies and has served on the Committee for Testing of the National Council of Social Studies. His article on social studies testing has been published in *Social Education,* the country's leading social studies journal. In addition, Mr. Killoran has won a number of awards for outstanding teaching and curriculum development, including, "Outstanding Social Studies Teacher" and "Outstanding Social Studies Supervisor" in New York City. In 1993, he was awarded an Advanced Certificate for Teachers of Social Studies by the National Council of Social Studies.

Stuart Zimmer, a retired New York City Social Studies teacher, has written *Ohio: Its Land and Its People; Ohio: Its Neighbors, Near and Far; Mastering Ohio's 9th Grade Citizenship Test;* and *Mastering Ohio's 12th Grade Citizenship Test.* In addition, he has written *Mastering Global Studies; Mastering U.S. History and Government; Government and You; Economics and You; The Key To Understanding Global Studies; The Key To Understanding U.S. History and Government; Nuestro Mundo: Su Historia, Sus Culturas; Los Estados Unidos: Su Historia, Su Gobierno; Principios De Economía;* and *Historia Y Gobierno De Los Estados Unidos.* Mr. Zimmer has served as a test writer for the New York State Board of Regents in Social Studies, and has written for the National Merit Scholarship Examination. He has published numerous articles on teaching and testing in Social Studies journals. He has presented many demonstrations and educational workshops at state and national teachers' conferences. In addition, Mr. Zimmer's achievements were recognized by the New York State Legislature with a Special Legislative Resolution in his honor.

Mark Jarrett is a former Social Studies teacher and a practicing attorney at the San Francisco office of Baker and McKenzie. He has written numerous books, among them *Ohio: Its Land and Its People; Ohio: Its Neighbors, Near and Far; Mastering Ohio's 9th Grade Citizenship Test;* and *Mastering Ohio's 12th Grade Citizenship Test.* In addition, he has written *Mastering Global Studies; Mastering U.S. History and Government; The Key To Understanding Global Studies; The Key To Understanding U.S. History and Government; Nuestro Mundo: Su Historia, Sus Culturas; Los Estados Unidos: Su Historia, Su Gobierno; Principios De Economía;* and *Historia Y Gobierno De Los Estados Unidos.* Mr. Jarrett has served as a test writer for the New York State Board of Regents, and has taught at Hofstra University. He was educated at Columbia University, the London School of Economics, the Law School of the University of California at Berkeley, and Stanford University, where he is a doctoral candidate in history.

PHOTO CREDITS

This book includes written material and pictures from many different sources. Occasionally it is not possible to determine if a particular source or picture is copyrighted, and if so, who is the copyright owner. If there has been a copyright infringement with any material produced in this book, it has been unintentional. We extend our sincerest apologies and would be happy to make immediate and appropriate restitution upon proof of copyright ownership.

TDOT=Texas Department of Transportation; IOTC=Institute of Texan Cultures; LOC=Library of Congress; NA=National Archives; t=top; m=middle; b=bottom; r=right; l=left; c=center

Cover: Battle of San Jacinto Monument, San Jacinto Battlefield State Park (TDOT)

Chapter 2 / Geography. **Page 18:** TDOT; **Pg. 30:** TDOT; **Pg. 32:** TDOT; **Pg. 37:** TDOT; **Pg. 39:** (t) TDOT, (b) TDOT; **Pg. 40:** TDOT; **Pg. 42:** TDOT; **Pg. 43:** (t) TDOT, (b) TDOT; **Pg. 44:** (t) TDOT, (b) TDOT; **Pg. 46:** (t) TDOT, (m) TDOT, (b) TDOT; **Pg. 52:** TDOT; **Pg. 54:** Mexican Government Tourism Office; **Pg. 56:** Ford Motor Corp.; **Pg. 65:** LOC.

Chapter 3 / American Heritage. **Page 73:** (t) IOTC, (l) IOTC, (b) IOTC; **Pg. 75:** IOTC; **Pg. 76:** (t) LOC, (b) IOTC ; **Pg. 78:** IOTC; **Pg. 79:** (t) IOTC, (b) NA; **Pg. 80:** LOC; **Pg. 81:** (t) LOC, (b) IOTC; **Pg. 83:** (t) IOTC, (b) IOTC; **Pg. 84:** IOTC; **Pg. 85:** (t) IOTC, (b) IOTC; **Pg. 87:** (t) IOTC, (b) IOTC; **Pg. 91:** Bureau of Engraving and Printing; **Pg. 92:** IOTC; **Pg. 94:** NA; **Pg. 95:** LOC; **Pg. 96:** NA; **Pg. 97:** LOC; **Pg. 99:** IOTC; **Pg. 100:** LOC; **Pg. 102:** IOTC; **Pg. 103:** (t) IOTC, (b) LOC; **Pg. 105:** (t) TDOT, (b) TDOT; **Pg. 106:** IOTC; **Pg. 108:** IOTC; **Pg. 109:** LOC; **Pg. 110:** IOTC; **Pg. 111:** (l) LOC, (r) LOC; (b) LOC; **Pg. 114:** IOTC; **Pg. 115:** LOC; **Pg. 117:** New York Public Library; **Pg. 118:** NA; **Pg. 122:** TDOT; **Pg. 123:** LOC; **Pg. 126:** NA; **Pg. 130:** IOTC; **Pg. 135:** TDOT; **Pg. 137:** LOC; **Pg. 138:** IOTC; **Pg. 139:** IOTC; **Pg. 141:** LOC; **Pg. 142:** LOC; **Pg. 146:** LOC; **Pg. 151:** IOTC; **Pg. 155:** NA; **Pg. 156:** IOTC; **Pg. 158:** (t & b) Six Flags Over Texas, Corporation; **Pg. 159:** TDOT; **Pg. 160:** (l & r) Six Flags Over Texas Corporation; **Pg. 164:** TDOT; **Pg. 172:** TDOT; **Pg. 173:** TDOT; **Pg. 175:** Mexican Government Tourism Office; **Pg. 176:** Peter Fleck Collection; **Pg. 180:** TDOT.

Chapter 4 / People In Society. **Page 183:** (t) LOC, (m) TDOT, (b) IOTC; **Pg. 187:** TDOT; **Pg. 188:** (t) TDOT, (b) TDOT; **Pg. 189:** (t) IOTC, (b) TDOT; **Pg. 190:** TDOT; **Pg. 191:** TDOT; **Pg. 192:** TDOT; **Pg. 194:** (t) TDOT, (b) TDOT; **Pg. 195:** TDOT; **Pg. 196:** (t) TDOT, (b) TDOT; **Pg. 199:** TDOT; **Pg. 200:** IOTC; **Pg. 202:** TDOT; **Pg. 203:** TDOT; **Pg. 204:** IOTC; **Pg. 205:** LOC; **Pg. 206:** IOTC; **Pg. 207:** LOC; **Pg. 208:** (t) TDOT, (b) IOTC; **Pg. 209:** TDOT; **Page 210:** (t) TDOT, (b) IOTC; **Pg. 211:** (t) IOTC, (b) IOTC; **Pg. 212:** (t) LOC, (b) TDOT; **Pg. 213:** IOTC; **Pg. 214:** TDOT; **Pg. 216:** (t) LOC, (b) United Nations; **Pg. 222:** (t) IOTC, (b) NA; **Pg. 223:** L.B.J. Presidential Library; **Pg. 229:** LOC; **Pg. 230:** (t) LOC (b) IOTC; **Pg. 232:** (t) Zimmer Collection, (b) TDOT; **Pg. 234:** (t) Jarrett Collection, (b) IOTC; **Pg. 235:** TDOT; **Pg. 236:** IOTC; **Pg. 240:** Collection of the U.S. Supreme Court.

Chapter 5 / Economics. **Page 243:** (t) TDOT, ((b) TDOT, (m) TDOT; **Pg. 246:** (l) TDOT, (r) TDOT; **Pg. 251:** TDOT; **Pg. 255:** (t) TDOT, (b) TDOT; **Pg. 256:** (t) TDOT, (m) Zimmer Collection, (b) Ford Motor Company; **Pg. 257:** Zimmer Collection; **Pg. 259:** TDOT; **Pg. 262:** TDOT; **Pg. 263:** (l) TDOT, (r) TDOT, (b) TDOT; **Pg. 264:** TDOT; **Pg. 265:** TDOT; **Pg. 266:** TDOT; **Pg. 267:** (t) TDOT, (b) TDOT; **Pg. 268:** TDOT; **Pg. 273:** TDOT; **Pg. 274:** TDOT; **Pg. 275:** Stewart Milstein, photographer; **Pg. 276:** Japanese National Tourist Office.

Chapter 6 / Government. **Page 283:** (t) TDOT, ((b) IOTC, (m) White House; **Pg. 286:** Stewart Milstein, photographer; **Pg. 287:** LOC; **Pg. 288:** (t) United Nations, (m,t) LOC, (m,b) LOC, (b,r) LOC; **Pg. 289:** (t) LOC, (m) LOC, (b) LOC; **Pg. 290:** (t) LOC, (m) LOC, (b) LOC; **Pg. 291:** (t) LOC, (m) LOC, (b) LOC; **Pg. 296:** (t) Bureau of Engraving and Printing, (b) NA; **Pg. 297:** IOTC; **Pg. 298:** (t) LOC, (m) IOTC, (b) IOTC; **Pg. 301:** Zimmer Collection; **Pg. 308:** IOTC; **Pg. 311:** IOTC; **Pg. 312:** IOTC; **Pg. 316:** United Nations; **Pg. 320:** Stewart Milstein, photographer.

Chapter 7 / Citizenship. **Page 322:** (t) TDOT, (b) NA, (m) Collection of the U.S. Supreme Court; **Pg. 324:** NA; **Pg. 331:** LOC; **Pg. 330:** IOTC; **Pg. 332:** (t) LOC, (b) LOC; **Pg. 334:** (t) Lyndon B. Johnson Presidential Library, (b) IOTC; **Pg. 335:** LOC; **Pg. 337:** NA; **Pg. 338:** LOC; **Pg. 339:** (l & r) Stewart Milstein, photographer; **Pg. 345:** United Nations; **Pg. 346:** LOC; **Pg. 349:** United Nations.

Closing Activity. **Pg. 362:** TDOT.

TABLE OF CONTENTS

OPENING ACTIVITY

THE IMAGE I HAVE OF TEXAS IS __?__.

This school year you will learn about the state where you live—Texas. The authors of this book hope you will enjoy your journey through its pages. As you travel through this book, you will be involved in many new and interesting learning activities.

IMPORTANT NOTE

This is an interactive textbook. It asks you to participate in many exciting activities as you learn the information in the chapters. Even though there are empty spaces on some pages, this book is **not to be written in.** Instead, all writing should be done on a separate piece of paper or in a notebook.

WHAT DOES "TEXAS" MEAN TO YOU?

Before we start our journey together, let's find out what images or thoughts **you** have about Texas. Millions of people around the world have an image of Texas as a place where cowboys ride horses. When some people hear the word "Texas" they may think of Tex-Mex food. Others think about a huge state—big and bold. Still others think of oil and millionaires. But let's find out what you think—What does Texas mean to **YOU?**

THINK ABOUT IT

When you hear the word "Texas" list the images and thoughts this word brings to mind.

When I think of Texas, I think of ...

After you have completed your list of images and thoughts, compare your thoughts about Texas with those of your classmates.

Now you are ready to begin your journey. The first chapter of this book will give you some handy tools to help you study—making your trip a more pleasant one. Later chapters will introduce you to the geography, history, culture, government and economy of Texas.

CHAPTER 1

STUDYING FOR SUCCESS

Social Studies is exciting and fun because it teaches you about people and how they relate to one another. You also learn about the past and how we came to be what we are today. In this book, you will learn about Texas and the Western Hemisphere. There will be many facts and ideas for you to learn and digest. You will need to participate actively in the learning process by reading, by doing activities and by studying. This chapter focuses on ways to study for success. You can learn new information both by visualizing this information and by using mnemonics—hints to help you remember facts.

VISUALIZING IMPORTANT INFORMATION

Social Studies involves knowledge of many important terms and ideas. How can you be expected to remember them all? To help learn new information, you will be asked to complete two **Vocabulary Cards** at the end of each activity in this book.

Vocabulary Cards are index cards with information on them. They are used to summarize important terms and ideas. As you go through this book, you will develop your own set of cards to use for studying. The Vocabulary Cards are divided into two parts:

- ☆ **Front of the card.** This is for writing about the term or idea.
- ☆ **Back of the card.** This is used to draw a picture about the term or idea.

THE FRONT OF THE CARD: WRITTEN INFORMATION

On the front of each card, you will be asked to describe or define a term or idea. Based upon what the term or idea is, each card asks you for different information. The following are two examples of Vocabulary Cards.

When you have to learn a specific term, like the **Texas Declaration of Independence,** you should describe it and then explain its importance. Often, these Vocabulary Cards will have specific questions for you to answer.

Example #1

Texas Declaration of Independence

What is it? (Description)

A document written mainly by George Childress on March 2, 1836 that declared Texas free from Mexican control.

Why was it written? (Question)

The Anglo-American colonists in Texas wanted to announce to the world their reasons for declaring independence from Mexico, and their ideas about how governments should act.

When you are learning about an idea, like **democracy,** you will usually be asked to define the idea and to give an example of it.

Example #2

Democracy

What is it? (Definition)

Democracy is a form of government in which citizens have a voice in the decisions that are made. This is usually done by citizens voting for people to represent them in the government.

Give an example: (Example)

The government of Texas

THE BACK OF THE CARD: VISUAL INFORMATION

Pictures are often easier to remember than words. You are asked to draw a picture on the back of each card, illustrating the information on the front. Making your ideas into pictures will help test your understanding and help you to remember. Let's see what the information on these two Vocabulary Cards might look like when put into picture form.

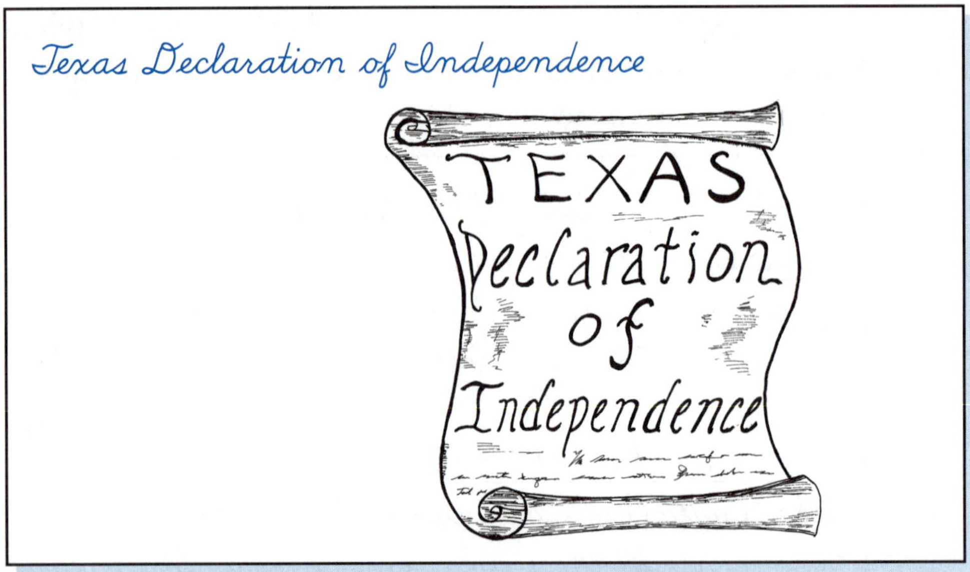

At the end of each activity in this book, you will find two terms or ideas to use for filling out Vocabulary Cards. By the end of this book, you will have a complete set of cards to help you prepare for any test in fourth grade Social Studies.

USING MNEMONICS

Another way to learn and remember factual information is to use mnemonic devices. **Mnemonics** are rhymes and other verbal tricks that help you to remember things. Mnemonic devices are especially useful when you have to learn the names of items on a list—such as planets, continents, cities, rivers or important historical events.

THE KEY WORD METHOD

With the key word method, you think of a key word for each name you must learn. For example, you might have to learn the names and locations of three cities in Texas—Amarillo, El Paso and Brownsville.

1. **Think of a word that rhymes with or reminds you of the name of each city:**
   - ☆ Amarillo–armadillo
   - ☆ El Paso–elbow
   - ☆ Brownsville–down
2. **Now visualize these rhyming words together to form a common picture that will help you to remember them. For instance:**

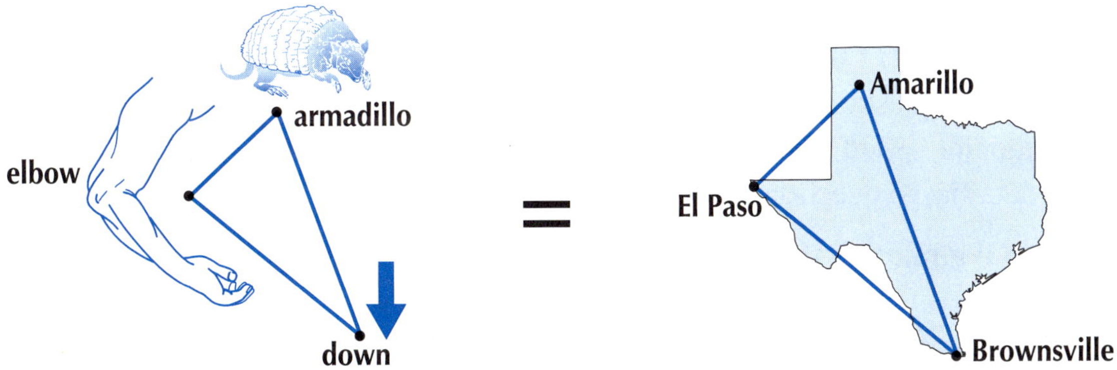

THE KEY SENTENCE METHOD

A second mnemonic technique is to take the first letter of each name you have to learn, and make a sentence or a word with all the first letters. **States Bordering Texas**

- ☆ New Mexico
- ☆ Oklahoma
- ☆ Arkansas
- ☆ Louisiana

Create a key sentence, such as "**N**ine **o**wls **a**re **l**ate." This is done by using the first letter of each name on the list. The key sentence helps your memory recall the four states that border Texas.

Another helpful mnemonic is to form a word by using the first letter of each name on the list. The word might be one such as L-O-A-N. Using the letters as clues, it will help you to recall the whole list.

ANSWERING MULTIPLE-CHOICE QUESTIONS

Taking tests is one of the tasks all students must do. Many of these tests will have multiple-choice questions. Following are some hints for answering them.

WHAT THE QUESTION WILL LOOK LIKE

A multiple-choice question is usually followed by a list of four possible answers. Only one of the answers is correct. The others are wrong. You must choose the correct answer.

There are two kinds of multiple-choice questions: statement questions and data-based questions.

☆ **STATEMENT QUESTIONS.** These questions test your knowledge of specific information. The question will be either a complete sentence or an incomplete one, followed by a list of possible answers. Here is an example of a statement question.

1. Which of the following people is producing something?

A. Joan is playing with her cat.
B. Sam is building a house.
C. José is eating lunch.
D. Fran is watching a movie.

> The answer is **B.** Sam is the only one producing, or making, something.

☆ **DATA-BASED QUESTIONS.** Some data or information is used to introduce a data-based question. The data can be a map, a timeline, a graph or a reading. You will then be asked to use the data to choose the right answer. Here is an example of a data-based question:

2. Use the map on the right to answer question 2.

You live in San Antonio. If you wanted to visit an aunt in Wichita Falls, in which direction would you need to travel?

A. north
B. south
C. east
D. west

> The answer is **A.** To travel from San Antonio to Wichita Falls, you have to go north.

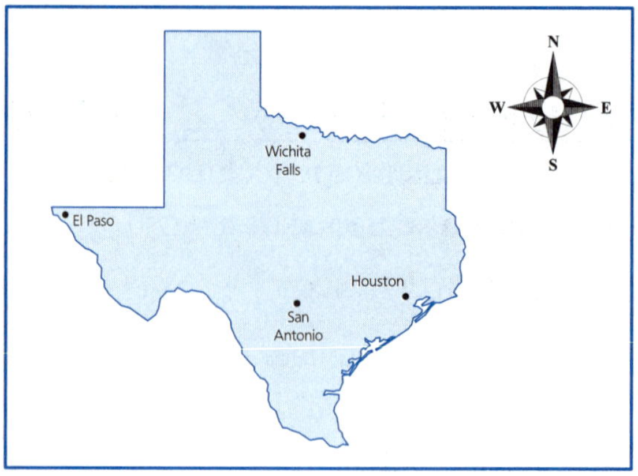

MAIN SUBJECTS OF MULTIPLE-CHOICE QUESTIONS

Most multiple-choice questions will be about the following:

☆ **RECOGNIZING TERMS, IDEAS AND PEOPLE.** This type of question tests your knowledge about a term, an idea or a person. The following is an example:

3. One of the main powers of the Governor of Texas is to

A. make national laws
B. carry out state laws
C. interpret city laws
D. enforce county laws

> The answer is **B.** The main power of the Governor of Texas is to enforce the laws of the state. The President carries out national laws, while a mayor carries out city laws.

To help you recognize the most important terms, ideas and people, they are presented in **bold print** throughout this book.

☆ **RECOGNIZING CAUSES AND EFFECTS.** Cause-and-effect questions test your understanding of how two or more events are related. The ***cause*** is the event or condition that happened first. The ***effect*** is something that happened because of the first event or condition. Another way to understand this is to remember that the cause is the *reason* for the effect. Here is an example of this type of question:

4. The city of Houston is one of the most important economic centers in Texas. A major reason for this is because Houston

A. is located near the Gulf of Mexico
B. is the capital of Texas
C. has tall buildings
D. was the first city in Texas

> The correct answer is **A.** Houston is located near the Gulf of Mexico. Being close to a large body of water brought trade and business to Houston. This helped make Houston one of Texas's largest cities.

To help you answer cause-and-effect questions, important causes and effects are identified in each chapter of this book. Activity 3F also examines cause-and-effect relationships in greater detail. Here are some key words or phrases to look for:

Causes	*Effects*
☆ Because of	☆ As a result of ....
☆ A main reason for	☆ This led to ....
☆ On account of	☆ This affected ....

WHAT LIES AHEAD IN THIS BOOK

You have now learned some practical study strategies to help you remember information and answer test questions. In the following chapters, you will learn about Texas and the Western Hemisphere. To help you remember what you learn, there will be a *Reviewing Your Understanding* section at the end of each activity and a *Summarizing Your Understanding* section at the end of each chapter.

CHAPTER 2

GEOGRAPHY

Where we live often determines "how" we live. The study of geography developed from the need to know "where." It tells us where different places are and what these places are like. It also explains how natural and human resources caused them to become as they are. This is important to know because we come into contact with people and products from many places. This chapter also covers the basic terms and ideas of geography.

2A

CAN YOU GIVE ME SOME DIRECTIONS, PLEASE?

In this activity, you will learn some of the ways that geographers locate places on the Earth. Look for the following important words:

★ North and South Poles	★ Sphere	★ Equator	★ Prime Meridian
★ Continent	★ Region	★ Country	★ State

To help you, the ★ symbol appears in the margin where the term is first explained.

It is the year 2100. Friendly life-forms have been discovered on a far-off planet. They are eager to learn about the Earth. They even understand our languages. These life-forms encourage their children to become pen pals with children from Earth. Imagine that you have been communicating with your pen pal, Wedosh, for almost a year.

Wedosh would like to visit with you this summer. However, he needs to know exactly where you live in order to locate your house. You decide to use a computer to help write directions for Wedosh. You hit the keys of your computer to bring up the instructions on the Geography-Information Program. Here is the first screen you see:

SCREEN 1: OUR SOLAR SYSTEM

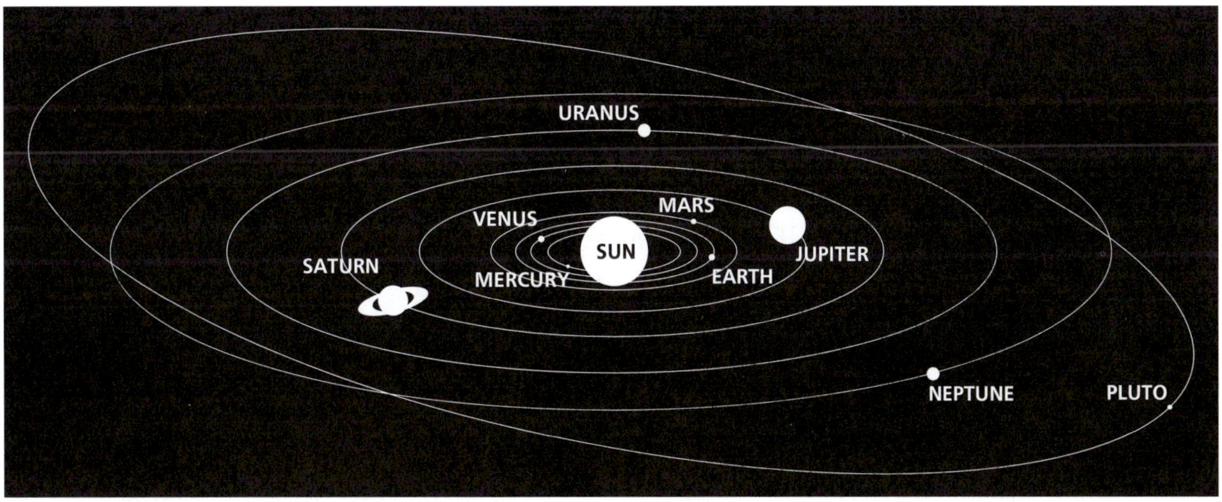

In our solar system there are nine planets moving around a star we call the **Sun.** We live on one of these planets. Each planet moves around the Sun in an **orbit** (*an oval path*). It takes our planet one year to make a complete orbit around the sun. The nine major planets are listed on the next page. An easy way to remember their names is to memorize the sentence: "**M**y **V**ery **E**ducated **M**other **J**ust **S**erved **U**s **N**ine **P**izzas."

1. Mercury	**4. Mars**	**7. Uranus**
2. Venus	**5. Jupiter**	**8. Neptune**
3. Earth	**6. Saturn**	**9. Pluto**

> NOTES
>
> The name of the planet I live on is __?__ .

SCREEN 2: OUR PLANET

Our planet is a somewhat flattened **sphere** (*an object shaped like a giant ball or globe*).
★ It spins on an imaginary line called an **axis.** The north (*top*) end of the axis is called
★ the **North Pole.** The south (*bottom*) end of the axis is called the **South Pole.** It takes our planet 24 hours to make one full turn on its axis.

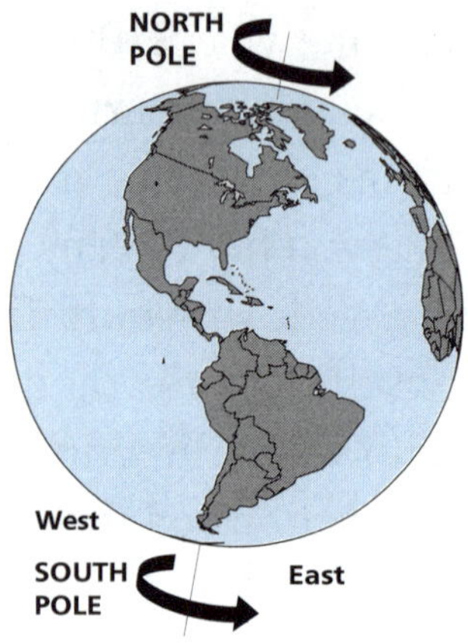

1 rotation=24 hours or 1 day

★ To make it easier to find real places on this large **sphere,** geographers divide the Earth into halves—first across, then up and down. Each of these halves are known as a **"hemisphere"** (*half of a sphere*).

☆ First, an imaginary line is drawn around the middle of
★ the Earth. This line is called the **equator.** It divides the Earth into two halves. The half above the equator is called the **Northern Hemisphere.** The half below the equator is called the **Southern Hemisphere.**

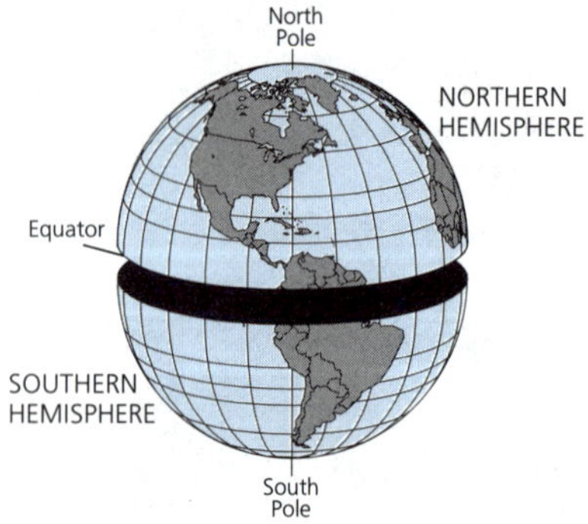

☆ Second, another imaginary line is drawn from the top of the Earth (*called the North Pole*) to its bottom (*called the South Pole*). This line is called the
★ **Prime Meridian.** When extended it also divides the Earth into halves. The half to the right of the Prime Meridian is called the **Eastern Hemisphere,** while the half to the left of the Prime Meridian is called the **Western Hemisphere.** Often, mapmakers will show the division between the Eastern and Western Hemispheres slightly west of the Prime Meridian. This is done to keep Europe and Africa in the same hemisphere.

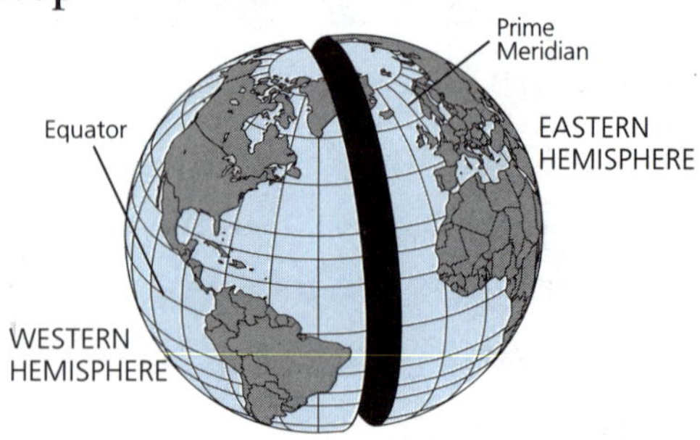

> NOTES
>
> I live in both the __?__ Hemisphere and the __?__ Hemisphere .

SCREEN 3: CONTINENTS AND OCEANS

Continents are the major land masses of the world. They are surrounded by water. Geographers have named the seven continents. In order of size, they are: **Asia, Africa, North America, South America, Antarctica, Europe** and **Australia.** ★

The continents of North America, South America and part of Antarctica make up the Western Hemisphere. Europe, Africa, Asia, Australia and part of Antarctica are the continents found in the Eastern Hemisphere.

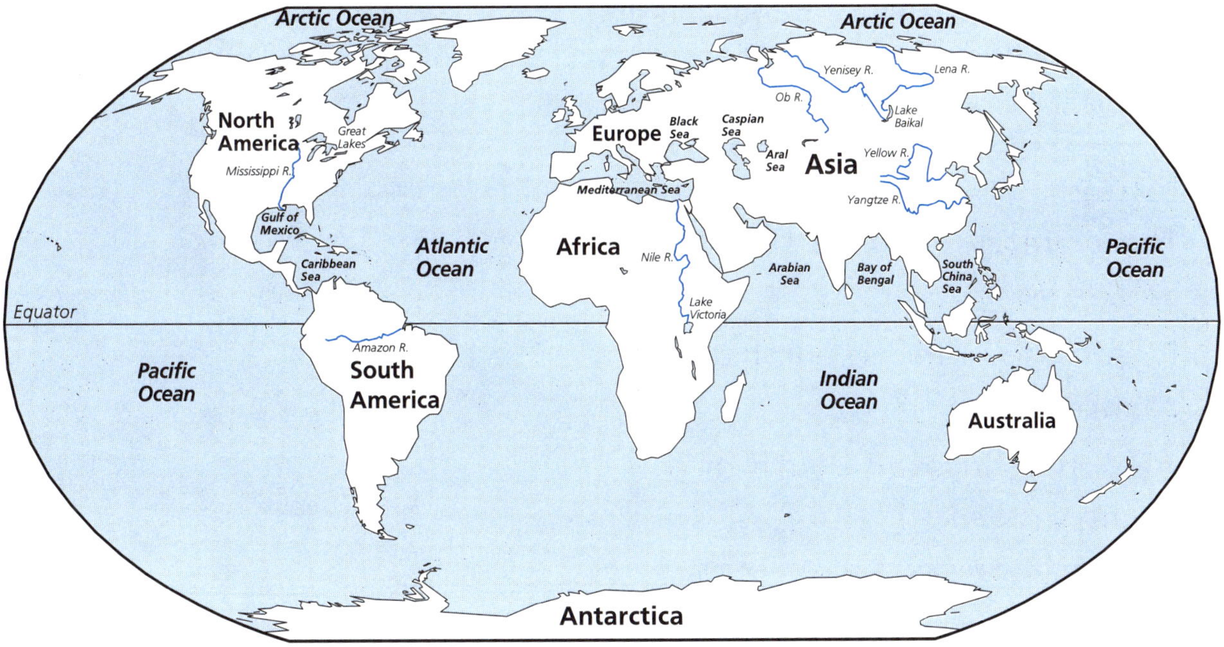

The Earth is the only planet in our solar system with a lot of water. It has fresh water in lakes and rivers, and salt water in oceans. Human life depends on water—for drinking, farming, fishing, manufacturing and for transportation.

Most of the Earth's surface is covered by oceans. An **ocean** is an extremely large body of salt water. There are four main oceans: the **Atlantic Ocean,** the **Pacific Ocean,** the **Arctic Ocean** and the **Indian Ocean.**

> NOTES
>
> I live on the continent of __?__, located between the __?__ Ocean and the __?__ Ocean.

★ CHECKING YOUR UNDERSTANDING ★

Use the map above to answer the following questions:

1. Which continents are located completely in the Northern Hemisphere?

2. Which continents are located completely in the Western Hemisphere?

SCREEN 4: COUNTRIES

Rules are needed to settle disagreements among people. They also protect people from those who break the law. **Governments** make and carry out these rules. Governments also draw imaginary boundaries (*borders*) around their areas. The areas within these ★ boundaries are often known as **countries.**

Each country has its own people, land, borders and form of government. Because things having to do with governments are known as **politics,** boundaries of countries are sometimes called **political boundaries.**

NOTES

The country in which I live is called the ___?___ .

It is located directly north of a country called ___?___ .

Also, it is located south of a country called ___?___ .

SCREEN 5: REGIONS

Most countries can be divided into smaller areas known as ★ regions. **Physical regions** are areas that usually have similar geographical features or climates. People develop different ways of adapting to the region in which they live. Within a region, they often have similar foods, customs, ways of speaking and ways of earning a living. Our country is often divided into four main regions.

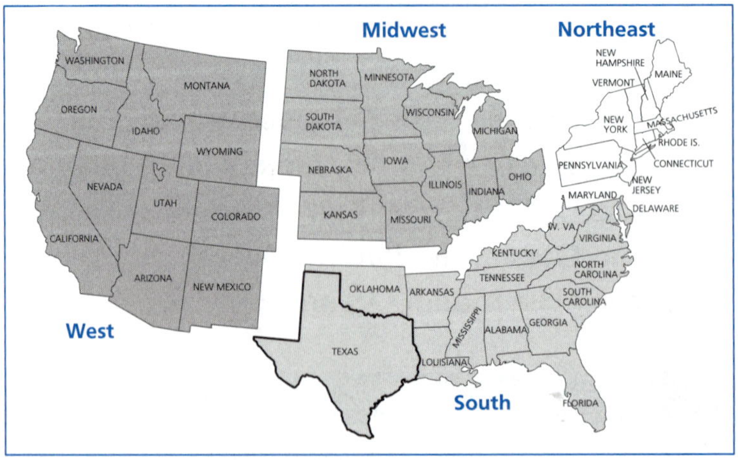

There are other ways of dividing our country into regions. For instance, many Texans refer to Texas as being part of the Southwest.

NOTES

The region I live in is known as the __?__. The number of states in the region in which I live is __?__. The names of these states are __?__.

SCREEN 6: GEOGRAPHIC FEATURES

Each place has its own combination of **geographic features** (*major land forms*). These features help us to identify the place. Here are some main types of geographic features:

MAJOR LAND FORMS

- **Mountains** are huge masses of earth and rock that rise high above the land. **Mountain ranges** are groups of mountains. In the United States, the major mountain ranges are the **Rocky Mountains** and the **Appalachian Mountains. Hills** are masses of earth and rock that are not as high as mountains.
- **Plateaus** are large highland areas that are flat on top. At the edge of a plateau are steep slopes or cliffs, often known as **escarpments.** In Texas, the **Cap Rock Escarpment** separates the Great Plains from the North Central Plains.
- **Canyons** are deep, narrow valleys with very steep sides formed by running water that has eroded the ground over thousands of years.
- **Valleys** are areas of low land between mountains or hills. A valley often has a river running through it. **Plains** are large areas of flat or slightly hilly land. The **Great Plains** are in the central part of the United States.

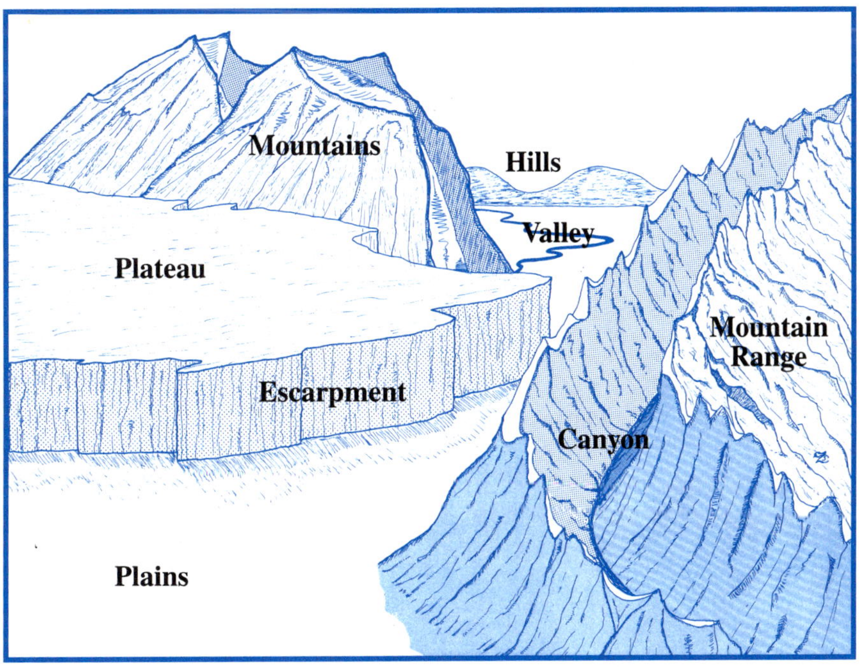

MAJOR BODIES OF WATER

- **Harbors** are protected bodies of water on coastlines. Usually a piece of land stands between a harbor and the larger body of water.
- **Gulfs** are a part of an ocean or sea, surrounded on three sides by land. The **Gulf of Mexico,** off the southern shore of the United States, lies southeast of Texas.
- **Rivers** are long, narrow bodies of fresh water that flow into the ocean or another river. In the United States, the largest river is the **Mississippi River.** The **Amazon River** is largest river in South America.
- **Lakes** are bodies of water completely surrounded by land. The major group of lakes in the United States is known as the **Great Lakes:** Lake Superior, Lake Huron, Lake Erie, Lake Michigan and Lake Ontario. A mnemonic to help you remember the names of the Great Lakes is HOMES.
- **Islands** are pieces of land surrounded by water on all sides. **Barrier islands** are created when waves push sand to form huge pieces of land that rise above the ocean surface. Barrier islands protect coastlines from **erosion** (*wearing away*) by ocean waves. Padre, Mustang, and Galveston are barrier islands along the coast of Texas. Also found along coastlines are peninsulas. **Peninsulas** are pieces of land surrounded on three sides by water. Florida is an example of a peninsula.

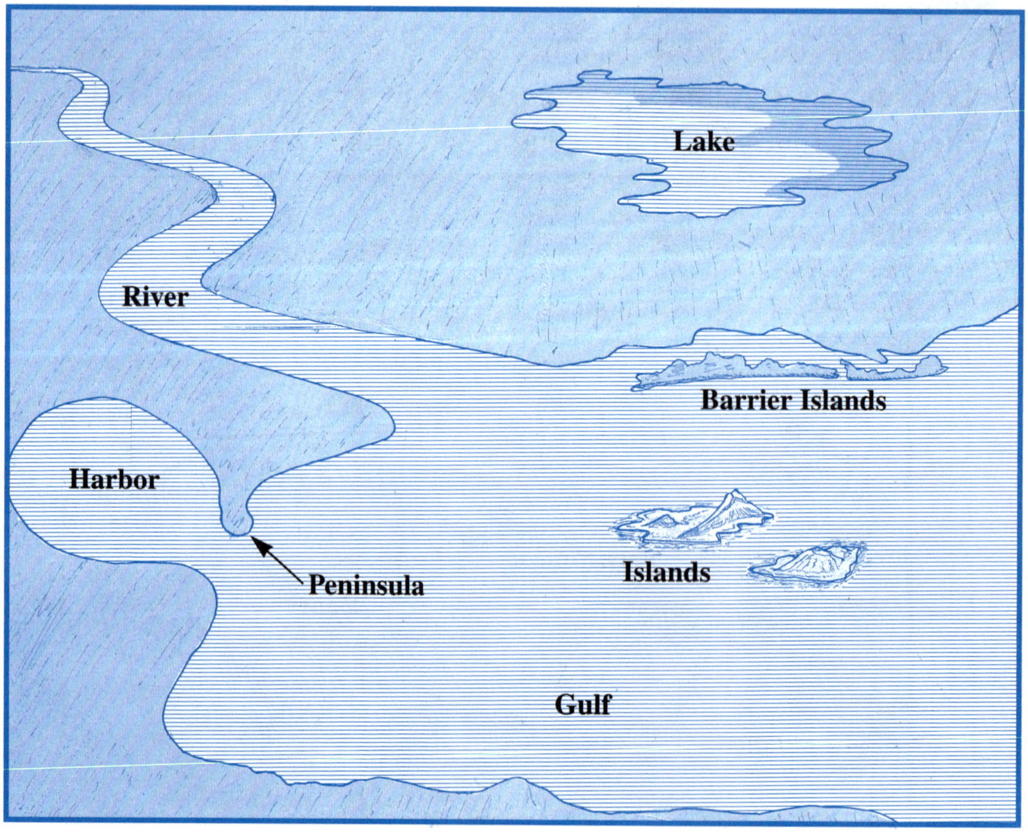

NOTES

You can recognize the country I live in by some of its geographic features. The geographic features are: ___?___

SCREEN 7: STATES AND COUNTIES

Most countries are divided into smaller political units usually called states or provinces. Smaller units of government often respond better to the special needs of a particular area. The country you live in is divided into 50 smaller units known as **states.** Can you locate your state? ★

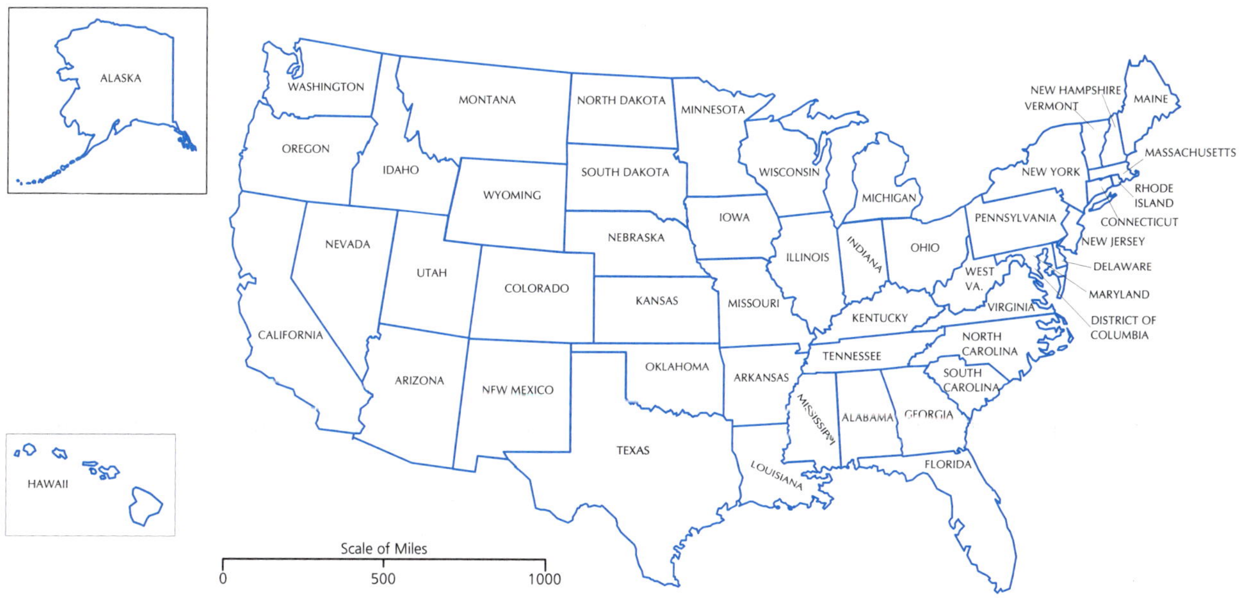

Sometimes an even smaller unit of government is more practical. This is because local units of government are more likely to know the needs of their people best. For example, a farm community might allow 14-year-olds to drive tractors. However, in a big city it would be too dangerous to let them drive motor vehicles. Therefore, each of the 50 states in your country is further divided into smaller units called **counties** (*parishes, in Louisiana*). Texas is divided into 254 counties—more counties than any other state. What is the name of your county?

NOTES

I live in the state of __?__ and the county of __?__ .

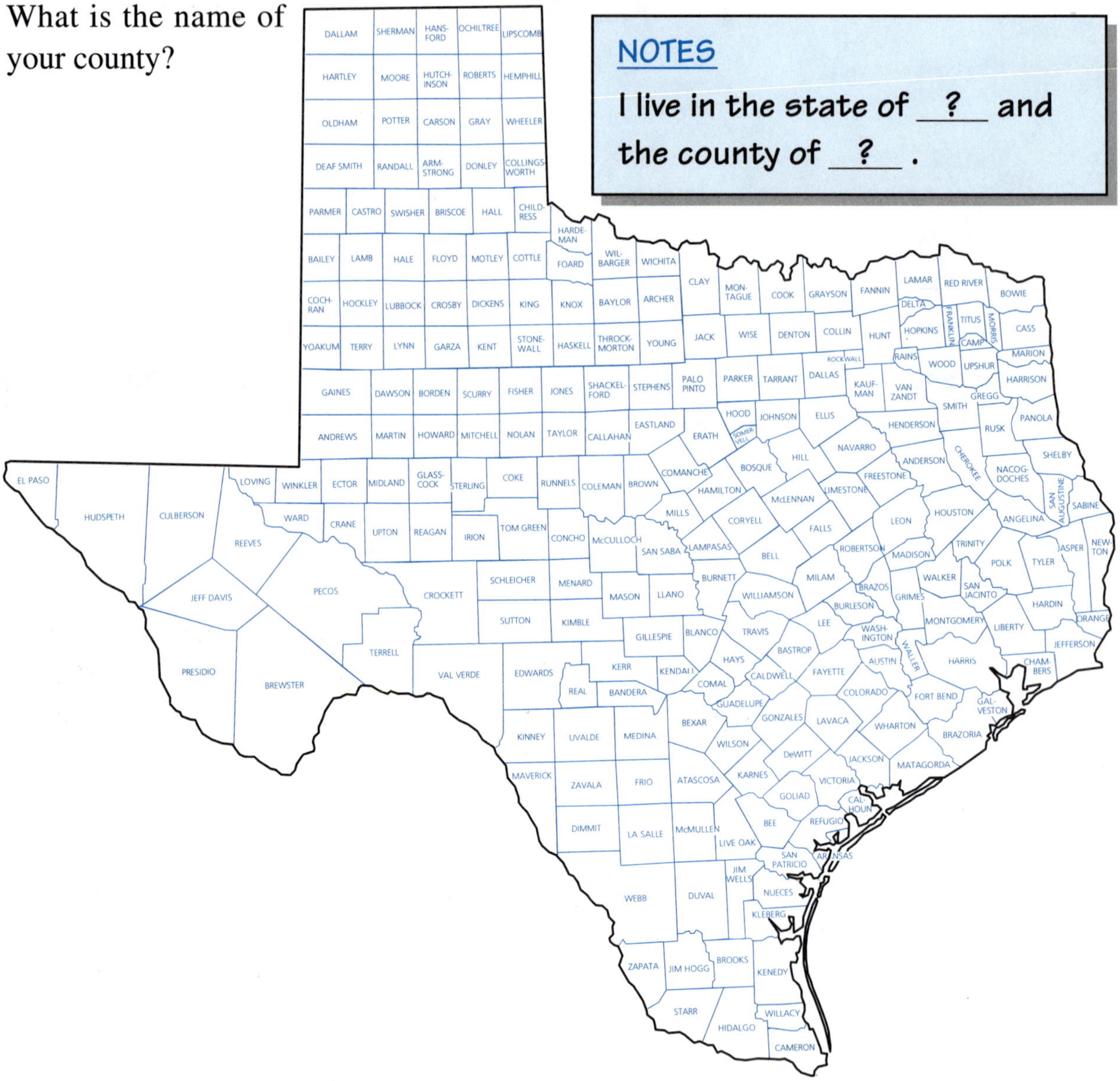

SCREEN 8: CITIES

Within most counties are smaller governing units called **cities** or **towns.** Whether you live in a city, a town or a rural area, there are roads and streets that allow you to reach your home.

By knowing what street you live on, you can tell where you are in relation to other places in the same area. Houses and apartments on a street have numbers, so that a visitor can find a specific house. The house number and street name are called its address.

Sometimes it helps to describe where you live by naming a cross-street. For example, you could tell a friend that your house is on Main Street, close to where Main Street crosses Second Avenue.

NOTES

I live in __?__ . The street on which I live is called __?__ . The nearest cross street is __?__ . My house or apartment number is __?__ .

You now have enough information for Wedosh to find your house. On a separate sheet of paper, write the directions following the form below. Giving directions is similar to any writing that explains **"how to"** do something. You explain to the reader what he or she will be doing, and then provide step-by-step directions. In this letter, start with the name of your street, and move outward to your city or town, county, state, country and planet.

INTER-GALACTIC COMMUNICATION

Dear Wedosh,

Getting to my house should be quite simple. These directions will tell you how to do it. First, I live on __?__ (street) in the (city/town) of __?__. This is located in the county of __?__, which is in the state of __?__. My state is located in the country called __?__.

You can recognize my country by some of its geographic features. They include __?__, __?__ and __?__.

My country is part of the continent of __?__. This is located in both the __?__ hemisphere and the __?__ hemisphere. The planet is called __?__.

Your Pen-Pal,

_____(sign your name)_____

EXTENDING THE ACTIVITY

THE FIVE THEMES OF GEOGRAPHY

In ancient times, **geography** meant to write or draw about the earth. Today geography includes the study of people and how the location, natural features and resources of where they live affect their lifestyles.

Geographers have identified **five major themes** to help us understand how the world and its peoples are linked. Each theme highlights one part of the study of geography. These five themes are *location, place, region, human-environment interaction* and *movement.* Let's see how you can apply these themes to a study of your school.

LOCATION

Location is where something can be found in relation to other things. Each continent, country, state and county has its own unique "location." Even buildings have a location.

- ☆ **Absolute Location** is the exact position of a mountain, lake, city or building on the Earth's surface. For example, the absolute location of your school is a unique address. On a map, your school occupies a single place.
- ☆ **Relative Location** is the position of a location on the Earth's surface in relation to other locations. Relative location uses such terms as *near, by* or *at the corner of* to identify the location. The relative location of your school tells us more information about your school. It tells us if it is in the center of a city or in the countryside. It tells us if it is near a highway, or how far it is from the nearest bus stop.

★ CHECKING YOUR UNDERSTANDING ★

- What is the absolute location of your school?
- What is the location of your school relative to the nearest fire station?

PLACE

"Place" refers to the special features of a location that make it different from other locations. A place is described by its **geographic features** such as climate, mountains, deserts, bodies of water, plants and animals. What is the place like? Is it hot or cold? Dry or humid? Rocky or flat?

Chalk Bluff, Nueces River
What geographic features does this place have?

You will learn more about the geographic features that make a place unique later in this chapter. Buildings are also "places" with features. How would you describe what kind of place your school is?

> **★ CHECKING YOUR UNDERSTANDING ★**
>
> - Is your school made of brick or wood?
> - How many floors does it have?
> - How many classrooms are there?

REGION

Regions are areas that are near each other and have similar characteristics or features. People within a region usually have more contact with each other than they do with people outside it. One region often belongs to an even larger region. For example, your community is part of a region called a **county.** The county, in turn, is part of a larger region called a **state.** The state is part of an even larger region called a **nation.**

> **★ CHECKING YOUR UNDERSTANDING ★**
>
> - In which county is your school located?
> - In which state is your school located?
> - In which nation is your school located?

HUMAN-ENVIRONMENT INTERACTION

This interaction refers to the way in which the physical features of a place affect its people, and how the people affect their environment. For example, people turn forests and hilly grasslands into cities and farms. On the other hand, the environment also shapes what people do. How might life in a desert be different from life in a city?

> **★ CHECKING YOUR UNDERSTANDING ★**
>
> - How do students in your school dress in the winter months?
> - Is it too hot in the summer to play outdoor sports?

MOVEMENT

People must interact with each other—trade, travel and communicate to get what they need. The *movement* of goods, ideas and people from place to place is an important theme of geography. It is likely that some of your schoolmates originally came from other places. The ideas you learn about in school are also the product of different lands and cultures.

> **★ CHECKING YOUR UNDERSTANDING ★**
>
> - Name a product used in your school that was made in another country.
> - Do you know any people in your school who were not born in Texas? If so, where did they originally come from?

REVIEWING YOUR UNDERSTANDING

Directions: Use the terms and questions on the small cards below to create your own Vocabulary Cards. Then answer the questions that follow.

Equator

What is the equator?

What is its purpose?

Prime Meridian

What is the Prime Meridian?

What is its purpose?

Locating Places on Maps

Use the map below to answer questions 1 and 2:

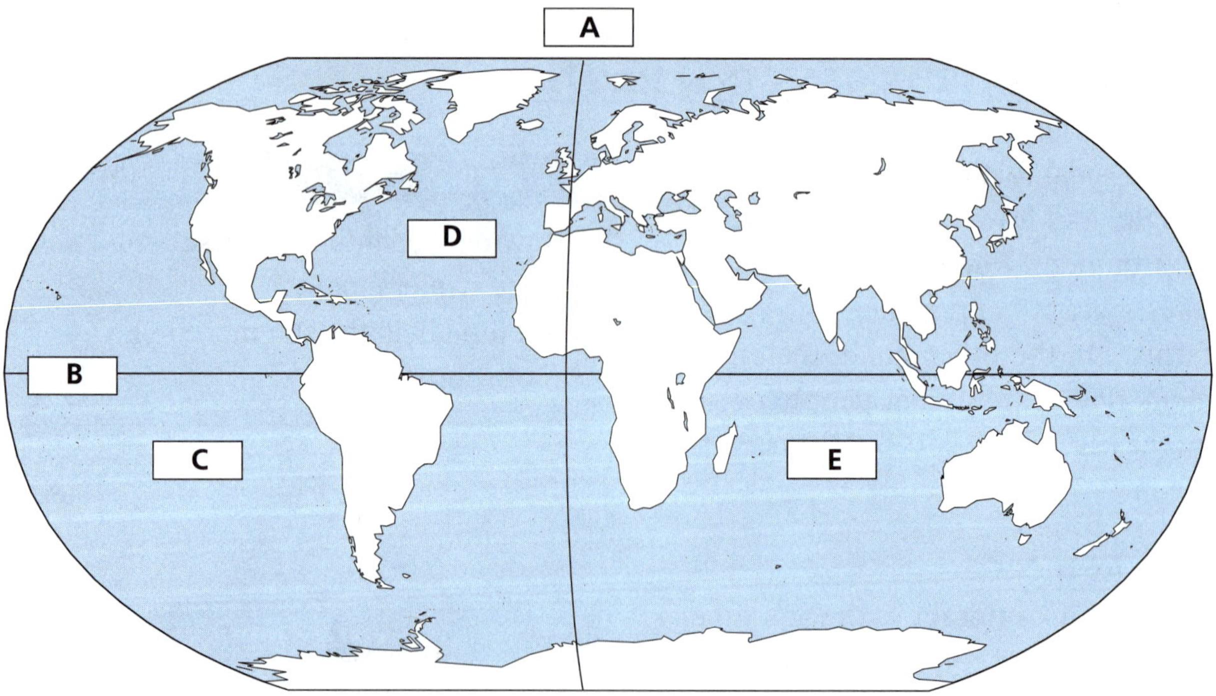

1. Which letter on the map represents the equator?

A. letter A
B. letter B
C. letter C
D. letter D

2. Which letter represents the Prime Meridian?

A. letter A
B. letter B
C. letter C
D. letter D

Use the map below to answer questions 3 through 5:

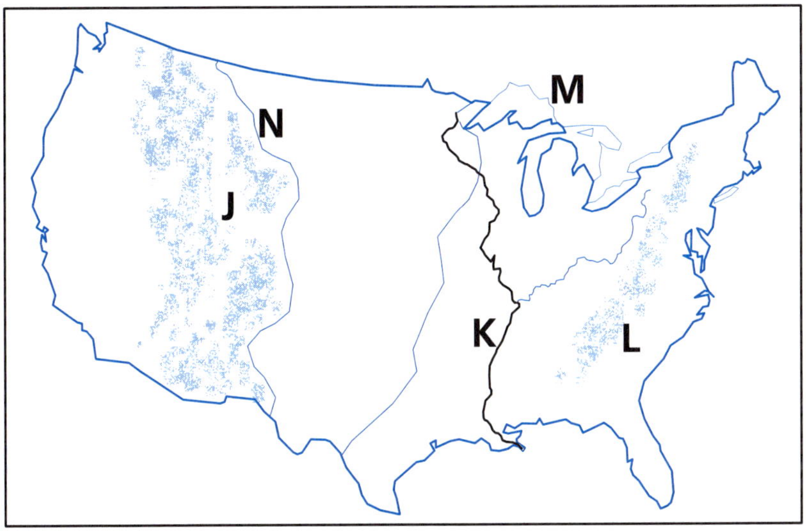

3. The Great Lakes are represented by
A. letter J
C. letter L
B. letter K
D. letter M

4. The Mississippi River is represented by
A. letter J **C.** letter N
B. letter K **D.** letter M

5. The Appalachian Mountains are represented by
A. letter J **C.** letter L
B. letter K **D.** letter M

Use the map below to answer questions 6 and 7:

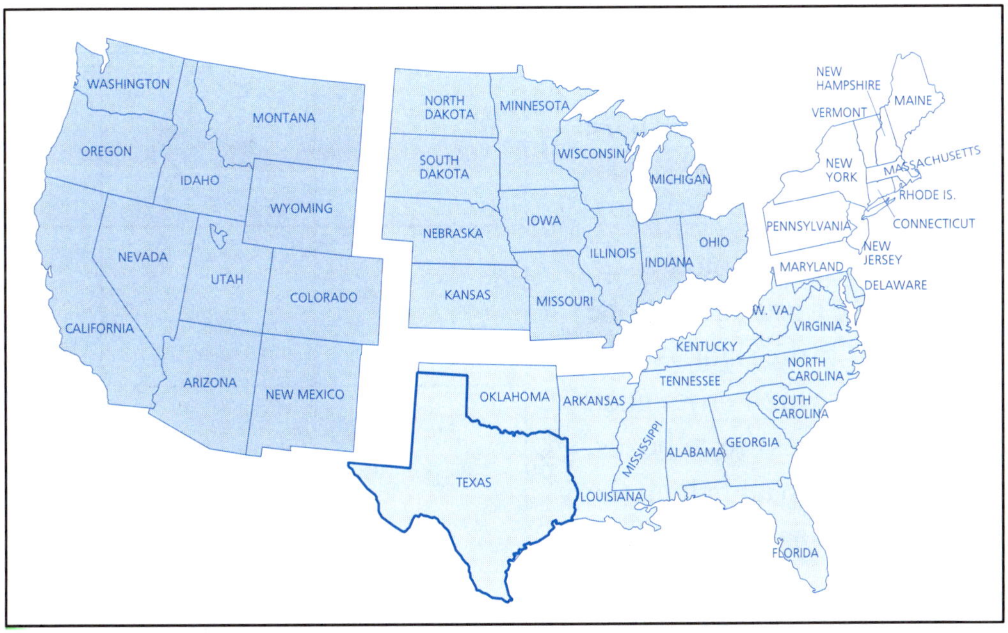

6. Texas is part of which region?
A. the Northeast **C.** the South
B. the Midwest **D.** the West

7. Which state does NOT border Texas?
A. Pennsylvania **C.** Oklahoma
B. Louisiana **D.** Arkansas

2B HOW WOULD YOU MAP YOUR COMMUNITY?

In this activity, you will learn how maps help us to locate places. Look for the following important words:

- ★ Map
- ★ Symbol
- ★ Legend (Key)
- ★ Scale
- ★ Latitude
- ★ Longitude

Your friend in California has sent you a map of an imaginary community which he made as a school project. He asks if you can also make a map of an imaginary community and send it with your next letter. You would like to make a map that is as good as your friend's. You ask your teacher how to begin.

★ Your teacher explains that **maps** are like the language of geography. Each map is really a small picture or diagram of a place. It shows where things are located. She says the easiest way to understand maps is by mapping things in a small area. She suggests you start by making a map of your desktop.

You draw a picture of your desktop. Your teacher then puts three objects in different locations on your desk. She says, "Now pretend you are a bird, flying over the desk. Can you describe exactly where the objects on your desk are located?"

You find it hard to do. Your teacher agrees that it is not easy. Your teacher tells you that **cartographers** (*people who make maps*) have the same problem.

To help locate places on a map, cartographers make a grid like the one on the "desk map" to the right. A **grid** uses straight lines which cross each other. The crossing lines create boxes. The rows along the top and along the side are given letters and numbers.

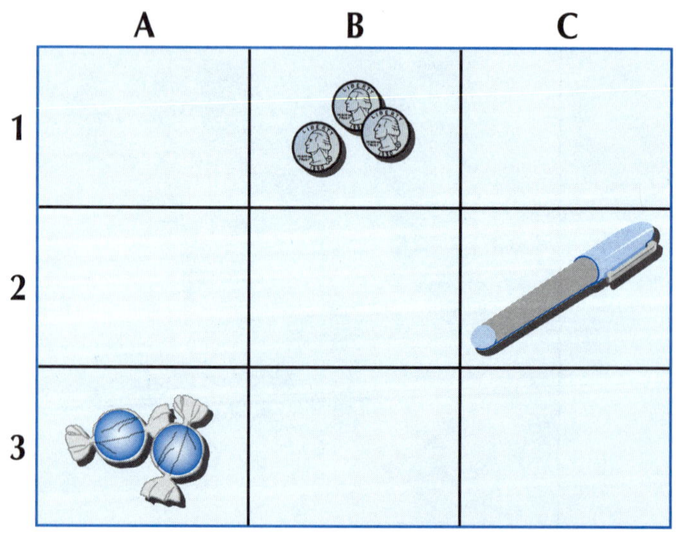

★ CHECKING YOUR UNDERSTANDING ★

Write down the number and the letter of the grid box that contains:

- the candy
- the coins
- the pen

WHAT ARE MAPS AND WHAT DO THEY SHOW?

Maps are drawings of a part of the Earth. They come in different sizes and shapes. Maps can be used to show countries, states or cities. These maps will show political boundaries. Other maps show geographic features such as mountains, oceans and rivers. Still others show airports, parks and schools. A **globe** is a special kind of map. It is a three-dimensional representation of the entire Earth. To understand a map, first look at its **title.** The title tells you what the map is about.

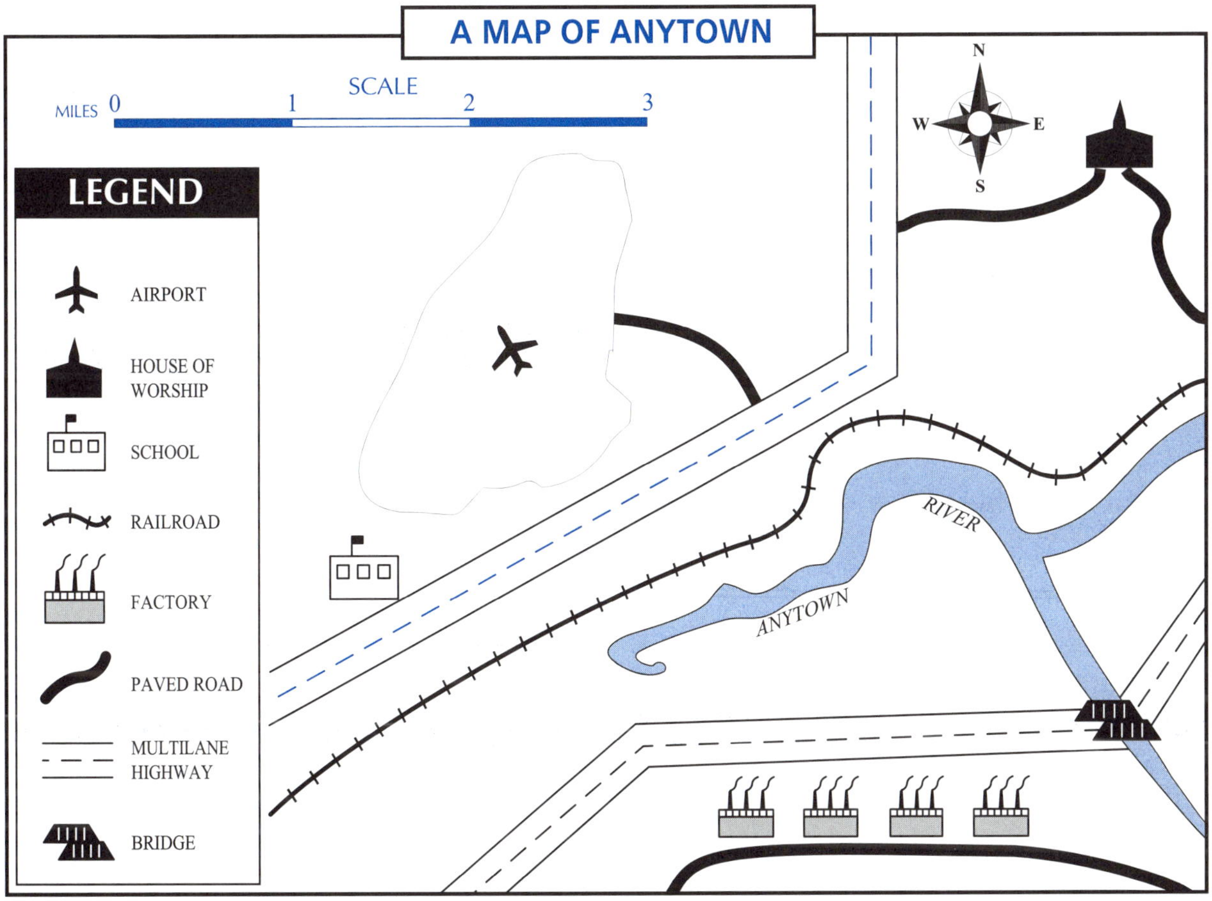

The secret to using any map is to understand its symbols. Instead of writing the word "highway," "railroad," "airport" or "school," mapmakers use symbols to represent these things. A map **symbol** is a drawing that stands for an actual place or a real thing.

Mapmakers provide a **legend** to explain each symbol in words. The legend unlocks the meaning of the symbols used on a map. The legend is sometimes called the "key." In the Anytown map, the symbol may appear as shapes, lines, dots,

> **★ CHECKING YOUR UNDERSTANDING ★**
>
> There are 8 symbols on the map of Anytown. On a separate piece of paper, draw the symbol used for a:
>
> • factory • school • bridge

dashes or drawings. On another map, the school symbol might be drawn differently. Each symbol is always explained in the legend, so you can tell what it means. Be sure to look for the legend or key whenever you are reading a map.

FINDING DIRECTIONS

To make it easier to use directions on a map, mapmakers provide a **direction indicator.** It is shown as a small **compass,** often called a **compass rose.** It shows the four cardinal (*basic*) directions:

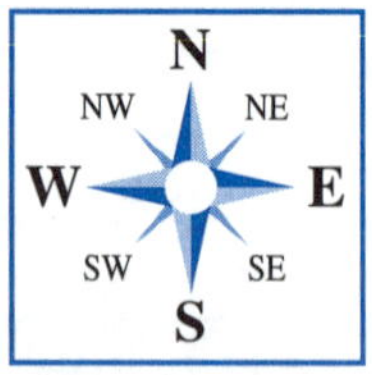

- **north** (N) • **east** (E) • **south** (S) • **west** (W)

A compass can also show other directions. Sometimes we need to find places that fall in between the four basic directions. A compass rose shows the intermediate (*in-between*) directions:

- **northeast** (NE) • **northwest** (NW) • **southeast** (SE) • **southwest** (SW)

Most maps show north at the top and south at the bottom. Look at the compass in the Anytown map. It can be found in the upper right-hand corner. If you traveled from the bridge (*in the eastern part of Anytown*) to the school (*in the western part*) you would be traveling west.

★ CHECKING YOUR UNDERSTANDING ★

In which direction would you be traveling if you went from the:

- airport to the bridge?
- school to the airport?
- factories to the river?

MEASURING DISTANCES ON A MAP

Just as a model airplane is a small version of a large, real airplane, a map is a small drawing of a large, real place. If a map were the same size as the area it shows, it would be too big to use—imagine a map the actual size of your school! Mapmakers use a device called a **scale** to show how much the drawing was reduced. The larger the area represented, the less detail the map can have. For example, a map of the United States can only show broad outlines of the individual states. A map of your school can show more detail, such as individual rooms. The scale also shows what distances the measurements stand for in real life.

The scale can be used to figure out the distance between any two places on a map. Scales tell us the real distance, usually in miles or kilometers. Map scales are usually shown as a line marked: **"Scale of Miles."** The mapmakers may use 1 inch to stand for 1 real mile. Or, on a map of a very large area, 1 inch may stand for 100 miles.

Let's see how we go about finding the approximate distance from El Paso to Austin. First, put a ruler under the scale on the map. You'll see that one-inch on the scale of miles stands for a real distance of two hundred thirty miles. Using this information, you can now find the distance from El Paso to Austin. On the map, line up the edge of a piece of paper with Austin. Move the paper to the left until it touches El Paso. Mark both spots with a pen or pencil. Now use a ruler to measure this distance. It measures about $2\frac{1}{2}$ inches. The scale shows us that 1 inch equals 230 miles. Since the distance between El Paso and Austin measures $2\frac{1}{2}$ inches, it is about 575 miles from El Paso to Austin.

★ CHECKING YOUR UNDERSTANDING ★

What would the distance be from El Paso to Brownsville?

DRAWING YOUR IMAGINARY MAP

Now you have enough information to draw a map at least as good as your friend from California has. You decide you will map an imaginary town named after you. For example, if your name is Brian, you'll call the town Brianville. If your name is Maria, the town will be called Mariaville. Remember, that like all good maps, your map should include:

1. symbols and a legend or "key" that explains things found on your map

2. a direction indicator (*compass rose*)

3. a scale of miles

Make your map on a separate piece of paper, starting with the title at the top:

MY MAP OF __?__ VILLE

USING LATITUDE AND LONGITUDE

EXTENDING THE ACTIVITY

Geographers have created two sets of imaginary lines—called "latitude" and "longitude" —to help us determine the exact location of any place on a map or globe.

LATITUDE

★ **Latitude** is the name given to imaginary horizontal lines that run *across* the Earth. A mnemonic device would be to think of the steps of a **<u>lad</u>**der because lines of latitude run horizontally. They are sometimes called **parallels** because like parallel lines, latitude lines run parallel to each other, and never meet.

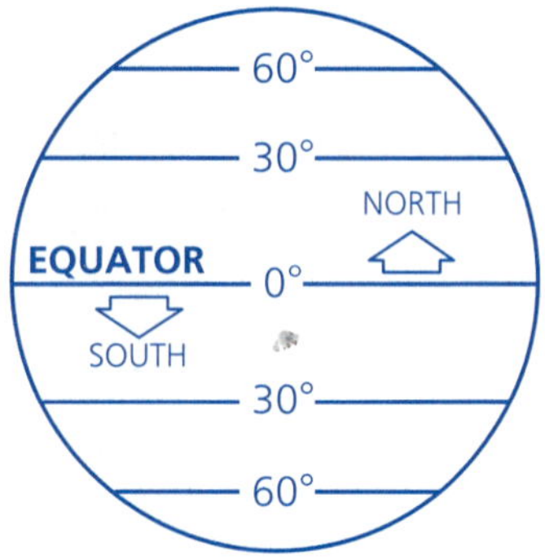

LATITUDE

Since a map or globe would be too crowded and confusing if *every* line of latitude were shown, mapmakers draw only some of the latitude lines. The **equator** is the most important latitude line. It stretches all around the middle of the Earth. It is the same distance from the North Pole as it is from the South Pole.

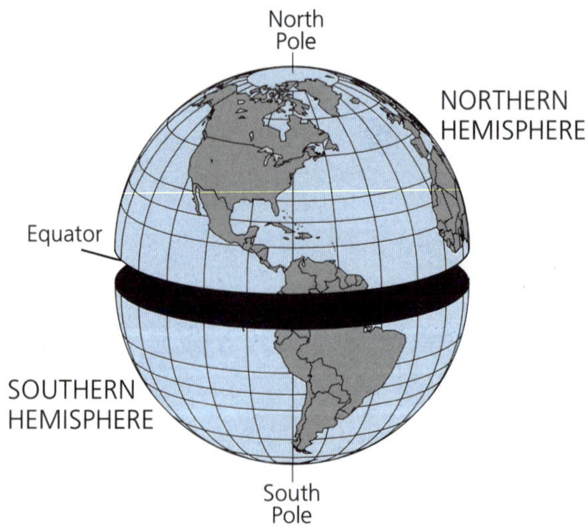

All other latitude lines are identified by how far north or south of the equator they are. The lines of north latitude are shown on land and water north of the equator (the **Northern Hemisphere**). The lines of south latitude are shown on land and water south of the equator (the **Southern Hemisphere**).

Each latitude line is assigned a number—in "degrees"—to help indicate its distance relative to the equator. The symbol for **degrees** is °. Going in either direction from the equator, we mark latitude lines from 1° to 90°, adding "N" or "S" to indicate if the line is north or south of the equator. For example, the latitude line 87° north of the equator is written as 87° N. Lines south of the equator have an "S" after the degree sign.

At zero degrees latitude (the equator) the weather is generally hot. Since the sphere of the Earth curves away from the Sun as you go towards the North and South Poles, the higher the latitude number, the colder the climate.

The angle of the Earth's tilt as it revolves around the Sun makes the seasons change. At the equator, there is no seasonal change. When it is winter north of the equator, it is summer south of the equator.

LONGITUDE

★

Longitudes are a set of imaginary lines that run north and south (*up and down*) on a map or globe. Lines of longitude run from the North Pole to the South Pole. These lines are used to indicate distances in an east to west direction.

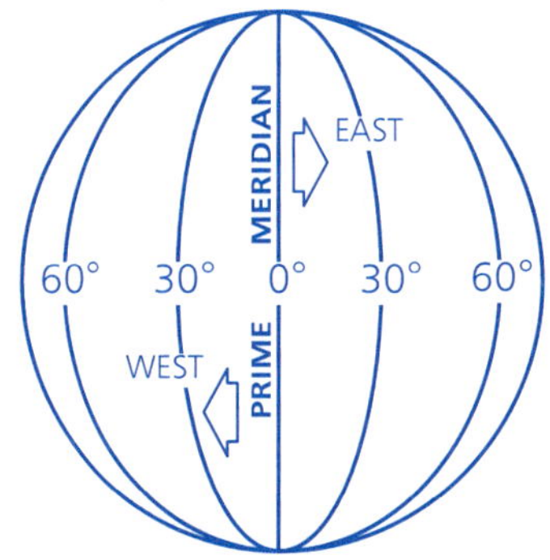

The **Prime Meridian** is the most important longitude line. The Prime Meridian divides the Earth into two hemispheres (east and west) and marks the starting line of longitudes. All areas west of the Prime Meridian are known as the **Western Hemisphere.** All areas east of the Prime Meridian are known as the **Eastern Hemisphere.** As you learned earlier, mapmakers often draw the division between the hemispheres slightly west of the Prime Meridian to show Europe and Africa in the same hemisphere.

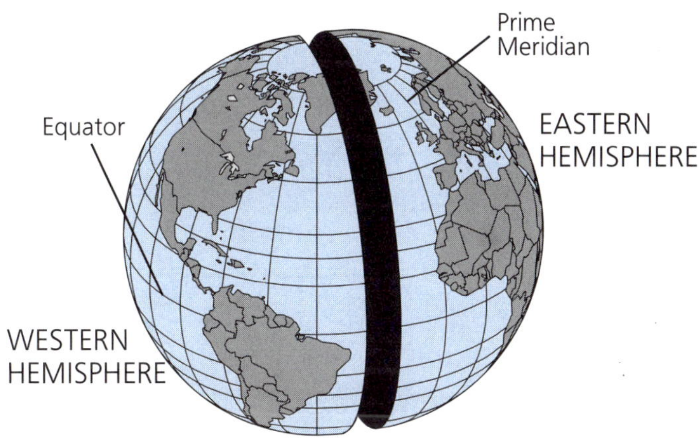

Like the equator, the Prime Meridian is also identified as zero degrees (0°). Going in either direction from the Prime Meridian, we mark longitude lines from 1° to 180°, adding **"E"** or **"W"** to indicate if the line is east or west of the Prime Meridian.

Longitude lines are not parallel like lines of latitude. As a result, they are not always the same distance from one another. At the equator, each degree of longitude is about 69 miles apart. As one moves closer to the North or South Pole, each degree of longitude measures fewer and fewer miles. Finally, all the longitude lines meet at both the North and South Poles.

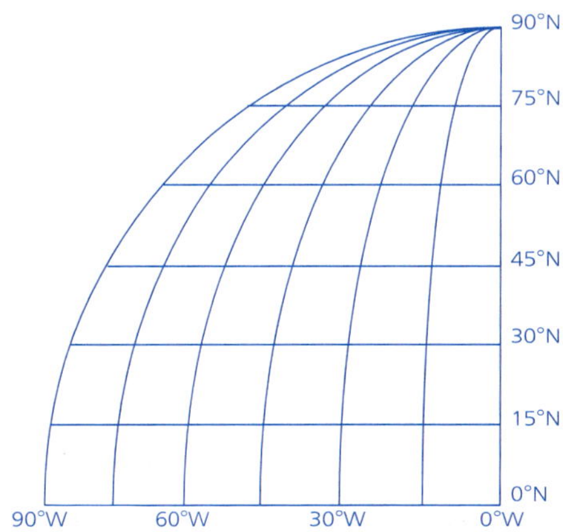

When latitude and longitude lines both appear on a map or globe, they form a grid pattern. By knowing the points at which latitude and longitude lines meet, we can locate any place on the surface of the Earth.

★ CHECKING YOUR UNDERSTANDING ★

Look at the map on the right. What is the approximate latitude and longitude of the city of Midland? To find out, put your finger on the dot representing Midland. Move your finger slightly up until it touches the 32°N latitude. This line is 32° **north** of the equator. Next, move your finger from Midland slightly to the left, until it touches 102°W longitude. This line is 102° **west** of the Prime Meridian. Midland's approximate latitude and longitude are where these two lines cross: at 32° N. latitude and 102° W. longitude. What are the approximate latitudes and longitudes of:

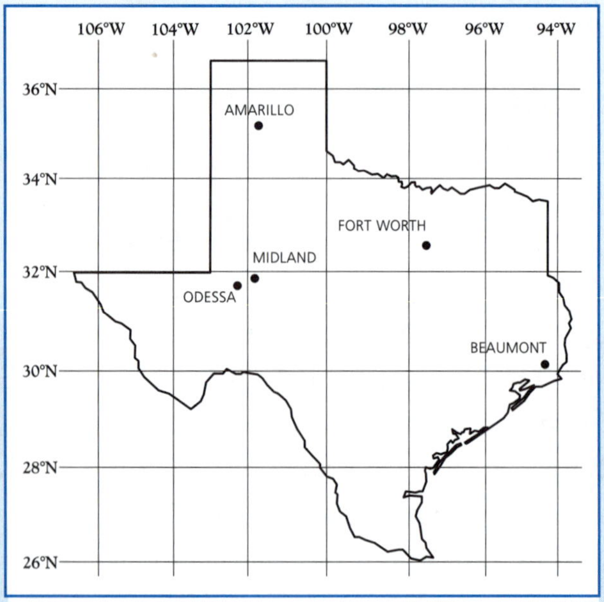

1. Odessa?
2. Fort Worth?
3. Beaumont?
4. Amarillo?

REVIEWING YOUR UNDERSTANDING

Directions: Fill in your Vocabulary Cards and complete the exercises that follow.

Maps
What is a map?
Name 4 items used on a map to
help locate places:

Latitude and Longitude
What is a latitude line?
What is a longitude line?
What are they used for?

Creating Symbols On A Map

Make a map of an imaginary island. On your map, create at least seven symbols to show where such things as parks, stores, schools, banks and highways are located.

Traveling Around Your Neighborhood

Examine the following community map. Then answer the questions.

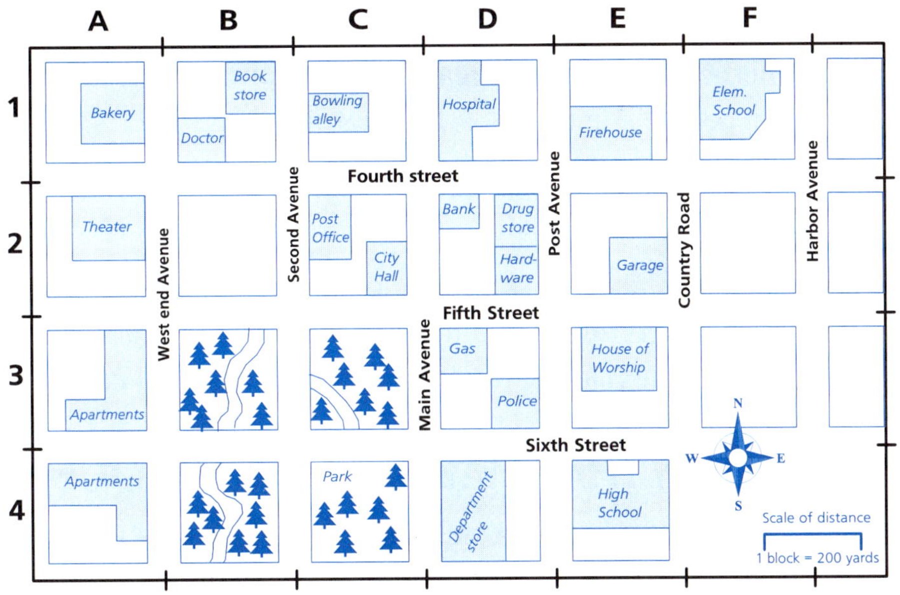

1. Which street is directly north of Sixth Street?
2. In which grid is the hospital located?
3. In which grid is the high school located?
4. How many avenues do you cross in going from the firehouse to the doctor?
5. Which stores are located on Post Avenue?
6. The hospital is 3 blocks from the department store. How many yards apart are they?

Finding Direction and Distance

Follow the line to find the direction you are traveling. Use the compass rose and scale to help you answer the questions.

1. In which direction must you travel to get from **A** to **B**?
2. In which direction must you travel to get from **B** to **C**?
3. In which direction must you travel to get from **F** to **G**?
4. How many milcs would you travel to get from **A** to **B**?
5. What is the total distance you would travel from **E** to **G**?

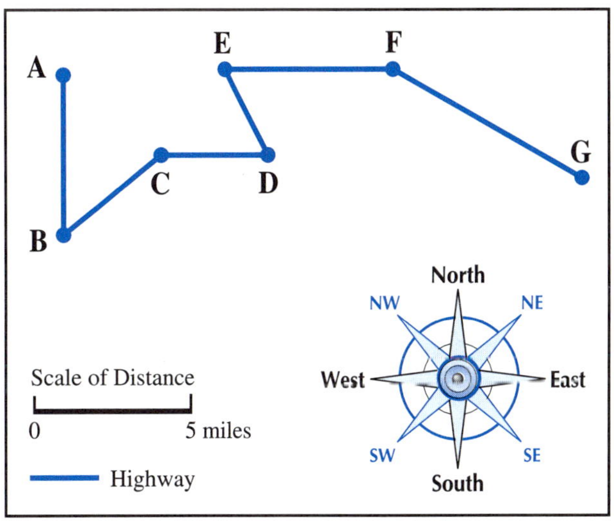

2C WHAT ROLE DOES "PLACE" PLAY IN PEOPLE'S LIVES?

In this activity, you will learn about the important role that "place" has in people's lives. Look for the following important words:

★ Climate ★ Population Density ★ Urban ★ Atlas

The Earth is a wonderful planet. It is a place of breath-taking beauty—lush green forests, dazzling white glaciers and brilliant desert sunsets. The Earth has climates and land features where life for human beings can be comfortable and easy, or quite harsh.

FEATURES THAT MAKE A PLACE UNIQUE

Each location on Earth has its own special features. These special features make it different from other places. **Geographers** study a location to determine what kind of **place** it is. The special features of a place include the following:

- ★ **climate** (*weather conditions of an area*): how hot or cold the place is, and how much rainfall it receives over a period of time.
- **topography** (*a land's natural features*): whether the place is in the mountains, in a valley or on a plain.
- **plants and animals:** the kinds of plants and animals that live there.
- **natural resources** (*something provided by nature that is useful to people*): whether the place has valuable minerals, timber, fertile soil or other resources.
- **nearness to water:** whether the place has rivers and lakes, is on the coastline, or is far from any bodies of water.
- ★ **population density:** how many people live there, in relation to the size of the place.
- **features of surrounding areas:** whether the place is next to mountains, deserts, forests or other types of areas.

Canyons along the Rio Grande
What is the terrain like where you live?

THINK ABOUT IT

Which feature do you think has the greatest effect on how people live?

A LOOK AT THREE PLACES IN THE WESTERN HEMISPHERE

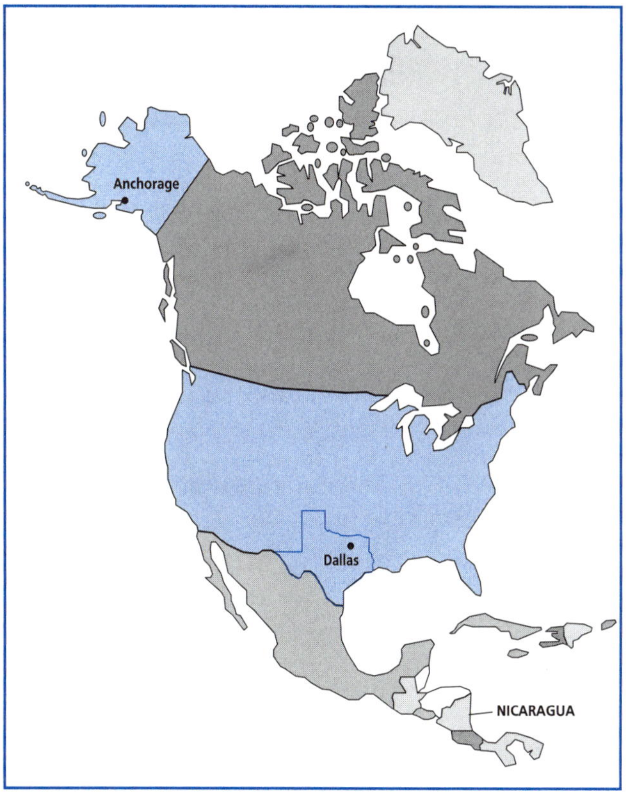

The kind of place we live in often determines **how** we live. If we live in the city of Anchorage, Alaska, the weather is very cold in the winter and for much of the fall and spring. The city is covered by snow for most of the year. Even parts of the ocean freeze over. The mountains surrounding the city of Anchorage look like massive snow drifts. Daylight is short: only five hours in December. Despite the bitter cold, one can still spot moose, eagles and sheep just outside the city. In the late spring, the snows melt. Summers are hot, and the sun does not set until after midnight. After a few hours, it rises again.

Anchorage is a large city because of Alaska's valuable natural resources—especially oil and gas. Many large oil companies have headquarters in Anchorage. They employ thousands of workers. The cold climate affects people's activities as well as their work. Most food has to be shipped or flown to Alaska from the south. In winter, people bundle up in heavy coats, boots, hats and gloves. Many Alaskans enjoy winter sports, such as skiing. In the summer months, they can go hiking and fishing.

A quite different place in the Western Hemisphere is the rain forest of Nicaragua. The weather is hot all year long. There are frequent rain showers. A large variety of tropical trees grow in the rain forest. Their interlocking tops form a dense umbrella-like covering over the forest. Many plant and animal **species** (*groups with similar characteristics*) are found only in this rain forest.

Life in the Nicaraguan rain forest is far different from life in the city of Anchorage, Alaska. The native people wear light clothing because the climate is so warm. They can pick fruits and go fishing and hunting all year long. They grow corn and sweet potatoes. However, active volcanoes in eastern Nicaragua remain a constant danger to the people living there.

THINK ABOUT IT

How is the food people eat and the clothes people wear different in the two places described?

A third place in the Western Hemisphere is the city of Dallas. Life in Dallas is very different from life in Anchorage or the rain forest of Nicaragua. Dallas is Texas' second largest city, with over one million people. ★ Many Texans regard it as the state's most **urban** (*city*) and **cosmopolitan** (*worldly*) city. Attractions in Dallas draw visitors from everywhere. People come to see the downtown skyline of **skyscrapers** (*tall office buildings*), the Dallas Zoo, Biblical Arts Center, State Fair Park, World Aquarium and the John F. Kennedy Memorial. Others are attracted by the Dallas Arts District, the shopping centers, parks and sports teams.

The city of Dallas
Does your city have a trolley car and skyscrapers?

The city of Dallas is the nation's southwest center for international business, oil, cotton, finance, fashion and culture. Many large corporations have their headquarters in the city, providing good career opportunities. Dallas has a mild climate, encouraging outdoor activities. Dallas has residents of many different backgrounds. This adds to the diversity and excitement of city life. At the same time, they must put up with crowds and heavy traffic, and are less close to nature.

THINK ABOUT IT

How is life for people living in Dallas different from that of the people who live in Anchorage or the rain forest of Nicaragua?

As you can see, the place you live in—its climate, topography, natural resources, population density and nearness to water—can greatly affect how you live. For example, in the city of Anchorage you might use a 4-wheel drive vehicle to get around. In the rain forest of Nicaragua, you would be more likely to travel on foot or to use a boat. In the city of Dallas, you would probably travel by car or bus.

THE "MAGIC" OF READING A BOOK

Have you ever listened to a grandparent explain what it was like growing up in a far-off land? Or maybe listened to a parent who visited a unique and exciting country? Wouldn't it be nice if you could visit some of the places you have heard about?

Sometimes it's not possible to travel. You may not have the time or money to journey to these far-off lands. But there is a way to visit these unique places without ever leaving home. Reading books is one of the best and easiest ways to "travel" to other places around the globe. Books let you visit a place without having to pack anything more than your imagination.

Let's take a look at some of the books available to you. On the next few pages are several books about places to visit. Choose **one** book from the list, or that your teacher or school librarian recommends. Take the book out of the library, so you can "visit" the place described. After reading the book complete the following Book Evaluation Form on a separate sheet of paper.

Book Evaluation Form

Title of the book: ____________________

Author's name: ____________________

Publisher: ____________________

Place described in the book: __________ Part of which continent? __________

How did the characteristics of the "place" affect the lives of its people? ________

Would you recommend the book to others? ____________________

Here are some suggested books you may wish to choose from:

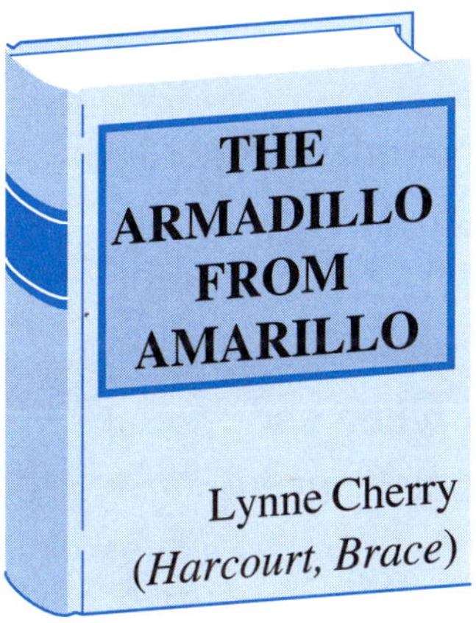

This story is about Sasparillo, an armadillo and his travels through Texas. In order to find out where on Earth he is, Sasparillo leaves his home in San Antonio and travels through the praries and canyons of western Texas.

This book, written in free-style verse, is about a wonderful town in the Texas Hill Country. Free-style verse is poetry in which the lines do not rhyme. The book shows that the best town in the world may not bc far from home.

MY TWO WORLDS

Ginger Gordon
(Clarion)

This is the story of a young girl, 8 years old, who lives in New York City. For Christmas, she returns to her other home in the Dominican Republic. The story is about her life in these two worlds.

THE REINDEER PEOPLE

Ted Lewin
(MacMillan)

This is a story about the region above the Arctic Circle. On this journey you will experience some of the unique sights and very cold weather of this land. The story is about the Lapp people (sometimes called the Sami).

NAOMI'S ROAD

Joy Nozomi Kogawa
(Oxford Univ. Press)

This is the story of Naomi Nakane. It tells about her childhood experiences facing prejudice and hardship during World War II. The story deals with Naomi's experiences when she is sent to an internment camp in Canada.

GOODBYE USA— ¡HOLA MEXICO!

Anne Bovaird
(Barrons)

Tom is a young boy who lives in Chicago. One day, he visits his cousin and other relatives in Mexico. On his trip, he explores the sights of Mexico City. Although Tom does not speak Spanish, he learns many Spanish words and phrases on his trip.

HOW MANY DAYS TO AMERICA

Eve Bunting
(Clarion)

This is the story of a family forced to flee their Caribbean island. Along with other refugees, they are crowded into a boat. The boat tries to reach America where the people hope to start a new life.

GOING HOME

Nicholas A. Mohr
(Bantam Skylark)

This is the story of a twelve-year old girl named Felita. She returns to Puerto Rico for a visit. There she faces both admiration and jealousy. By the end of the summer, she learns much about her Hispanic heritage.

WITH LOVE FROM GRAN

Dick Gackenbach
(Clarion)

This is the story of a boy and his grandmother. She goes on a trip around the world and sends him presents from every place she visits.

AROUND THE WORLD IN EIGHTY DAYS

J. Burningham
(Jarrold)

This book recreates the classic story of Phileas Fogg and his famous trip "around the world in eighty days." The author gives his impressions as he travels through 24 countries on a 44,000 mile journey.

EXTENDING THE ACTIVITY

LEARNING TO USE AN ATLAS

ATLAS

An **atlas** is special type of book that contains many different kinds of maps. A world atlas will have a map of every nation in the world. If the atlas is printed in the United States, it will probably have maps of each of the 50 states.

The maps will also show where counties and important cities in each state are located. In addition, an atlas will contain specialized types of maps:

- **Physical Maps.** These show land features such as mountains, and may even include the depths of the oceans and other bodies of water.
- **Political Maps.** These show the boundaries of countries or states—where one country or state ends and another begins.
- **Theme Maps.** These usually deal with a single item or theme. They are used to show rainfall, population distribution, food production, religions or other special information.

An atlas will also have an **index.** The index is used to find information. The index will tell you on which page of the atlas to look for a particular country, state, body of water, mountain range or other place. An atlas will also have a **gazetteer.** This is a geographical dictionary that often lists the longitude and latitude of cities.

Make a copy of the outline map of Texas. Then use an atlas to find and mark the following cities, rivers and mountains on the map:

Cities: **1.** Lubbock **2.** Midland **3.** Texarkana **4.** Arlington **5.** Beaumont **6.** Odessa

Rivers: **1.** Neches River **2.** Sabine River **3.** Colorado River **4.** Canadian River

Mountains:

1. Chisos Mountains **2.** Guadalupe Mountains **3.** Hueco Mountains **4.** Davis Mountains

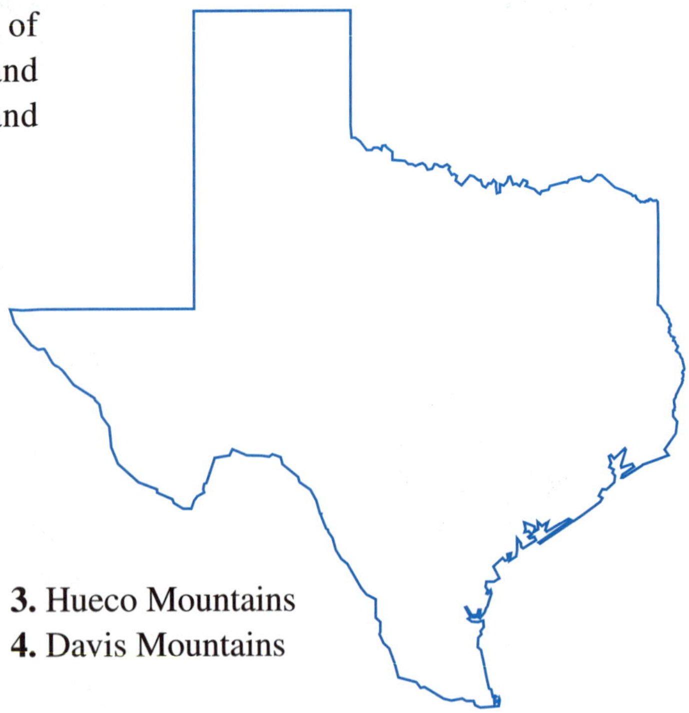

Using your atlas, answer the following questions:

1. What are some of the main farm products grown in Texas?
2. What are some of the major manufacturing cities in Texas?
3. What are some of the natural resources found in Texas?
4. In what part of Texas are most of its mountains located?

REVIEWING YOUR UNDERSTANDING

Directions: Fill in your Vocabulary Cards and complete the exercise that follows.

Urban
Define the word urban:
Name 2 urban areas in Texas:

Atlas
What is an atlas?
List some information you might
find in an atlas:

Describing the Place Where You Live

What are some of the special features of the place where you live? In your answer be sure to include the following:

- ☆ Climate
- ☆ Plants and animals
- ☆ Natural resources
- ☆ Topography
- ☆ Nearness to water
- ☆ Population density

Understanding Topography

What types of topography (land features) are shown in the photograph below?

Guadalupe National Park

Making A Collage About a "Place"

In this activity you read a book about a "place." Make a collage about that place. A collage is made by pasting a collection of items onto a piece a paper. Your collage can be made up of drawings, pictures or other materials. When these are pasted on a sheet of paper, they will tell about the story you read for this activity.

2D WHAT DOES TEXAS "LOOK" LIKE?

In this activity, you will learn to identify the physical features of Texas and its regions. Look for the following important words:

- ★ Panhandle
- ★ North Central Plains
- ★ Mountains and Basins
- ★ Gulf Coastal Plains
- ★ Great Plains Region
- ★ Almanac

Cartographers are people who make maps. In this activity, you will play the role of a junior cartographer. Let us begin with a simple question:

> To learn new information, do you think it is better to see a picture showing this information or to read a description of the information?

Let's check your answer by using the geography of Texas as a test case. You will be given descriptions of Texas and its regions. You will then be asked to convert these written descriptions on to a map of Texas.

TEXAS GEOGRAPHY AT A GLANCE

SIZE

Texas is the largest state in area in the continental United States. Of all the 50 states, only Alaska is larger. Texas is far larger than a great number of countries. In fact, Texas is so large that New York, New Jersey, Ohio, Illinois and Wisconsin could fit inside its borders—with room to spare.

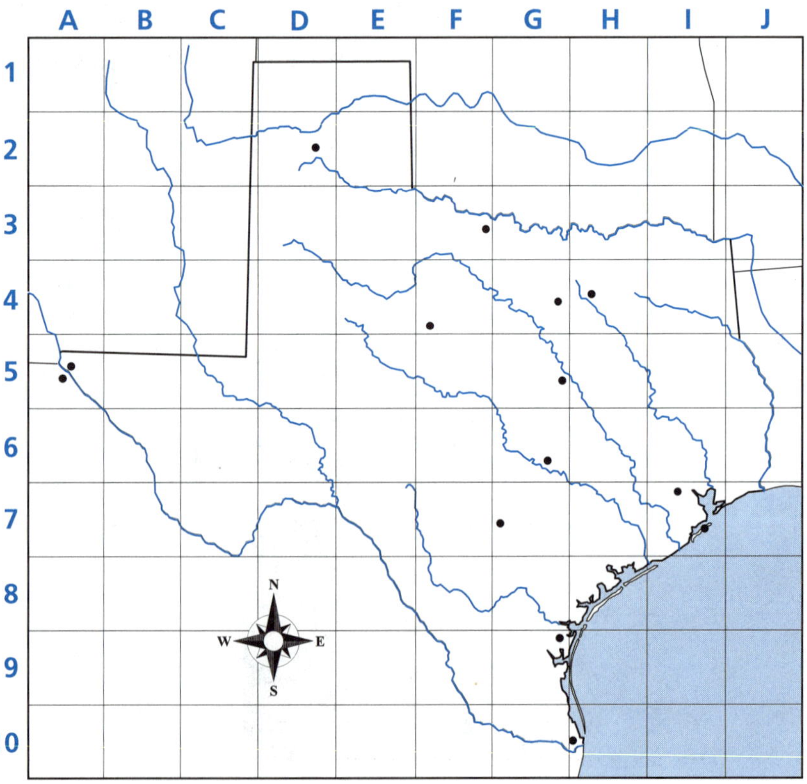

Texas is the second largest state in the United States in terms of population. In fact, three of the nation's largest

urban (*city*) areas are found in Texas. Texas often does things in a "big" way. The state raises more cattle, has more ranches and farmland, and produces more oil and gas than any other state. It also leads all other states in the length of its railroad tracks and roads.

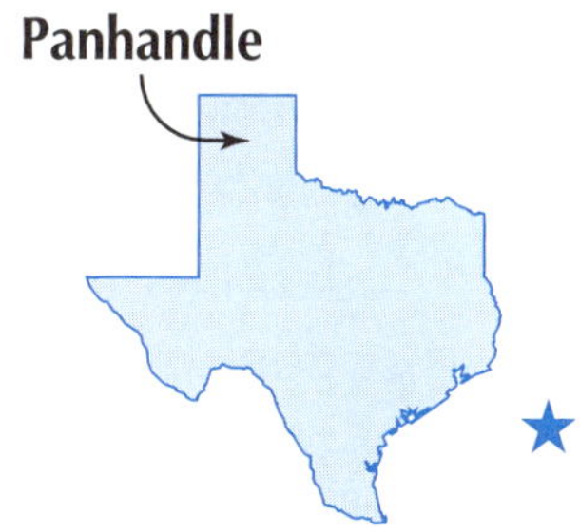

COASTLINE AND BORDERING STATES

Texas forms a rough triangle along the southern border of the United States. Jutting out at the top of the state is an area shaped like a **panhandle.** Texas is bordered by **Mexico** and the **Gulf of Mexico** to the south. Texas shares its other borders with several states. To the west, is **New Mexico.** Directly north of Texas is **Oklahoma.** To the north-east is **Arkansas. Louisiana** is just south of Arkansas.

Texas has one of the longest coastlines and some of the busiest ports in the United States. Its coastline along the Gulf of Mexico stretches 367 miles, from Louisiana to Mexico, with many deep-water ports.

Corpus Christi is a city on the Gulf of Mexico.
Do you live near any large bodies of water?

THE AMATEUR CARTOGRAPHER

Make a copy of the map of Texas found on page 38. Then, identify the following on your map:

- Mexico and the Gulf of Mexico
- New Mexico, Oklahoma, Arkansas and Louisiana

RIVERS AND LAKES

Three rivers serve as state borderlines. The **Rio Grande** forms the border between Texas and Mexico. It is the longest river in Texas. The **Red River** separates Texas from Oklahoma. In the east, the **Sabine River** separates Texas from Louisiana. Most of the rivers in Texas flow southward and empty into the Gulf of Mexico.

A bluff of the Canadian River
What other land forms can you identify?

The **Canadian River** flows eastward, across the top of the Texas Panhandle. Located due south of the Canadian River, in west Texas, is the **Pecos River.** It is the major river feeding into the Rio Grande.

The **Colorado River** flows through central Texas. (*To help you locate places on the map on page 38, grid coordinates have been supplied.*) The Colorado River is located on the map where the river begins, at E4. The **Nueces River** (which starts at E7) is located in the southern part of the state. Where the Nueces River flows into the Gulf of Mexico, the city of Corpus Christi (G9) is located. The **Brazos River** (which starts at D3) also flows through south Texas. The **Trinity River** (which starts at H4), is located in east Texas and flows through the city of Dallas.

In addition to its many rivers, Texas has thousands of lakes. These lakes range in size from small ponds to major bodies of water. Many lakes have been artificially created to irrigate farmland and provide flood control. During periods of little rainfall, especially in western Texas, water evaporates quickly. Rivers often dry up for weeks at a time. As a result, water is a precious and sometimes scarce natural resource.

THE AMATEUR CARTOGRAPHER

On your Texas map, identify the rivers of Texas described in this section.

★ CHECKING YOUR UNDERSTANDING ★

At the start of this activity, you were asked which was a better way of learning information—a word description or a picture description. Based on what you have just done, would you change your answer?

CLIMATE

We often hear people talk about the weather. How is *weather* different from *climate?* **Weather** is a description of an area's day-to-day conditions. One important condition in determining an area's weather is its temperature—how hot or cold it is. We use a **thermometer** to measure the outside temperature.

A summer rainstorm in the Davis Mountains
Does it rain much where you live?

Besides temperature, weather also takes into account such conditions as **precipitation.** Precipitation is the moisture that falls to the Earth in the form of rainfall, snow, hail and sleet. **Climate,** on the other hand, is the average of all of these weather conditions over a period of years.

Texas is thought of by many outsiders as being a hot, dry state. This is accurate for some but not all parts of the state. In some parts of Texas, like the northern plains, there can be winter blizzards. In the southeastern part of the state, the climate is damp with heavy rainfall. This type of climate helps farmers grow crops.

Temperatures vary in the state from north to south. In the Panhandle, winter temperatures average 35°F. (2°C.), while summers average 79°F. (24°C.). This limits crop growth to the spring and summer months. The highest temperatures in the state are found in the southwest in the Rio Grande valley. Here winter temperatures average about 60° F. (14°C.) As a result, grains and vegetables can be grown all year round.

THE AMATEUR CARTOGRAPHER

On your Texas map, label the average winter and summer temperatures in the Panhandle and the Rio Grande valley.

THINK ABOUT IT

Look out your classroom window. Describe today's weather. Now, describe the climate of your area during the winter months. Then, describe the climate of your area during the summer months. How is climate different from weather?

THE FOUR MAIN REGIONS OF TEXAS

As you would expect, a state the size of Texas has more than one climate or region. A **region** is an area of land that has similar geographic features. Places within a region are more like one another than areas outside the region. Texas can be thought of as consisting of four major land regions—the Gulf Coastal Plains, the North Central Plains, the Great Plains, and the Mountains and Basins region.

Each of the four regions of Texas can be thought of as a giant step on an imaginary staircase. As one moves westwards from the southeast coast, each region becomes higher in **elevation** (*height*)—ending in the high plains of the west and northwest.

THE AMATEUR CARTOGRAPHER

In the next few pages, you will read about each of the four regions of Texas and find a blank outline map for each region. Make a copy of each map before you read about the region. You might wish to trace the outline of each region, since they are all drawn to scale. You will be asked to give a title to your map and to label the cities and rivers in that region.

GULF COASTAL PLAINS

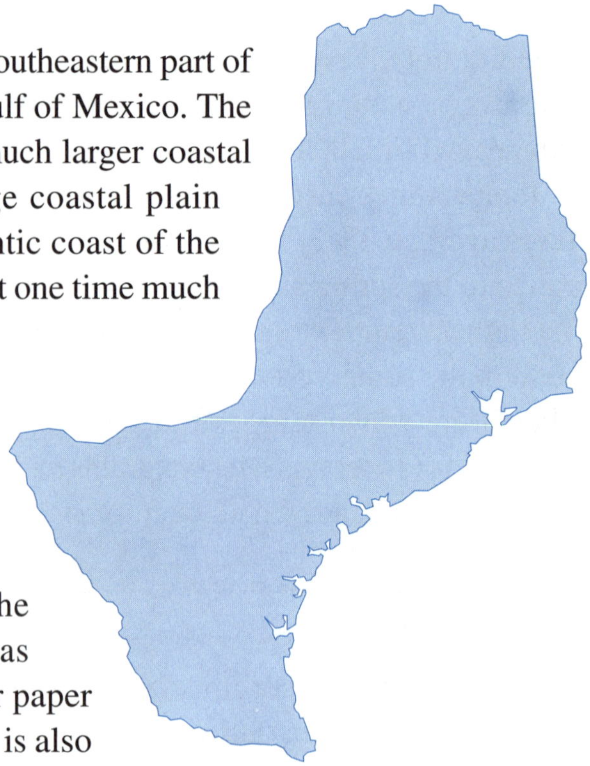

★ The **Gulf Coastal Plains** are located in the southeastern part of the state. They run along the coast of the Gulf of Mexico. The Gulf Coastal Plains of Texas are part of a much larger coastal plain—the largest in the world. This large coastal plain stretches from New Jersey, along the Atlantic coast of the United States, through Texas into Mexico. At one time much of this area was covered by sea water.

Along the shoreline of the Gulf Coastal Plains, a series of sandy **barrier islands** act as barriers between the bays and the seas. Today, many of these barrier islands are beaches and centers of recreation.

In the northeast of this region, along the border with Louisiana, is the area known as the Piney Woods. Its pine trees are used for paper and timber. **Big Thicket National Preserve** is also located here. To the west of the Piney Woods is the Post Oak Belt. Many of its oak trees have been cut down to make way for farms and ranches. Even further west, but still part of the Gulf Coastal Plains, is a strip of land known as the Blackland Prairie. Its rich black soil is fertile and covered by grass that is used for cattle raising.

The city of Galveston
Have you ever visited Galveston?

In the years before the 1860s, the Gulf Coastal Plains were the center of Texas' thriving cotton agriculture. In 1901, oil was discovered here. Since then, this region has been at the center of Texas' oil and gas industry. Because of the availability of water, nearness to the coast, and valuable raw materials, the Gulf Coastal Plains have the greatest concentration of industry and population in the state.

The three main urban areas of Texas—Houston, Dallas and San Antonio—are all found in the Gulf Coastal Plains. So are many other important cities, including Brownsville, Corpus Christi, Waco and the state capital at Austin.

Houston (I7) is the state's largest city, and the fourth largest city in the United States. Houston is located close to the Gulf Coast and north of Galveston (I7). The climate is humid and hot. Houston's Ship Channel allows large ships to sail into Houston, making

Houston skyline
What information in the photo tells you Houston is a major city in Texas?

it one of the nation's busiest seaports. During World War II, Houston became a center for manufacturing and petrochemicals. Today, it remains the center of the petrochemical industry. **Petrochemicals** are the products made from oil, such as nylon and plastics. The city is also the financial and industrial center for much of the state. Visitors to Houston enjoy the Astrodome, the Lyndon B. Johnson Space Center and the gardens of Bayou Bend.

Dallas (H4) is the state's second largest city in size. It is located on the edge of the Gulf Coastal Plains, just east of the North Central Plains. The city was built on what was once wooded prairie land. Dallas was originally founded as a trading post. It has since grown to become the southwest's leader in banking, wholesale business and insurance. The city has a large number of parks as well as the Museum of Natural History, an aquarium and a Museum of African-American Life and Culture.

President Johnson Library in Austin
Why do you think the library is located in Austin?

In 1839, **Austin** (G6) was chosen as the capital of Texas. The city was named after Stephen F. Austin, the "Father of Texas." It is the northeastern gateway to the Texas Hill Country. Austin is home to the President Lyndon B. Johnson Library and Museum, the State Capitol building and the University of Texas.

San Antonio (G7) is one of the oldest cities in Texas. It was founded in 1718 as a Spanish mission, where priests attempted to teach Christianity to the Native Americans. Later, it became the Spanish and then Mexican capital of Texas. Today, San Antonio is the third largest city in Texas and a center for industry. Visitors can see the River Walk, the Hemis Fair Plaza, the missions and the restored old town of La Villita.

Three other important cities in this region are Brownsville, Corpus Christi, Waco and Galveston. The city of **Brownsville** (H10) is located on the border with Mexico. It is the state's southernmost city and a major crossing point into Mexico. It was founded in 1846, to secure the Rio Grande as the nation's southern boundary. Today, Brownsville serves as an electronics, food processing and petrochemical center.

Corpus Christi (G9) is the largest city on the Texas Gulf Coast. It was first established as a frontier trading post. Today, it is one of Texas' most popular seacoast cities. **Waco** (G5) is located along the Brazos River. Today, Waco is noted for its educational, cultural and recreational facilities. **Galveston** (I7) is an important city located on a barrier island. It serves as a busy shipping port with many miles of attractive beaches.

The San Antonio River Walk
Which features in San Antonio make it modern even though it is one of the oldest cities in Texas?

THE AMATEUR CARTOGRAPHER

On your map identify the region and its major rivers and cities. Can you also identify the Piney Woods, the Post Oak Belt and the Blackland Prairie?

NORTH CENTRAL PLAINS

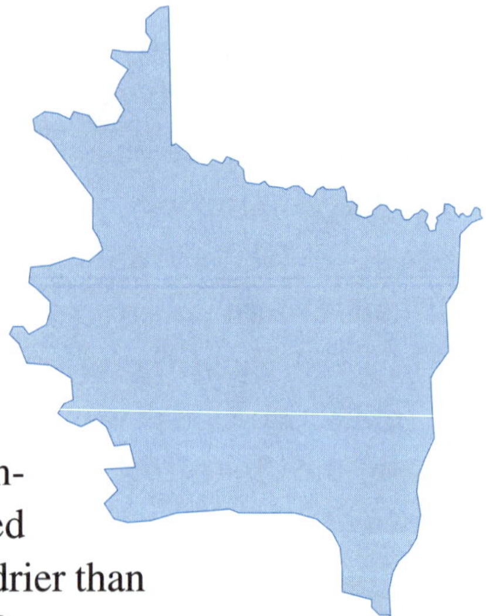

At the western edge of the Gulf Coastal Plains stands a line of hills. These balcony-like hills are called the **Balcones Escarpment** (*steep slopes or cliffs*). These hills mark the boundary between lowland and upland Texas. The cliffs extend the whole length of the state from Oklahoma south into Mexico. To the west of the ★ cliffs are the **North Central Plains.**

The North Central Plains of Texas are actually an extension of the prairies that dominate the Midwestern United States, and extend as far north as Canada. The climate is drier than in the Gulf Coastal Plains. These rolling grasslands have few trees, but provide excellent grazing for cattle. The North Central Plains region continues to be a center for cattle ranching, and the farming of cotton, wheat, peanuts and **sorghum** (*grain fed to livestock*).

The Ft. Worth stockyards.
Why do you think some people call Ft. Worth "Cowtown?"

The chief cattle trails and stagecoach routes once crossed this region. As a result, cities developed along its edge. **Fort Worth** (G4) was originally established in 1849. Since then it has grown to become an industrial center with a wide range of industries. Forth Worth and Dallas (across from Ft. Worth on the other side of the Balcones Escarpment) have grown so large, that they now form one urban center known as the **Metroplex.** The Metroplex thus stretches over into two regions of Texas: the Gulf Coastal Plains (Dallas) and the North Central Plains (Fort Worth).

Another city in this region is **Wichita Falls** (F3), near the Oklahoma border. Today it is the gateway to North Texas and a major trade and industrial center. A third important city is **Abilene** (F4). Cattle have always been important to this city. Abilene was established in 1881 by cattle ranchers as a major railroad shipping point. In more recent times, oil has become important to the city's economy.

THE AMATEUR CARTOGRAPHER

On your map identify the region, the Balcones Escarpment and the region's rivers and cities.

THE GREAT PLAINS REGION

The **Great Plains** of the Texas Panhandle start at the **Cap Rock Escarpment**—found along the western edge of the Central Lowlands. This natural boundary is two hundred miles long. The cliffs of the escarpment rise 1,000 feet in some places. To the west of the escarpment, the land rises again. This marks the beginning of dry grasslands, that extend all the way north to Canada. In Texas, most of this region is extremely flat. Although the climate is dry, fertilizers and irrigation have allowed farmers in the Panhandle of Texas to develop productive farms—specializing in cotton, grain and raising livestock.

The northern part of this region is known as the *Llano Estacado,* which is Spanish for "staked plain." According to tradition, the land was so flat and without landmarks that the early Spanish explorers drove stakes in the ground to mark their location. South of the *Llano Estacado* is the Edwards Plateau. The soil is thinner and mainly good for grazing. This region is known for its angora goats, that produce the wool for mohair sweaters. The hill country is found to the southeast, bordered on the south by the Balcones Escarpment.

The Great Plains are not as densely populated as eastern Texas. The largest and best well-known city in this region is **Amarillo** (D2). It has cold winters and cool nights. Amarillo is famous for its livestock auction, where cattle are bought and sold.

Snowfall in the Panhandle region
Does it snow where you live?

THE AMATEUR CARTOGRAPHER

On your map, identify the region and its major rivers and cities. Can you also identify the Cap Rock Escarpment, Llano Estacado and Edwards Plateau?

MOUNTAINS AND BASINS REGION

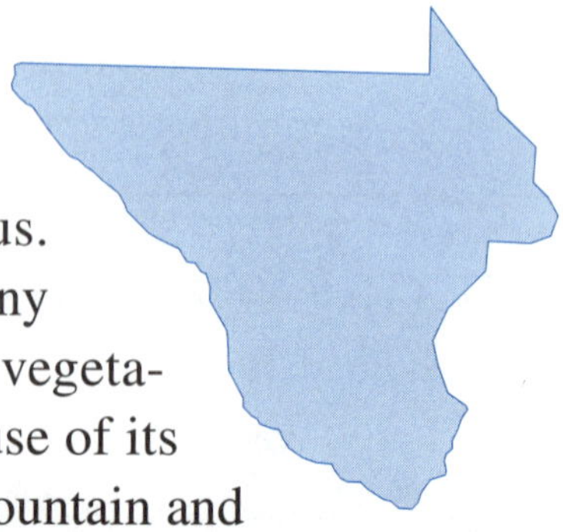

★ The **Mountains and Basins Region,** sometimes also called the Trans-Pecos Region, is located in the state's southwestern corner. The area is very dry and mountainous. The region contains all of the state's major mountains. Many people believe the blue skies, deserts, red soils and desert vegetation of this rugged area make it extremely beautiful. Because of its dry climate, this region is very sparsely populated. In the Mountain and Basins region are two national parks. **Guadalupe Mountain National Park** is a blend of deserts and wooded mountains. **Big Bend National Park** is made up of rugged riverbanks, deserts and mountains.

Guadalupe Peak, the highest point in Texas
Do you live near any mountains?

In the very western corner of this region is **El Paso** (A5), the fourth largest city in Texas. The city is one of the oldest in Texas and boasts several old Spanish missions and a Native American reservation. El Paso and its Mexican counterpart across the border, **Juarez** (A5), have benefited greatly from trade between the United States and Mexico.

The city of El Paso at night
Have you ever crossed into Mexico from El Paso?

THE AMATEUR CARTOGRAPHER

On your map, identify the region and its rivers and cities. Also identify Guadalupe Park and Big Bend Park.

TESTING YOUR EARLIER ANSWER

At the start of this activity, you were asked which was a better way of understanding information—through a word description or a picture. Based on what you have just done, would you change your answer?

THE AMATEUR CARTOGRAPHER

After reading about each region in Texas, you completed a regional map. Now cut out and combine all four sections to form a map of the whole state. Compare this map to the map of Texas that appears on page 368. Are your rivers, cities, and adjoining states the same as those shown on this map?

LOCATING PLACES

EXTENDING THE ACTIVITY

An **almanac** is another important reference tool. Let's look at how to use an almanac. ★

ALMANAC

An almanac is a book of facts. A new edition is published every year, so its information is always up to date. An almanac has a wide range of subjects—such as art, astronomy, business, countries of the world, education, entertainment, farming, geography, history and religion. Almanacs also contain lists of movie stars, explorers, musicians, writers, Nobel prize winners and athletes. A variety of information can be found in an almanac. For example, you can find which team won the football Super Bowl last year or which city in Texas has the largest population. Although many almanacs exist, two of the best known are:

- *The World Almanac and Book of Facts*
- *The Information Please Almanac*

Now let's put your knowledge about almanacs and atlases to work. In using these references, it is important to know the difference between relevant (*pertinent*) and irrelevant (*not pertinent*) information.

- **Relevant information** is information connected to the topic you are interested in. Relevant information is useful, appropriate and has some connection with what you are looking for.
- **Irrelevant information** is information not related or connected to the topic you are interested in. It is either not useful for solving the problem you are working on or it has no bearing on what you are looking at.

How well do you understand the difference between relevant and irrelevant information? Imagine that you wanted to identify one state from the following information. Which clues would be relevant and which would be irrelevant?

A. This state borders Texas.

This information is relevant. It narrows your search from 50 states to the four states that border Texas—(1) New Mexico, (2) Oklahoma, (3) Arkansas and (4) Louisiana.

B. This state has a governor.

This information is true, but irrelevant. Since every state in the United States has a governor, the information is not helpful.

C. This state borders the Mississippi River.

This information is relevant. Only two of the four states that border Texas also have borders along the Mississippi River—Arkansas and Louisiana. This piece of information further narrows your search to these two states.

D. This state has a state flag.

This information is also true, but irrelevant. Every state has its own state flag. This clue does not help you to narrow down the number of states.

E. This state was named after a King of France.

This final piece of information is relevant. Louisiana was named after King Louis XIV of France. Arkansas, on the other hand, received its name from the Quapaw Native Americans. Therefore, the answer is Louisiana.

Now that you understand the difference between relevant and irrelevant information, let's put your knowledge to use. Use the information below to identify the mystery city that is being referred to in the clues.

IDENTIFY THE MYSTERY CITY:

1. This city is located in Texas.
2. This city is located in the Gulf Coastal Plains.
3. This city is one of the three largest cities in Texas.
4. This city is **not** the capital of Texas.
5. Both English and Spanish are spoken in this city.
6. People in this city often celebrate weddings with large parties.
7. The city was founded as a Spanish mission in 1718.

★ CHECKING YOUR UNDERSTANDING ★

A. Can you name the mystery city?
B. Was clue #1 relevant? If so, why?
C. Was clue #2 relevant? If so, why?
D. Was clue #3 relevant? If so, why?
E. Was clue #4 relevant? If so, why?
F. Was clue #5 relevant? If so, why?
G. Was clue #6 relevant? If so, why?
H. Was clue #7 relevant? If so, why?

REVIEWING YOUR UNDERSTANDING

Directions: Fill in your Vocabulary Cards and complete the chart that follows.

Panhandle

What is the Panhandle?

In which region of Texas is it located?

Almanac

What is an almanac?

List some of the information you might find in an almanac:

Geographic Sections of Texas

Geographic Region				
Its Location in Texas	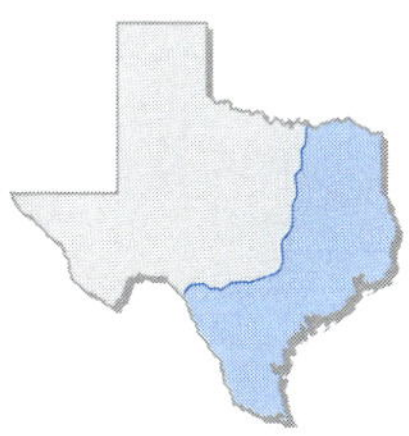			
Describe Its Main Physical Features				
Identify Its Major Cities				

Learning More About The Cities Of Texas

The cities of Texas have acted as human magnets attracting people. Today, these cities have become a mixture of tall buildings, convention and cultural centers and sprawling shopping malls. Let's take a closer look at some of the cities mentioned in this activity. Complete the information called for in the chart. The first city has already been done for you. To find this information consult as many of the following sources as needed:

- ☆ an almanac
- ☆ **Texas State Travel Guide** (Published by the *Texas Department of Transportation.* Phone: 1-800-452-9292)
- ☆ **Texas Almanac** (Published by the *A.H. Belo Corp.* Dallas, Texas. Phone: 1-800-642-6480)
- ☆ **Texas Facts: A Comprehensive Look At Texas Today** by John Clements Published by *Clements Research, Incorp.* Dallas, Texas)

City	Population	When Founded	Economic Activities	Region	Interesting Sites and Places of Interest
Abilene	*107,707*	*1881*	*cattle, farming, oil*	*North Central Plains*	*Abilene Zoo, Dyess Air Base, Ft. Phantom Hill, Shore Art Gallery*
Amarillo					
Austin					
Brownsville					
Corpus Christi					
Dallas					
El Paso					
Fort Worth					
Galveston					
Houston					
San Antonio					
Waco					
Wichita Falls					
Your City					

★ Checking Your Understanding ★

1. Which source did you find most helpful in locating information?

2. Look over the list of cities and the information you gathered about each city. Do these cities have anything in common?

2E WHAT DO SOCIAL SCIENTISTS DO?

In this activity, you will compare the work of geographers with the work of other social scientists. You will also discover how the geographical features of a place are often connected, and how people can be affected by their environment. Look for the following important words:

★ Social Scientist ★ Physical and Cultural Regions ★ Ecosystem

THINK ABOUT IT

On a separate sheet of paper, describe what you see in this illustration.

You may answer that you see a boy and a girl. However, other people might look at the same picture and focus on something else. For example, a very young child might look and "see" an older brother or sister. A teacher might "see" students while a store-owner might "see" possible customers. *Who* we are often determines *what* we focus on.

In this activity, you will explore how different social scientists look at physical and cultural regions of the world with a different focus. A **social scientist** is someone who studies human activities in a scientific way. Social scientists record facts and attempt to understand why things happen the way they do. We will start by examining what is meant by physical and cultural regions.

NOTES ABOUT REGIONS

A **region** is a group of areas sharing common features and characteristics. There are physical regions and cultural regions.

PHYSICAL REGIONS

A **physical region** is an area that shares the same climate, plant and animal life or land forms. It is different from areas outside the region. A physical region can be quite large—like Antarctica, one of the seven continents. It can also be small like the Panhandle region.

CONTINUED

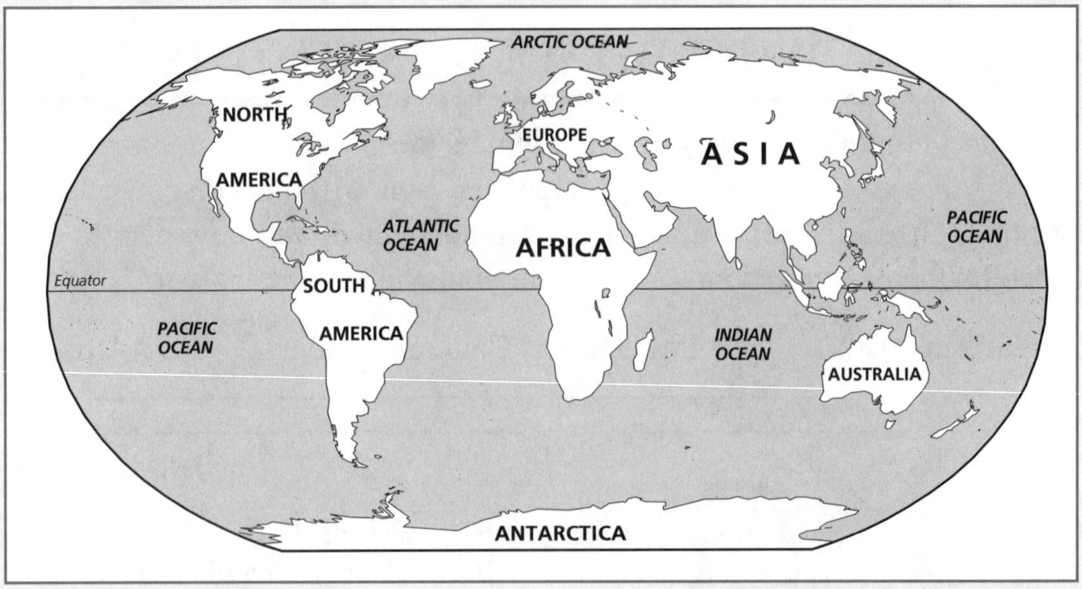

The Amazon Rain Forest in South America is another example of a large physical region. Throughout this vast area, the climate is hot all year long, with frequent rain showers. Many tropical trees grow in the Amazon region, and a great number of plant and animal species are unique to this area.

The four regions of Texas—the Gulf Coastal Plains, the North Central Plains, the Great Plains and the Mountains and Basins Region—are also examples of physical regions.

The Great Plains, where many farms in Texas are located
Do you live near a farm area?

CULTURAL REGIONS

Culture refers to a people's way of life. You can think of culture as the ABCs of human society: **a**ttitudes, **b**usinesses, **c**ustoms, **d**ress, **e**xpressions, **f**ood, **g**overnment, **h**ousing, **i**nteresting manners, **j**... (*How many more can you add?*) **Cultural regions** are areas in which people share common cultural characteristics—such as language, history or religious beliefs.

A cultural region can be small, like the Amish community in Pennsylvania. A cultural region can also be quite large, like Latin America. Several features make Latin America a cultural region. The great majority of people in the area are Catholics. The main language spoken is Spanish. Finally, the peoples of Latin America communicate more with one another than they do with people from countries outside this region.

CONTINUED

Cultural regions can be grouped according to a variety of characteristics. This map shows one way some geographers have grouped the world's cultural regions:

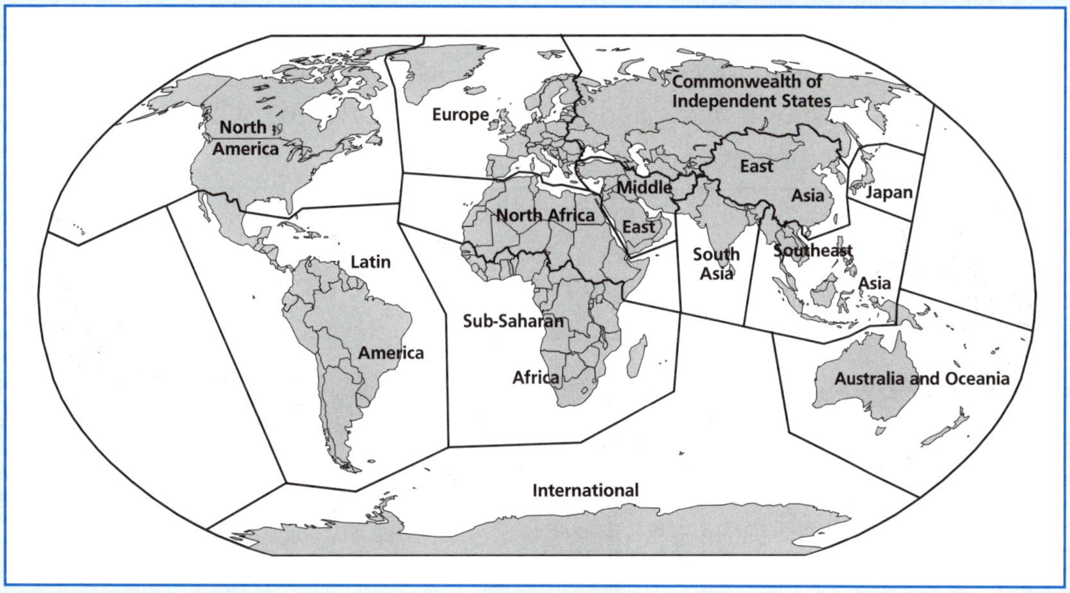

LOOKING AT NORTH AMERICA

Let's explore the idea of seeing things with a different focus by examining how three different kinds of social scientists might view North America and the countries found within it.

★ CHECKING YOUR UNDERSTANDING ★

1. Archeologists, anthropologists, political scientists and historians are also social scientists. Look in a dictionary to find out what each of these social scientists does.
2. Which countries are located in North America?
3. Which two major bodies of water border North America?

WHAT WOULD A GEOGRAPHER FOCUS ON?

There are many different types of social scientist. One type is a **geographer.** A geographer studies the physical and cultural features of an area. Geographers are especially concerned with the five themes of geography: location, place, region, human-environmental interaction and movement. For example, a geographer might describe the mountains, rivers and climate of a place and how they have affected where people live, how they use the land, how they travel and what they trade.

THINK ABOUT IT

What do you think a **geographer** might focus on in North America?

A geographer would focus on the fact that North America is the third largest continent, after Asia and Africa. North America makes up about 16% of the Earth's land. It occupies over 9.4 million square miles. Geographers look at North America as a continent bordered by three oceans—the Pacific, Atlantic and Arctic.

Corpus Christi is located near the coast of the United States.
How far do you live from the coast?

A geographer would note that North America's size gives it a wide range of climates. In the north, near the Arctic Ocean, it is almost always cold. In the south, where North America joins South America, it is generally hot, except in mountain areas. In between, there is a wide range of different climates.

A geographer would also note that North America has a long coastline, with many excellent harbors. There are two major mountain ranges—the **Rocky Mountains** in the west and the **Appalachian Mountains** in the east. Between these mountain ranges are vast grasslands, a dry plateau and North America's largest deserts.

A geographer might also be interested in patterns of human settlement and urbanization. Many large urban centers, like New York City, Houston and Vancouver are on coasts. Climate also affects where people live. For example, in Mexico, most people live on a high **plateau** (*an area of elevated, flat land*). There, temperatures are cooler and more comfortable than near the coasts. As a result, Mexico's **population density** (*average number of people living in an area*) is greatest there, even though this city is located inland.

WHAT WOULD A SOCIOLOGIST FOCUS ON?

A **sociologist** studies how societies work and the relationships among groups in a society. For example, a sociologist would be interested in the roles that society expects us to play, and in social units like the family. Sociologists look particularly at social structure and social change. They might divide a society into its main groups, and see which group has the most influence and power. They would also look at how some groups keep other groups under control. They look at **social mobility**—how easy it is to move from one social group to another. Finally, sociologists would examine whether any groups in the society are gaining or losing power.

THINK ABOUT IT

What do you think a **sociologist** might focus on in North America?

A sociologist would focus on the fact that North America is a continent with over 430 million people. A sociologist would be interested in what holds these societies together and how different groups in these societies deal with each other.

For example, many people in Canada and the United States are of European and African origins. In Mexico, most of the people are **mestizo**—of mixed European and Native American-ancestry. In Central America and the Caribbean, people of European origin are in the minority. A sociologist might be interested in how these different ancestries affect social relations in these areas.

Mexico City has more people than any other city in the world.
What is the population of your city?

Another item of interest to a sociologist would be the degree of **urbanization** (*living in cities*). Most people in North America live in cities. The largest cities in North America are Mexico City, New York City, Los Angeles, Chicago, Houston and Toronto. How does this affect how people relate?

A sociologist would also find that more than 85% of the people living in North America are Christians—either Roman Catholic or Protestant. The principal languages spoken are English (*in Canada and the United States*), Spanish (*in parts of the United Sates, Mexico and most of Central America*), Portuguese (*in Brazil*) and French (*in parts of Canada*).

Sociologists might examine North American sports like baseball, football, basketball, soccer and ice hockey. A sociologist might wish to study how all these different customs developed.

WHAT WOULD AN ECONOMIST FOCUS ON?

An **economist** studies the kinds of goods and services a society produces, how they are made, and how they are used. Economists are especially concerned with knowing *who* makes decisions about *what* a society will make, *how* it will be made and *how* it will be used. Economists study things like the total production of a society, the ways people earn a living, how much money people earn, and how the government affects what people produce and earn.

THINK ABOUT IT

What do you think an **economist** might focus on in North America?

An economist would be impressed with the fact that North America produces most of the world's wheat, corn, peanuts, oats, apples, potatoes, cotton, soybeans, tobacco and meat. North America is also rich in mineral resources. These resources include coal, iron, bauxite, copper, natural gas, petroleum, mercury, nickel, potash and silver.

An auto assembly plant in Detroit
What would an economist ask about this picture?

An economist would also note that most of the countries of North America have a highly-educated work force. The factories of North America provide many manufactured products. However, most people in the United States and Canada actually provide services to others rather than working in factories.

An economist would be especially interested in knowing how the people in each country in North America decide what goods and services to make and how they choose to sell them. Most of these countries follow the **free enterprise system** (*also known as capitalism*). People are free to make and buy whatever they can. The government provides services to help people, while it regulates business and trade.

PLAYING THE ROLE OF A SOCIAL SCIENTIST

Now it's your turn to pretend you are a social scientist. What might different social scientists focus on in looking at a country in South America? To find out, your teacher will divide the class into groups. Students in the group should each take the role of a different type of social scientist. Each group will investigate a different country in South America, and report back to the other students in the class.

Social Scientists	Questions A Social Scientist Might Ask About This Country In South America	What Would A Social Scientist Focus On In Looking At This South American Country?
Geographer	**1.** What are the main physical features of the country? **2.** What is the climate?	
Sociologist	**1.** What are the chief social groups? **2.** What is the role of women?	
Economist	**1.** What goods and services are made in this country? **2.** What goods are exported?	

To find information for this assignment, you may wish to:

- look up the country in an **encyclopedia.**
- check the facts and statistics of the country in an **almanac** listed under the heading: "Countries" or "Nations of the World."
- consult an **atlas** to find some of the geographic features of the country.
- find **books** in the library that deal with that country.
- use **magazines** such as *National Geographic*. Your librarian can help you find particular articles on individual countries.
- view a **video** about your chosen country.

THE IMPACT OF GEOGRAPHY ON PEOPLE'S LIVES

EXTENDING THE ACTIVITY

In this activity, you learned about physical and cultural regions. Within a physical region such as a rain forest, a desert or a mountain range, there are important relationships between climate, land forms, water, plants and animals. For example, in a desert, plants that do not need much water can thrive. Similarly, animals that can withstand intense cold are able to live in icy climates like the Arctic.

Even the Earth's water has a natural cycle. Clouds of water vapor move from areas above oceans to areas above land. When they reach mountains, they often turn to rain or snow. The rain washes down the mountains, forming streams, rivers and vast underground water systems. This fresh water is used by both plants and animals. Eventually it flows downhill, back to the sea. The world's oceans depend on river water to keep them filled. At the same time, the world's rivers depend on rain from clouds of water vapor coming from the ocean. All plants and animals depend upon this natural cycle for their existence.

OUR FRAGILE ECOSYSTEMS

★ Within a physical region, there is usually a balanced relationship known as an **ecosystem.** "Ecosystem" refers to the way living things in a region interact with each other. The same nutrients and energy flow through the different levels of the ecosystem. Thus, a prairie's ecosystem would include coyotes, the rabbits on which they feed, and the grasses that feed the rabbits. Energy flows from the Sun to the grasses, from the grasses to the rabbits, and from the rabbits to the coyotes. When the rabbits and coyotes die, they in turn enrich the soil for the grasses.

People, like plants and animals, are affected by land forms, climate and the availability of water. They develop different life-styles in response to their physical surroundings. Where people settle is also influenced by geographic factors. They often live along rivers. They frequently settle where there is a moderate climate.

However, by adapting to their environment, humans can live virtually anywhere. For example, warm clothing can be worn to make extremely cold climates bearable. Humans also have the power to alter their environments. For example, the Israelis have turned desert into fertile farm land by using new irrigation methods.

In this activity, you and your classmates looked at various countries in South America from three different viewpoints. The outline map of South America on the right shows its major land forms and bodies of water. Make a photocopy of this map. Then shade in the areas of the map where you think most people in South America live.

THINK ABOUT IT

Explain why you selected those areas to shade in on the map:

GEOGRAPHIC FEATURES OF SOUTH AMERICA

South America is a large continent surrounded by the Pacific and Atlantic Oceans. Because South America lies near the **equator,** much of it has a warm climate. Up in the hills and mountains it is cooler because of the elevation and ocean winds. Along the western side of the continent rise the **Andes Mountains.** This mountain range is among the world's highest. **Tropical rain forests** occupy much of the northeast region of the continent near the equator. These forest areas have warm, humid climates and receive a great deal of rainfall.

The **Gran Chaco** is an extremely hot lowland plain in Argentina, Brazil, Bolivia and Paraguay. Most of the Gran Chaco is dry land, dotted with swamps during the rainy season. Some areas are thick jungle.

The **Amazon Rain Forest** is the world's largest rain forest. The **Amazon River,** flowing 2,300 miles, is the world's second longest river. Two other important rivers in South America are the **Rio de la Plata** and the **Orinoco.** They provide important links in the area's transportation system.

Mountains, rain forests and poor soils make much of South America's land unsuitable for farming. However, large grassy, treeless plains in the southeast (*the **pampas** of Argentina*) and northwest (*the **llanos** of Venezuel*a) contain very fertile land. These lands are similar to the prairies of North America. They are used to raise crops and graze cattle.

The map on the right shows where most of the population of South America has settled. Compare this map with your own predictions from page 58.

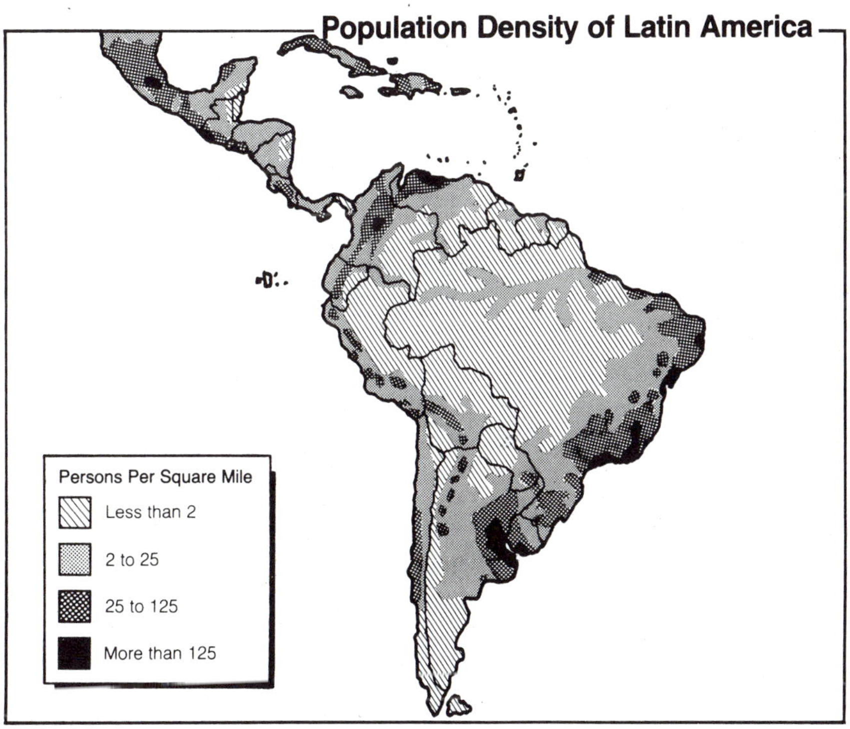

★ CHECKING YOUR UNDERSTANDING ★

1. Draw the symbol used to show an area with a population of:
- ☆ less than 2 people per square mile
- ☆ more than 125 people per square mile

2. Which areas of South America appear to have the highest population density?
❑ Coastal areas ❑ Central areas

3. Look at your own map on page 58, where you shaded in areas where you thought most people in South America live.
A. How accurate was your map? ❑ Accurate ❑ Not Accurate
B. If your earlier map was not very accurate, why do you now think most South Americans live where they do?

SKILL BUILDER: POPULATION DENSITY MAPS

Maps provide many types of information. One common use of maps is to show how many people live in a particular area. A **population density map** tells us the average number of people who live in a given space. To understand population density better, let us look at two imaginary cities that are identical in area.

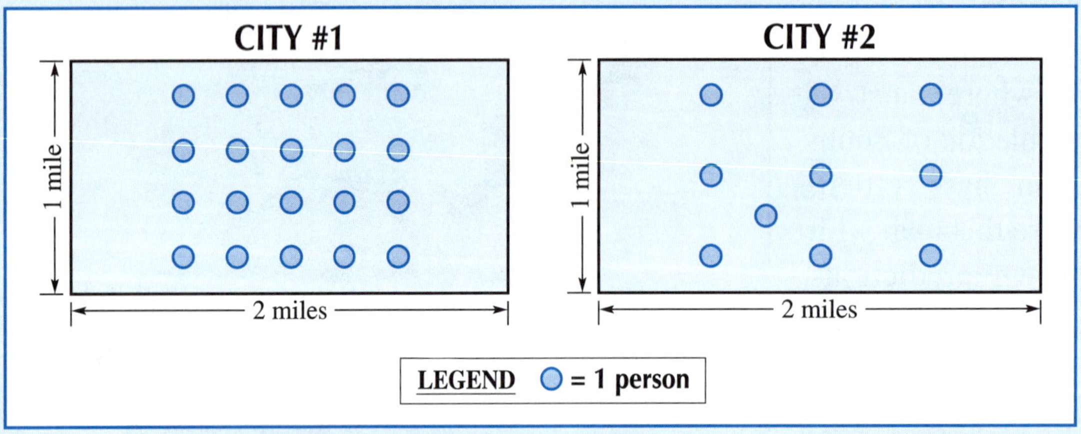

In City #1, there are 20 people living in an area of 2 square miles. City #2 has 10 people living in the same area. City #1 is more crowded, because there are twice as many people living in the same area. Another way of saying this is that City #1 has a higher population density than City #2.

To figure out the population density of any place, we divide the number of people by the space they occupy. For example, let's look again at both cities. Both cities are 2 square miles in area. Since City #1 has 20 people living in it, we can

CONTINUED

find its population density by dividing its number of people (20) by the number of square miles (2) in its area. Thus, its population density is 10 people per square mile. This means that every square mile in City #1 has, on average, 10 people living in it.

The population density for City #2 is the number of people (10) divided by the number of square miles (2), or 5 people per square mile. From this, we see that City #2 is exactly twice as crowded (*or densely populated*) as City #1.

Let's put your knowledge about population density maps to use. Study the population density map of Texas in 1990, and then answer the questions that follow:

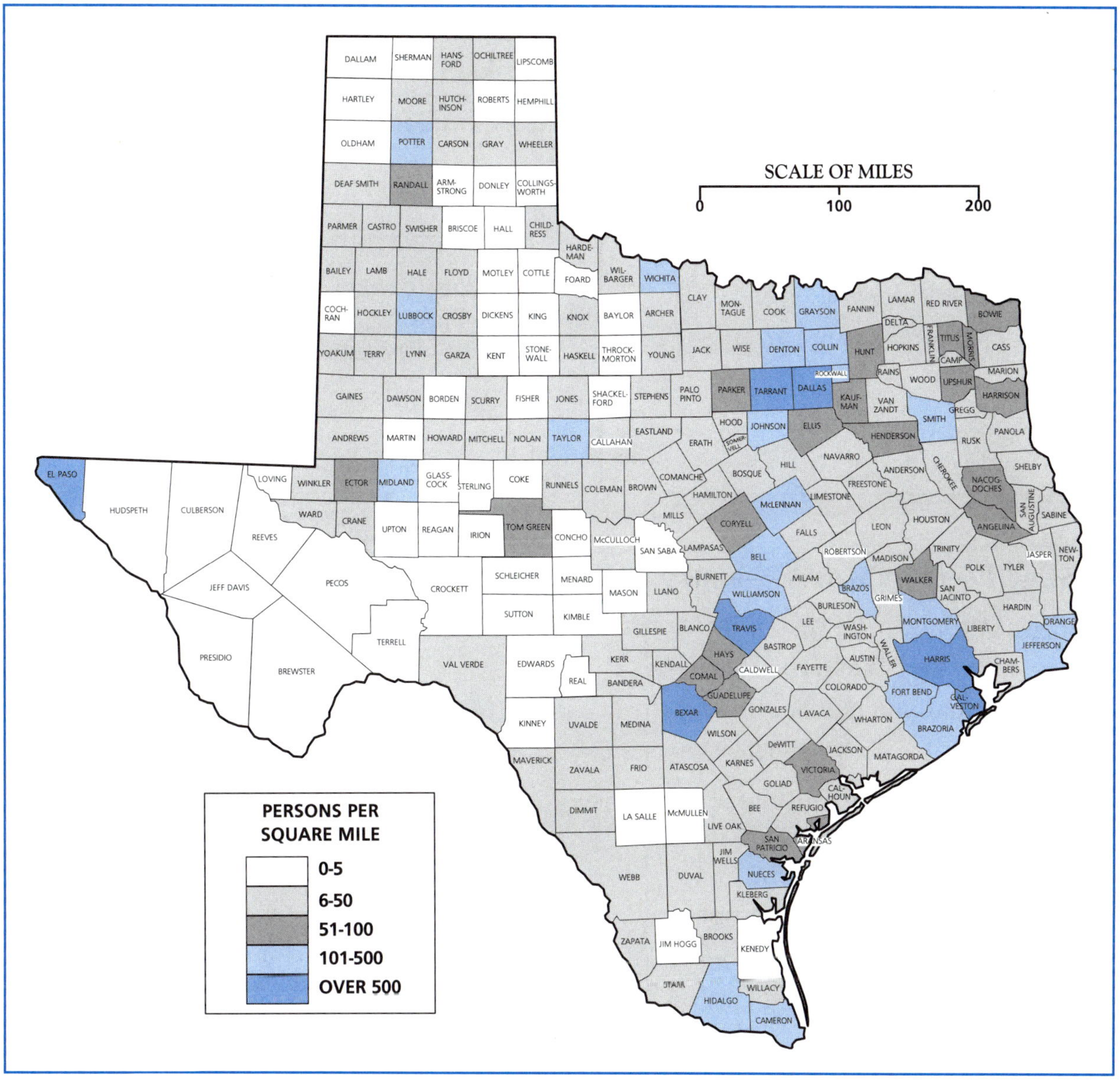

★ Checking Your Understanding ★

1. What are population density maps used for?

2. Name a county in Texas in which the population density is:
- less than 5 persons per square mile
- over 500 persons per square mile

3. Which parts of Texas are most densely populated?

4. Which parts of Texas are least densely populated?

5. What factors can you think of to explain why some areas of Texas are more heavily populated than others?

REVIEWING YOUR UNDERSTANDING

Directions: Fill in your Vocabulary Cards, then complete the project that follows.

Physical and Cultural Regions

What is a physical region?

What is a cultural region?

Ecosystem

What is an ecosystem?

Describe the relationship of plants and animals in an ecosystem:

Writing Poetry About A Country In the Western Hemisphere

Can you create a poem about a country in the Western Hemisphere? Actually, it can be fun and informative. To do so, write the name of a country vertically. Then, for each letter, select a phrase that provides information about the country you selected. For example, if you selected Mexico:

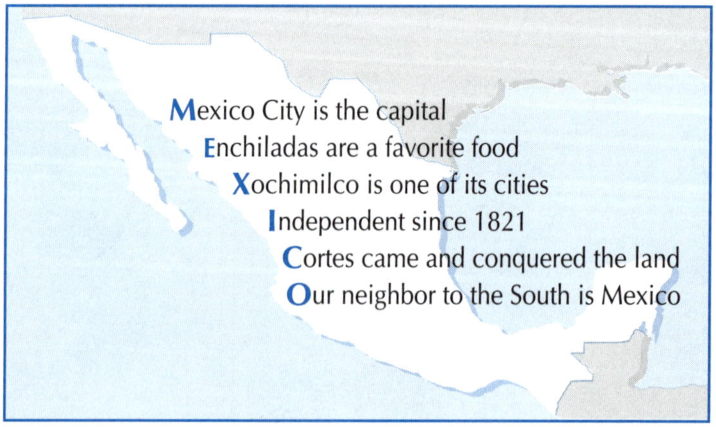

2F WHERE WOULD YOU LOCATE YOUR BASEBALL TEAM?

In this activity, you will apply your knowledge of geography to a specific purpose: choosing the best city for a new baseball team. Look for the following important words:

★ Per Capita Income ★ Chart ★ Latin America

Wow! It is hard to believe your good fortune in the last two weeks. First, you won the Lotto Texas for over $100 million. Then, you successfully bid on buying a new baseball team. All your life you have been a baseball fan, and at last your dream has been realized. You are now the proud owner of a team. There is just one small problem. You must find a city in which to locate your baseball team.

THINK ABOUT IT

In which city would you like to locate your baseball team?
Why would you want to locate the team in that city?

CHOOSING A CITY FOR A BASEBALL TEAM

You decide to hire a panel of experts to help you with such an important decision. They tell you that the location of your team requires a great deal of thought and investigation. The final decision depends on many factors. For one thing, you cannot choose a city that already has a major league team. Your experts give you a list of those cities that already have major league baseball teams.

Make a copy of the map on page 64. Then, using an atlas, mark the location of each city that has a major league team. This will allow you to see where all current baseball teams are located.

CITIES WHERE MAJOR LEAGUE BASEBALL TEAMS ARE LOCATED	
Atlanta *Braves*	Baltimore *Orioles*
Chicago *Cubs*	Boston *Red Sox*
Cincinnati *Reds*	Calif. (Anaheim) *Angels*
Colorado (Denver) *Rockies*	Chicago *White Sox*
Florida (Miami) *Marlins*	Cleveland *Indians*
Houston *Astros*	Detroit *Tigers*
Los Angeles *Dodgers*	Kansas City *Royals*
Montreal (Canada) *Expos*	Milwaukee *Brewers*
New York (City) *Mets*	Minnesota *Twins*
Philadelphia *Phillies*	New York (City) *Yankees*
Pittsburgh *Pirates*	Oakland *Athletics*
St. Louis *Cardinals*	Seattle *Mariners*
San Diego *Padres*	**Texas (Arlington) *Rangers***
San Francisco *Giants*	Toronto (Canada) *Blue Jays*

(Arizona *Diamondbacks* and the Tampa Bay *Sting Rays* begin play in 1997).

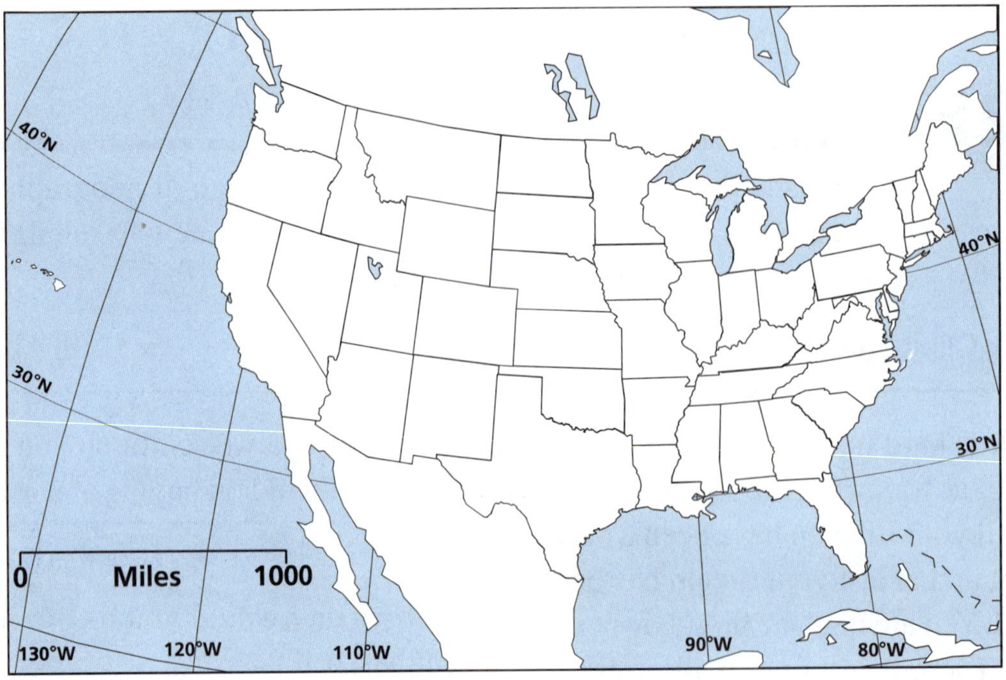

RESEARCHING THE CITIES YOU SELECT

As the owner of a baseball team, you will need fans to come to the games to help pay your costs. Your experts now tell you there are other factors to think about. These include:

1. **Population.** The city should have a population large enough to support a baseball team.
2. **Population Density.** This means the average number of people living in an area. The city should have a high population density—where the population is concentrated rather than spread out over a large area. Finding the population density of a city is fairly simple. You need to divide the number of people living in the city by the size of its land. For example, Austin is the capital of Texas. It has a population of 465,648. The size of Austin is 116 square miles. To find its population density, use a calculator to divide the number of square miles into the size of the population:

   $\frac{465,648}{116}$ = 4,014. Thus, Austin has about 4,000 people per square mile.

3. **Growth.** The city should have a growing population. A city that loses population each year would not be a good place to locate a baseball team.

★ CHECKING YOUR UNDERSTANDING ★

Galveston, Texas has a population of 217,396. It is about 400 square miles in area. What is the approximate population density of Galveston?

4. **Unemployment.** The city should have a low unemployment rate. This means that most people are working and can afford to attend some games each year or to buy products from advertisers sponsoring games.
5. **Per Capita Income.** This means the average amount of income for each individual. The city should have many people who earn a reasonable income to spend on activities like attending a baseball game or on buying advertisers' products.
6. **Climate.** The city should have mild weather between April and September. This is normally when most baseball games are played.

A plane about to land
Does your city have an airport?

7. **Transportation.** The city should have a good transportation system—including an airport, a bus terminal and a major railroad line.
8. **Attractions.** The city should have interesting tourist attractions. This will encourage people in surrounding areas to visit the city. While they are visiting, they may want to attend a baseball game.

You ask the experts, "Where am I going to find that kind of information about each city?" They tell you that this information is readily available in *The World Almanac and Book of Facts,* or other popular almanacs. Just look in the index to find "Cities of the U.S."

To simplify matters, you should limit your search to **three** cities. Look over the following chart:

AMERICA'S LARGEST CITIES WITHOUT A MAJOR LEAGUE BASEBALL TEAM			
Akron, Ohio	Fort Wayne, Indiana	Long Beach, California	Sacramento, California
Albuquerque, N.M.	Fort Worth, Texas	Louisville, Kentucky	St. Paul, Minnesota
Anchorage, Alaska	Fremont, California	Lubbock, Texas	St. Petersburg, Florida
Aurora, Colorado	Fresno, California	Madison, Wisconsin	San Antonio, Texas
Austin, Texas	Glendale, California	Memphis, Tennessee	San Jose, California
Bakersfield, California	Grand Rapids, Michigan	Mesa, Arizona	Santa Ana, California
Baton Rouge, Louisiana	Greensboro, N.C	Mobile, Alabama	Shreveport, Louisiana
Birmingham, Alabama	Hialeah, Florida	Montgomery, Alabama	Spokane, Washington
Buffalo, N.Y.	Honolulu, Hawaii	Nashville, Tennessee	Stockton, California
Charlotte, N.C.	Huntington Beach, California	Newark, N.J.	Tacoma, Washington
Columbus, Georgia	Indianapolis, Indiana	New Orleans, Louisiana	Toledo, Ohio
Columbus, Ohio	Jackson, Mississippi	Norfolk, Virginia	Tucson, Arizona
Corpus Christi, Texas	Jacksonville, Florida	Oklahoma City, Oklahoma	Tulsa, Oklahoma
Dallas, Texas	Jersey City, N.J.	Portland, Oregon	Virginia Beach, Virginia
Dayton, Ohio	Las Vegas, Nevada	Raleigh, N.C.	Washington, D.C.
Des Moines, Iowa	Lexington, Kentucky	Richmond, Virginia	Wichita, Kansas
El Paso, Texas	Lincoln, Nebraska	Riverside, California	Yonkers, N.Y.
	Little Rock, Arkansas	Rochester, N.Y.	

KEEPING TRACK OF THE INFORMATION

While gathering your information, you should fill in a copy of the chart on the bottom of this page to keep track of the data.

SKILL BUILDER: CHARTS

★ A **chart** is an arrangement of words or numbers in columns. It is used for organizing large amounts of information so that they can be easily located and compared. The chart usually shows different categories of information. These categories are named in the headings found across the top of the chart and down the left-hand side. In this case, the categories listed along the top row of the chart below are: *City #1, City #2* and *City #3.* Categories down the left-hand side include: *population, population density, growth rate,* and so on.

After you have completed the chart, you can find specific information by looking where the rows and columns meet. For example, assume that Corpus Christi. Texas was City #1 (the first column on the top). How would you find Corpus Christi's rate of unemployment? Place your finger at the top of the City #1 column. Slide your finger down the column until you reach "rate of unemployment." Where this row meets the first column should be a number that tells you the rate of unemployment in Corpus Christi.

	CITY #1	CITY #2	CITY #3
NAMES OF CITIES			
Population			
Population Density			
Growth Rate			
Rate of Unemployment			
Per Capita Income			
Climate			
Transportation			
Major Tourist Attractions			

After you have completed your research and filled in the chart, answer the following questions:

1. In which city would you now locate your new baseball team?
2. Why did you finally decide on that city?
3. Is this city different from the city you first selected? If so, what factors made you change your mind?

CREATING A TEAM NAME AND LOGO

Selecting a city for your team is only part of the fun of owning a team. Each major league baseball team must have a name, such as the Texas Rangers or the Houston Astros. Houston plays its home games in the world's first indoor stadium—the Astrodome. As a result, it chose the name Astros, short for Astrodome.

THINK ABOUT IT

What will you call your new team? Why did you choose that name?

In addition to a name, each team must have its own **logo,** or team symbol. For example, the baseball team in Miami, Florida, uses the marlin—a large fish found in the waters off the coast of Florida—as its logo. What will your logo look like? Make a copy of the baseball cap. Then design your team's new logo to fit the front of the cap.

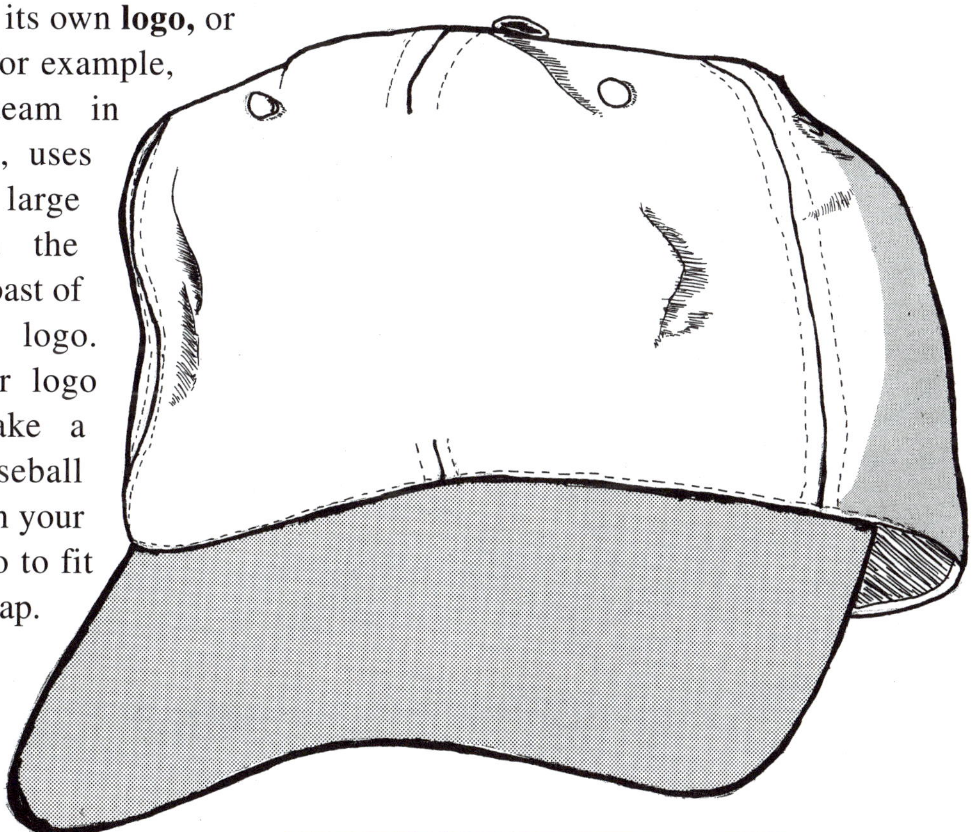

THINK ABOUT IT

Why did you decide on that particular logo?

USING AN ALMANAC TO COMPARE AND CONTRAST

EXTENDING THE ACTIVITY

It has just been announced that the baseball owners want to increase the number of major league baseball teams. They want to select a country in **Latin America** (*Mexico, Central America, parts of the Caribbean and South America*) for a team. Which Latin American nation would you suggest?

One of the things you might consider is how that nation compares with the United States and Canada—two countries that already have major league teams. An almanac can be a helpful reference for deciding in which country to locate the new team. Almanacs can be used to **compare** and **contrast** (*seeing how two or more items are alike and different from each other*). We compare and contrast things to better understand what each item is really like, and what is unique about each.

You will need to find information in an almanac on **two countries** in Latin America. Then compare and contrast the United States, Canada and the two countries you have selected. This information can be found by looking in the "Nations" or "Countries of the World" section of the almanac. You can also use the "Yearbook" of an encyclopedia to find this information.

	U.S.A.	CANADA	Country from LATIN AMERICA	Country from LATIN AMERICA
Population				
Population Density				
Land Area				
Capital City				
Type of Government				
Major Industries				
Language Spoken				
Number of Motor Vehicles				
Number of Telephones				
Life Expectancy at Birth				
Literacy Rate				

★ Checking Your Understanding ★

1. Which two countries are most similar? Explain.
2. Which two countries are most different? Explain.
3. Which Latin American country would you select for a baseball team? Explain.

REVIEWING YOUR UNDERSTANDING

Directions: Fill in your Vocabulary Cards, and complete the project that follows.

Population Density
Define population density:
Why might a business be
interested in this information?

Per Capita Income
Define per capita income:
Why might a business be
interested in this information?

Where Do Most Texans Live?

In this and Activity 2D, you learned about the climate, rivers, cities and regions of Texas. The map on page 61 shows the population density of Texas—where Texans live. Which factors do you think have been most important in determining where Texans have settled?

- topography of the land
- rainfall and availability of water
- location of mineral resources
- nearness to rivers
- fertility of the soil
- location by major intersections of railroad lines
- nearness to the Gulf coastline
- areas of early Native American settlement
- areas first explored and settled by Spaniards
- location along major cattle trails
- direction from which American settlers first came

SUMMARIZING YOUR UNDERSTANDING

Directions: Make a copy of the following organizer. Use your knowledge to fill in the blanks.

HOW THE FEATURES OF A MAP HELP US TO UNLOCK ITS MEANING

A TITLE helps us by...

A LEGEND (KEY) helps us by...

A SCALE helps us by...

A DIRECTION INDICATOR helps us by...

IDENTIFYING ITEMS ON A MAP AND GLOBE

Directions: Make a copy of the map below. Then label each of the following areas on the map of the world: (1) Northern Hemisphere; (2) Southern Hemisphere; (3) Eastern Hemisphere; (4) Western Hemisphere; (5) North Pole; (6) South Pole; (7) equator; and (8) Prime Meridian.

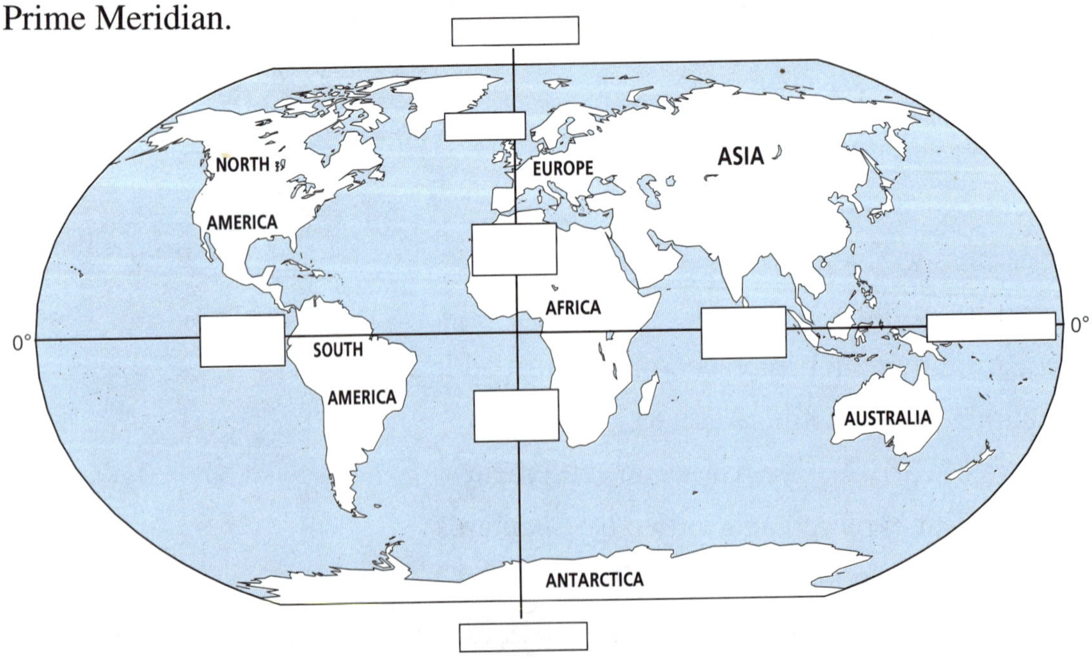

IDENTIFYING GEOGRAPHIC FEATURES OF THE UNITED STATES

Directions: Place the number of each of the following items on a copy of the map of the United States: (1) Great Lakes; (2) Mississippi River; (3) Gulf of Mexico; (4) Rocky Mountains; (5) Appalachian Mountains; (6) Great Plains; (7) Atlantic Ocean; (8) Pacific Ocean; and (9) Rio Grande.

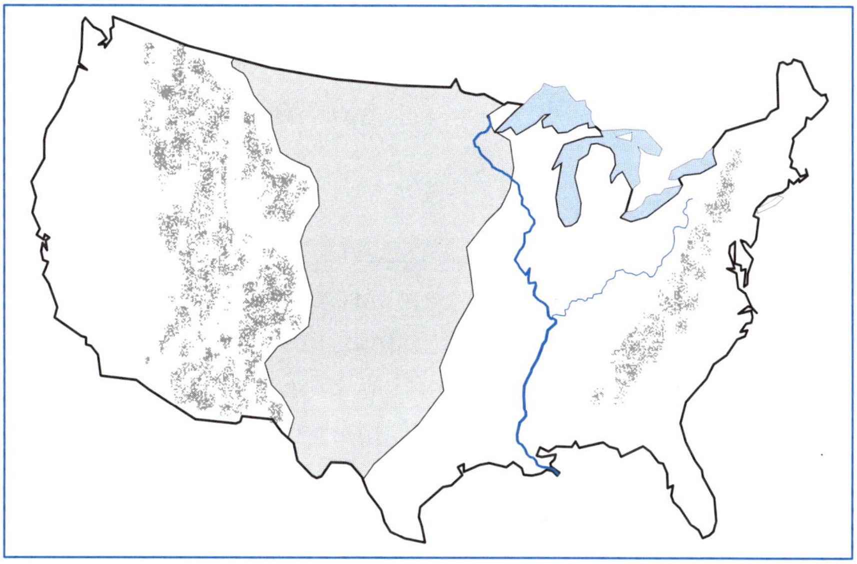

WHICH REFERENCE BOOK WOULD YOU USE?

Directions: In this chapter you learned about atlases and almanacs. Each of these reference books has a specific use. Below is a list of factual questions you might be interested in answering. Determine which would be the better book to use, and then write:

☆ **AT** if the information can be found in an **atlas.**

☆ **AL** if the information can be found in an **almanac.**

1. What was the winning team of the baseball World Series in 1900?

2. What are the names of all countries bordering Costa Rica?

3. What is the easternmost city of Alaska?

4. What are the major bodies of water connected by the Panama Canal?

5. What is the name of the present Prime Minister of Great Britain?

6. Which are the five longest bridges in North America?

7. What are the burial places of all deceased Presidents of the United States?

8. What is the exact latitude and longitude of Houston, Texas?

9. Which states in the United States touch the Mississippi River?

FACTS AND FIGURES ABOUT TEXAS GEOGRAPHY

Land Area: 262,017 square miles
Dimensions: 733 miles (east to west)
801 miles (north to south)
Rivers: 80,000 miles of rivers
Road Miles: 305,951 miles
Highest Point: Guadalupe Peak (8,749 feet)
Lowest Point: Sea level along the Gulf Coast

Highest Temp: 120° F in Seymour (August 12, 1936)
Lowest Temp: –23° F in Tulia (February 12, 1899)
Most Rainfall: 109.38 inches of rain in Clarksville in 1873
Most Snowfall: 65 inches in Romero in 1923-1924

WHAT'S IN A NAME?

Where did the name Texas come from? A Caddo tribe, called the Hasinai, in what is now East Texas, used the word "tashas" for "friend." The Spanish had difficulty pronouncing this. Instead, they used the word "tejas." Eventually, the word "tejas" through misuse, became Texas.

FOREIGN WORDS?

Most people know that San Antonio was named by Spanish settlers. Many other cities in Texas also have exotic names—such as Anahuac (Aztec), Aspermont (Latin), Concan (Mexican), Danevang (Dutch) and Waka (Native American).

TEXAS—THE "BIG" ONE

Texas is the second largest state in the United States. In population, Texas ranks second with 17 million inhabitants. In addition, Texas occupies 7% of the total land and water area of the United States.

COULD YOU REPEAT THAT?

The Rio Grande stretches 889 miles. It was named the "River of great water" by the Pueblo Indians. In 1598, when Juan de Oñate landed on its banks , he called it the Rio Grande, or "big river." So, if you call it the Rio Grande River, you are really saying "big river river."

CHAPTER 3

AMERICAN HERITAGE

Early immigrants to Texas

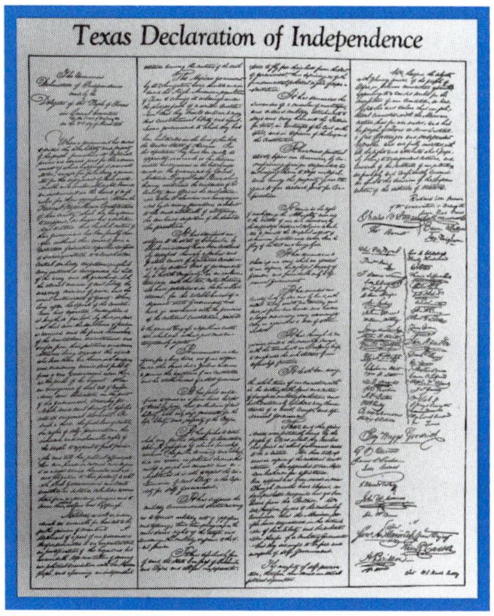
Texas Declaration of Independence

Texas Declaration of Independence (1836)

Troops parade in Ft. Worth (1918)

The term "American Heritage" refers to what we have gained from the past. We enjoy the life-styles we lead today because of the sacrifices, struggles and accomplishments of those who lived before us. In this chapter, you will learn about the lives and achievements of some famous Texans. You will also see how people's personalities are influenced by the times in which they live. Finally, you will learn new ways to organize and to think about your knowledge of the past.

3A

PART I: HISTORY

ARE YOU A GOOD HISTORIAN?

In this activity, you will read about some exciting events in Texas' past. Look for the following important words and names:

★ Stephen F. Austin	★ Sam Houston	★ Goliad
★ Law of 1830	★ The Alamo	★ Primary/Secondary Sources

To help you find these terms, the ★ symbol will appear in the margin where the term first appears.

A historian tries to determine the truth of what happened in the past. A historian also tries to understand what it was like to live in the past. Historians want to know how people in past times felt about the events that were taking place around them. In addition, you will learn how a historian uses primary and secondary sources as clues to find out what really happened.

As you read the following pages you will be asked to use your imagination to think what it would have been like to live in past times and to experience certain events. To help you with this, after each group of paragraphs you will be asked to exercise your historical imagination as an amateur historian by "Recreating The Past."

THE EARLY HISTORY OF TEXAS

THE FIRST PEOPLE IN TEXAS

Many historians believe that at least twelve thousand years ago, people from Asia crossed the narrow plain that once connected Asia to Alaska (*see map on page 75*). The new arrivals hunted animals for food, moving from place to place in search of good hunting areas. These people spread southwards from Alaska into North and South America. They are now known as the **Native Americans** because they were the first people to live in America. Wherever they settled, they developed their own unique ways of life.

A Note On Names: The earliest settlers in the Western Hemisphere have been identified by different names throughout history. Christopher Columbus called them ***Indians*** because he thought he had landed in India. In the 1960s, the term ***Native Americans*** began to be used to show that these people were the first to live in the Americas. More recently, some people have called them ***Indigenous Peoples.***

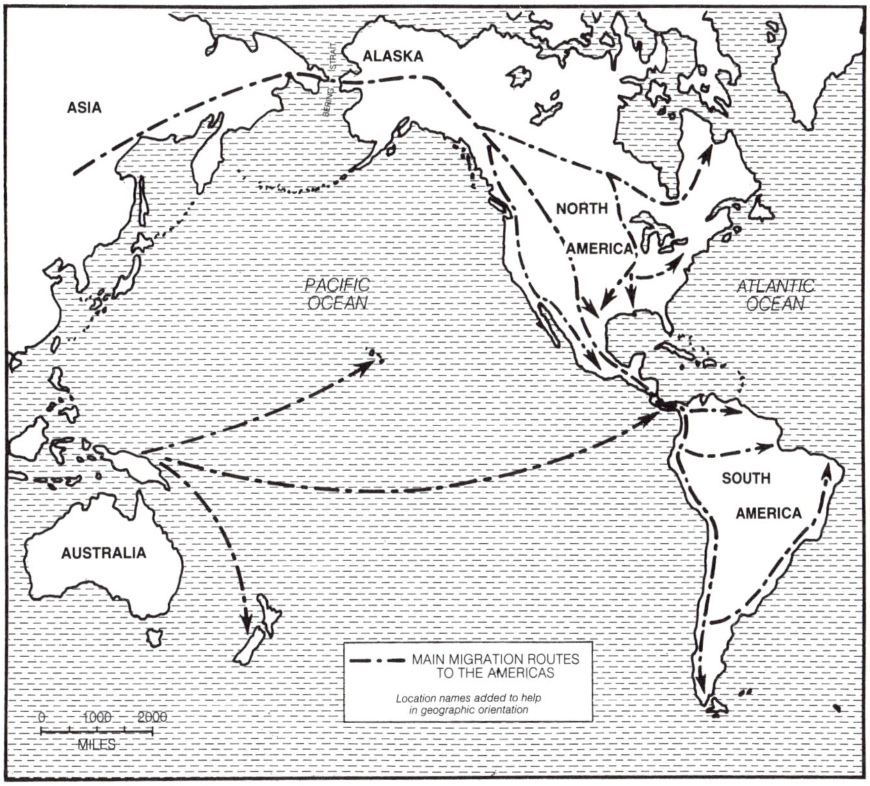

By the time Europeans arrived in Texas, several tribes of Native Americans had settled there. A **tribe** (*or nation*) is a group of related people with their own way of life. The most important tribes in Texas were the Caddo, Karankawa, Tonkawa, Wichita, Comanche, Apache and Jumano. Unfortunately, many of the Europeans who came had been exposed to diseases such as smallpox and measles. These diseases were common in Europe, but were unknown in North and South America. Because the Native Americans had no resistance to these diseases, large numbers of them soon died from these illnesses. You will learn more about the Native Americans later in this chapter.

Some of the first Europeans to arrive in Texas.
Why did many Native Americans die from contact with Europeans?

1. Where did the Native Americans originally come from?

2. In what parts of the Americas did the Native Americans eventually settle?

3. Which Native American tribes lived in Texas before the arrival of the Europeans?

EUROPEANS EXPLORE TEXAS

Europeans did not know about the land which is now called America until Christopher Columbus sailed to it in 1492. Once Europeans learned about these lands, they sent explorers searching for gold and other riches. Spain claimed control of most of the "New World" based on the voyages of Columbus. In 1521, the Spanish conquered the powerful Aztec Empire in central Mexico. In 1533, the Incas of Peru also fell to the Spanish.

At first Europeans coming to the Americas were few. Soon the trickle turned into a flood.
What were they searching for?

Spain wanted to extend its rule from Mexico to the north. Spanish explorers were sent to investigate the coast of Texas. One explorer, **Alvar Núñez Cabeza de Vaca,** was captured by the Karankawas and spent six years in the interior of Texas. A slave named **Esteban** traveled with Cabeza de Vaca. *(See page 77 for details).* He is the first black person known to have visited Texas. Esteban shared some of his knowledge of African medicines with the Karankawas.

Cabeza de Vaca eventually escaped and returned to Mexico. Based on his reports, the Spanish government sent **Francisco Vásquez de Coronado** and **Hernando de Soto** to the southwest of the present-day United States. They came in the 1540s, but failed to find "cities of gold." A later expedition led by **Don Juan de Oñate** also failed to discover any riches. When these explorers found no treasure, the Spanish government lost interest in Texas.

Francisco Vásquez de Coronado
What does this picture tell you about the explorers?

1. Who were some of the early European explorers of Texas?
2. What were these early explorers looking for in Texas?
3. Why did the Spanish government lose interest in Texas?

THE TRAVELS OF CABEZA DE VACA

In 1528, about 400 Spaniards sailed from Cuba to Florida in search of gold. After traveling in the interior, they returned to the coast where they found they had no ships. The men built new ships in order to float along the coast until they reached Mexico. Unfortunately, most of their makeshift boats were lost at sea. About 80 expedition members finally landed on Galveston Island in November, 1528.

Alvar Núñez Cabeza de Vaca, treasurer to the original expedition, assumed command. The Karankawa Native Americans came upon the Spaniards and helped them by giving them food. In return, the Spaniards gave the Karankawa bells, beads and other trinkets. Cabeza de Vaca and his men then loaded their belongings onto a clumsy raft, which immediately crashed. The Karankawas again gave the stranded men food and shelter.

The friendly relationship between the Karankawas and the newcomers did not last long. A number of Karankawas became ill from diseases caught from the Europeans. They blamed Cabeza de Vaca and his men, and enslaved them. Most of the men died, but Cabeza de Vaca, Esteban and two others survived for six years. They were treated as slaves, but also acted as medicine men and traders with other tribes. Finally, the four escaped and began the long journey southwards to Mexico. They walked over 2,000 miles on their journey.

On their travels, they saw herds of buffalo on the Great Plains and observed other Native American tribes. They also heard rumors of legendary cities to the north made of gold. They finally reached Mexico City in 1536. Later, Esteban returned with an expedition in search of the golden cities, but was killed by Native Americans. Cabeza de Vaca published an account of his travels in Texas. He was later appointed as a royal governor and made further explorations in South America. Cabeza de Vaca died in Spain in 1560, at the age of 70.

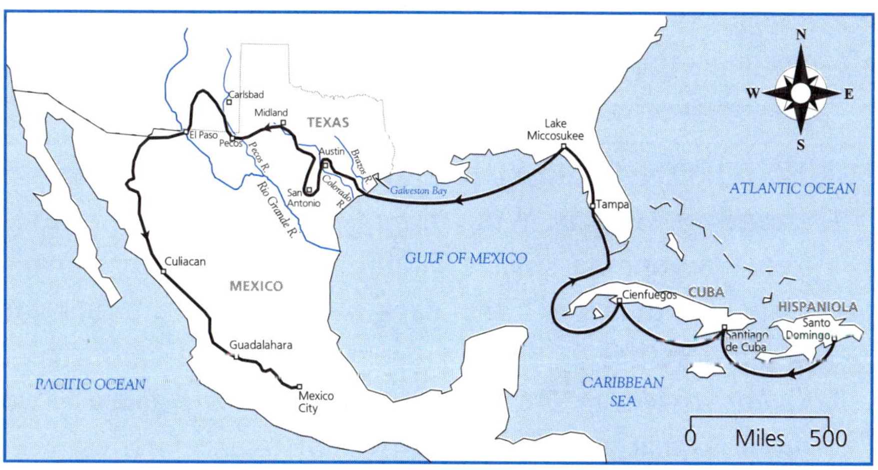

THE SPANISH MISSIONS

In the 1680s, Spanish interest in Texas revived. The French explorer **René Robert de la Salle** established a colony of 280 settlers at Matagorda Bay in 1684. The colony, Fort St. Louis, failed because the colonists were either killed by hostile Native Americans, died from disease or fled. The Spanish government feared that France wanted to become a colonial power in the region.

Residents of a mission in prayer
What were the purposes of missions?

Spanish authorities decided to establish several missions in Texas. **Missions** were settlements organized by Spanish priests who hoped to convert the Native Americans to the Roman Catholic religion. Usually, the mission was a large building with an inner patio at its center. At one side of the mission was a church. Crops were grown on the surrounding fields, and livestock were raised. Water was brought to the mission from wells and **aqueducts** (*pipes or channels carrying water from distant places*).

The Native Americans who came to the missions were given food and shelter. In exchange, they had to work. They awoke each morning to the sound of church bells calling them to prayer. After church, they had breakfast and went to work. Men and older boys worked in the fields and in the mission workshops, or constructed buildings. Women made clothes and cooked meals. Children went to school, where they were taught by the priests.

Although some of the missions were successful, others were attacked by hostile Native American tribes. As a result, many missions were abandoned in the late 1700s. By 1800, there were fewer than 5,000 Spaniards living in all of Texas.

1. What did the Spanish missionaries want to accomplish?

2. Why were aqueducts important to the missions?

THE AMATEUR HISTORIAN: RECREATING THE PAST

1. Creating Models. What did a typical Spanish mission look like? You and your classmates should build a model or draw a picture of a Spanish mission. Label each building and the function it played in mission life.

2. Creating Maps. On a map of Texas, locate at least two of the 30 missions that were founded by Spanish missionaries.

ANGLO-AMERICAN SETTLERS COME TO TEXAS

Some people in the Spanish colonies became more and more unhappy with the colonial government administered by Spain. In 1810, Mexican leaders began a war against Spanish rule. By 1821, Mexico had won its independence from Spain.

STEPHEN F. AUSTIN STARTS A COLONY

Moses Austin
Why is he famous?

While the Mexican revolution was still in progress, an American, **Moses Austin,** as an empresario proposed to bring 300 families to Texas. An **empresario** was a land agent who brought settlers to Mexico in exchange for land. Austin asked that the Mexican government give him 200,000 acres of land to start a colony. In 1821, the Spanish authorities, and then the new Mexican government, approved his plan. They wanted to see Texas become prosperous and filled with settlers.

Moses Austin died before he could carry out his project. His son, **Stephen F. Austin,** took his father's place. Austin chose the fertile lands between the Colorado and Brazos Rivers for his colony. The colonists had to promise to become Mexican citizens and Roman Catholics before they were given land. Because of Austin's success, other empresarios were given land for settlement. By 1830, as many as 30,000 Anglo-American colonists had settled in that part of Mexico which is now Texas.

1. What is an empresario?

2. Why did the Mexican government give land to the empresarios?

3. What promises did settlers have to make when coming to live in Texas?

PIONEER LIFE-STYLES

A pioneer family
Why was life difficult for early pioneers in Texas?

After finding a good spot to settle, a pioneer family would buy its land from an empresario. Next, the pioneer had to find fresh water and build a log cabin. The first cabins were often small, with no windows and a dirt floor. Later, the pioneer would build a larger log cabin with windows, doors, a fireplace and a wood floor. Bark was stripped from the logs, and the spaces between the logs were filled with mud and rock.

Frontier settlers clearing the land
What were some of the responsibilities of women in these frontier settlements?

To clear land for planting, the pioneers in East Texas had to cut trees and pull stumps out of the ground. The pioneers then plowed the soil with iron-tipped plows. Once the land was prepared, they planted corn and other crops. They also hunted and fished. Women helped men in the fields and had other duties, like washing and sewing clothing. Clothing was usually made from animal skins and homespun cloth. Women often grew vegetables in a family garden and cooked the meals. A typical meal consisted of roasted meat, corn bread and black coffee. As busy as they were, the pioneers also had to protect themselves from Native American attacks.

Some of the early pioneers became very successful. They planted **cash crops**—products such as cotton and sugar cane—that could be sold for money. Some settlers brought slaves to help with farm work and chores. By the time Texas became independent, almost one in every seven Texans was an African-American slave.

1. What obstacles were faced by the early pioneers in Texas?
2. How did the early pioneers overcome these obstacles?
3. What were some of the cash crops planted by the early settlers?

THE AMATEUR HISTORIAN: RECREATING THE PAST

1. Writing Letters. You and your classmates should each pretend to be an early settler in Texas. Write a letter to friends describing what life was like in Texas in those days.

2. Writing An Essay. What was life like for children growing up in Texas during this early period? Write an essay comparing and contrasting your life today with that of a typical young person growing up in Texas in the early 1800s.

THE TEXAS REVOLUTION BEGINS

Many Anglo-American colonists were happy in Texas. But others disliked Mexican rule. For example, some of the Anglo-American settlers had slaves, which were illegal in Mexico.

THE LAW OF 1830

Brownsville, Texas in the early 1800s
Why did Mexico fear Anglo-American settlers moving into Texas?

At the same time, the Mexican government was not entirely happy with the new settlers in Texas. As the number of Anglo-Americans settlers increased, Mexican authorities feared losing control of Texas to colonists who came from a different culture. This fear was strengthened when an important Mexican general reported on his travels to Texas. He stated that the Anglo-Americans were not following Mexican laws or customs. In fact, they appeared to be more loyal to the United States.

To prevent this situation from getting worse, the Mexican government passed the **Law of 1830.** This law prevented additional settlers from the United States from coming to Texas. The law also prohibited Texans from owning slaves. Finally, the new law required Texans to pay special taxes on goods brought from the United States. ★

1. Why did the Mexican government pass the Law of 1830?

2. What were some of the most important parts of the law?

TEXANS DEMAND GREATER RIGHTS

Texans holding a convention
Why did Texans oppose the Law of 1830?

In 1832, the Anglo-Americans in Texas held a convention. A **convention** is a meeting of representatives. The convention requested the **repeal** (*end*) of the Law of 1830 and greater powers of self-government for Texas.

In Mexico City, General **Santa Anna** of the Mexican army took control of the government early in 1833. Because of this change in government, Texans held a second convention. The **Convention of 1833** again requested the repeal of the Law of 1830. The members also wrote a proposed constitution for themselves as a new state government within Mexico.

Stephen F. Austin was sent to Mexico City to give these demands to the Mexican government. The Mexican government repealed the Law of 1830, but refused to make Texas a separate state within Mexico. Austin wrote home urging Texans to establish a separate Mexican state on their own. For writing this letter, Austin was put in prison in Mexico City for more than a year.

1. What were the main goals of the Conventions of 1832 and 1833?
2. Why was Stephen F. Austin sent to Mexico?
3. Why was he imprisoned in Mexico City?

FIGHTING BEGINS AT GONZALES

After getting out of prison, Austin returned to Texas in 1835. Shortly afterwards, the Mexican government sent a small force to the town of Gonzales to take back a cannon. This cannon had been given to the town to fight off Native American attacks. The Anglo-Americans of Gonzales refused to surrender the cannon. They made a flag that read "Come and Take It," and used the cannon to fire on the approaching Mexican soldiers. With these shots, the Texas Revolution began.

1. How did the people of Gonzalez respond to the Mexican request to return their cannon?
2. Why did the issue of the cannon become important to the history of Texas?

THE BATTLE OF SAN ANTONIO

Texans called a new convention to meet, while a force of volunteers surrounded Mexican troops in San Antonio. After many weeks of hesitation, the Texans eventually attacked. The final battle lasted several days. The Mexicans retreated into the Alamo and finally surrendered. The Texan commanders then let the Mexican prisoners go home. Before releasing them, they made the prisoners promise not to fight in Texas again.

Meanwhile, the delegates to the **Convention of 1835** still did not want to declare independence from Mexico. Instead, they voted to seek separate statehood and greater ★ self-government within Mexico. **Sam Houston** was a former governor of Tennessee who had moved to Texas. The Convention made him the commander-in-chief of the Texas forces.

1. What did the delegates to the Convention of 1835 decide?
2. What job was Sam Houston given by the Convention of 1835?

THE AMATEUR HISTORIAN: RECREATING THE PAST

1. **Writing Speeches.** How did Stephen F. Austin feel about events taking place in Texas? Write a speech that Stephen F. Austin might have delivered to the Convention of 1835 about whether or not Texas should break away from Mexico and declare its independence.

☆ CONTINUED

2. Creating A Visual Biography. Sam Houston held many important jobs during his lifetime. Create a visual biography of the jobs he held. HINT: In the middle of a page, put a photocopy of Sam Houston's picture. Then, in lines radiating out from this picture like the spokes of a wheel, describe each job he held and when.

The Jobs of Sam Houston

THE BLOODY ROAD TO INDEPENDENCE

General Santa Anna wanted revenge for the Mexican defeats at Gonzalez and San Antonio. He decided to take a large force of 6,000 soldiers into Texas to defeat the Texans once and for all.

THE ALAMO PREPARES FOR BATTLE

Santa Anna crossed the Rio Grande into Texas early in 1836. By then, most of the Texans who had captured the city of San Antonio had gone home. Others had marched south to Goliad, where a force was gathering under **Colonel James Fannin.** Fannin was preparing to attack a nearby Mexican town. As a result, there were only just over a hundred men to defend the Alamo and San Antonio.

James Fannin

The Alamo was originally a Spanish mission named **Mission San Antonio de Valero.** It was called the **Alamo** (Spanish for cottonwood) after it became a fort. The Alamo would not be easy to defend. A young lawyer named Green Jameson helped fortify the Alamo by building platforms for several cannons. He also had a wooden barrier built along a 75-foot gap in the Alamo's walls.

Sam Houston sent the legendary knife-fighter **James Bowie** to the Alamo with instructions to abandon the fortress and blow it up. However, when Bowie arrived, he found the defenders of the Alamo prepared to sacrifice their lives before surrendering the fortress. Bowie decided to stay and help defend the Alamo.

James Bowie
What role did Bowie play at the Alamo?

Two other famous arrivals to the Alamo were William B. Travis and David Crockett. **William B. Travis** was a young but daring Texan who had led a successful raid against Mexican officials in 1835. He soon took joint command of the Alamo with Bowie. When Bowie fell sick, Travis took chief command of the garrison. The other arrival, **Davy Crockett,** was probably the most famous of all the Alamo defenders. He was known for his skill as a marksman. He had also served three times as one of the U.S. Congressmen from Tennessee.

1. Why did General Santa Anna march against Texas?

2. Who were some of the more famous defenders of the Alamo?

THE ALAMO IS ATTACKED

As Santa Anna's large army approached, William Travis realized that the small garrison in the Alamo would be fighting a much larger force. Travis sent out desperate messages for reinforcements. Volunteers from Gonzalez came, bringing the number of defenders to just over 180. Additional forces from Goliad never arrived. One of these messages was carried by the tejano **Juan Sequín,** the leader of the Mexican-American volunteers. *Tejano* is a Spanish word that means "Texan." Many Mexican tejanos, like Sequin, helped fight for Texas independence.

Historic Document of Texas: *William Travis Asks For Help Defending the Alamo*

To the people of Texas and all Americans...

I am besieged (surrounded) by a thousand or more of the Mexicans under Santa Anna. I have sustained a continual bombardment... for 24 hours and have not lost a man. The enemy has demanded a surrender..., otherwise the garrison (defenders) are to be put to the sword, if the fort is taken. I have answered the demand with a cannon shot, and our flag still waves proudly from the walls. I shall never surrender or retreat. Then, I call on you in the name of liberty, of patriotism and everything dear to the American character to come to our aid... If this call is neglected, I am determined... to die like a soldier who never forgets what is due to his own honor and that of his country—victory or death.

William B. Travis, Commander of the Texas Army

The Alamo is attacked

Why was the Alamo of such importance in the fight for Texas independence?

Meanwhile, Mexican cannons pounded away at the Alamo for almost two weeks. Travis held a meeting of the defenders. He told them that the situation was desperate and asked them who wanted to remain. All but one man chose to defend the fortress, even though it meant probably sacrificing their own lives.

On the morning of March 6, 1836, Santa Anna and his forces attacked. Two waves of soldiers were thrown back. The third wave of Mexican troops managed to cross over the walls of the Alamo. Eventually, all but one slave and a handful of women and children were killed. The final battle lasted only 90 minutes. Almost 1,500 Mexicans were killed. The heroism of the defenders stirred Texans everywhere. These men had willingly sacrificed their lives in the cause of Texas independence.

1. What did William Travis say in his call for help that might have inspired people to come and fight at the Alamo?

2. What happened to the defenders of the Alamo?

3. If you had been at the Alamo, would you have voted to leave or to stay and possibly sacrifice your life? Explain your answer.

THE MASSACRE AT GOLIAD

Shortly after the fall of the Alamo, Colonel Fannin decided to retreat from **Goliad.** His men were soon surrounded on the open prairie by three times as many Mexican troops. After two days of heavy fighting, Fannin surrendered. One week later, on Santa Anna's orders, the prisoners were shot as rebels. Only about 60 of Fannin's force of 400 managed to escape.

The march of Fannin's men

What happened to these captured prisoners?

1. Why did Colonel Fannin surrender?

TEXAS DECLARES ITS INDEPENDENCE FROM MEXICO

While these events took place in San Antonio and Goliad, a new convention was held. Representatives met in Washington-on-the-Brazos. Texans called the new convention a **Consultation** because the will of the people was being consulted. On March 2, 1836, the Consultation voted to declare independence from Mexico.

The next day, the delegates signed the **Texas Declaration of Independence.** Written mainly by **George Childress,** the declaration was based on the principles of the American Declaration of Independence of July 4, 1776. The Texas Declaration of Independence stated that the Mexican government had failed to protect the lives, liberty and property of the Texans. The Declaration listed the many disagreements that Texans had with the government of Mexico. Lastly, it announced that Texans now had the right to form their own government.

Historic Document of Texas: *The Texas Declaration of Independence*

The Texas Declaration of Independence

When a government has ceased (stopped) to protect the lives, liberty and property of the people, and when that government has become a military dictatorship, it becomes the right of the people to abolish (end) such a government and create another to secure their future welfare and happiness. The Mexican nation has allowed General Santa Anna to overturn the constitution of the country. He now offers us the cruel choice of either abandoning our homes or submitting to his tyranny (cruel government).

We, therefore, the delegates of the people of Texas... do hereby resolve and declare that our political connection with the Mexican nation has forever ended; and that the people of Texas do now [make up] a free... and independent nation.

Richard Ellis, President of the convention and Delegate from Red River.

Charles B. Stewart
John S.D. Byrom
J. Antonio Navarro
Wm. D. Lacey
Jno. Fisher
William Mottley
Stephen Everitt
Elijah Stapp
Wm. B. Scates
A.B. Hardin
Thos. J. Gazley
Sterling C Robertson
Edwin Waller
Geo. C. Childress
Rob. Potter

JB Woods
Chas. S. Taylor
Robert Hamilton
Albert H Latimer
Sam Houston
Edwd. Conrad
Edwin O. LeGrand
Jas. Gaines
Sydney Penington
Jno. Turner
G.M. Barnett
Jesse Grimes
John W. Moore
Saml. A. Maverick
Sam P. Carson

Thos. Barnet
Franco Ruiz
Jesse B. Badgett
William Menefee
Mathew Caldwell
Lorenzo de Zavala
Geo. W Smyth
Claiborne West
M.B. Menard
J.W. Bunton
R.M Coleman
Jas. Collingsworth
Asa Brigham
Bailey Hardeman
A. Brisco

Thomas J. Rusk
John S. Roberts
Collin McKinney
James Power
David Thomas
Martin Parmer
Stephen W. Blount
Wm. Clark, Jr.
Wm. C. Crawford
Benj. B. Goodrich
James G. Swisher
S Rhoads Fisher
John W. Bower
(from Bejar)

H.S. Kemble, Secretary

After the Declaration was adopted, the Consultation began work on the Texas Constitution. A **constitution** is a plan establishing a system of government. The Consultation also sent Sam Houston to re-organize the Texas army. Finally, its members elected **David G. Burnet** as the interim (*temporary*) President of Texas.

Davis G. Burnet
What post was he chosen to fill in the new government of Texas?

1. How many names of the signers of the Texas Declaration of Independence do you recognize?
2. Why do you think Texans declared independence in 1836, when they had refused to do so in 1835?
3. Were Texans justified in declaring independence from Mexico in 1836? Explain why or why not.
4. What do you think is the main message of the Texas Declaration of Independence?

THE BATTLE OF SAN JACINTO

The Battle of San Jacinto
Why was the battle important to Texas?

Sam Houston retreated with his army into East Texas. This retreat brought fear to many Texan families, who now believed that they would no longer be protected. Some fled from their homes, seeking safety. This was called the **Runaway Scrape.** Houston spent the next several weeks drilling and training his men. Houston then learned that Santa Anna had separated from the main Mexican army. Santa Anna had taken a smaller force to try to capture President Burnet and the Texas government. Houston saw this as his chance to fight Santa Anna on equal terms.

Houston ordered his army on a rapid march. Both armies met along the banks of the San Jacinto River. On the afternoon of April 21st, while many of the Mexicans were taking a siesta (*an afternoon nap*), Houston attacked. The Mexicans were taken completely by surprise. Nearly half of the Mexican force was killed, and most of the others were captured. Santa Anna tried to escape disguised as a common soldier in his own army, but was caught the next day. Houston spared his life but demanded that he withdraw all Mexican forces from Texas.

Historic Document of Texas: *The Treaty of Velasco*

Following the defeat of Mexican forces at San Jacinto, President David G. Burnet and General Santa Anna negotiated a final settlement. In this treaty, Santa Anna agreed in:

The Treaty of Velasco

- ☆ *Mexico would recognize the independence of Texas*
- ☆ *The southern boundary of Texas would be the Rio Grande*
- ☆ *Mexican forces would be withdrawn from Texas*
- ☆ *Mexico would not attack Texas again*

1. How did Houston hope to achieve victory over Santa Anna's forces?

2. What were the main terms of the Treaty of Velasco?

3. Why was this treaty of such importance to Texas?

THE LONE STAR REPUBLIC

After Santa Anna was freed, he quickly spoke out against the Treaty of Velasco. The Mexican government therefore never accepted it. They claimed that Santa Anna had been forced to sign it while he was still a prisoner. Even so, the treaty marked the end of Mexican rule in Texas. Texas was now an independent country.

The government of Texas was patterned after that of the United States. It had a President, Congress and a separate court system. Sam Houston became the first popularly elected President of the new Republic. Stephen F. Austin was chosen by Houston as the first Secretary of State. Soon after independence, Texans asked to be **annexed** (*become a part*) by the United States. The government of the United States refused.

WHY THE UNITED STATES AT FIRST REFUSED TO ANNEX TEXAS

- ✗ Many Northerners spoke against annexation because they were morally opposed to slavery in Texas.
- ✗ If Texas was admitted as a slave state, it would upset the balance of free and slave states in Congress.
- ✗ If the United States annexed Texas, Mexico might threaten war.

The Texas Constitution forbade President Houston from serving two terms in a row. The next person elected President of the Republic of Texas was **Mirabeau B. Lamar.** In 1839, President Lamar approved an act that established the Texas system of public education. The act stated that land in each county be set aside for primary education (*kindergarten through 12th grade*) and for colleges and universities. For this reason, President Lamar is known as the "Father of Texas Education."

1. How did the new Republic of Texas organize its government?
2. Why did Texas select Sam Houston as its first President?
3. Why were some Americans opposed to the annexation of Texas?
4. What arguments can you provide for and against annexation by the United States?
5. What contribution did Mirabeau Lamar make to education in Texas?

THE AMATEUR HISTORIAN: RECREATING THE PAST

1. Building a model. Historians often need to "see" places from the past. Sometimes a model or diorama helps us to imagine how things actually looked. The following illustration shows the layout of the Alamo. Build your own model of the Alamo following this plan.

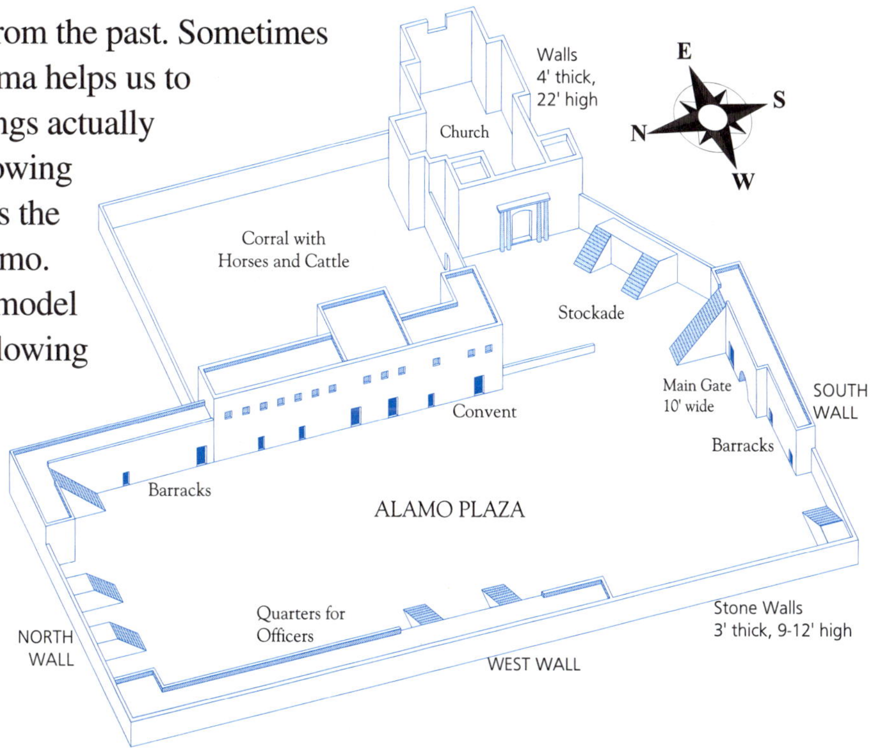

2. Writing a song. Besides being a famous fighter, Davy Crockett was also an excellent fiddle player. At the Alamo, Crockett kept up everyone's spirits by playing his fiddle. Write the words to an imaginary song that the defenders of the Alamo might have sung while they were waiting for the Mexican attack.

THE DIFFERENCE BETWEEN PRIMARY AND SECONDARY SOURCES

EXTENDING THE ACTIVITY

A skilled historian is like a good detective. A detective arrives after a crime has taken place. The detective tries to figure out who committed the crime by looking for clues. The detective may interview witnesses, examine evidence and check facts.

Historians also look for clues when trying to figure out what happened in the past. Both a detective and a historian must look through many sources to find accurate information. In this section, you will be challenged to act as a historian by looking at clues. Historians rely on two types of sources for gathering information:

★ PRIMARY SOURCES

Primary sources are original records of an event. They include eyewitness reports, official records made at the time of the event, letters, speeches, diaries, photographs or audio and video tapes by people involved in the event. Most of the facts we know about past events originally came from primary sources.

★ CHECKING YOUR UNDERSTANDING ★

Can you think of another example of a primary source?

★ SECONDARY SOURCES

Secondary sources are the writings and viewpoints of historians and other people written after an event. The author of a secondary source usually does not have first-hand experience of the event. Secondary sources, such as textbooks and magazine articles, often provide summaries of the information found in primary sources. Historians sometimes read these writings to learn about other historians' ideas.

★ CHECKING YOUR UNDERSTANDING ★

Can you think of some other examples of a secondary source?

The following source is about Texas joining the Union. Read this imaginary selection carefully and answer the questions that follow:

Diary of Thomas Galloway

September 30, 1835. This month we voted to become part of the United States. It seems only natural that we should want to do this since we share their culture and beliefs.

March 18, 1836. On the 2nd of this month, President Andrew Jackson recognized Texas as an independent republic. But the U.S. Congress still refuses to admit us into their Union. They fear this will lead to a war with Mexico. In addition, the Northern states do not allow slavery. They feel a conflict will come about if they admit Texas, which does allow slavery. Meanwhile, our Lone Star Republic faces many problems. Our government has no money to pay its debts, to maintain its army, to build roads or to meet its other needs. We also worry about an invasion from Mexico.

November 29, 1844. Thank goodness James Polk was elected President of the United States. President Polk has promised voters he will annex Texas. Most Americans now believe they will rule from the Atlantic Ocean to the Pacific. They call this their "Manifest Destiny" (future). It seems that the admission of Texas into the Union is now only a matter of time.

President Polk

March 1, 1845. Events have taken place even faster than I expected. The U.S. Congress just passed a resolution making Texas part of the Union. The resolution annexes Texas as a state, not just as a territory. Texas could, if it so decided, divide into as many as five states. All of this has occurred even before President Polk has taken office.

December 29, 1845. President Anson Jones of Texas held a convention to decide whether we should accept the invitation of the U.S. Congress to join the United States. The delegates from Texas quickly voted to accept the invitation. We then sent our state constitution to the U.S. Congress for approval. Finally, we are to be admitted as the 28th state today.

President Anson Jones lowers the flag of the Republic of Texas for the last time. *Why did he pull down the flag?*

June 19, 1846. No sooner are we admitted into the United States then we face a new crisis. Mexico never fully recognized our independence. An argument has developed between Mexico and the United States over the southern border of Texas. We claim it is the Rio Grande, based on the Treaty of Velasco. The Mexicans claim the boundary has always been the Nueces River. President Polk sent troops into the disputed territory for our protection. The Mexicans attacked these soldiers. As a result, Congress declared war on Mexico. It seems Texas may again become a battlefield.

March 12, 1848. At last the Mexican War is over! Our Texan soldiers played a major role in the fighting. General Zachary Taylor invaded Mexico from the North in 1846. Even after he defeated Santa Anna, Mexico refused to surrender. Then General Winfield Scott sailed to the coast of Mexico and his troops marched into Mexico City itself. Santa Anna fled. The Mexican government had little choice but to accept the Rio Grande as its border with Texas. Under the terms of the Treaty of Guadalupe Hidalgo, Mexico gave up the immense territories of Upper California and New Mexico to the United States.

★ CHECKING YOUR UNDERSTANDING ★

1. If the diary on pages 91–92 were real, would it be a primary or a secondary source? How would you tell?
2. Why did many people in Texas want to join the United States?
3. Why did Galloway believe some Americans opposed the annexation of Texas?
4. How did the U.S. election of 1844 change the course of Texas history?
5. Why might a Mexican disagree with Galloway's diary entry of June 19, 1846?
6. What were some of the political effects of the Mexican-American War of 1846-1848?
7. What other sources might a historian look at to write a history of the Mexican-American War?

REVIEWING YOUR UNDERSTANDING

Directions: Fill in your Vocabulary Cards. Then answer the questions that follow.

Primary Sources

What are primary sources?

Give two examples:

Secondary Sources

What are secondary sources?

Give two examples:

Primary and Secondary Sources

Below are listed some sources that historians might use in writing a history of Texas. Copy the list down on a separate sheet of paper. Then, if the item is:

☆ a **primary source** write the letter **P** ☆ a **secondary source** write the letter **S**

1. A letter written by René Robert de la Salle about his journey to Texas.
2. A diary written by Sam Houston.
3. A painting made 6,000 years ago discovered on the wall of a cave.
4. A modern copy of a Bowie knife.
5. A newspaper from 1900, describing a flood in that year.

3B CAN YOU "SPOT" THE MAIN IDEA IN A PARAGRAPH?

In this activity you will learn about the history of Texas from the time of the Civil War to the defeat of the Native Americans on the Great Plains. Look for the following important words.

- ★ Abolitionists
- ★ Civil War
- ★ Reconstruction
- ★ Indian Wars
- ★ Freedman's Bureau
- ★ Sharecroppers

Although you have probably been reading since the first grade, did you ever stop to think what a complicated process reading is? What does it mean to "read" something?

> Describe what you do when you "read" something.

When you read, you are trying to understand the meaning of a group of words. Understanding what you read takes time and practice. As with every important activity, you need some basic skills to perform it well.

A reading selection is usually made up of a series of paragraphs that deal with a common theme. Each paragraph will contain a main idea. The **main idea** is the major point made in the paragraph. The other sentences usually provide details that support or describe the main idea more fully. The following paragraph is an example:

> Before the Civil War, some people in Texas and other Southern states disagreed with many Northerners about whether the national government should allow slavery to continue. ★ Northern **abolitionists** (*people who wanted to end slavery*) believed that slavery was wrong and should be prohibited by the national government. Many Southerners believed they had the right to determine their own way of life. They believed that the national government should not tell states what to do. They also felt that Southern slaves were often better off than factory workers in the North.

John Brown was an abolitionist who led an uprising to free slaves.

Notice that in this example, the main idea—"Before the Civil War, some people in Texas and other Southern states disagreed with many Northerners about slavery"—helps us to understand what the paragraph is about. The rest of the sentences are **supporting details**—*specific examples* that support the main idea.

Let's see what this reading might look like if it were put into a diagram.

MAIN IDEA

Before the Civil War, some Texans and other Southerners disagreed with some Northerners about whether the national government should allow slavery to continue.

Northern abolitionists believed that slavery was wrong and should be prohibited.

Southerners believed that they had the right to determine their own way of life.

Most Southerners felt that the national government should not tell states what to do.

Supporting Details

It often helps to understand what you read if you create a diagram of the reading. Read the following selection about Texas. After reading the selection, use the last paragraph and create a diagram showing the main idea and **three** supporting details.

TEXAS DURING THE CIVIL WAR

The **American Civil War** (*a war between people of the same nation*) was a major event in the history of Texas.

The conflict over slavery heated up when **Abraham Lincoln** was elected President in 1860. Southerners feared Lincoln would try to end slavery. Several Southern states left the United States and formed their own country. This new country was called the **Confederate States of America.**

Abraham Lincoln.
Why did his election as President lead the South to form its own country?

CONTINUED

A state convention was held in Texas in January, 1861. The convention voted to join the Confederacy. Afterwards, a special vote by all Texans supported the convention's decision. Sam Houston resigned as Governor, however, because he could not support the secession of Texas from the Union (*the United States*).

When President Lincoln refused to agree that the South had the right to leave the Union, the Civil War began. Although the most important fighting took place outside of Texas, Union forces occupied Galveston for part of the war. A large number of Texans—almost 60,000—fought in the Confederate Army. By 1865, Texas and the South had lost the war. Defeat came about, in part, because of the North's larger population, industrial resources and naval power.

Charleston, South Carolina in 1865.
How did losing the Civil War change life in the South?

Texas' way of life was changed forever by the Civil War. Many Texans died or lost their property. Farms and businesses were neglected. Texans suffered from shortages of food and other supplies. Many families lost their savings when Confederate money became worthless. Slavery was abolished in Texas and the rest of the nation.

Let's see what this reading might look like when you put it into a diagram. Copy the following diagram onto a separate sheet of paper and then fill in each part.

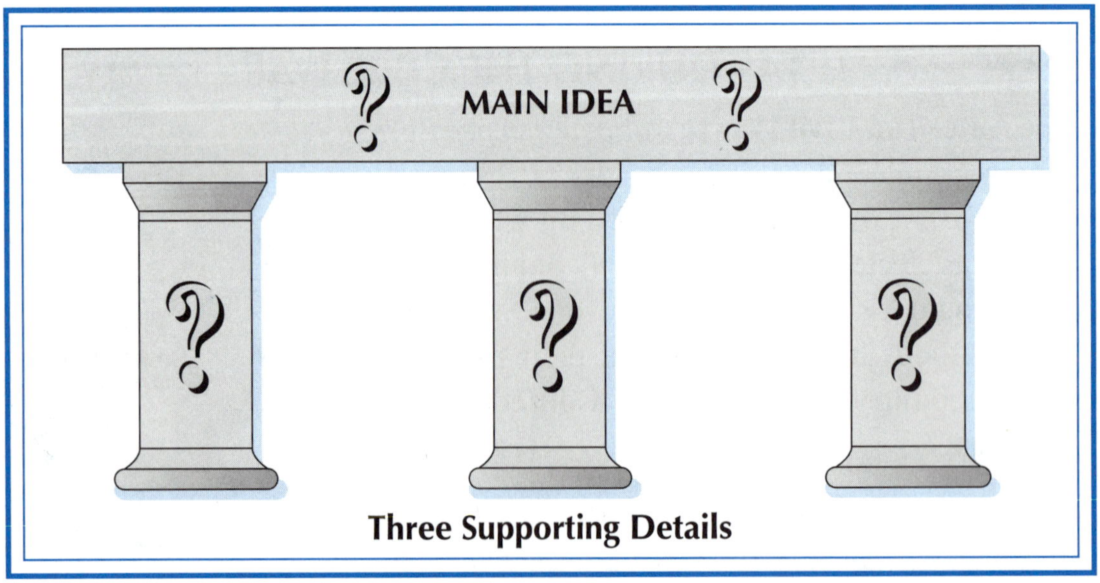

Another way to make it easier to understand what you have read is to create a schematic or concept "map." This is done by dividing the topic of the reading into smaller and smaller parts. You begin by putting the main idea in the middle and surrounding it with the main points or chief supporting details. Then add other details that further explain these main points or chief details. Let's look at an actual reading passage and see how it can be turned into such a "schematic map."

RECONSTRUCTION IN TEXAS

The period of **Reconstruction** refers to the rebuilding of the United States after the Civil War. During Reconstruction, Texans overcame many immediate problems as they adjusted to new ways of life. ★

When the war ended, the Southern states had to be readmitted into the United States. There was a shortage of food and clothing. Many public services—courts, postal services and law enforcement—were disrupted by the war. On June 19, 1865, the Union General in Galveston announced the Emancipation Proclamation, freeing the slaves of Texas. African Americans were freed from slavery, but lacked land or a place to go.

Sharecroppers harvesting cotton.
What is a sharecropper?

The Union army occupied the South after the war. Troops gave food to many of the needy, protection to the former slaves and helped to get things running again. The **Freedmen's Bureau** was created to help the former slaves. It set up schools for African Americans. Many poor whites and blacks became **sharecroppers.** A sharecropper is allowed to use an owner's land in return for giving the owner a share of his or her crop. ★ ★

Soon after the start of Reconstruction, Texas was placed under military control. Former Confederate soldiers and government officials were not allowed to vote. Local and state governments were controlled by those Texans who had sided with the North, and by freed slaves and people from the North. The Reconstruction governments passed many reforms. They built new schools, roads and public

CONTINUED

buildings. They encouraged the freed slaves to participate in public life. However, they were often accused by Texans of corruption and over-spending.

In 1869, Texas drafted a new constitution. Texas also approved the 14th and 15th Amendments to the U.S. Constitution, guaranteeing equal rights to men of all races. Reconstruction in Texas officially ended in 1870. Not long afterwards, Texas was allowed back into the Union.

In the new Texas, former Confederates regained the right to vote. Members of the Reconstruction governments soon lost their jobs. African Americans were discouraged from voting. In 1875, another state Constitution was adopted. It added a new bill of rights and made state officials more responsible to voters. In the following years, the state passed new laws limiting the rights of African Americans. These laws undid much of the work of the Reconstruction period.

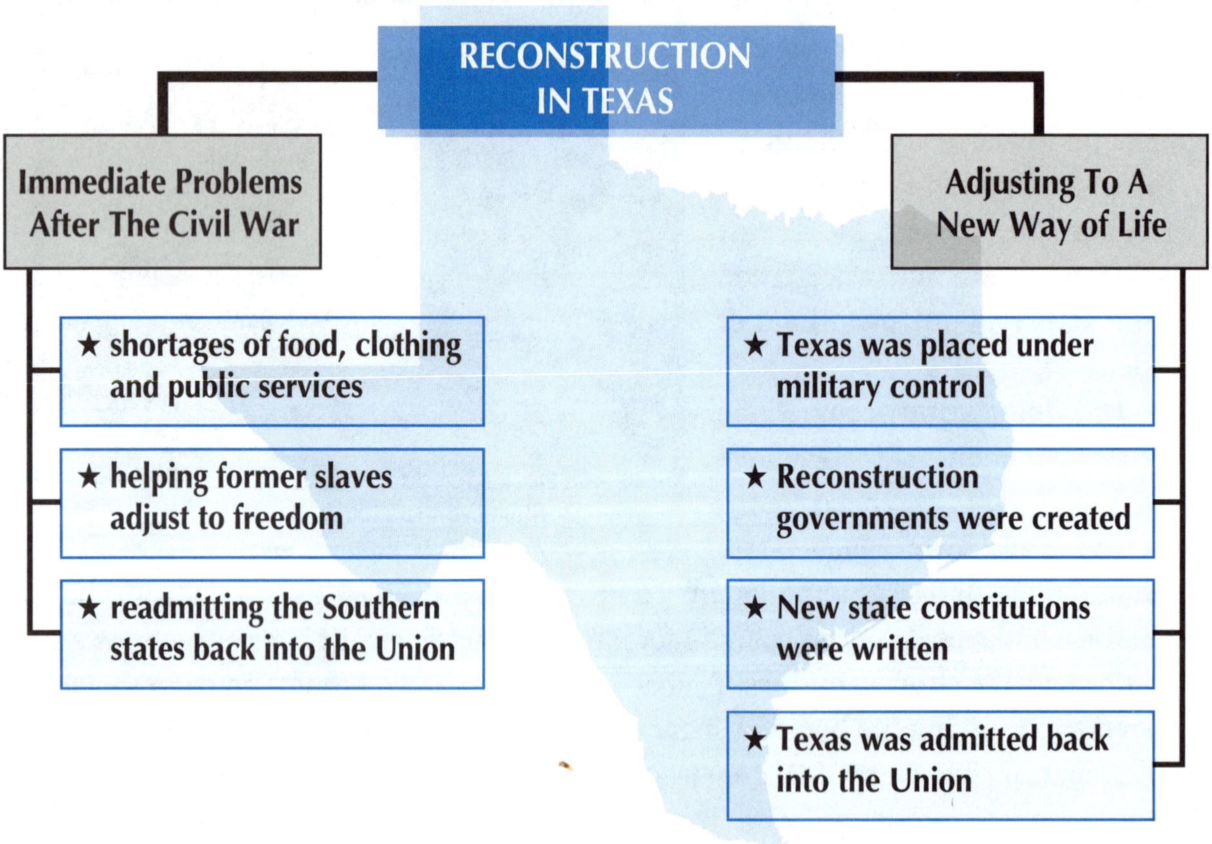

How well are you at creating your own schematic map? Read the next selection about the Indian Wars. Then put the reading in the form of a "schematic" map, like the one above.

THE "INDIAN WARS"

Following the end of the Civil War, a series of key events resulted in the removal of the remaining Native American tribes from Texas. Before the war, few Anglo-American settlers had been interested in occupying the Great Plains since land was still available in East Texas. Native American tribes such as the Comanche, Apache and Kiowa roamed the Great Plains of West Texas in search of herds of buffalo. These tribes depended on the meat and skins of buffalo for most of their needs—food, clothing and shelter.

Quanah Parker.
What role did he play in the Indian Wars?

During the Civil War, there was little protection for settlers on the edge of the Plains. Comanches and Apaches attacked their farms and ranches at will. Soldiers from the Texas Frontier Regiment tried to protect the settlers, but they could not stop all the attacks. When the Civil War ended in 1865, new arrivals, looking for cheap land, began to settle on the vast grazing lands of the **Great Plains** in West Texas. This increased hostilities between the Native Americans and the settlers.

However, now that the Civil War was over, the U.S. Army became directly involved in the struggle against the Native Americans. U.S. soldiers had better rifles and learned to fight on horseback like the Plains tribes. At the same time, the railroads began to spread through Texas. The railroads brought hunters who killed the buffalo for their hides. By wiping out the buffalo herds, the hunters destroyed the main source of food for the Plains Indians.

In 1867, the Comanches signed a treaty in which they agreed to move to a **reservation** (*land set aside by the U.S. government*) in Oklahoma. They were promised that they would be given food and supplies. Despite this, many Comanches did not move and the Comanche raids continued. In 1874, Chief **Quanah Parker** and other Comanche leaders attacked a group of buffalo hunters at Adobe Walls in Texas.

In response, the U.S. Army sent 3,000 troops to destroy the Comanches' winter camp. The U.S. troops mounted a surprise attack, and the Comanches fled. The U.S. Army then burned all the Comanche tepees and food supplies and shot over a thousand horses. The next summer, a half-starved Chief Parker surrendered and agreed to move to the reservation. By 1881, the Comanches were defeated and the Native American stronghold in West Texas was permanently ended.

REVIEWING YOUR UNDERSTANDING

Directions: Fill in your Vocabulary Cards. Then complete the exercise that follows.

Civil War
What is a civil war?
Name two reasons for the start of the American Civil War:

Reconstruction
What was Reconstruction?
Name an agency that helped African Americans during Reconstruction.

Find the Main Idea and Supporting Details

After you read the following passage, answer questions 1 and 2:

(1) After the Civil War, Texas experienced hard times. (2) Texas did not suffer as much damage as other Southern states. (3) Despite this, Texas experienced much turmoil and lawlessness. (4) Outlaws were active throughout the state. (5) Native American attacks were common along the frontier of Texas. (6) Racial violence was carried out by the Ku Klux Klan. (7) Federal troops occupying Texas during Reconstruction often met with local hostility.

KKK meeting to induct new members
What was the KKK known for?

1. Which sentence expresses the main idea?

A. After the Civil War, Texas experienced a period of hard times.
B. Texas did not suffer as much damage as other Southern states did.
C. Federal troops in Texas often met with local hostility.
D. Racial violence was carried out by the Ku Klux Klan.

2. Which sentence does NOT contain a supporting detail?

A. sentence (2)
B. sentence (4)
C. sentence (5)
D. sentence (6)

3C HOW GOOD ARE YOU AT DIAGRAMMING WHAT YOU READ?

In this activity, you will learn about the history of Texas from the end of Reconstruction to World War II. You will read about the cowboys on the open range, the growing of cotton, the growth of cities, two World Wars and the Great Depression. You will also learn some additional techniques to improve your reading skills. Look for the following important words:

- ★ Cowboys
- ★ Long Drive
- ★ Vaqueros
- ★ Wranglers
- ★ Cities
- ★ Dust Bowl

It would be very hard for us to recognize other people if we didn't know the general pattern of the human face. We focus on the things that make each person's face unique—the eyes, facial shape, nose and mouth. Knowing the general pattern of the human face helps us to detect very slight differences in key features.

It's the same with reading. We can better understand reading selections if we recognize their general patterns or basic forms. Three major forms of reading selections you will learn about in this activity are:

- ☆ descriptive readings
- ☆ problem-solution readings
- ☆ sequential readings

You will learn about a fourth form, cause-and-effect readings, in the next activity.

A reading may sometimes combine two or more of these forms. However, it will primarily be organized as one of them. For example, if a reading poses a problem and reviews some solutions, it is mainly a problem-solution reading—even though it may contain descriptions as well. Let us now examine each of these forms of reading.

A DESCRIPTIVE READING

A descriptive reading *describes* a person, place or object. The main idea or topic sentence usually states what is being described. The rest of the selection moves from one description to another, providing the main characteristics of the thing being described.

Often, it helps to understand a descriptive reading if you can "diagram" what is being described. Begin by reading the following selection. As you read, look for topic sentences and descriptive details. Then examine the diagram that follows the reading.

CATTLE AND COTTON

In the late 1800s, the economy of Texas was largely based on cattle and cotton. Cattle were first brought to the Americas by the Spaniards. By the end of the Civil War, large herds of wild longhorn steers roamed the Great Plains. These steers were claimed by ranchers, giving rise to the Texas cattle boom.

From the 1860s to the 1880s, Texas ranchers relied on the **"open range"** where cattle grazed freely on the grasses of the Great Plains. In the spring, **cowboys** rounded up the cattle to **brand** the skin of the calves with a hot iron showing the mark of the owner. The cattle were then released to feed further on the grasses of the range. In the fall, the cattle were rounded up for the **"long drive"** north to the stockyards and railroad stations of Kansas, Missouri, Nebraska and Wyoming.

The cowboys who herded these cattle were Anglo-Americans, Mexican Americans, African Americans and European immigrants. They learned their ways of ranching and dressing from the Mexican **vaqueros** (*cowboys*).

Cowboys used special clothing. They wore broad-rimmed hats to protect themselves from the sun. They also wore neckerchiefs or bandannas to serve as washcloths and to cover their faces when riding in dust. Leather chaps protected their legs from thorns. Leather gloves allowed them to handle a lariat without rope burns. High-horned saddles made it possible for the cowboys to hold the horn while galloping, or to attach their lariats to something when roping a steer.

Out on the range, a dozen cowboys could handle as many as a thousand cattle. On the "long drive" a few cowboys rode in front of the herd, with others on the sides and rear. A **wrangler** was in charge of the spare horses, since each cowboy rode several horses in the course of a day. Finally, they were accompanied by a cook and a "chuck wagon." On the trail, cowboys ate beef, corn, beans, smoked meats, game and coffee.

An early cattle drive

Describe some of the special clothing worn by cowboys.

By the 1880s, the "long drive" ended as railroads extended into Texas. The open range was divided into farms and ranches, each protected with barbed wire fences. Cattle raising, however, did not

CONTINUED

come to an end. Ranchers now raised cattle on their own property instead of on the open range. Texas continued to be the leading producer of cattle in the United States.

Cattle being rounded up
Why did the long drive end when railroads extended into Texas?

Like cattle, cotton was very important to the Texas economy. In the late 1800s, more Texans worked in growing, picking and processing cotton than at any other job. Cotton agriculture began in Texas with the first Anglo-American settlers. The climate and soil of East and Central Texas were well suited to growing cotton. Settlers from Southern states such as Georgia built plantations in Texas, using slaves to grow, harvest and transport the crop.

On June 19th, 1865, often referred to as "Juneteenth," slavery in Texas was abolished. Cotton production collapsed. Cotton-growing revived gradually, as landowners introduced the **sharecropping** system to work their lands. Sharecroppers farmed the land and in return gave the landowner a share of the crop. Planting cotton soon spread further west, onto the prairies and Great Plains. Railroads carried the cotton to Houston or Galveston, where it was transferred to ships bound for England or the northeastern United States.

Cotton pickers in Corpus Christi, Texas, 1942
Why was harvesting cotton such hard work?

Harvesting cotton was a backbreaking job. The plant grew only a couple of feet tall, and the pickers had to bend over all day long. In addition, cotton burrs cut the pickers' hands. Afterwards, the cotton was cleaned and the seeds were removed with a cotton "gin."

Texas also became an important center for processing the cotton seeds. The seeds were crushed to squeeze out cottonseed oil. The ground-up seeds were then used to feed livestock.

Now let us see how the previous reading could be presented in the form of a diagram.

KEYSTONES OF THE TEXAS ECONOMY IN THE LATE 1800s

CATTLE

- Developed out of wild herds on the Great plains
- Ranchers made use of the "open range" from 1860s–1880s
- Cowboy life was hard and required special clothing
- *What would you include here?*

COTTON

- Developed before the Civil War with plantations using slave labor
- *What would you include here?*
- Still the major employer of Texans in the late 1800s
- *What would you include here?*

THE AMATEUR HISTORIAN: RECREATING THE PAST

1. **Branding.** The branding of cattle identifies the owner of the animal. For example, the "XIT" brand identifies the XIT ranch. The "X" stands for the ten members of the group who originally put up the money for the ranch. The "IT" is for "in Texas." Make up a brand for an imaginary ranch using your initials. Explain why you selected the design that you did and what it means.
2. **Cowboy "lingo" (*language*).** Cowboys often spoke their own unique language or lingo. For example, *grub* meant food; *varmint* was a small, harmful animal; *I reckon* meant I think so. Make up a short dictionary of other words and phrases used by cowboys in Texas.
3. **Cowboy clothing.** Cowboys in Texas often dressed in a unique style. Draw a typical cowboy and use lines to point to each item of clothing. State what each item of clothing was called and how it was used by the cowboy.
4. **Role-playing.** In the late 1800s, ranchers used large unsettled areas for grazing their cattle. Settlers took small areas of land and fenced them in to make farms. Sometimes conflicts developed between the two groups. Members of the class should divide into ranchers and farmers. Each side should present its views. Then the class should hold a "town meeting" at which the entire class, acting as ranchers and farmers, should try to resolve their differences.

A PROBLEM-SOLUTION READING

Texas was largely agricultural until well into the twentieth century. In 1900, only 17 out of every hundred Texans lived in a large city. At the beginning of the twentieth century, Texas **cities** began to grow. From the 1870s onwards, cities developed along major ★ railroad lines. As profits from farm products fell, some farmers moved to cities in search of work. Immigrants from Europe and Mexico also came to cities such as Houston, Dallas and San Antonio. The movement of people to cities is called **urbanization.**

The Ft. Worth skyline
What attracted Texans to move to cities?

Cities offered new opportunities for culture and entertainment. They had their own newspapers, universities, libraries, churches, theaters, hospitals and sports teams. They were the first places to have telegraphs, telephones, streetcars and electricity. Cities were also financial centers, where loans could be obtained. Later, the oil boom and the growth of local manufacturing further fueled the growth of cities in Texas. However, the bringing together of such large numbers of people created many new problems.

The growth of cities in Texas gives us an opportunity to examine another type of reading—the **problem-solution reading.** This form of reading identifies problems. The reading provides details about these problems and describes attempts at solutions. The following reading looks at the problems and some of the solutions that resulted from the growth of cities in Texas. Afterwards, you will see how a diagram approach can also work for a problem-solution reading.

The Grace Cultural Center in Abilene
What did this structure have to offer Texans?

PROBLEMS OF URBAN GROWTH IN TEXAS

The coming together of large numbers of people created many new problems for the cities of Texas. Some of these problems were physical ones: how to meet the needs of so many people living in one place. Other problems were moral: how to prevent the spread of corruption and abuse.

One serious problem was that many cities in Texas at first lacked fresh drinking water. These cities now drilled new wells and pumped water through pipes to homes. Another problem facing cities was how to handle large amounts of sewage. Houston had been dumping sewage into the Buffalo Bayou, which also provided the city's water supply. In 1902, Houston completed a new sewage system that became a model for other cities in the nation. Other Texas cities followed this example. Unpaved roads presented yet another physical problem for cities. They were dusty in the summer and became mud tracks when it rained. In the final years of the nineteenth century Galveston, Houston and Dallas used wooden planks, bricks, gravel and asphalt to pave their roads.

Workers at a door factory in San Antonio (1918). *What problems do you think city factory workers faced?*

Education posed special difficulties. There were not enough schools for the growing numbers of children. In addition, supplies such as textbooks were very expensive. To solve this problem, new laws were passed to build more schools. State laws required children ages 8 to 14 to attend school. Children were also provided with free textbooks.

Government corruption in the cities presented another problem. New forms of city government in Texas were designed to be more efficient and less corrupt. For example, in 1900 Galveston was destroyed by a powerful hurricane. The Governor appointed new officials to take over the city government, giving rise to the **commission system**—where the city was governed by a group of commissioners. Each commissioner acted as a legislator, and was given control over a different part of city government, such as finance, the police or the fire department. This system was soon adopted by other cities.

Many workers living in cities faced harsh working conditions. To prevent abuses by new industries, laws were passed limiting the number of hours that people had to work. Child labor laws prohibited children from working in factories.

The following graphic organizer diagrams this problem-solution reading:

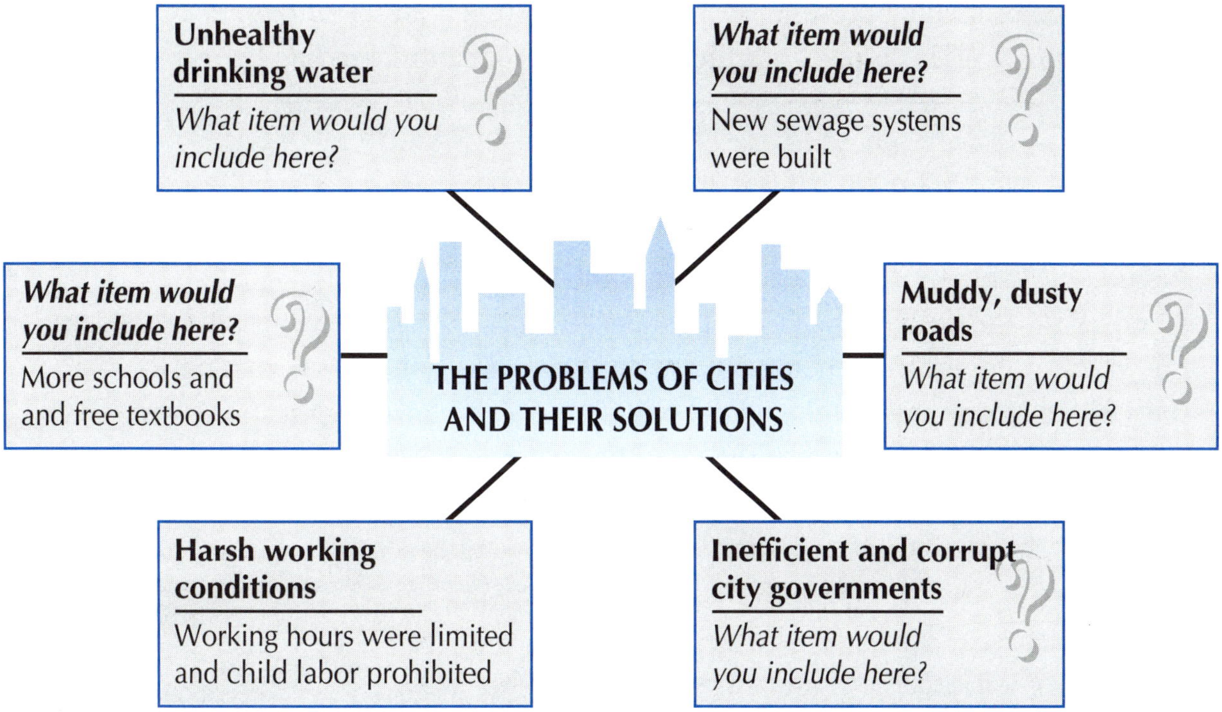

THE AMATEUR HISTORIAN: RECREATING THE PAST

1. Completing a chart. Complete the chart of the major cities in Texas in 1850, 1860, 1990 and today.

THE MOST POPULOUS CITIES IN TEXAS

1850		1860		1990		This Year
Galveston	4,117	San Antonio	8,235	Houston	1,629,902	?
San Antonio	3,488	Galveston	7,307	Dallas	1,007,618	?
Houston	2,396	Houston	4,845	San Antonio	835,393	?
New Braunfels	1,727	Austin	3,494	El Paso	515,342	?

A. Which have always been the most populated cities in Texas?

B. What factors do you think caused some cities to grow but not others?

C. Locate and mark each of these cities on a map of Texas.

2. Writing speeches. Pretend you are a candidate seeking election as the mayor of your town in 1900. Read about the history of your town in the local or school library to learn about the problems it faced at that time. Then write a short campaign speech describing those problems and proposing your own solutions.

A SEQUENTIAL READING

Another type of reading presents events in chronological order (*the order in which they occurred in time*). This type of reading is called a sequential reading.

TEXAS IN THE AGE OF GLOBAL POWER

In the early twentieth century, the United States became a world power. This brought Texans, along with other Americans, into a number of crises. These included World War I, the Great Depression and World War II.

In 1914, the countries of Europe went to war. At first, the United States kept out of the fighting. But when the Germans began sinking American ships in 1917, the United States entered the war. About 200,000 Texans fought in the war. Over 5,000 of them died. Texas became an important training area for American troops. Military bases were located at Waco, Houston, Fort Worth and San Antonio. **World War I** ended when Germany surrendered in November 1918.

Soldiers returning to Texas after W.W. I (July 4, 1919)

Why did the U.S. enter the war?

Following the war, the 1920s brought good times to Texas and the rest of the nation. Women won the right to vote. Americans began buying a new invention—the automobile. The rise of the automobile created a demand for gasoline, which was made from Texas oil. People enjoyed other new inventions such as motion pictures, radios, vacuum cleaners and refrigerators. The 1920s also saw an increase in violence. The **Ku Klux Klan** started up again and committed crimes against African Americans, Jewish Americans and Catholic Americans. When alcoholic drinks were prohibited throughout the United States, Texas became one of the places where these beverages were illegally brought into the country.

Then in the 1930s, Texas and the nation were hard hit by the **Great Depression.** The U.S. economy suddenly turned bad. Millions of people could not find work. Families depended on relatives, charity groups and government programs for money to live. Many people became homeless. Farmers in West Texas faced special problems. The lack of rain made the soil so dry that it turned to dust and was blown away by the wind. The Great Plains turned into a vast **"Dust Bowl."**

During the mid-1930s, the government started to spend money on public programs to put people back to work. This government policy became known as the **New Deal.** The federal government spent nearly $1.5 billion in Texas, building

CONTINUED

roads, bridges, parks, schools and other public buildings. This spending allowed many Texans to earn a living again.

In Europe, the Great Depression led the German people to support the dictator **Adolf Hitler.** Hitler started World War II in 1939, when his armies invaded Poland. Dictators in Italy and Japan soon joined Hitler. When Japan attacked the American navy in 1941, the United States entered the war. Texans again fought all over the world—in Asia, Africa and Europe. Nearly 750,000 Texans joined the military. About 23,000 of them were killed in the war. **Audie Murphy,** of Farmersville, Texas, received more medals than any other soldier in the war. Meanwhile, Texas factories were kept busy producing airplanes, ships and other goods for the war. Peace finally came in 1945 when Germany and Japan surrendered.

A Texas farm during the Dust Bowl in 1938
What caused the soil to turn to dust?

Convert the words in this reading into a diagram by completing the following graphic organizer:

- In 1914, World War I broke out in Europe.
- ***What item would you include here?***
- W.W. I ended in 1918 when Germany surrendered.
- The 1920s were a time of world peace, change, new inventions and violence.
- ***What item would you include here?***
- In the mid 1930s, the government spent billions of dollars putting people to work.
- World War II began in 1939 when Hitler's soldiers invaded Poland.
- ***What item would you include here?***
- ***What item would you include here?***

THE AMATEUR HISTORIAN: RECREATING THE PAST

1. **Writing a letter.** Pretend you are a farmer in West Texas during the Depression. Write a letter to your friend in California narrating your experiences in fighting the bad economic conditions. Describe your experiences in chronological order. Try to answer the questions **who, what, where** and **when** for each event. *Who* was involved? *What* happened? *Where* did it happen? *When* did it happen?

Unemployed workers line up in San Antonio (1934) looking for jobs. *What problems existed during the Great Depression?*

2. **Drawing pictures.** Look at photographs of Texas during the Great Depression. These can be found in books at your library. Then draw a picture that you think describes Texas during this period.

INTERPRETING HISTORICAL ILLUSTRATIONS

EXTENDING THE ACTIVITY

Historians look at many types of sources to determine what happened in the past. They review written records and also look at artifacts. **Artifacts** are things that people made and used in their daily lives. Another tool that helps us to understand the past are old pictures and photographs. They tell us how people looked and dressed. Often pictures express the feelings of the people who lived at the time.

During the years when the "long drive" played an important role in the Texas economy, cameras were just coming into use. Surviving photographs of cowboys let us "see" what life was like on the "open range." But the first cameras were large, heavy and clumsy to use outside of a studio. And of course, outside was the only place to photograph the cowboy in his natural setting.

As a result, there are few photographs of cowboys on the open range in the 1870s and 1880s. Instead, we depend mainly on drawings of cowboy life. Illustrators drew events as they saw them.

THINK ABOUT IT

Describe a photograph from your home that you would use to best illustrate your own lifestyle.

In this *Extending The Activity,* you will play the role of a junior historian. You will examine two drawings and one photograph showing the life of Texas cowboys. Carefully examine each of these, in order to learn what each tells you about the life of the cowboy in Texas.

Picture #1 (drawing)

Driving cattle into a corral

Picture #2 (photograph)

Cowboy driving a long line of cattle

WRITING A DESCRIPTION OF COWBOY LIFE ON THE OPEN RANGE

As you learned in this activity, a descriptive paragraph describes a person, place or object. To **describe** is to draw a mental picture with words. You can describe what something looks like or what it does. If you are describing a person, you tell how the person looks or what that person thinks or feels. When writing a description, try to provide as many details as you can.

Pictures often tell us about what life was like in the past. In this exercise, describe exactly what you see in each picture. Then, conclude each description by adding something about what the picture tells us about cowboy life.

Be sure to look at the caption under each picture. It provides important information about the illustration. Try to determine what is happening in each illustration. For example, what is the cowboy in the center of Picture #1 doing with his whip? Also look at how the people are dressed. What do their clothes tell us about their life?

Picture #3 (drawing)

Depositing a letter in a mailbox

REVIEWING YOUR UNDERSTANDING

Directions: Fill in your Vocabulary Cards. Then complete the project that follows.

Cowboys

What is a cowboy?

Describe how a cowboy might have dressed:

Cities

What problems did Texas cities face as they were developing?

How were some of these problems solved?

Creating Your Own Readings

In this activity you learned about three types of readings—descriptive, sequential and problem-solution. How good would you be at creating one of these types of readings? Let's find out. Next to each type of reading is a list of topics.

TYPE OF READING	TOPICS
Descriptive	★ The members of my family ★ The life of a cowboy in Texas today
Sequential	★ My life from birth to the fourth grade ★ The history of the Dallas Cowboys
Problem-Solution	★ How to improve my school ★ The problems facing my community

Select **one** topic from the list and write a short essay about it. Make sure that your essay corresponds to the type of reading it has been matched with. For example, if you write about the members of your family, be sure you write a descriptive essay.

3D WHAT EFFECT HAVE KEY EVENTS HAD ON TEXAS?

In this activity, you will read about some of the causes and effects of key events in Texas during the 20th century. You will learn how events can sometimes have important effects. Look for the following important words:

- ★ Cause and Effect
- ★ Petroleum
- ★ Spindletop
- ★ Civil Rights Movement
- ★ Segregation
- ★ Integration

In 1963 President John F. Kennedy was assassinated when he visited Dallas. How might history have been different if you could go back in time and stop him from making that trip? Changing just one past event might change the whole course of history.

This is because every event has effects. Some events can affect the entire future of a society. For example, suppose a leader decides that his or her nation should go to war. That decision could change a country's entire development. Historians often study the events of the past to better understand cause-and-effect relationships.

- The **cause** of something is *what made it happen.* For example, turning on a light switch makes electricity flow to the bulb and lights it up. The *cause* of the light's going on was that someone turned on the switch.
- An **effect** is what happens *because of* a situation, action or event. For example, the light's going on was the *effect* of turning on the switch. Sometimes a single cause can have a whole chain of many effects.

CAUSE
Someone turned on the switch.

EFFECT
The light went on.

Let us look at another example. Imagine that one morning you get up late for school. Usually, you walk to the corner and wait to meet your school bus. But because you are late, you miss the bus. This makes you late for school. A diagram of these cause-and-effect relationships might appear as follows:

***Event:* Missing The School Bus**

CAUSE
Getting up late in the morning.

EFFECT
Being late for school.

In this activity, you will read about three events in the history of Texas. You will learn how each of them involved **causes** and **effects.**

KEY EVENTS IN TEXAS HISTORY

★ **Petroleum** *(oil)* is one of our most valuable natural resources. It is created by decaying plants and animals that once lived in the sea. The petroleum holds the energy the plants once captured from the sun. This energy is released when the oil is burned.

In 1894, workers in Corsicana discovered oil while drilling a water well. The town later built the first oil refinery in Texas. An **oil refinery** breaks up oil into usable products like kerosene and fuel oil.

Oil gusher.
How did the discovery of oil affect Texas?

In 1899, a mining engineer, Patillo Higgins, began drilling for oil around Beaumont. His studies showed that petroleum should gather near salt domes because they trapped the oil. Higgins was not successful in finding oil. Underground areas of quicksand prevented his drill from working. His work was then taken up by Anthony Lucas. On ★ January 10, 1901, Lucas hit oil in the **Spindletop** well. The pressure of this oil well was so powerful that half a million barrels of oil blew out from the well before it could be capped. In the nine days it took to bring it under control, the well spurted out as much oil as the Corsicana field had produced the entire previous year.

The discovery of the Spindletop oil field had many effects in Texas. People shifted from lamp oil to fuel oil. Trains were converted to burn oil instead of coal. The coal industry declined. New companies like the Gulf Oil Company were formed. Other companies arose to take care of the oil industry's needs. These companies produced wooden and iron derricks to hold the drilling equipment. Other new companies made pipes, drills and storage tanks. The discovery of oil also led to the construction of more oil refineries, especially along the Gulf Coast.

Boom towns grew up overnight in places where oil was found. Houston offered oil companies a place to load their ocean-going ships and became a major port. The city grew further when many other oil companies moved their main offices there. A few years later, the discovery of oil on lands owned by the University of Texas made that college one of the richest in the nation.

If we put this information into a graphic organizer, this cause-and-effect reading would look something like this:

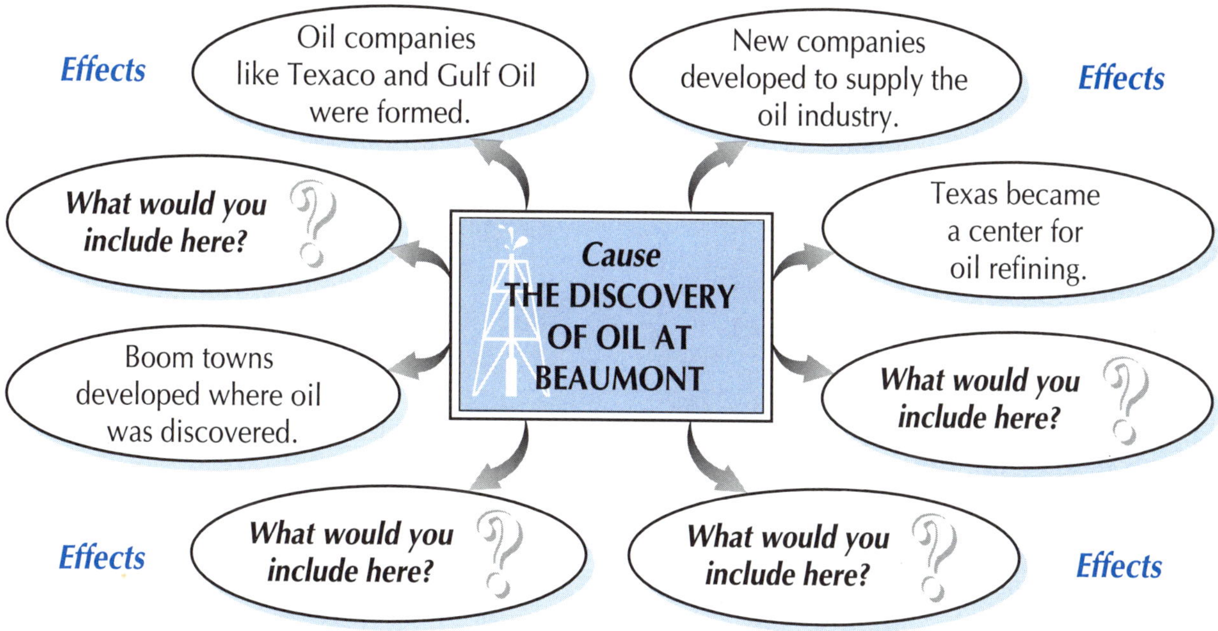

Let's try converting another cause-and-effect reading into a graphic organizer.

THE OIL DISCOVERY AT KILGORE, TEXAS

Spindletop's success encouraged others to look for oil in Texas. An even greater oil discovery was made several years later by Columbus "Dad" Joiner at Kilgore in October 1930. This discovery in East Texas was the largest oil field ever found in the state. By 1931, it was producing 109 million barrels of oil a year.

One effect of this discovery was that oil prices suddenly fell. People with property at Kilgore were drilling their own wells. Too many investors were producing oil. They had to lower their prices to less than it actually cost to produce the oil. Eventually, the Texas state government stepped in to regulate production. Oil producers had to cut back production, so that oil was sold at a fair price. Oil wells had to be spaced apart, allowing producers to bring out the maximum amount of oil from the field.

A residential section of Kilgore (1939).
What effect did the production of so much oil have on its price?

CONTINUED

Meanwhile, continued production in East Texas provided jobs for many people and eased the Great Depression in Texas. Oil also provided tax money that paid for many government programs.

The economy of Texas soon came to depend heavily on the success of the oil industry. Texas also became a leading producer of **petrochemicals** (*chemical products made from petroleum*) such as explosives, plastics and synthetic materials.

In the 1970s, when oil prices rose, Texas enjoyed boom times. In the 1980s, when oil prices fell, Texas experienced a weak economy. Texas continues to produce large amounts of oil and natural gas. However, the Texas economy no longer depends on oil as heavily as before. Manufacturers of other products now produce more revenue for Texas than the oil and gas industry.

Cause
THE DISCOVERY OF OIL AT KILGORE

Effects

- Oil prices fell.
- The state government of Texas stepped in to regulate production.
- Many new jobs were created in Texas.
- Texas became a center for petrochemicals.
- ***What would you include here?***
- ***What would you include here?***
- ***What would you include here?***

THE AMATEUR HISTORIAN: RECREATING THE PAST

1. Visiting places. What was life like during the oil boom? An interesting way to find out is to visit one of the following:

- **Lucas Gusher Monument** (Beaumont): marks the beginning of the world's modern petroleum industry.
- **Texas Energy Museum** (Beaumont): highlights the discovery of oil and also includes exhibits on energy science and the environment.
- **Felty Outdoor Oil Museum** (Burkburnett): you can see early oil field equipment from the oil boom days.
- **Trails and Tales of Boomtown USA** (Burkburnett): has tours through oil fields and an outdoor oil museum.
- **Permian Basin Petroleum Museum** (Midland): you can see paintings, 3-D models and hardware from the early days of oil pumping.
- **Crackaxle Canyon** (San Antonio): you can visit an imaginary 1920s boom town at Fiesta Texas.

2. Writing a diary. Pretend you are Anthony Lucas. Write a diary entry or a letter to a friend describing your discovery at Spindletop.

You have just had some practice in completing two graphic organizers on cause and effect. Let's put your knowledge to a test one more time. Read the following selection. Then complete the graphic organizer for this cause-and-effect reading.

THE CIVIL RIGHTS MOVEMENT IN TEXAS

There were many reasons for the start of the **Civil Rights Movement** in the 1950s and 1960s. First, the Civil War and Reconstruction had promised equality to African Americans. However, in Texas and other Southern states, equality had been withheld for almost another hundred years.

Racial discrimination in the South. *How does this picture reflect racial discrimination?*

Another cause was the continuing **discrimination** (*treating people unfairly because of their race*) and violence against African Americans. After slavery ended in Texas, African

CONTINUED

Americans continued to be shut out from white churches and schools. Separate schools were set up for African Americans, which were often not as good as those for whites. In the 1890s, the Texas legislature passed laws, known as **Jim Crow laws,** requiring separate railroad cars, public parks and beaches for blacks and whites. In addition, African Americans were often the victims of violence. The Ku Klux Klan terrorized African Americans who spoke out for their rights.

One of the key causes of the Civil Rights Movement was an important decision by the Supreme Court. In 1954, the Supreme Court ruled that **segregation** (*separation of races*) in public schools was against the U.S. Constitution. Public schools were told to **integrate**—bringing black and white students together.

Dr. Martin Luther King, Jr.
How did he contribute to the Civil Rights Movement?

The Civil Rights Movement was led by the Reverend **Dr. Martin Luther King, Jr.** In 1955, he helped organize a boycott of segregated buses in Montgomery, Alabama. Other civil rights leaders also attempted to end the segregation of public facilities. African Americans protested segregation by taking **"freedom rides"** on segregated buses. They held sit-ins at segregated lunch counters and marched to demand equal voting rights. These protests led to the end of segregation in Texas and other Southern states. Lunch counters, buses, restaurants and theaters all became integrated.

Integration was greatly helped by new federal laws. In 1964, President **Lyndon B. Johnson,** a Texan, proposed a new **Civil Rights Act.** The new law prohibited discrimination in employment or places open to the public because of race, age, religion or nationality. It also established a new federal commission to make sure that minorities were fairly treated.

In 1965, Congress passed the **Voting Rights Act.** This act ended special taxes and other devices used to prevent African Americans from voting. President Johnson also introduced an **Affirmative Action Program,** requiring employers, universities and local governments with federal contracts to hire more minority and women employees.

The Civil Rights Movement served as an important example for many other groups. Women, Hispanic Americans, Native Americans and people with disabilities soon followed the example of African Americans in demanding more rights and greater opportunities. These changes had the effect of turning Texas and the rest of the nation into a more open society.

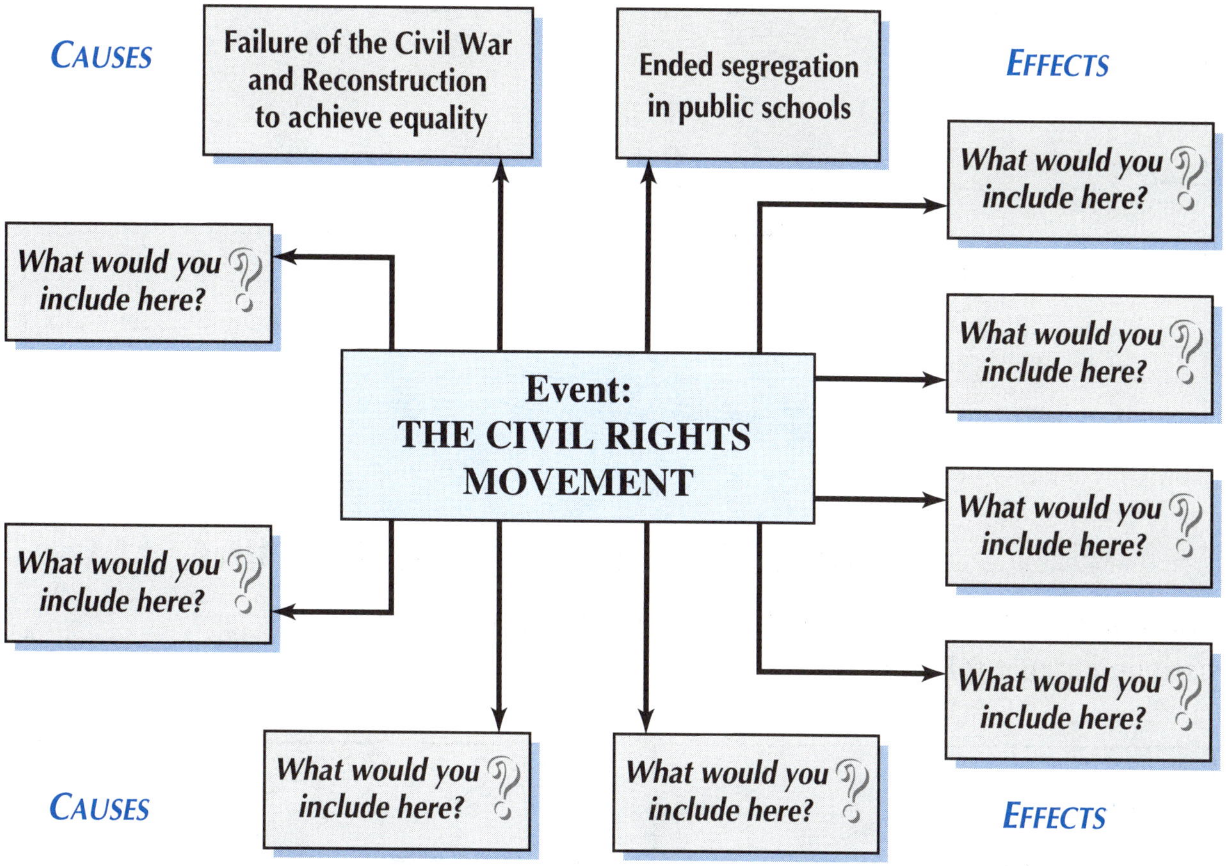

THE AMATEUR HISTORIAN: RECREATING THE PAST

1. **Interviewing eyewitnesses.** Interview your parent, guardian, grandparent or other adult. Ask them what they remember about life in Texas before the Civil Rights Movement. Explore with them how this compares with life in Texas today. Write a brief one page summary of the interview.

FINDING CAUSE-AND-EFFECT IN YOUR NEWSPAPER

EXTENDING THE ACTIVITY

How events are reported in our daily newspapers often involves cause and effect relationships. Select any event described in an article in a recent Texas newspaper. Then, on a separate sheet of paper, copy the chart found on the next page. Complete the chart, using the newspaper article you have selected.

Event: ?

Causes	Effects
☆ ?	☆ ?
☆ ?	☆ ?
☆ ?	☆ ?

REVIEWING YOUR UNDERSTANDING

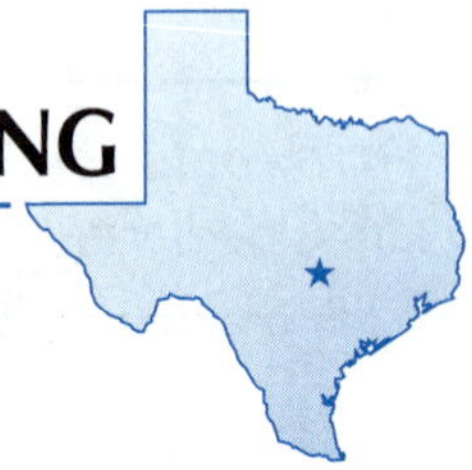

Directions: Fill in your Vocabulary Cards. Then complete the assignment that follows.

Cause

Define cause:

Provide an example of a cause:

Effect

Define effect:

Provide an example of an effect:

Finding Cause and Effect

Use this reading selection to answer the question that follows:

> Arthur "Jack" Johnson was an African American who was born in Galveston in 1878. As a young man, he worked on the Galveston docks lifting 500-pound bales of cotton. He soon decided to put his strength to a different use. He became a boxer. In 1908, he knocked out Tommy Burns and became America's first black heavyweight boxing champion.

Which was an effect of "Jack" Johnson's lifting weights on the docks of Galveston?

- **A.** Johnson was an African American.
- **B.** Johnson was born in Galveston, Texas.
- **C.** Johnson was born in 1878.
- **D.** Johnson became a successful boxer.

3E HOW WOULD YOU OUTLINE THIS READING?

In this activity, you will learn about Texas today. Look for the following important words and people:

- ★ Outline
- ★ Arabic Numerals
- ★ Barbara Jordan
- ★ Roman Numerals
- ★ High-Tech Industry
- ★ Oral History

In this activity, you will learn about outlines, another tool to help you understand a reading. An **outline** is a brief plan in which a topic is divided up into smaller parts. The purpose of an outline is to show how a topic and its parts are related. An outline serves as a plan to help guide you through a reading.

Outlines begin with general topics and then provide specific details. The major topics of an outline are numbered with **Roman numerals** (I, II, III). If a topic listed by a Roman numeral needs to be further divided, its sub-topics are identified by **capital letters** (A, B, C). If these sub-topics need to be further divided, each smaller subject is given an **Arabic numeral** (1, 2, 3).

Let's look at how this process of outlining works. Assume you want to create an outline about your own life. This topic might be outlined as follows:

MY LIFE → **(Title)**

I. Early Childhood → **(Main Topic)**

- **A.** Family → **(Sub-Topic)**
  - **1.** Parents
  - **2.** Brothers and Sisters
  - **3.** Grandparents

  } **(Parts of Sub-Topic)**
- **B.** Playmates → **(Sub-Topic)**
- **C. Neighborhood** → **(Sub-Topic)**

II. Elementary School Years → **(Main Topic)**

- **A.** Kindergarten → **(Sub-Topic)**
- **B.** Early Grades → **(Sub-Topic)**
  - **1.** Teachers
  - **2.** Friends

  } **(Parts of Sub-Topic)**

Notice that, in this example, each smaller part helps us to understand a larger idea. For example, "Teachers" and "Friends" help us to understand the larger topic "Early Grades." "Kindergarten" and "Early Grades" help us to understand the "Elementary

School Years." This larger sub-topic is one of the two main parts that make up the general theme of "My Life."

Now let's look at a reading about Texas today. After reading the passage, you will be asked to complete the outline that follows.

TEXAS TODAY

In recent years, Texas has undergone many important changes. The rise of cities has been an important part of recent Texas life. Today, more than 80% of Texans live in cities or suburbs. Most of these residents work in manufacturing, oil or service industries. Texas city-dwellers and suburbanites also enjoy similar life-styles. They share information and ideas communicated by television, radio, newspapers, magazines, books and the mail. They travel frequently by automobile, train, bus or airplane. They are united as members of a consumer society, with many products and vast shopping malls at their command.

The rise of new scientific methods of ranching and farming has been another important part of modern Texas life. New machinery and better business methods are now used to run farms and ranches. These require large amounts of money, so many smaller farms and ranches have been unable to compete. Today, only a small part of the Texas population is involved in ranching or farming. Yet they produce more than a much larger number of farms and ranches did 20 years ago.

Another recent development has been the fall in oil prices. In the early 1980s one-quarter of all income in Texas was related to oil. With the drop of oil prices, property lost much of its value. Many banks in Texas failed. The state government nearly ran out of money.

LBJ Space Center

What other high-tech industries besides the space industry exist in Texas?

Texas has gradually recovered from the oil slump. Manufacturing now produces more income for Texas than oil and gas. ★ Today, **high-technology industries** like electronics and aircraft production are found throughout the state. Major companies like Texas Instruments, Lockheed, General Dynamics, Compaq and Tandy have made Texas their headquarters.

Because of its warm climate, employment and cultural opportunities, Texas has become one of the fastest growing states. It attracts many newcomers from other parts of the United States and Mexico. Between 1950 and 1980, the population of Texas doubled.

CONTINUED

Texas has become an important part of a vast world economy. The rise of the state as a major oil, manufacturing and agricultural center has occurred in part because of the state's transportation and communication links with the rest of the world. This has made it possible for Texans to do business with other places. Texans now depend upon goods and services from other areas. They also depend on their ability to sell Texas goods and services throughout the nation and abroad.

A final important change in Texas has been the growth of individual civil rights over the past 30 years. African Americans, women, Hispanic Americans and Native Americans have all benefited. For example, **Barbara Jordan,** an African American, was elected to the U.S. Congress. **Ann Richards,** a woman, was elected Governor of Texas. A Mexican-American, **Henry Cisneros** became Mayor of San Antonio. Throughout Texas, citizens of all races and backgrounds have made the state of Texas into a truly multicultural society.

SMS Ranch in Spur, Texas
Why are ranches and farms becoming more scarce in Texas?

Here is what this reading would look like in outline form. Notice that some items have been omitted. Complete any omitted items in the outline.

TEXAS TODAY

I. The Rise of Cities and Their Effect On Texas Life
- **A.** Most Texans live in cities or nearby suburbs
- **B.** Most Texans work in manufacturing, oil or service industries
- **C.** *What do you think goes here?*
- **D.** *What do you think goes here?*

II. *What do you think goes here?*
- **A.** Smaller farms and ranches were unable to compete
- **B.** Therc are now less ranches and farms than before, but they produce more

III. The Decline in Oil Prices Affected Texans in the late 1980s
- **A.** Real estate lost its value
- **B.** Large numbers of Texas banks failed
- **C.** *What do you think goes here?*

IV. The Gradual Recovery of the Texas Economy

- **A.** Manufacturing developed
- **B.** *What do you think goes here?*
- **C.** Major companies made Texas their headquarters

V. Texas As a Fast Growing State

- **A.** Climate, employment and cultural opportunities helped Texas grow
- **B.** Newcomers have been attracted to the state
- **C.** *What do you think goes here?*

VI. Part of a Vast World Economy

- **A.** Transportation and communications link Texas with the nation and world
- **B.** *What do you think goes here?*
- **C.** *What do you think goes here?*

VII. The Expansion of Civil Rights

- **A.** Women and minority groups in Texas have benefited
  - **1.** Barbara Jordan was elected to Congress
  - **2.** Ann Richards was elected Governor
  - **3.** *What do you think goes here?*
- **B.** Texas has grown into a multicultural society

BECOMING AN ORAL HISTORIAN

EXTENDING THE ACTIVITY

In this activity, you learned about the recent history of Texas. Can you recall a time when you heard a grandparent or other adult family member speak about what it was like when he or she was growing up in Texas? Or can you remember when this family member spoke about living through an important event in Texas history?

> On a separate sheet of paper, describe what this family member spoke about.

If you recorded your grandparent or other adult family member's story, you were ★ participating in a special process. Historians call this **"oral history"**—collecting and keeping records of memories of the past through interviews of living eyewitnesses.

Some people believe that the importance of oral history is increasing with each new generation. We live in a fast-paced society. People seem to have less time to keep diaries or to write journals. There is also a greater use of the telephone and computer services. These developments make communication more convenient. However, they often leave no record of what was said or done. Many historians believe that there is a growing need to preserve the personal or human side of history for future generations. At the same time, many people are living longer. They provide a rich resource for historians because some of these people actually experienced the past that historians describe.

In this *Extending The Activity,* you will be given an opportunity to become an oral historian. Remember, however, that your oral interview only records a person's memories of the past. A person's memories are often not the whole story, but only that person's own view of the story. Also, a person's memory of events often changes over time and may contain some inaccuracies.

PREPARING FOR THE INTERVIEW

Acting as an oral historian involves more than just turning on a tape recorder or video recorder and letting someone talk. Careful planning and research are needed to conduct a successful interview.

SELECTING AN ORAL HISTORY PROJECT

The first step is to decide which person to interview and why. The most common type of oral history involves interviewing a family member, neighbor or other person about his or her life. In this interview, gather as much information as you can about that person's life. Focus on how the person's culture (*language, attitudes, customs and beliefs*) has influenced his or her life.

RESEARCHING YOUR PROJECT

Do not rush off to conduct your interview. You should first look at books, newspapers, and other written sources. This will allow your interview to go smoothly and help you jog the memory of the person you interview. If you select a family member to interview, speak with other relatives and friends to gather information about him or her.

DEVELOPING A QUESTIONNAIRE

After you have completed your research, you should create a questionnaire. A **questionnaire** is an outline of topics you wish to cover during your interview. Each questionnaire will be different, since it must be designed to fit the particular person being interviewed.

Your interview questions will differ from topic to topic. Your questionnaire should use "leading" words—such as **describe, explain** and **discuss.** Remember, you want to "open up" the memories of your interviewee. Here is a sample questionnaire that asks a subject about his or her reactions at the time of the dropping of the atomic bomb on Hiroshima, Japan, in 1945—an event that helped end World War II:

QUESTIONNAIRE

I. Biographical Questions

Name: _______ Address: ____________

II. Topical Questions

- How old were you when the atom bomb was dropped on Hiroshima?
- Were any of your family members directly involved in World War II? If so, **describe** who they were and what role they played in the war.
- **Describe** how you first learned the news that the bomb was dropped.

A destroyed city in Japan after the bomb was dropped.
What questions might you ask?

- **Discuss** what you remember about the reactions of those around you.
- **Describe** your other memories from that period in your life.
- At the time, did you agree with the decision to drop the bomb on Hiroshima?
- President Truman made the decision to actually drop the bomb. If you had been an advisor to the President in 1945, **describe** what you might have told him to do at that time.
- Have your ideas on this topic changed since 1945? If so, **describe** how your ideas changed and **explain** what caused them to change.

CONDUCTING THE INTERVIEW

A successful interview will also depend in large part on how you behave during the interview itself. Here are some helpful hints to keep in mind:

☆ **Make An Appointment.** Make an appointment several days in advance. Allow at least 30 minutes for the interview. Bring along a tape recorder or video recorder that you are familiar with. Be sure to test it before going to the interview.

☆ **The Start of the Interview.** Try to arrange it so that only you and your subject are present. Start by chatting informally with the person being interviewed to set yourselves at ease. Begin the interview with a short introduction, such as:

> "This interview is being conducted with Mrs. Barbara Neuman at her home. It is Thursday, March 3, 1996. It is 4:30 in the afternoon."

Begin the interview with easy questions. Avoid questions that require simple yes or no answers. Ask questions that call for descriptive answers.

- ☆ **Stay On The Topic.** If your subject strays from the topic, try to re-focus him or her as soon as possible. Follow up important information and details with new questions that may not be on your questionnaire.
- ☆ **Closing The Interview.** Always end the interview by thanking your interviewee. If you feel the interview has gone on too long, pick an appropriate time to end. If necessary, arrange another time for a follow-up interview. For example, you might say:

> "I would like to end the interview now. However, this was so interesting I would like to return to talk more about what else you remember about your reactions to the bomb's being dropped. Is that all right?"

CREATING A COVER SHEET FOR THE TAPES

Looking at the tape of your interview would not allow anyone to understand what the tape is about. You will need to create a cover sheet that explains the themes and ideas that are discussed in your taped interview. Use the following guide to create your cover sheet.

COVER SHEET FOR THE TAPED INTERVIEW

Topic of the Interview ______________________

Person Being Interviewed ______________________

Signature Granting Permission
For Educational Purposes. ______________________

RUNNING TIME AND IDEAS COVERED

Minutes: 1–4 General background information about the subject

Minutes: 5–8 Immediate reactions to the bombing

Minutes: 9–15 Personal opinions about the need to drop the bomb

OBTAINING PERMISSION TO USE THE TAPED INTERVIEW

You might decide to donate your taped interview to the school library. If so, you need to get permission from the person you interviewed. After you have prepared your cover sheet, have your subject sign it.

REVIEWING YOUR UNDERSTANDING

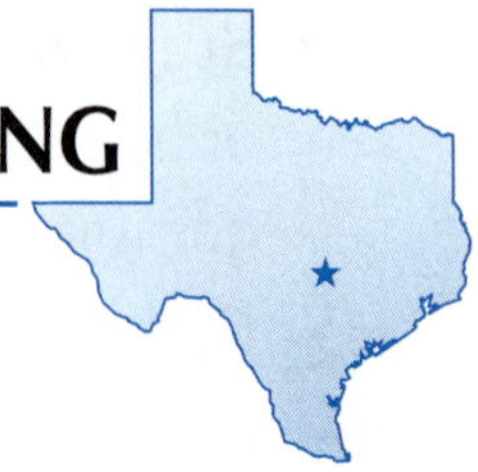

Directions: Fill in your Vocabulary Cards. Then complete the assignment that follows.

Outline
What is an outline?
What is an outline used for?

Oral History
What is oral history?
Why is oral history important?

Creating an Outline of Texas History

Let's practice your outlining skills. Look over the first activity in this chapter in order to practice them. The outline for this activity has been started for you. Complete it.

THE HISTORY OF TEXAS

I. The Early History of Texas
- **A.** The First People in Texas
- **B.** Europeans Explore Texas
- **C.** *What do you think goes here?*

II. Anglo-American Settlers Come to Texas
- **A.** *What do you think goes here?*
- **B.** *What do you think goes here?*

III.
- **A.**
- **B.**
- **C.**
- **D.**

IV.
- **A.**
- **B.**
- **C.**
- **D.**
- **E.**
- **F.**

3F

WHICH EVENTS WOULD YOU PLACE ON THE TIMELINE?

In this activity, you will learn about and create a timeline using key events in Texas history. Look for the following important words:

★ Timeline ★ Chronological Order ★ Decade ★ Century

Reading about the history of Texas allows your imagination to wander back in time. It is exciting to read about the people and events of Texas in the past. Often, while important events are taking place in one part of Texas, other important events are happening elsewhere. In order to see these connections, historians use a timeline.

TIMELINES AND THEIR MAIN PARTS

A **timeline** is a type of graph. It shows a group of events arranged along a line in ★ **chronological order.** "Chronological order" means the order in which the events ★ actually happened.

A timeline can cover anything—from a very short period to several thousand years. Its purpose is to show a sequence of events. To understand a timeline, first look at its main parts—its title, the events and the dates.

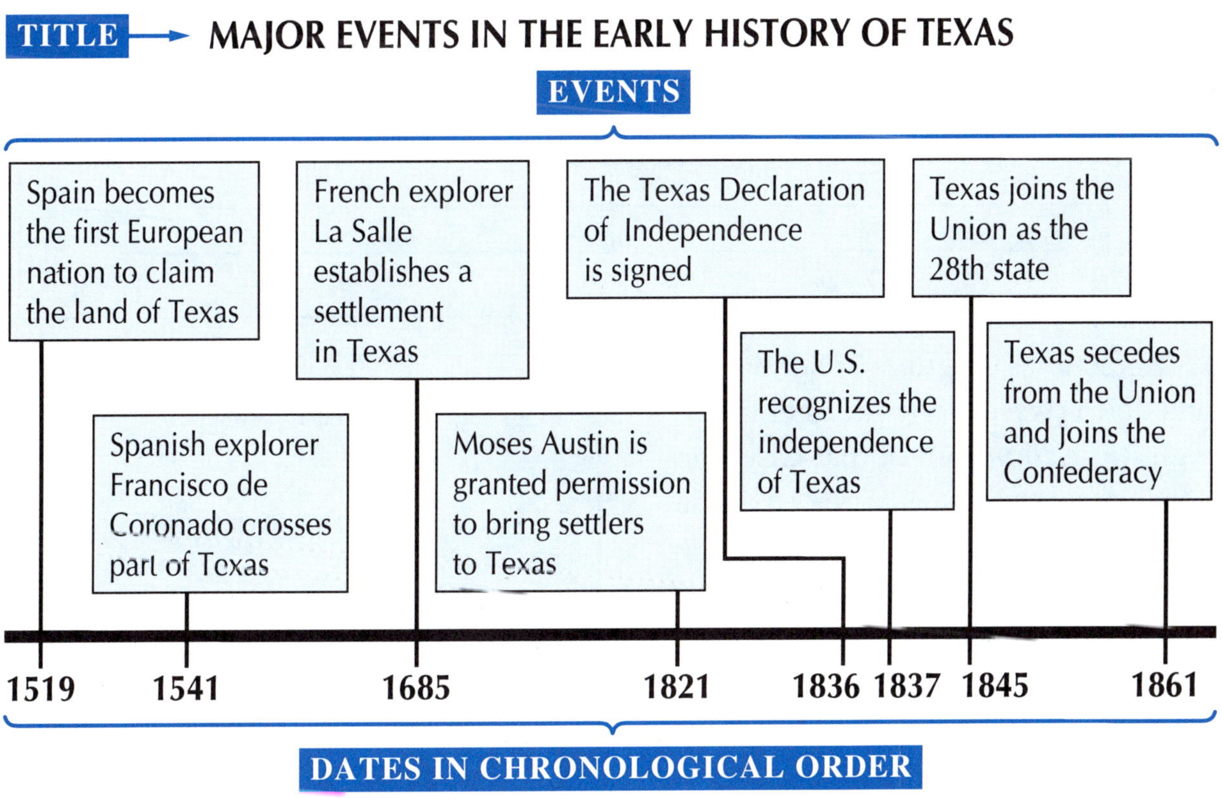

TITLE

The title tells you the overall topic of the timeline. In the timeline on page 129, the title means that the listings are important events that occurred in the early history of Texas.

★ CHECKING YOUR UNDERSTANDING ★

Selecting a title. A series of events is listed below. What title would you give a timeline that had these events on it?

Your Timeline Title: ______ ? ______

- In 1846, **James P. Henderson** was the first person to serve as Governor of Texas.
- In 1853, **James W. Henderson** served as Governor of Texas for only 28 days, when he took office to fill the seat of a Governor who had resigned.
- In 1891, **James S. Hogg** became the first Governor of Texas who had been born in Texas.
- In 1925, **Miriam A. Ferguson,** known as "Ma" for the initials in her name, became the first woman Governor of Texas.

Governor James S. Hogg

TIMELINE DESIGN

On a timeline, the earliest event usually appears on the far left. The rest of the events are placed to the right of it, in the order in which they occurred.

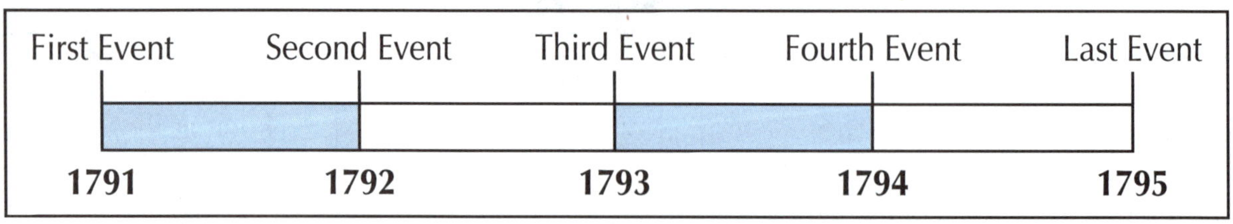

Sometimes timelines are drawn up and down (*vertically*) instead of left to right (*horizontally*). In that case, the earliest event is usually placed at the bottom of the timeline. The rest of the events are placed above the first event, in the order in which they occurred.

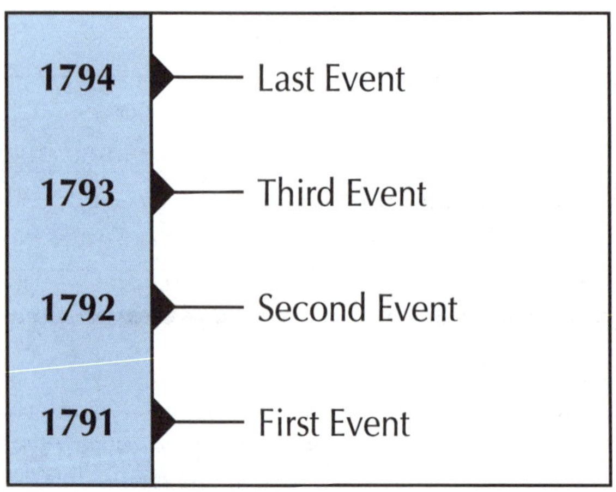

PERIODS OF TIME

To fully understand timelines you must know about time periods. For short periods of time, you can divide a timeline into one year intervals. For example:

Now you try it. Make a copy of the timeline and then place the years from 1952 to 1958.

For longer periods of time, you can divide a timeline into decades. A **decade** is a period of ten years. For example: ★

Now you try it. Make a copy of the timeline and place the years from 1930 to 1990 by decades.

An even longer period of time is a century. A **century** is a period of 100 years. For example, the following timeline shows several centuries of time. ★

Now you try it. Make a copy of the timeline and put in the years from 1300 to 1900, by centuries:

How we identify centuries may seem confusing at first. The "20th century" means the 100 years from 1901 to 2000. The 1990s, therefore, belong to the 20th century. Let's see why. Our dates are based on when it is believed Jesus Christ was born. The first 100 years after the birth of Jesus were the years 1–100. This is called the first century. Look at the following centuries to see more:

1–100	First Century	201–300	Third Century
101–200	Second Century	301–400	Fourth Century

1. Which century is: 701–800?

2. Which century is: 1501–1600?

3. What is the present century, 1901–2000?

4. What will the next century be called?

You may wonder how we record dates before the first century. These dates are called B.C. for the time Before Christ's birth. Many historians use the letters B.C.E. They stand for Before Common Era. You will learn more about these dates in later grades.

MEASURING THE PASSAGE OF TIME

To measure the number of years from one date to another, just subtract the smaller date from the larger date. Assume the year is 1996. How long ago was 1500? By subtracting 1500 from 1996, we arrive at 496 years ago.

1996	(1996 years since the birth of Jesus)
– 1500	(1500 years since the birth of Jesus)
496	Years ago

★ CHECKING YOUR UNDERSTANDING ★

Texas became a state in 1845. How long has Texas been a state?

EVENTS

Events on a timeline are related to its title. Each event is an example of the general topic in the title. For instance, if the title of a timeline were "Wars That Texans Have Fought In," each listed event should be one of the various wars that Texans have fought in throughout history.

Let's practice this skill by choosing events on a timeline called "Selected Events In The History of Texas." HINT: Look for events that are related to the title. If you look at the list of events on the next page, you will notice that **not every event** is related to the history of Texas. Decide which events you think are related to the title of the timeline. Then, on a separate sheet of paper, make a timeline of these events in chronological order.

Note: Often you will have to list a date that falls between two dates shown on a timeline. For example, 1903 is between 1900 and 1910. Since 1903 is closer to 1900 (*3 years*) than it is to 1910 (*7 years*) on the timeline, put it closer to 1900 than to 1910.

SELECTED EVENTS IN THE HISTORY OF TEXAS

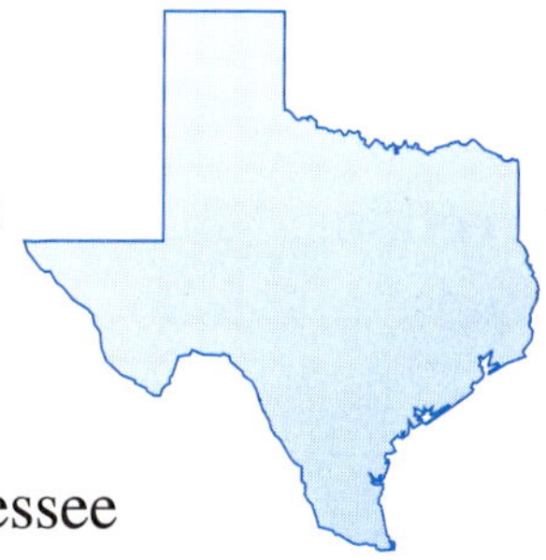

- 1901 The great oil field at Spindletop is discovered
- 1874 Gail Borden, the inventor of condensed milk, dies
- 1892 Sculptor Elisabet Ney moves to Texas
- 1889 H.L. Hunt, Texas oilman, is born
- 1819 Sam Houston becomes Attorney General of Tennessee
- 1776 American colonies declare their independence from Great Britain
- 1812 War breaks out between the United States and Great Britain
- 1920 The Nineteenth Amendment gives women the right to vote
- 1861 The Civil War begins

MAKING A TIMELINE ABOUT YOUR LIFE

EXTENDING THE ACTIVITY

Often, certain things that happen during a person's lifetime stand out. For example, your parents probably remember what they were doing when astronauts Neil Armstrong and Buzz Aldrin first stepped onto the surface of the moon in 1969.

In this section you will need to think back to important events that have happened to you. Choose the three most important events of your life and put them on the timeline. Make the first year the one on which you were born.

IMPORTANT EVENTS IN MY LIFE

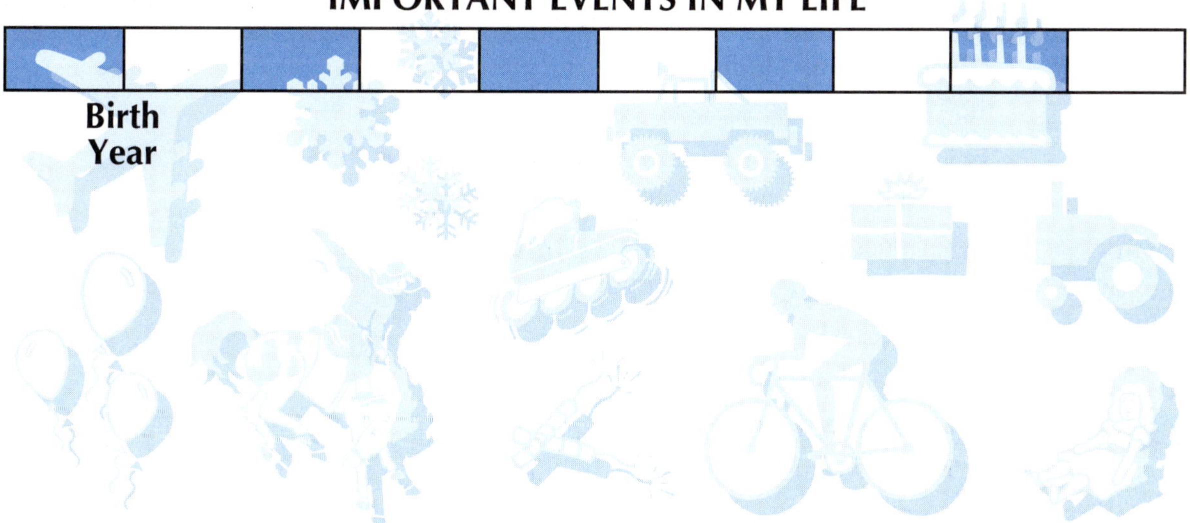

Ask your parent or guardian for three important events that happened to them in the last ten years. Add those events to your timeline.

REVIEWING YOUR UNDERSTANDING

Directions: Fill in your Vocabulary Cards. Then complete the exercise that follows.

Timeline

What is a timeline?

Why are timelines used?

Chronological Order

What is chronological order?

Arrange the following dates in chronological order: 1903, 1864, 1987, 1745.

Arranging Dates in Chronological Order

Following is a list of events from the history of Texas that were mentioned in this chapter. The events are not arranged in chronological order (*the order in which they happened*). Your task is to:

A. Find the date each event occurred.

B. Arrange the events in chronological order. Write (1) next to the event that happened first. Then write (2) next to the event that happened second, and so on. Continue numbering each event.

Date	Event	Chronological Order
?	Texas joins the Union as the twenty-eighth state of the United States.	?
?	Texas withdraws from the Union and joins the Confederate States of America.	?
?	Texas declares its independence from Mexico and becomes an independent republic.	?
?	Cabeza de Vaca and other members of a Spanish expedition land in Texas.	?
?	An assassin kills President Kennedy in Dallas and seriously wounds Governor Connally.	?
?	Moses Austin receives permission from the Spanish government to set up a colony in Texas.	?

PART II: PEOPLE AND PLACES

3G WHAT GENERALIZATIONS CAN YOU MAKE ABOUT NATIVE AMERICANS IN TEXAS?

In this activity, you will learn about a group of people that has had a major influence on the history of Texas—the Native Americans. Look for the following important words:

- ★ Generalization
- ★ Nomadic
- ★ Caddo
- ★ Comanche
- ★ Karankawa
- ★ Aztec

Generalizations are powerful organizing tools. We use them to put large amounts of information into manageable form. In this activity, you will examine how generalizations are formed and practice making your own generalizations.

WHAT IS A GENERALIZATION?

Look at the following list:

- ☆ **Galveston** is located on the **Gulf of Mexico.**
- ☆ **Brownsville** borders the **Rio Grande.**
- ☆ **Austin** is on the **Colorado River.**
- ☆ **Dallas** is located on the **Trinity River**.

It might be hard to remember all of these separate facts. But if you look at them as a group, you will start to see a pattern. The pattern shows something these four facts about cities in Texas have in common. This pattern may actually be more important than any specific fact.

THINK ABOUT IT

What do the four facts on the list have in common?

View of the Port of Beaumont
Near what body of water is Beaumont located?

HOW GENERALIZATIONS ARE FORMED

The list shows that *major cities are located next to large bodies of water.* This general statement describes what each of the specific examples have in common. When a general statement identifies a common pattern, it is called a **generalization.**

A generalization shows what several facts have in common. A generalization can also help us to make predictions. Each of the previous examples showed a major city next to a large body of water. We might now guess or predict that if we look at any major city, it will be located next to a large body of water.

Let's see how this particular generalization might be presented in a diagram.

Major cities are located next to large bodies of water.				← ***Generalization***
Galveston: *Gulf of Mexico*	Brownsville: *Rio Grande*	Austin: *Colorado River*	Dallas: *Trinity River*	← ***Specific Examples***

Although generalizations are useful tools, we must be careful in applying them. For example, is our generalization really true for all large cities? Suppose we applied it to Lubbock, a large city in Texas. If you look at a map, you will find that Lubbock is **not** located next to a large body of water. This means we have to change our original generalization. Based on all the facts we now know, we can say that *most,* but not all, major cities are located next to large bodies of water.

When you are asked if a generalization is true, you must look at specific examples and facts for support. Remember, generalizations are always subject to change and improvement as new information is learned. Now let's see how this modified generalization might be presented in a diagram:

Most major cities are located next to large bodies of water.					← ***Generalization***
Galveston: *Gulf of Mexico*	Brownsville: *Rio Grande*	Austin: *Colorado River*	Dallas: *Trinity River*	Lubbock: ***not** next to a large body of water*	← ***Specific Examples***

You have just learned how a generalization is formed and changed. Can you form your own generalizations? Let's apply what you have just learned by seeing if you can make some generalizations about early Native American groups in Texas. First, let's look at early U.S. government policy towards Native American groups in general.

EARLY U.S. GOVERNMENT POLICY

Various groups of **Native Americans** once occupied all of the present-day United States. The Native Americans consisted of many different groups, sometimes called **tribes** or **nations.** They spoke hundreds of languages and followed many different ways of life. Contact between Native Americans and Europeans created problems for the tribes. For example, they were exposed to serious European diseases such as smallpox, and many of the Native Americans died.

During the 1800s, the U.S. government followed a policy of moving Native Americans from their traditional lands onto government lands in the West. The government often broke its promises and allowed citizens to move onto these "Indian" lands. This forced the Native Americans to move still further westward. The U.S. occupation of western lands was also speeded up by the completion of the transcontinental railroad in 1869, and by a series of wars between Native Americans and federal troops.

Native Americans who went along with U.S. government policy were moved to **reservations,** often on undesirable land. Only three reservations still exist in Texas: the Alabama-Coushatta in the east, the Tigua in the west and the Kickapoo in the southwest.

Native Americans hunting buffalo. *Which type of Native Americans do these hunters represent?*

Next, you will read about some Native American groups who lived in Texas. There were two major types. One type was **agricultural.** They stayed in one place and planted food. The other type was made up of hunters and gatherers. Usually they led a **nomadic** lifestyle roaming from place to place in search of food and good hunting grounds.

After reading about the tribes of each of these two types, you will be asked to list some facts about them. Then you will make some generalizations about all of the tribes of that type. As you read these sections, you should therefore look for those characteristics that different Native American tribes had in common.

AGRICULTURAL NATIVE AMERICAN TRIBES IN TEXAS

THE CADDO

Location. The Caddo were actually a large group of several tribes who lived in the forested areas of East Texas. Today, this area is known as the Piney Woods region. Other Caddo tribes lived in parts of Louisiana and Arkansas.

How They Obtained Their Food. Thanks to their farming skill, the Caddo were able to grow corn, squash, beans, melons and tobacco. They cleared their fields by setting them on fire and then mixing the ashes with the soil to make it fertile. The Caddo also hunted deer, rabbits, turkey, buffalo and other animals. They later obtained horses from the Spaniards, which helped them in their hunting. They were also excellent fishermen.

Native Americans celebrating mass. *Why did the Spanish missionaries want to convert them to Catholicism?*

Shelter. The Caddo built round huts which looked like beehives. They were made of poles covered with grass. Their beds were made of reeds covered with buffalo hides (*skins*).

Other Customs. The Caddo lived in villages, where they grew food and built temples. Because they had extra food, they could support a special class of priests and chiefs. The Caddo believed in an all-powerful God and so built special holy fires. They also made clay pots and musical flutes. The Caddo tattooed their bodies. They were known for treating their women with great respect. For amusement, they played a game much like field hockey.

Traditional Enemies. Apaches often attacked the Caddo, making hostages of those they captured. Although also enemies of the Comanches, the Caddo helped them push the Apaches southward.

★ CHECKING YOUR UNDERSTANDING ★

1. Where did the Caddo live?
2. How did they obtain their food?
3. What were their shelters like?
4. What were some of their customs?
5. Who were their traditional enemies?

THE WICHITA

Location. The Wichita were a group of nine tribes related to the Caddo. They lived in northeast Texas, just north of the Caddo. In this area today are the cities of Dallas, Fort Worth, Waco and Wichita Falls.

How They Obtained Their Food. The Wichita way of life was similar to that of the Caddo. Although they were close to the Great Plains and sometimes hunted buffalo, they were mainly agricultural. They grew large fields of corn, melons, pumpkins, beans and squash.

Shelter. Like the Caddo, the Wichita built round huts covered with grass. They were not nomadic, and lived in permanent villages.

Other Customs. The Wichita believed in several gods and goddesses. They also believed that all things had their own spirits. They were especially known for their elaborate tattoos. The Wichita tattooed lines on their faces, circles on their chests and special symbols on their arms and hands. They often renamed their children after something their children did or were especially good at.

Traditional Enemies. The traditional enemy of the Wichita were the Apache, who often raided their camps. They also feared the Osage and the Comanche.

Native Americans digging an irrigation ditch at a mission.
Why were Native Americans sometimes used as slaves by the Europeans?

★ CHECKING YOUR UNDERSTANDING ★

1. Where did the Wichita live?
2. How did they obtain their food?
3. What were their shelters like?
4. What were some of their customs?
5. Who were the traditional enemies of the Wichita?

THE JUMANO

Location. The Jumano lived in the dry Trans-Pecos region, along the Rio Grande. Because of their location, they were strongly influenced by the Pueblo Native Americans of the Southwest.

How They Obtained Their Food. The Jumano knew how to grow their own food. They grew corn, which they often ground into flour to make cakes. The Jumano also hunted buffalo and small animals.

In the late 1400s, changes in climate brought less rainfall to the Trans-Pecos region. As a result, the Jumano faced a crisis—even before the arrival of the Spaniards. Unable to grow enough food, the Jumano began eating the seeds needed to grow future corn crops. The Jumano disappeared in the 1500s, and much remains to be learned about them.

Shelter. Like the Pueblo tribes, the Jumano lived in rectangular-shaped houses made of sun-baked adobe brick. Adobe brick is made of clay and baked in the sun instead of in an oven. Jumano houses were built close together. This permitted them to stay cool in summer and warm in winter.

Other Customs. Each Jumano village was governed by its own chief. The Jumano were skilled at making clay pottery.

Traditional Enemies. After they migrated into the Southwest, the Apache became enemies of the Jumano.

★ CHECKING YOUR UNDERSTANDING ★

1. Where did the Jumano live?
2. How did they obtain their food?
3. What were their shelters like?
4. What were some of their customs?
5. Who were the traditional enemies of the Jumano ?

CREATING A GENERALIZATION

Can you think of a general statement that is true for the Caddo, Wichita and Jumano? You might recall that all three of these tribes grew some of the food they ate. Such a statement is a generalization.

Some Native American tribes in Texas lived by growing food. ← ***Generalization***

Caddo:	*Wichita:*	*Jumano:*	
planted corn, squash, beans, melons and tobacco	planted corn, melons, pumpkins, beans and squash	planted corn	← ***Specific Examples***

★ CHECKING YOUR UNDERSTANDING ★

Can you make **one** other generalization about these Native American tribes? Think about any other similarities between the three groups. Then write your generalization on a separate sheet of paper, using the following guide:

Your Generalization ← ***Generalization***

Caddo	*Wichita*	*Jumano*	
?	?	?	← ***Specific Examples***

HUNTERS AND GATHERERS IN TEXAS

THE COMANCHE, KIOWA AND APACHE

Location. The Comanche lived on the Great Plains in northwest Texas. They occupied a large territory known as the **Comancheria.** The Apache lived southeast of them, between the Pecos and Colorado Rivers. Other Apache tribes lived in present-day New Mexico and Arizona. The Kiowa lived mainly in the Panhandle area of the northern plains.

How They Obtained Their Food. The Apache, Comanche and Kiowa, like most Plains tribes, lived off the millions of buffalo that once grazed the Great Plains. They did not grow their own food. They sometimes raided other tribes or traded buffalo hides for corn and tobacco. Sometime in the 1700s, these three tribes got horses from the Spaniards in Mexico. They soon developed into expert riders. Boys were trained to become tough hunters and fierce warriors. Comanche men used spears and short bows and arrows that they could shoot from a galloping horse. While riding, they lived on a special mix of nuts, berries, dried buffalo meat and buffalo fat.

Shelter. The tribes of the Great Plains lived in cone-shaped tents made of buffalo hides stretched over long poles. Their tents were known as **tepees.** A fire pit in the center of the tepee was used for cooking and to keep the tepee warm. The floor of the tepee was covered with buffalo hides. When the tribe needed to move in order to follow the buffalo herd, they simply packed up their tepees and carried them along.

The coming of the railroad was a threat to their lifestyles.
Was the railroad a threat to tribal lifestyles?

Other Customs. To the Native American tribes on the Great Plains, the buffalo was all-important. They used every part of the animal to provide food, clothing and shelter. The hide was used to make tepees, clothes and boots. Buffalo hair was used to make rope and decorations on shields and clothing. The sinews (*tissues attached to the muscles*) were used to make bowstrings. The bones were used to make tools and arrowheads.

The Comanche language was understood by many other tribes in the Southwest and was sometimes used as a common language for trading. The Comanche made decisions for each tribe in councils, attended by the men. Warriors were permitted to organize their own raiding parties.

The Apache in Texas followed a way of life similar to the Comanche. Among their special customs, the Apache poured water over the heads of children if they misbehaved. Apache boys were trained to be brave and to put up with many hardships. Girls were taught to be able caregivers—both for their families and for other tribe members.

Traditional Enemies. War was an important part of life for these tribes. The Comanche, Apache and Kiowa were often disliked by other tribes. The Comanche were the most feared warriors in Texas.

★ CHECKING YOUR UNDERSTANDING ★

1. Where did the Comanche, Kiowa and Apache live?
2. How did they obtain their food?
3. What were their shelters like?
4. What were some of their customs?
5. Who were some of their traditional enemies?

★ THE KARANKAWA AND TONKAWA

Location. The Karankawa lived along the Gulf Coast between Galveston Bay and Corpus Christi. The climate was warm, with lots of rain. In this region there were plenty of fish, wild animals, berries and nuts. The Tonkawa lived just north of the Karankawa. The cultures of these two groups were very similar. The Tonkawa were also influenced by the Plains tribes to the west.

How They Obtained Their Food. The Karankawa and Tonkawa did not raise crops, but lived by hunting, fishing and gathering nuts and fruits. Because the Karankawa lived on the coast, they ate large amounts of oysters, clams, turtles and fish. To catch fish and to travel, they used stone tools to carve out the insides of logs to make canoes. The Karankawa did not use fish hooks to catch fish; they caught them with traps. The Tonkawa were known as tough hunters and warriors. They ate buffalo and small animals, including rats and skunks.

U.S. Army Cavalry chasing Native Americans
Why was there hostility between these two groups?

Shelter. Karankawa houses were made of animal skins stretched over poles or logs. These houses were temporary, because the Karankawa often moved in search of the animals they hunted. The Tonkawa lived in caves or in round houses covered with grass.

Other Customs. The Karankawa were tall and strong. They wore few clothes because of the hot, humid weather along the Gulf Coast. To prevent mosquito bites, they rubbed themselves with strong-smelling alligator fat and the insides of fish. The Tonkawa practiced **cannibalism** (*eating of other human beings*) during some of their religious ceremonies. Sometimes this involved eating parts of a killed enemy in order to receive the "spirit power" of that warrior.

Traditional Enemies. The Karankawa often fought other Native American groups who came into their territory. The Tonkawa were enemies of the Comanche. By the late 1800s, most of the Tonkawa had died from fighting or disease. Some of the remaining Tonkawa served as scouts for the U.S. Army against the Comanche during the Indian Wars.

★ Checking Your Understanding ★

1. Where did the Karankawa and Tonkawa live?
2. How did they obtain their food?
3. What were their shelters like?
4. What were some of their customs?
5. Who were some of the enemies of the Karankawa and Tonkawa?

CREATING ANOTHER GENERALIZATION

Can you make any generalizations about the Apache, Comanche, Kiowa, Karankawa and Tonkawa? For example, you might recall that most of these tribes were nomads. They went in search of food by hunting.

Some Native American tribes in Texas obtained their food by hunting. ← *Generalization*

Karankawa:	*Tonkawa:*	*Comanche:*	*Apache:*	*Kiowa:*
hunted and fished	hunted and fished	hunted buffalo	hunted buffalo	hunted buffalo

← *Specific Examples*

★ Checking Your Understanding ★

Can you make **one** other generalization about these Native Americans? Think about any similarities between the five groups. On a separate sheet of paper, write out your generalization using the following outline:

Your Generalization ← *Generalization*

Karankawa	*Tonkawa*	*Comanche*	*Apache*	*Kiowa*
?	?	?	?	?

← *Specific Examples*

LOOKING AT OTHER NATIVE AMERICAN GROUPS

EXTENDING THE ACTIVITY

In this activity, you made several generalizations about the Native American tribes of Texas. Are these same generalizations true of Native American cultures found in other parts of the Western Hemisphere?

Let us try to find out. Your class should be divided into eight groups of students. Each group will research **one** Native American culture from the following list:

- Inca
- Iroquois
- Maya
- Cherokee
- Sioux
- Navajo
- Pueblo
- Eskimo *(Inuit)*

After you have investigated this Native American group, you should decide whether your generalizations would be true for them. One place you can find information about Native Americans is an **encyclopedia.**

ENCYCLOPEDIA

Encyclopedias contain articles with information on many topics. You can find out about history, science, music and current events. They also have articles about countries, states and famous people. Encyclopedias usually have many volumes. Articles are arranged in alphabetical order. The first volume starts with "A," and the last volume ends with "Z." Each volume has guide words or letters on the spine, to help you locate topics.

Let's use an article from an encyclopedia for practice. The following article is about the Aztecs—a Native American culture from central Mexico.

AZTECS (1200-1521 A.D.). The Aztecs were actually three different native peoples who formed an alliance in the late 1200s. The principal group called themselves the Mexica. The Mexica were originally a nomadic people who lived northwest of the Valley of Mexico. They lived by hunting and gathering plants. Their legendary early home was Azlan, from which the name Aztec was taken.

CONTINUED

The Aztecs Move To The Valley of Mexico. The Aztecs gradually began to move into the Valley of Mexico, during which time they learned how to grow corn and other skills from neighboring peoples. Around 1325 they settled on an island in Lake Texcoco. At that time, this was the largest fresh-water lake in the center of the Valley of Mexico. In their new location the Aztecs were surrounded by older, hostile city-states. Over the next century, they developed alliances with some of these neighboring states through marriages with their ruling families.

Cortez and soldiers battle the Aztecs.

Aztecs As Warriors. In 1426, the Aztecs became involved in a dispute with their neighbors. The Aztecs and their allies won the war that followed. For the next 90 years, they were involved in frequent wars to conquer other peoples in the central Valley of Mexico. These wars continued right up until the time of the Spanish conquest. In 1521, Hernando Cortez and his soldiers conquered the Aztec Empire.

Aztec Society. The Aztecs developed a highly complex society. The men were responsible for the well-being of the family. Women spent their time caring for the household, cooking and weaving cloth.

In general, each person was born into a particular social class. A person could move to a higher class after performing some special act, such as capturing enemy

CONTINUED

warriors in battle. At the very top of Aztec society were the rulers, headed by the emperor. Below the rulers were the nobles. Many of these nobles were relatives of the ruling family. They often held high positions in the government, army or priesthood. Some nobles served as advisers to the rulers, or as tax collectors. They owned large estates and received payments from the people who farmed on their lands. Most people were commoners, working as farmers, fishermen, craftsmen, or as warriors in the Aztec armies.

If a person committed a crime or could not pay his debts, he could become enslaved. Slavery was not hereditary, but in times of food shortages, people would sell themselves into slavery in order to eat. In Aztec society, slaves could buy back their freedom if they could save enough money.

Aztec Beliefs and Practices. The Aztecs believed in a large number of gods. They believed that the world had passed through a number of "ages." The present age was ruled by the Sun God. This age would eventually end in a series of earthquakes, after which monsters would come down from Heaven to eat all remaining humans.

The Aztecs believed that the Sun God wanted human blood as the price for continuing his daily journey across the sky. For this reason, the Aztecs practiced human sacrifices. Their victims were usually prisoners from other tribes they had conquered. The Aztecs believed such sacrifices were necessary to satisfy the Sun God and to keep the universe alive.

At the top of Aztec society was the emperor. *What do you think is taking place in this illustration?*

★ Checking Your Understanding ★

On a separate sheet of paper, write again your generalizations about Native American tribes in Texas.

- Which of them would also apply to the Aztecs?
- Can you think of any new generalizations that would apply to both the Aztecs and the tribes of Texas?
- Would these apply to any of the other Native American peoples listed at the top of page 144?

REVIEWING YOUR UNDERSTANDING

Directions: Fill in your Vocabulary Cards. Then complete the exercise that follows.

Generalization
What is a generalization?
Provide an example of a generalization:

Nomadic
Define the term:
Give an example of a nomadic group:

Practice in Using an Encyclopedia

The following drawing shows a set of 12 encyclopedia volumes. Each volume has guide words or letters on its spine.

Guide words or guide letters (*parts of words*) help you locate information about certain topics. For example, suppose you wanted to find information on Brazil, a country in South America. You would use Volume 2 (BAS to CAV), because in the alphabet **BRA** comes after **BAS** but before **CAV.**

★ CHECKING YOUR UNDERSTANDING ★

Which volume would you use to find information about …

1. the names of different types of **dogs?**
2. **George Washington,** the first U.S. President?
3. the names of the major **rivers in Texas?**
4. how much gasoline the country of **Saudi Arabia** sells in a year?
5. the name of the first Governor of **Texas?**
6. the main products manufactured in the city of **San Antonio?**
7. the distance from the **Sun** to the planet Earth?

3H

WHO IS THE WOMAN YOU MOST ADMIRE?

In this activity, you will look at the roles of some typical and not so typical women from Texas. Look for the following important words:

★ Essay ★ Elisabet Ney

One day your friend asks you to help clean out his parent's attic. While cleaning, you find a copy of an old newspaper. You flip through the pages, curious about what stories such an old newspaper might have. You come across an interesting article about an essay contest for students. The theme of the contest was: "A Woman I Admire." Here are two of the essay winners you find in the newspaper:

MAMA'S DARK WORLD

Amelia H. Chamberlain

It is 10 o'clock, time to wake up Mama. I open my bedroom door into a wall of darkness. I creep into the living room. The lights are off and the shades are drawn. On the couch lies Mama. Her hair is standing on all ends and her face is a mask of peace. I give her shoulder a shake, telling her that it's 10 o'clock. Instantly, her eyes open and she starts to get up.

I turn to go back to my room, when she asks me to make her a cup of coffee. I swivel around, and a spark of anger flicks through my eyes. Guilt quickly replaces it. How can I be angry? Every day she gets up and goes to work on four or five, sometimes only two hours of sleep. She even works overtime every chance she gets. I tell her not to push herself, but she says we need the money. All she's asking me for is a cup of coffee. So I go into the kitchen. I leave the lights off, as if light would be an intrusion on Mama's dark world. I pour a cup of coffee. I take it to her. She's already dressed and sitting up on the couch. I hand her the cup of coffee and she thanks me.

All too quickly, she has to leave. She hands me money for school and kisses me on the cheek. As always, she tells me she loves me. Then she walks out the door, off to her job. I watch from the door in wonder. How does she do it? How does she always remember to leave me money for school? How does she always remember to tell me that she loves me? How does she work all night and do errands all day? How does she raise me and my sisters on her own? She never gives up or says "I can't go today." She never, ever, doesn't get up, no matter how little sleep she's gotten.

I shut and lock the door. I walk silently through Mama's dark world and go back to my bright room. I turn my eyes toward God and silently thank the Lord for Mama.

★ **CHECKING YOUR UNDERSTANDING** ★

1. Why do you think Amelia is in such wonder of her mother?
2. Why do you think Amelia gave this essay the title she did?

THE STORYTELLER

Deepti Thomas

I would rather forget my elementary school years. They were full of unpleasant people and unhappy days. I can still name most of the kids who were in my class. They were all part of the loneliness I felt that came with unacceptance and ridicule. I was one of the few kids from India. I tried my hardest to fit in with my "friends."

The gray clouds that hung around me were blown away whenever I entered the school library. It was here that I found encouragement from a very special woman, Mrs. Miller, the school librarian. She was small-framed, always wore make-up, and had thick brown hair. Her smile was her signature. From ear to ear, it was a smile that showed her whole personality, her values and her dedication to her job and to us.

I had the chance to know her better when I entered the storytelling contest. It was the librarian's task to train me for the contest. We often had lunch together in the library, me with my peanut butter and jelly sandwich and she with her ham on rye. We didn't talk much because she was usually doing paperwork. But it didn't matter. It was the plain fact that I was in her company that thrilled me. Her eyes always promised trust, and her voice had a sad tone about it that was soothing, like a mother singing her baby to sleep.

I never told her any of my problems, about how humiliated I was when some boys would whoop, hop about on one leg and ask me to do the rain dance. I didn't need to tell her; she read it my eyes. I practiced my story over and over, making sure I did it to her satisfaction. When I won, she hugged me, an expression of pride and warmth I had never before experienced.

After I graduated, I never came back to the school. Mrs. Miller told me to visit but I never did. It would have meant walking through halls that held many sad memories. As the years passed, I heard she left the school and went back to college. She probably thinks I forgot all about her. But I will always carry her, my pillar of hope, with me wherever I go.

★ **CHECKING YOUR UNDERSTANDING** ★

1. Why do you think Deepti was so sad when she went to school?
2. Why do you think Mrs. Miller played such a key role in Deepti's life?

WRITING ABOUT A WOMAN YOU ADMIRE

These two stories affect you so much that you decide to write an essay of your own entitled, "The Woman I Most Admire." Before you begin, read the following ideas about organizing an essay.

WRITING AN ESSAY

★ **Essays** are short compositions that express a writer's views about a particular subject. Essays can be written about almost any topic and can take many different forms. Essays can describe, narrate, compare and contrast, persuade and even show how to do something. In general, essays are used to provide information, to persuade the reader to adopt your viewpoint or simply to entertain. Essays are usually organized into three parts:

- ☆ **Introduction.** This introduces the reader to the general subject. It should make the reader want to read more of what you have written.
- ☆ **Body.** The main part of the essay is called the body. It usually has several paragraphs that develop and expand on the subject. It is here that you explain your views and give specific examples to illustrate your main points.
- ☆ **Conclusion.** This is the final part of the essay. It should briefly summarize what you have written, and explain its importance.

Now it is time to write your own essay. On a separate sheet of paper, write an essay entitled: "The Woman I Most Admire" using the form that follows. In the essay define what you mean by "admire."

The Woman I Most Admire...

Introduction:

Body:

Conclusion:

RESEARCHING A FAMOUS WOMAN FROM TEXAS

EXTENDING THE ACTIVITY

In this activity you wrote about a woman you personally admire. Throughout the history of Texas, a number of women have been especially admired for their achievements. Here is a partial list of some of those women:

- **Jan McManus Cazneau. Empresarios** were land agents given permission by the Mexican government to bring people to settle in Texas. Cazneau was the only woman among them. In 1833, the Mexican government gave Cazneau permission to settle German families near Matagorda Bay.
- **Jane Long** (1798-1880). She was one of the first pioneers to come to Texas. Jane Long was the wife of Dr. James Long, who entered Spanish Texas in 1819 in the hopes of establishing a republic. She was once referred to as the "Mother of Texas" by the Anglo-American community because she was the first known Anglo-American woman to give birth in Texas.
- **Suzanna Dickenson** (1817-1883). Although her husband was killed at the Alamo, she and her child managed to hide. She was one of the few survivors of the Alamo siege.

Miriam A. Ferguson and her husband. *What government office did both hold?*

- **Miriam "Ma" Ferguson** (1875-1961). She was the wife of Governor Jim Ferguson, who was removed from office for wrongdoing. She served as Governor of Texas from 1925 to 1927 and again from 1933 to 1935. Her election made her the state's first woman Governor.
- **Jovita Idar.** She was a leader in the fight to end discrimination against Mexican-American women in Texas in the early twentieth century. She served as president of *La Liga Feminil Mexicanista.* This was an organization dedicated to improving the rights of women and increasing their educational opportunities.
- **Elisabet Ney** (1883-1907). She was a German sculptress who emigrated to Texas in the 1870s. Her statues can be found in both the state capitol building in Austin and the U.S. capitol building in Washington, D.C.

- **Oveta Culp Hobby** (1905-present). During World War II, she commanded the Women's Army Corps (WACs). In 1953, President Eisenhower selected her as the nation's first Secretary of Health, Education and Welfare.
- **Mildred ("Babe") Didrikson Zaharias** (1914-1955). In the 1932 Olympics she won two gold medals in track and field. Then she began a new athletic career as a golfer. She founded the Ladies Professional Golf Association (LPGA), winning 82 tournaments, and every major golf title there was.
- **Doris Miller** (1919-1943). An African-American woman who in 1941, was on duty on the U.S.S. Arizona when it was attacked by the Japanese at Pearl Harbor. She shot down four Japanese attack planes, for which she was awarded the Navy Cross for her bravery.
- **Ann Richards** (1933-present). She was elected the State Treasurer of Texas in 1982, making her the first woman to hold that position. In 1990, she went on to be elected Governor of Texas.
- **Barbara Jordan** (1936-1996). In 1966, she was elected to the Texas Senate. This made her the first African-American woman to sit in the Texas legislature. She later became the first African-American woman to be elected in the South to the U.S. House of Representatives, where she served from 1973 to 1979.
- **Elma Salinas.** In 1983, Ms. Salinas was appointed the nation's first Mexican-American federal judge.
- **Selena (Quintanilla Perez)** (1971-1995). Born in Corpus Christi, Selena began her singing career with her family band at age 9. She popularized Tejano music and soon became the nation's best known Tex-Mex singer. Her rising career ended when she was tragically murdered at age 23.

YOUR TASK

Select **one** woman from this list **or** select any other Texas woman who has accomplished something significant. For the woman you select, write at least a **one** page essay. Your essay must summarize this woman's life and accomplishments. Be sure to describe any special difficulties the woman faced because she was female.

GATHERING INFORMATION

To research your subject, you should use:

- **Encyclopedias:** look for articles listed under the woman's name.
- **History books:** check the index for information about the woman.
- **Biographies:** find biographies written about the woman.
- **Autobiographies:** see if the woman has written a book about herself.

Earlier in this activity you learned how to organize an essay. Before you begin to write, you should assemble the information you will need. To help you, make a copy of the Research Guide to the right. After finding the information called for in the Research Guide, write your essay on a separate sheet of paper.

RESEARCH GUIDE

Name: ______?______

- Where was she born?
- Briefly summarize her life:
- Her major accomplishments:
- Difficulties she overcame:
- How did she break out of the traditional role of women?

REVIEWING YOUR UNDERSTANDING

Directions: Fill in your Vocabulary Cards. Then complete the assignment that follows.

Essay

What is an essay?

What are the three basic parts of a well-organized essay?

Elisabet Ney

Who was she?

Why was she famous?

Locating Information In A Book

Imagine reading a biography with the title, *Ann Richards: Governor of Texas.* Suppose you wanted to find out about Ann Richards' mother and father. One way might be to look through all the pages of the book, but that would take a long time.

- **The Table of Contents.** When searching for information, it is easier to look at the table of contents found in the first few pages of most books. The **table of contents** contains a list of the main topics of the book, divided into chapters, and the pages on which they can be found.

  The "main topics" deal with the major subjects of the book. The "chapters" cover more specific subjects. For example, in the book about Ann Richards, you might find the following main topics and chapters:

In which chapter would you look to find information about

1. her mother and father, Cecil and Iona Willis?

2. her involvement with the debating team at Baylor University?

3. her childhood friends?

4. the name of her husband?

5. which political office she held first?

☆ **The Index.** Another way to find information in a book is by using an **index.** The table of contents gives a reader a *general* idea of the contents of the book, while an index helps a reader locate *specific* information. For example, suppose you wanted to find out about Ann Richards' keynote speech at the 1988 Democratic National Convention in a biography about her.

The speech is not listed by name in the book's table of contents. You might try to find references to it by scanning every page of the book. This might take you a long time. To solve this problem, books usually provide an index. The index is arranged in alphabetical order at the back of the book. It tells readers on which pages to find information about names, places and events. Look at the index section on the right from a biography about Ann Richards.

This index tells you that information about Richards' keynote speech at the Democratic National Convention can be found on pages 134 to 137 of the book.

On which pages would you look to find information about

1. members who served in Governor Richards' Cabinet?

2. her campaign to win the office of Governor of Texas?

3. whom she ran against for the position of County Commissioner of Travis County?

31

WHAT SYMBOLS DO YOU IDENTIFY WITH TEXAS?

In this activity, you will learn about some of the symbols often identified with the state of Texas. Look for the following important words:

- ★ Symbols
- ★ Six Flags Over Texas
- ★ Texas, Our Texas
- ★ Texas Flag Pledge

Every country has what a French historian once called its "places of memory." These historic places or symbols help us identify the spirit of that nation and its people. A **symbol** is something that stands for (*represents*) something else. ★

Symbols take many forms. Some symbols are visual. For example, a red light means stop. Holidays, emblems, flags, songs, people and places can also be symbols. For example, the American flag is a symbol of the United States. The Statute of Liberty is another symbol of the United States. In this activity, you will look at some symbols that people often identify with the State of Texas.

THINK ABOUT IT

What other symbols can you think of that represent the United States?

THINK ABOUT IT

When you hear the name Sam Houston, what images come to your mind?

SAM HOUSTON

The name *Sam Houston* is one of the best-known names in Texas history. Houston served twice as the President of Texas when it was an independent country. As a boy he spent time living with the Cherokees. He became the governor of two different states, acted as an ambassador to the Cherokees and served as a U.S. Senator.

Andrew Jackson

How did Houston's friendship with President Jackson change Houston's life?

In 1813 a tribe of Creeks went on the warpath, attacking Tennessee settlers. Houston, at the age of 20, joined the U.S. Army. U.S. forces were then under the command of General Andrew Jackson. At the Battle of Horseshoe Bend, Houston was shot in the shoulder by a bullet and hit in the leg with an arrow. Despite his wounds, Houston kept on fighting. General Jackson was impressed by his bravery.

In 1832, President Jackson sent Sam Houston to negotiate with Native American tribes in Texas. Houston fell in love with Texas and decided to settle there. Soon, Texans began looking to Houston for leadership. In 1835, war broke out between Texas and the Mexican government. Houston was chosen to act as the chief commander of the Texas forces.

Historic Document of Texas: *General Order No. 17*

On March 2, 1836, as Commander-in-Chief of the Army of Texas, Sam Houston issued the following general order:

> *War is raging on the frontiers. Bexar [San Antonio] is [under attack] by two thousand of the enemy .... By the last report, our force at Bexar was only one hundred and fifty men. The citizens of Texas must rally to the aid of our army, or it will perish [die]. Let the citizens of the east march to combat. The enemy must be driven from our soil ....*

As commander-in-chief, Houston instructed the Texans defending the Alamo at San Antonio to abandon it. Refusing to follow Houston's orders, the defenders pledged to protect the Alamo with their lives. The Alamo defenders were soon overrun by Mexican soldiers. Two weeks later, Texans retreating from Goliad surrendered to a Mexican force.

While fighting was taking place at San Antonio and Goliad, delegates met at Washington-on-the-Brazos on March 2, 1836 for the Consultation. Houston attended the convention and signed the Texas Declaration of Independence, which proclaimed Texas as an independent nation.

Sam Houston
What role did he play in defeating General Santa Anna?

Houston felt that his best hope of winning the war was to draw Mexican General Santa Anna deep into Texas. Only then, with the Mexican army far from home, did Houston plan to attack. After Houston spent several weeks training and resting his troops, a Mexican messenger was captured. The messenger revealed that Santa Anna would be leading a smaller force in an attempt to capture the new government of Texas. Houston decided the time was right to face the Mexican general.

On April 20, 1836, the two armies met by the San Jacinto River. The following morning Houston refused to fight. The Mexicans began to relax. Later that day, while the Mexican army was enjoying an afternoon *siesta* (nap), Houston ordered a surprise attack. The Mexican army was defeated. Over 600 Mexican soldiers were killed, 280 wounded, and 730 captured. Only nine Texans were killed. Wounded in the leg, Houston continued to lead his forces—even though his boot was filled with blood.

Soon after, General Santa Anna was captured. Houston spared his life, but demanded that Santa Anna order his troops out of Texas. To make sure Santa Anna kept his word, the Texans held him prisoner for seven months.

When the first popular election was held, Houston was elected President of the independent Republic of Texas. Houston worked hard to make Texas a part of the United States. In 1845, his efforts were finally rewarded. Texas was admitted as a state in the United States. Houston was elected to the U.S. Senate and served from 1846 to 1859. In 1859, he was elected Governor of Texas.

Soon after Houston became Governor, Abraham Lincoln was elected President. Several Southern states voted to secede from (*leave*) the United States. They didn't want to remain a part of the United States with Lincoln as President. In Texas, public opinion favored secession.

Houston was against secession. He had devoted much of his life to bringing Texas into the United States. Houston refused to take an oath of allegiance to the Confederate States of America and resigned his position as Governor.

He spent his remaining years in retirement. He died in 1863. To many Texans, Houston came to symbolize the fighting, independent spirit of Texas.

THINK ABOUT IT

What images come to mind when you see the state flag of Texas?

THE SIX FLAGS OF TEXAS

During its history, Texas has seen many changes of power. Over the past 470 years, six flags have flown over Texas—the flags of Spain, France, Mexico, the Republic of Texas, the Confederate States and the United States.

From the 1500s to 1821, **Spain's** flag flew over Texas. The Spanish built missions in East Texas in an attempt to convert the Native Americans to Christianity. They called the territory San Francisco de los Tejas—in honor of Saint Francis. The name *Tejas* (or Texas) was taken from the Caddo language.

From 1685 to 1690, the royal flag of King Louis XIV of **France** flew over part of Texas. This flag had a snow white background with small golden fleur-de-lis (*lily flowers*). The flag was first raised over Texas in 1685 by the French explorer René-Robert Cavelier, Sieur de La Salle. His expedition had landed on the coast of Texas carrying four shiploads of people—soldiers, priests and almost 200 colonists. He established a colony in southeastern Texas, but it only lasted a few years.

The French flag under King Louis XIV.
When did this flag fly over Texas?

After 1690, Spain again ruled over all of Texas. However, by 1821, **Mexico** had become an independent nation and took over Texas from Spain. The bright Mexican flag of red, white and green flew over Texas from 1821 until 1836. During that time, many English-speaking colonists moved to Texas.

These colonists decided to break away from Mexico in 1836. The "Lone Star Flag" flew over Texas for the next ten years. The colors were red (*for bravery*), white (*for strength*), and blue (*for loyalty*). The flag had one white and one red stripe. It had a single white star on a blue background. The design of the flag was chosen in part to show the desire of Texans to associate with their northern neighbor, the United States.

The Mexican flag.
When was the last time this flag flew over Texas?

Texas' use of a single-starred flag was popular among several other Southern states in the early 1800s. Today, this flag remains the state flag of Texas. The star is used as a symbol on other Texas emblems also—the state seal, the Governor's flag and the badges of the Texas Rangers.

On March 1, 1845, Congress voted to annex Texas. Texans approved the annexation. On December 29, 1845 Texas officially became a state of the **United States.** The stars and stripes of the U.S. flag then flew over Texas. However, in 1861 Texas seceded from the United States and became a part of the **Confederate States of America.** For the next four years, the Confederate flag flew over Texas. In 1865, the Confederacy surrendered and the U.S. flag returned to Texas. It flies over Texas today.

THINK ABOUT IT

How do you feel when you sing the state song, "Texas, Our Texas," or the national anthem, the "Star Spangled Banner"?

"TEXAS, OUR TEXAS"

In 1929, the Texas legislature adopted a state song: "Texas, Our Texas." The music was composed by William Marsh. Gladys Yoakum Wright and William Marsh wrote the words. The song has been changed only once since it has been the state song. In the third line, the word "Largest" was changed to "Boldest." This change was needed when Alaska gained statehood in 1959, making it the largest state.

Texas, our Texas! All hail the mighty State!
Texas, our Texas! So wonderful, so great!
Boldest and grandest, withstanding every test;
O empire wide and glorious, you stand supremely blest.

Chorus: God bless you, Texas! And keep you brave and strong.
That you may grow in power and worth, throughout the ages long.

Refrain: Texas, our Texas! Your freeborn single star,
Sends out its radiance to nations near and far.
Emblem of freedom! It sets our hearts aglow.
With thoughts of San Jacinto and glorious Alamo.

Texas, dear Texas! From tyrant grip now free,
Shines forth in splendor your star of destiny!
Mother of Heroes! We come your children true.
Proclaiming our allegiance, our faith, our love for you.

San Jacinto Monument

Why do you think San Jacinto is mentioned in "Texas Our Texas"?

THE STAR-SPANGLED BANNER

At one point during the War of 1812, Francis Scott Key was held captive on board a British warship. This warship shelled Fort McHenry. The next morning, Key was so happy to see the American flag still flying over the fort that he wrote "The Star-Spangled Banner." In 1931, it became the National Anthem. Singing the national anthem is one way many people express their pride in being American.

Oh say, can you see, by the dawn's early light,
What so proudly we hail'd at the twilight's last gleaming,
Whose broad stripes and bright stars through the perilous fight,
O'er the ramparts we watch'd, were so gallantly streaming?
And the rockets' red glare, the bombs bursting in air,
Gave proof thru' the night that our flag was still there.
Oh say, does that star-spangled banner yet wave
O'er the land of the free and the home of the brave?

The flag of Texas

The American Flag

THINK ABOUT IT

How do you feel when you are asked to say the pledge to the Texas state flag or the pledge to our national flag?

TEXAS FLAG PLEDGE

The Texas Flag Pledge is similar to the Pledge of Allegiance to the Flag of the United States. Each pledge is intended to remind people of what the flag symbolizes. The Texas pledge indicates that Texas is one state and should not be divided. The national pledge is designed to tell people that the United States is one country, united and dedicated to the ideals of liberty and justice.

Texas Flag Pledge
Honor the Texas Flag.
I pledge allegiance to thee,
Texas, one and indivisible.

Pledge of Allegiance to the Flag
I pledge allegiance to the Flag of the United States of America, and to the Republic for which it stands, one Nation under God, indivisible, with liberty and justice for all.

THINK ABOUT IT

1. What do you think of when you celebrate Texas Independence Day or Martin Luther King, Jr.'s birthday?
2. Why do you think chili was chosen as the State Dish in 1977?

STATE HOLIDAYS

Martin Luther King, Jr.'s Birthday—Third Monday in *January*
Texas Independence Day—*March 2*
San Jacinto Day—*April 21*
Emancipation Day ("Juneteenth")—*June 19*
Lyndon B. Johnson's Birthday—*August 27*

TEXAS FAVORITES

(Year Adopted)

- State Flower—*bluebonnet* (1901)
- State Tree—*pecan* (1919)
- State Bird—*mockingbird* (1927)
- State Motto—*Friendship* (1930)
- State Gem—*Texas blue topaz* (1969)
- State Dish—*chili* (1977)
- State Fish—*Guadalupe bass* (1989)
- State Fruit—*Texas red grapefruit* (1993)

YOUR SYMBOL FOR TEXAS

In this activity, you looked at several symbols that people often identify with the State of Texas. Now let's look at what symbols **you** have for Texas:

- Which *person* do you most closely associate with Texas? Explain.
- Which *event* do you most closely associate with Texas? Explain.
- Which *object* do you think most closely symbolizes the State of Texas? Explain.
- Which *place* do you most closely associate with Texas? Explain.

Bring your four symbols to class and discuss them with your classmates. Also, ask your parent or guardian what symbols they most closely associate with the State of Texas.

1. What was the most popular symbol for Texas among your classmates?

2. What is your parent or guardian's favorite symbol for Texas?

REVIEWING YOUR UNDERSTANDING

Directions: Fill in your Vocabulary Cards. Then complete the assignment that follows.

Symbols
What is a symbol?
Why are symbols used?

Six Flags Over Texas
Name each of the six flags that have flown over Texas.
Why has Texas had so many different flags?

Identifying Other Symbols In Your Life

Sports teams often use a symbol to represent their team. For example, the Dallas Cowboys football team uses a lone star to represent the team. Can you name any other symbols associated with teams in Texas?

- Your school team
- A college team from Texas
- Another professional sports team from Texas

Symbols play an important part in our daily lives. They help us to record and recall certain information. How good are you at identifying some common symbols? Let's find out. On a sheet of paper, write down each of the numbers and identify the symbol if you know it.

Religious Symbols

(1)

(2)

(3)

Historic Symbols

(4)

(5)

(6)

On a sheet of paper, draw three more symbols and write down what each one stands for.

3J HOW WOULD YOU CLASSIFY THE LANDMARKS OF TEXAS?

In this activity, you will learn about some of the unique landmarks that reflect the heritage of both Texas and the rest of the Western Hemisphere. Look for the following important words:

★ Museum ★ Classify ★ Theme Maps

You are about to leave for school when the phone rings. Your older sister is calling from school. She says she forgot her report on "Landmark places to visit in Texas." She needs the report in school. "Can you get the report from my room and the notecards I left on top of the report?" she asks. "I need these notecards to finish typing my report. Meet me at the school library at 8:30." You agree to meet her.

Unfortunately, as you get off the school bus, you fall. You are not hurt, but the report and the notecards have scattered all over the ground.

Your sister will be furious. After picking the papers up, you realize that her notecards were not numbered. Quickly, you start reading your sister's report to find out how to arrange the notecards. Here is what you find on the first page of her report:

Texas As A Misunderstood State

Texas is one of the most misunderstood states in the United States. Many people identify Texas only with cow towns, forts and cowboys. No doubt these are important parts of Texas history. However, Texas is more than ranches, ranges and cowboys. It is a state with many important landmarks.

Our state has had a long and interesting history. It helped to develop and to change our nation. The focus of my report will be on examining many of Texas' unique landmarks. There are so many interesting places to visit in Texas that I have limited my list to just a few major categories.

CONTINUED

Places To Visit In Texas ______________________________

In this part of my report, I will look at each of these types of important Texas landmarks. These landmarks include:

- Historic Sites. This group includes places involved with the history and heritage of Texas. It also includes places that have been restored or rebuilt to show what life was like in the past. For example, the Alamo in San Antonio is one of our most famous missions. It served as a stronghold during the Texas Revolution.

The Alamo, San Antonio

★ • Museums. Museums are places where works of art and other valuable objects are displayed. For example, the Texas Ranger Hall Museum is located in Waco. It displays items from the history and heritage of the Texas Rangers—guns, weapons and other unique artifacts.

- Homes of Famous People. This group includes the birthplaces and homes of Texas' best known citizens. For example, in Bonham you can visit the home of Sam Rayburn. "Mr. Sam," as he was called, was the Speaker of the U.S. House of Representatives longer than any other person in history.

- Unique Places. This group includes unusual and one-of-a-kind places for sightseeing or amusement. For example, one unique place is the state capitol in Austin. The capitol building is located on 46 acres of beautifully landscaped trees and gardens. This large, classical-style structure is made from Texas pink granite. Other unique places to visit may be factories, businesses or amusement parks.

Now you know what you must do. Your sister's notecards deal with landmarks in Texas. You must classify her notecards into the types of landmarks she suggests. Before you start, you should understand something about classifying.

CLASSIFYING INFORMATION

To **classify** is to arrange, organize and sort information. When we classify pieces of information we identify each piece as belonging to a certain group or category. Classifying is especially helpful when we want to make sense out of many items that seem disorganized. Could you imagine shopping in a department store for a pair of sneakers if no one in the store knew in which department sneakers were sold? You would have to walk through the entire store, hoping to find the sneakers. To prevent this problem, store managers take each item in the store and decide in which department it should be sold. That is why, if you wanted to buy sneakers, you would know to look in the footwear department. If you needed a baseball glove, you would find it in the sporting goods section. Store managers classify goods by department. Grouping similar items together makes shopping easier. ★

THINK ABOUT IT

What other situations can you think of where classifying is used?

Luckily for you, your sister has already set up a classification system for the different types of landmarks—historic sites, museums, homes of famous people and unique places. Your task is simply to put each card into its correct category. How can you do this? Here is the procedure you should follow:

1. Look through **each** card.
2. Try to find the landmark's basic feature.
3. Categorize each card with the group where it belongs. For example, if a card is about the birthplace of a famous person, you should place that card in the group: "Homes of Famous People." At the end, you should find that all the cards in the same category have common features.

Note: A few of the cards may fit into more than one category.

Let's do the first card together:

A

Landmark: The Alamo (San Antonio) Category: ?

This landmark was first established in 1718. It was the scene of a famous battle during Texas' fight for independence. On March 6, 1836, a force of just over 180 Americans were killed by Santa Anna's Mexican army. The event showed the spirit and sacrifice of those determined to win independence for Texas. "Remember the Alamo" became a battle cry during the war for Texas independence.

Notice how the information on this card tells about important events that occurred at this place in the past. Since it relates the place to Texas history, it may be categorized as a "historic site." Make a copy of the following chart to help you keep track as you classify each card. Place a check mark (✓) in the appropriate column in which the card can be grouped. The first card has already been done for you.

	Historical Sites	Museums	Homes of Famous People	Unique Places
Card A	✔			
Card B				
Card C				
Card D				
Card E				
Card F				
Card G				
Card H				
Card I				
Card J				
Card K				
Card L				
Card M				
Card N				
Card O				
Card P				
Card Q				

B Lyndon B. Johnson Library and Museum (Austin).

Lyndon Johnson served Texas as a Congressman, Senator, Vice-President, and President. The museum highlights his career in government.

C Ranching Heritage Center (Lubbock).

This 12-acre site of 30 buildings represents 90 years of ranching history. You can visit a log cabin built in 1838, bunkhouses, blacksmith shops, and windmills that pump water.

D The Strand Historic District (Galveston).

After Texas became a Republic in 1836, Galveston grew into a major port. Today, the Strand is the commercial and financial Wall Street of the Southwest.

E Sam Houston Museum (Huntsville).

Sam Houston moved into Steamboat House in 1861. The house got its name from Dr. Bailey, who built it as a wed-ding gift for his son. It resembled a Mississippi River paddle boat. His son hated the way it looked and refused to live there.

F Astrodome (Houston).

The Astrodome Complex includes the Astrodome. the worlds first domed stadium. The stadium is so large that an 18-story building would easily fit inside. There is also a large exhibition center and a 6,000-seat theater.

G Sixth Floor Museum (Dallas).

An exhibit exists on the 6th floor of the old Texas School Book Depository building. From this site Lee Harvey Oswald shot and killed President Kennedy in 1963. The museum shows photos, artifacts and films about the life and death of President Kennedy.

H San Antonio Missions (San Antonio).

Starting in 1718, Spanish mission-aries built five missions in the city. At these missions, Christianity, the Spanish language, farming methods and ranching were taught to the Native Americans.

I LBJ Space Center (Houston).

The Space Center is the headquarters of America's manned space program. Its Mission Control guides astronauts during flights. Visitors can experience the past, present and future of NASA's space flight program.

J *USS Lexington Museum (Corpus Christi).*
The USS Lexington served in the U.S. Navy longer than any other aircraft carrier. It saw action during World War II. Today, it is a floating museum.

K *San Jacinto Battleground (Houston).*
In 1836, 900 men fought a battle by the San Jacinto River against the Mexican army. Houston and his men defeated the Mexican army. The next day Santa Anna agreed to grant Texas its independence.

L *Ysleta Mission (El Paso).*
In 1680, 300 Christian Native Americans established a mission in Texas. Today, the church is surrounded by the Tigua Indian Reservation.

M *Six Flags Over Texas (Arlington).*
This theme park has rides for the whole family. One of its attractions is a 17-story parachute drop. One of its most exciting rides is a roller coaster that goes through three loops—first forward and then backwards.

N *Judge Roy Bean Center (Langtry).*
In 1882, Roy Bean, a bar keeper, was named justice of the peace. He brought justice to this part of Texas. He claimed to be the "Law West of the Pecos."

O *Texas State Aquarium (Corpus Christi).*
The aquarium allows visitors to have an underwater experience without ever getting wet. Visitors delight in the marine wonders of the Gulf of Mexico. The aquarium has a 132,000-gallon water exhibit.

P *King Ranch (Kingsville).*
In 1853, Richard King bought a 15,500 acre ranch. Over the years, he continued buying land. His ranch grew to over one million acres, making it the largest ranch in America.

Q *La Villita (San Antonio).*
La Villita (little village) is a restored community established in 1722 around the Mission San Antonio de Valero. In one of its buildings, Mexican General Martin Perfecto de Cos signed a document surrendering San Antonio to Texas in 1835.

Once you are finished categorizing the cards, you have only one task left—to get to the library to meet your sister!

THINK ABOUT IT

Compare how you categorized the cards with what your classmates did.
1. Were your categorizations of the cards the same as those of your classmates?
2. Did any of the cards fit into more than one category? If so, which ones?

CREATING A THEME MAP

EXTENDING THE ACTIVITY

Have you ever gone to a "theme party?" A theme is picked, and everything about the party is in keeping with that theme. For example, at a sports theme party, everyone dresses in clothing associated with a sport.

Some maps also have a central idea or theme. **Theme maps** show information about a subject such as types of government, economic resources, physical features, languages or climate conditions.

The activity you have just completed was about major landmarks found in Texas. Extending that idea, create a theme map about landmarks found elsewhere in the Western Hemisphere. The map on the right shows the outlines of nations in the Western Hemisphere:

Here is what you need to do to create your theme map:

☆ For each of the following regions find **two** historic landmarks or famous attractions: (1) North America; (2) Central America; and (3) South America.

This information can be found by looking in an almanac, an encyclopedia or a travel guide book.

☆ For each landmark, complete the following card on a separate sheet of paper:

Name of Landmark

Description of landmark:

Location of landmark:
Region:
Country:
Town or City:

☆ Locate the approximate place of the landmark or attraction on the map. Then, mark its location with a star (★). Next, write the name of the landmark or attraction next to the star. Finally, give your map a title.

REVIEWING YOUR UNDERSTANDING

Directions: Fill in your Vocabulary Cards. Then complete the assignment that follows.

Museums

What is a museum?

Name two museums found in the Western Hemisphere:

Theme Maps

What is a theme map?

What themes might be found on a map?

Locating Landmarks On A Map Of Texas

Make a copy of the outline map of Texas on page 171:

A. Find the city or town where each landmark mentioned in this activity is located.

> **HINT:** These are found in parentheses next to the name of each landmark.

B. List the names of the landmarks on the outside border of the map. Then draw a line from the name of each landmark to the city where it is found.

C. Name two interesting landmarks where you live. Add their names to the outside border of the map. Place the name of your city on the map if it does not already appear there. Then draw lines from the names of your two landmarks to their location on the map.

D. Lastly, make a map **legend** or key. Create a symbol for each type of landmark on your map. For example, the location of museums might be shown as a large M inside a circle. For cities with several landmarks, put all of the symbols next to each other at the city's location on the map.

3K WHICH CITIES IN THE WESTERN HEMISPHERE WOULD YOU LIKE TO VISIT?

In this activity, you will compare and contrast several communities in the Western Hemisphere. Look for the following important words and city names:

- ★ Compare and Contrast
- ★ San Antonio
- ★ New Orleans
- ★ Mexico City
- ★ Mestizo
- ★ Buenos Aires

While you are in your room doing homework, you hear your mother shout. Running from your room, you find her laughing with joy. She's just received a letter informing her that she and the family have won a contest. The prize is an all-expense-paid trip to San Antonio or New Orleans, and then on to either Mexico City or Buenos Aires. She must inform the contest committee which cities your family would like to visit.

Your mother asks where you would like to go. "I'm not sure," you reply. She shows you the brochures the contest sponsors have sent, describing each city. "Wow," you say, "this would be a great time to use what I just learned in school: comparing and contrasting!"

Comparing and contrasting are important skills that can help you understand information and make decisions. To **compare** means to identify how things are alike. By focusing on their likenesses, you can see what things have in common. To **contrast** means to look at how things are different.

You look over the brochures that describe each city. Here is what you read:

★ SAN ANTONIO

Location and Climate. San Antonio is the third largest city in Texas. It is located on the banks of the San Antonio River. It has a warm and humid climate.

Mission San Jose in San Antonio
Which do you think is the most famous mission in San Antonio? Why?

History. The Governor of Spanish Texas first visited the site on Saint Anthony's Day in 1691, so he named the area "San Antonio." Between 1718 and 1731, the Spaniards built a fort and five missions in the area—one of which became known as the Alamo. In 1731, settlers from the Canary Islands established a town here. San Antonio became the capital of Spanish Texas. In 1836, San Antonio was the scene of the famous battle of the Alamo.

In the 1840s, a large number of German immigrants arrived. Other groups began moving into San Antonio once Texas became part of the United States in 1845. The city retains much of its Spanish flavor. In the 1860s, San Antonio became an important cattle town. It marked the starting point of the Chisholm Trail. San Antonio also became a key military center. Fort Sam Houston was built here in 1876. In the 1900s, four air force bases were located near San Antonio.

Economy. In the mid-1990s, San Antonio had over 1 million residents and stretched out over 320 square miles. The city's economy is based on business, manufacturing, education, government and tourism. Its airport, 8 television stations and 22 radio stations make San Antonio a major communications center.

San Antonio River
What other attractions does San Antonio have?

Tourist Sites. San Antonio is the most popular tourist attraction in Texas. The city is known for its relaxed and festive atmosphere. Flower gardens are found throughout the city and there are frequent festivals. Tourists are attracted to the Alamo and other San Antonio missions. The Spanish Governor's Palace, built in 1749, has been restored. The **Paseo del Rio,** or River walk, stretches for over two miles along the river. The banks of the river are lined with cobblestone walks and arched bridges. Restaurants, cafes and shops are found all along the walk. Another popular site is the King William Historic District, with its restored homes from the late 1800s. Sea World of Texas boasts a large number of performing whales, dolphins and other marine life. Fiesta Texas is a new theme park with rides, music and food. Its theme areas represent Hispanic Texas, German Texas, oil boom towns and a small Texas town in the 1950s.

You now turn to your next brochure. Here is what it tells you about New Orleans:

NEW ORLEANS

Location and Climate. New Orleans is located near the mouth of the Mississippi River. Because parts of the city are below sea level, the city is surrounded by walls to prevent flooding. It has a moderate climate and gets large amounts of rain.

History. New Orleans was founded by the French in 1718. Its early population included French Canadians, slaves and Native Americans. In 1762, New Orleans was given to Spain. North American settlers shipped their farm products down the

Mississippi River and deposited their goods at New Orleans for transfer to larger ships. In 1800, New Orleans became French again. Three years later, the French sold New Orleans to the United States as part of the Louisiana Purchase.

Economy. New Orleans has a population of almost half a million people. Its area is about 2,500 square miles. Before the Civil War, steamboats carried cotton from New Orleans to factories in England and the northeastern United States. After the Civil War, channels leading into New Orleans were deepened, so that ships could sail from the Gulf of Mexico right into the city. Today, New Orleans remains a major port. Exports from New Orleans include grain, animal feed, metal products, petroleum, chemicals and textiles. There are two airports, 7 television stations and 18 radio stations serving the city.

Tourist Sites. New Orleans is known for its lively cultural mix of French Canadian, West Indian, African American and North American traditions. The **French Quarter** is located in the center of town. Its buildings are based on French and Spanish architecture. New Orleans is the birthplace of modern jazz, developed by African American musicians. Its many jazz and night clubs along Bourbon Street are world famous. New Orleans is also famed for its spicy Cajun and Creole cooking. Finally, the city's annual **Mardi Gras** celebration—marking the last day before Lent—draws visitors from all over the world. On Mardi Gras a large parade takes place. Masked and costumed paraders march and dance down the streets of New Orleans.

Now, let's use the information in these two brochures to make a compare-and-contrast organizer:

SAN ANTONIO | **HOW THE TWO CITIES ARE ALIKE** | **NEW ORLEANS**

Both are located near rivers.
Both were Spanish cities at one time.
Both were settled by European immigrants.
What other items would you include here?

HOW THE TWO CITIES ARE DIFFERENT

San Antonio	New Orleans
Has a mostly Spanish flavor.	Has a mostly French flavor.
What item would you include here?	Climate is moderate.
First settled by Canary Islanders, Spanish and Germans.	First settled by French, French Canadians, African slaves and Native Americans.
Economy today is based on business, manufacturing, education and government.	***What item would you include here?***
What item would you include here?	Has French Quarter, jazz clubs, Creole and Cajun food and Mardi Gras celebrations.

THINK ABOUT IT

What would you suggest to your mother about which of the two cities to visit? Explain your choice.

Now let's look at the other two cities—Mexico City and Buenos Aires.

MEXICO CITY

Location and Climate. Mexico City is the capital of Mexico. It is the oldest city in North America and forms the world's largest metropolitan area. It is located in a valley in central Mexico, surrounded by mountains. Although it is in the tropical zone, its climate is moderate because of its high altitude. Located 7,200 feet above sea level, the climate of Mexico City is comfortably cool for most of the year.

History. The Aztecs founded the city in the 1300s. They ruled a great empire from an island in the center of a lake. However, in 1521, the Spaniards conquered and destroyed the Aztec capital. Where the main Aztec temple once stood, the Spaniards built the Metropolitan Cathedral. Mexico City soon became the capital and most important city of New Spain. By 1650, Mexico City was a well organized city of churches, public buildings and homes. Its light volcanic rock was used to carve many splendid public buildings. When Mexico became independent, Mexico City became the capital city of the new country.

Economy. In the 1800s, businesses were attracted to Mexico City, where government services were available. Food prices were controlled in the capital. Mexico City became the first place in Mexico to have electricity and street cars. People from the countryside moved to the city in search of jobs. Migrations to the capital increased further in the 20th century. With close to 20 million people, it is severely overcrowded today. The poor often live in shanty towns that lack sewers and running water. Mexico City accounts for one-third of all Mexican industry. The stock exchange, central bank and most major businesses are located in the capital. It is the heart of the country's transportation center, with all the country's major roads and railroads leading out from Mexico City. Its heavy concentration of industry and constant auto traffic have made the city one of the most polluted in the world.

A Mexican bullring
What other sites are popular among tourists visiting Mexico City?

Tourist Sites. Mexico City is very proud of its Aztec and Spanish heritage. It is the center of Mexico's political, economic and cultural life. In the heart of Mexico City is the Zócalo, the great square where one can see Aztec temple ruins, the Metropolitan Cathedral built in 1562, and the National Palace, which serves as the modern seat of government. Mexico's symphony orchestras, museums, universities and sports arenas are world famous. The Spanish custom of bullfighting has become a major sport in Mexico. Mexico City's bullring is the largest in the world, seating 50,000 spectators.

You next open the brochure about Buenos Aires:

BUENOS AIRES ★

Location and Climate. Buenos Aires, the second largest city in South America, is the capital of Argentina. It is located on the Rio de la Plata, a river in Argentina. Buenos Aires is hot and humid in the summer and mild in the winter.

History. Founded by Spain in 1580, it remained a small town for 200 years. In 1776, Spain made the area by the river the Viceroyalty of La Plata. Buenos Aires was made the capital of this new region. The city also became the center for shipping silver from northern Peru to Spain. In 1810, led by José de San Martin, this region declared its independence from Spain. The city became the capital of the new country, Argentina. In the 1800s, Buenos Aires was a leading port as well as a center for food processing. Large numbers of immigrants from Spain and Italy came to Buenos Aires. Smaller numbers of immigrants from Germany and Eastern Europe, including many Jews, also arrived. People of mixed Native American and Spanish ancestry, known as ★ **mestizos,** also began moving to the capital. Today, they represent about 30% of the city's population. Many live in shanty towns on the outskirts of the city. Their houses are often made of pieces of sheet metal, and they usually have no running water.

Wealthy residents of Buenos Aires (1870). *Which information in the picture lets you know they are wealthy?*

Economy. Surrounded by rich farmlands (*pampas*), Buenos Aires was once a center for shipping grain, cattle and dried beef to plantations in Brazil and the West Indies. Today, Buenos Aires remains the largest port in South America. It dominates Argentina's political, economic and cultural life. It is the nation's industrial center as well as home to the stock exchange, central bank and most businesses.

Tourist Sites. Today, the city's European heritage is evident in its architecture, language and customs. In many ways Buenos Aires still resembles a European capital city, with its beautiful buildings, broad avenues, hundreds of bookstores and lively night life. Its mansions are similar to the palaces of French nobles—making the city the "Paris of South America." Large modern apartment houses mix with older mansions in the city. Many people believe that Buenos Aires houses the finest opera house in Latin America. It is also the location of a national theater, a national library, several major art museums and a large number of universities.

Now, let's use information in these two brochures to make a compare-and-contrast organizer:

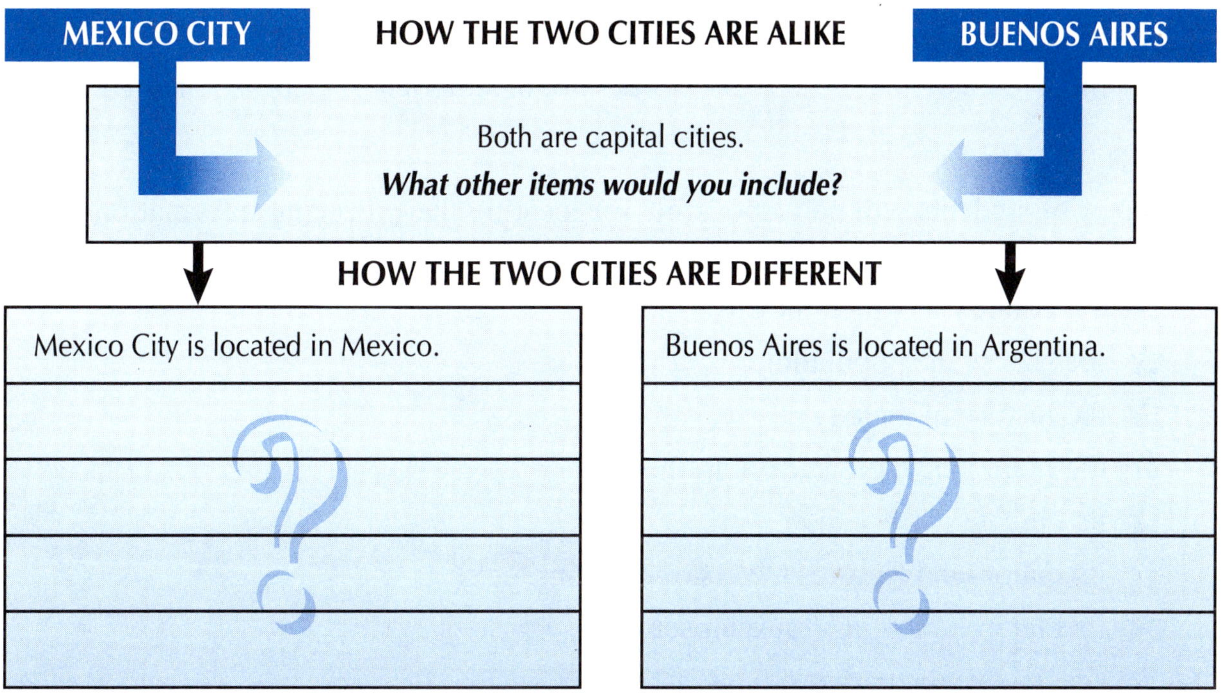

THINK ABOUT IT

What would you suggest to your mother about which of the cities to visit? Explain your choices in a brief essay using the outline above where you have compared and contrasted the two cities. When writing a **compare-and-contrast** essay, you should:

1. Begin by identifying the items you are comparing. In this case you are comparing and contrasting Mexico City and Buenos Aires.
2. Then, describe the similarities between these items. For example, both Mexico City and Buenos Aires are national capitals.
3. Finally, describe the differences between the items. For example, Mexico City is inland, while Buenos Aires is an important port.

LOOKING AT OTHER CITIES IN THE WESTERN HEMISPHERE

EXTENDING THE ACTIVITY

Tourism is a major industry, not only in Texas but throughout the Western Hemisphere. Now that you have become an "expert" about four major cities, you should learn more about some of the other important cities in the Western Hemisphere. Each student in your class should pair up with a partner. Each team of students should then select **one** city from **each** of the following locations:

- Texas
- the United States
- Canada or Mexico
- South America or Central America

YOUR TASK

Each pair of students will be responsible for locating the following information about each of the four cities:

- the country in which the city is located
- the size of the population
- the history of the city
- the main languages spoken in the city
- its climate
- its major land features (rivers, mountains, etc.)
- its major attractions (museums, etc.)
- special events (parades, fairs, etc.)

GATHERING INFORMATION

Where can you find this information? The following sources may be useful:

- look at various maps in an **atlas**
- check the "Cities" section of an **almanac**
- read **encyclopedia** articles about the city, as well as the country where the city is located
- refer to **travel guides** for tourists
- look at **reference books,** such as the *Texas Almanac* and *The Country Towns of Texas*. Both are available in libraries.

- write for a free **Texas State Travel Guide** from the:
  Texas Department of Transportation
  Travel and Information Division
  Post Office Box 5064
  Austin, Texas 78763-5064
- for cities in other states, call the state's **Office of Tourism.** They will often give you a toll-free phone number for contacting that city's Chamber of Commerce.
- for cities outside the United States, ask your parent or guardian for help in **calling the consulate** of that country for more information. Consulates are located in Washington, D.C., New York City and many large cities like Houston and Dallas.

COMPILING THE INFORMATION

There are several ways of compiling this information.

- You can write down on index cards the information that you find.

—or—

- If you have a computer, you can put your information into a data base. A **data base** is a computer program that allows you to store, sort and process large amounts of information. Once your information has been entered into the data base, you can then add, delete, search, sort and print it.

REVIEWING YOUR UNDERSTANDING

Directions: Fill in your Vocabulary Cards. Then complete the assignment that follows.

Compare
What do we do when we compare?
Why do we compare items?

Contrast
What do we do when we contrast?
Why do we contrast items?

Creating a Pamphlet for Your Community

What might interest someone visiting the area where you live? You are probably familiar with the main attractions of your own community. Use this knowledge to create a pamphlet that can be used by an imaginary "Tourist Center" in your community. Your pamphlet should have the following format:

Interior of the Stuermer Store which has been in operation for almost 100 years in Ledbetter. *What interesting sites exist in your community?*

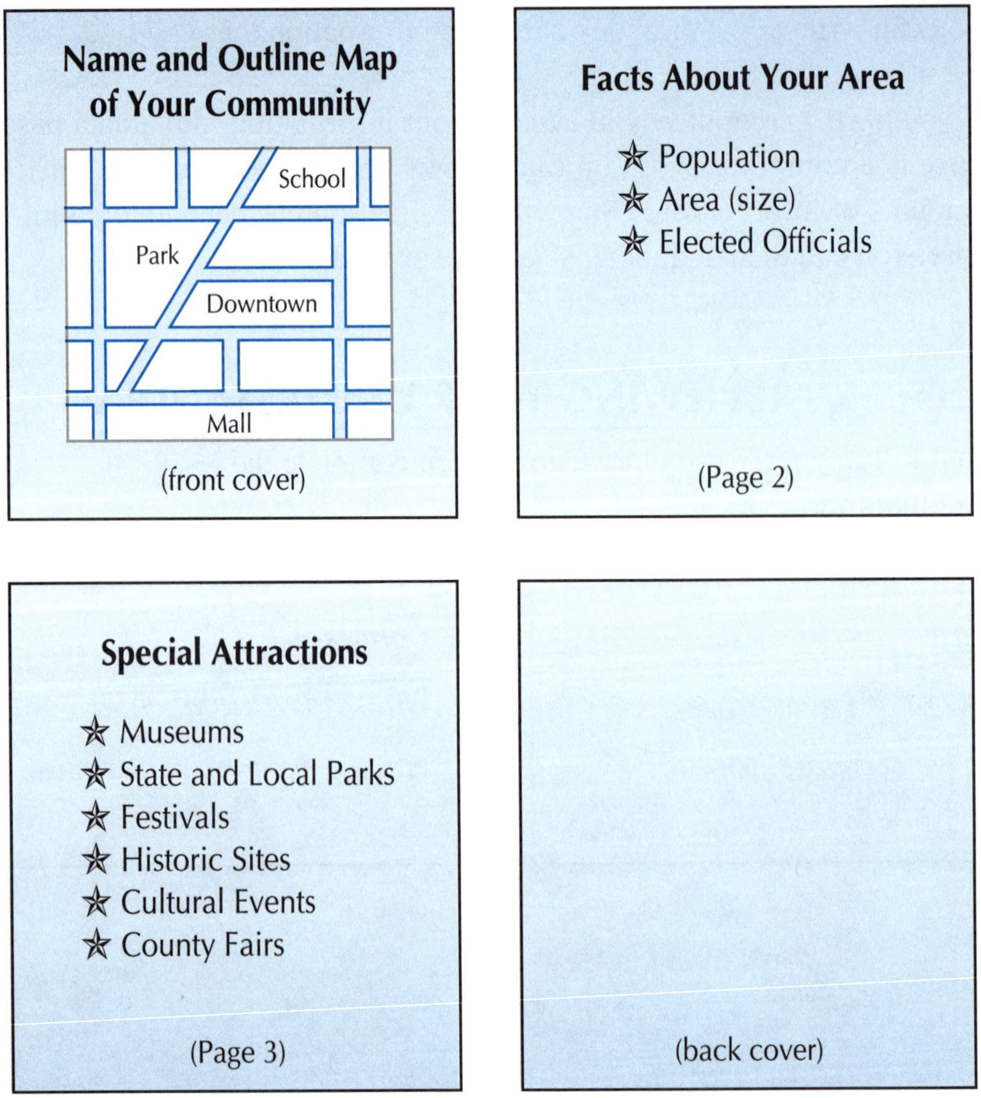

SUMMARIZING YOUR UNDERSTANDING

Directions: Use your knowledge to fill in the blanks in the following graphic organizers.

PEOPLE AND THE ROLE THEY PLAYED IN TEXAS HISTORY

1. **Person:**
   Role:
2. **Person:**
   Role:
3. **Person:**
   Role:
4. **Person:**
   Role:
5. **Person:**
   Role:
6. **Person:**
   Role:
7. **Person:**
   Role:
8. **Person:**
   Role:

PLACING EVENTS ON A TIMELINE

The timeline that follows is divided into 25-year segments.

1875	1900	1925	1950	1975	2000

Look over this chapter. Select **five** events that happened after 1875. Copy the chart below onto a separate piece of paper. Then, record these events on the timeline.

Event in History	Date
1.	
2.	
3.	
4.	
5.	

FACTS AND FIGURES ABOUT THE HISTORY OF TEXAS

DID YOU KNOW THAT …

THE SPANISH MISSIONS

After French rule ended, the Spanish Franciscans established thirty missions throughout Texas. Five of the most famous missions still exist along the San Antonio River. They were built with strong walls, and served as the spiritual and governmental centers for their surrounding areas. Each mission was supposed to be self-supporting, growing and providing everything needed by its residents.

THE CANNON THAT STARTED A WAR

In 1831, the settlement at Gonzales was given a small iron cannon as protection against Native American attacks. The cannon had been damaged. The best it could do was make a loud noise when fired. On October 2, 1835, Mexican troops tried to take the cannon back. The battle that followed, between the settlers and the Mexican soldiers, marked the start of the Texas Revolution. The cannon disappeared for almost a hundred years. In 1936 it was rediscovered after a flood exposed it; it had been buried in a nearby creek.

THE FIRST TO DIE FOR TEXAS

In one of the first battles between Texans and the Mexican army, 60 Mexican soldiers and one Texan were killed. **Richard Andrews** stepped out from his protected hiding place to shoot at the Mexican soldiers. Once exposed, he was shot, making him the first Texan casualty of the Texas Revolution.

THE START OF THE TEXAS RANGERS

In 1823, Stephen F. Austin needed help protecting settlers from Native American raids. Ten men were hired, marking the birth of the **Texas Rangers.** Soon after, the force was increased to 20 and then to 30. At the Consultation of 1835, the Texas Rangers were officially established. Their duties included acting as scouts, lookouts and spies during the Texas Revolution. They were paid $1.25 a day, and were expected to provide their own horses and guns. They still exist as a law-enforcement agency in Texas today.

CHAPTER 4

PEOPLE IN SOCIETY

Early settlers moving to Texas

Eating apples at the Texas Apple Festival

Tigua women dancing in El Paso

What is your favorite food? Do you like pizzas, tacos or hamburgers? Each of these foods was brought to Texas by a different ethnic group. An ethnic group is a group of people who share cultural traditions, customs, beliefs and ancestors. Texas has many ethnic groups—creating a colorful mix of cultures that makes our state an exciting place to live. In this chapter, you will learn something about the different cultures that have influenced the Texan way of life. This survey of ethnic groups will help you to appreciate how each group has contributed something special and unique to our state.

4A HOW WOULD YOU CATEGORIZE YOURSELF?

In this activity, you will see how people form groups based on race, nationality, ethnicity and religion. This activity will help you to understand what each of these terms mean. Look for the following important words:

★ Race ★ Nationality ★ Ethnicity ★ Religion

To help you find these terms, the ★ symbol will appear in the margin where the term first appears.

America is unique in many ways. One of the things that makes our nation special is its people. As of 1996, there were over 260 million people living in the United States. Each of us is a unique individual. Yet each of us also has some things in common with other people. Because people have things in common, Americans often identify themselves by their race, nationality, ethnic group, or religion.

HOW WOULD YOU GROUP YOURSELF?

In this activity, you will learn some of the ways in which people identify themselves. You will look at different racial groups, nationality groups, ethnic groups and religious groups. First let's see how you might "group" yourself:

☆ What is your race?
☆ What is your nationality?
☆ What is your ethnic group?
☆ What is your religion?

Did you group yourself correctly? The answer really depends on how you define these words. Each of these words—race, nationality, ethnicity and religion—is a concept. A **concept** gives a name to things that, although different, have something in common. For example, the word "bird" is a concept. An eagle is different than a mocking bird. However, they both share a characteristic common to all birds. They have feathers.

HOW ARE PEOPLE OFTEN GROUPED?

You have probably heard people use the words **race, nationality, ethnic group** and **religion.** But do you know what each of these terms really means?

RACE

Over the course of time, humans living in different regions of the world developed various physical and genetic differences. For example, some people have a light skin color; other people have a darker skin color. Sometimes these differences are used to identify groups of people.

Most people identify themselves with a racial group. A **race** is a group of people ★ who are identified by the color of their skin and other physical characteristics. The U.S. Census Bureau uses the following to classify people by race:

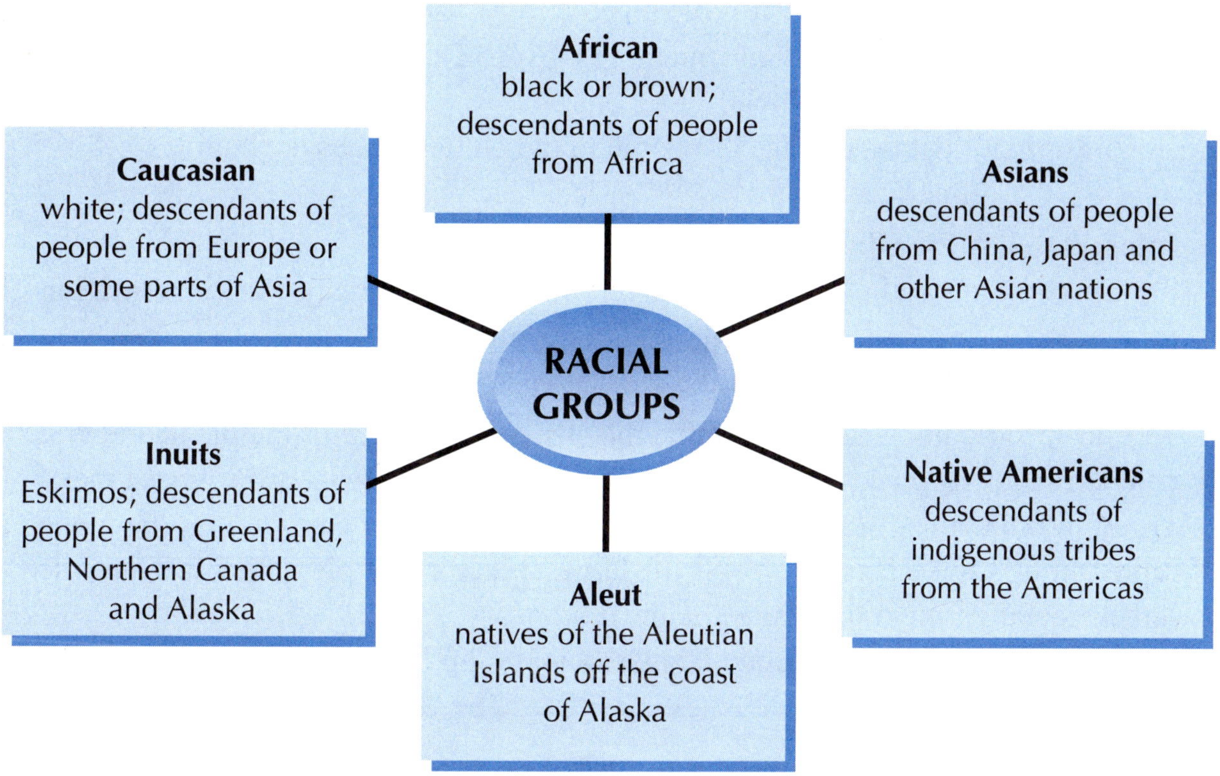

People from each of these racial groups have ancestors who came from different places. Some people have mixed racial backgrounds.

> Which racial group do you now think you belong to?

The United States is a **multi-racial society,** made up of many different races. The pie chart to the right shows the racial makeup of the United States in 1990.

U.S. RACIAL GROUPS, 1990

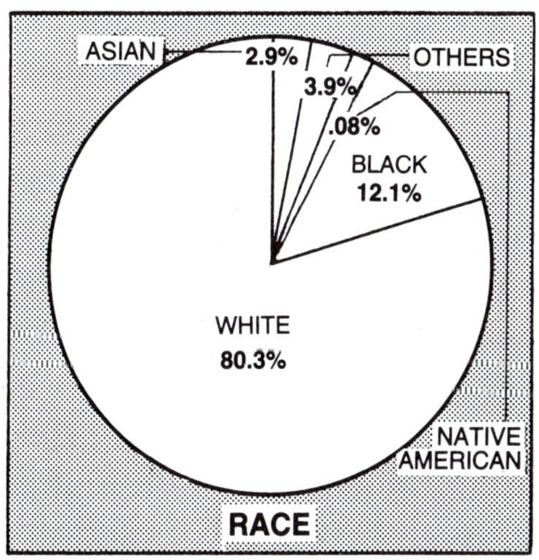

SKILL BUILDER: PIE CHARTS

What Is A Pie Chart?

A pie chart (*or circle graph*) is a circle diagram that is divided into different size slices. Its main function is to show how the parts are related to the whole pie. The pie represents 100% of something. If you add all the slices of the pie together, they total 100%.

Question: In the pie chart, what items are being compared?

Keys To Understanding A Pie Chart

Slices of the pie tell us what information is given. The pie chart also tells us how each slice is related to the whole.

Question: What percentage of people in the United States are Native Americans?

Interpreting A Pie Chart

Start by looking at the title. It will give you an overall idea of the information presented.

Question: What is the title of the pie chart?

To find specific information, examine the size of each piece of the pie and how it compares to other pieces or to the whole pie. For example, what is the largest racial group in the United States? If you look at the chart, you can see that the piece representing Caucasians (*whites*) is the largest piece of the pie—80.3%. Thus, the largest racial group in the United States is white.

Question: What is the second largest racial group in the United States?

NATIONALITY AND NATIONAL ORIGIN

★ The word **nationality** refers to the country in which a person is a citizen. Therefore, if you were born in the United States or became an American citizen, your nationality is American.

National origin sounds similar to nationality, but it means something different. National origin means the country your parents, grandparents or ancestors came from. **Ancestors** are members of your family who lived long ago, such as your great-grandparents. One example of national origin is German American. A German American is an American whose family (*parents, grandparents or ancestors*) originally came from Germany.

In the United States, people's national origin often forms the basis of their ethnic group. People who trace their ancestors back to Ireland, for example, often identify themselves as Irish-Americans.

Texans trace their roots back to many different countries. As a result, Texas is a state with people of many national origins.

THINK ABOUT IT

Ask your parents where your family's ancestors came from. What do you think they might say?

ETHNICITY

Ethnicity can be defined in several ways. Ethnic groups are people who have the same national origin, culture, language or race. For example, African Americans are of the same race. Irish Americans have the same national origin.

The people of Texas are multi-ethnic. *Where do you trace your roots?*

Sometimes members of different ethnic groups can come from the same country. For example, French Canadians and English Canadians are from different ethnic groups, but both have Canadian citizenship (*nationality*).

People who speak the same language may also be considered members of an ethnic group. **Hispanics** in Texas form the state's largest ethnic group based on language. Hispanics may come from or have ancestors from Central America, South America, the Caribbean or Spain. Most Hispanics in Texas are from Mexico.

Ethnicity may tell us something about a group's way of life. It may tell us what foods they prefer to eat, their dating patterns and their customs. Texas is a state with many ethnic groups. We can see this in the variety of foods we eat and the many kinds of music we enjoy listening to.

★ CHECKING YOUR UNDERSTANDING ★

1. What percentage of Texans trace their ancestry back to England?
2. From which continent do 20% of Texans trace their ancestry?

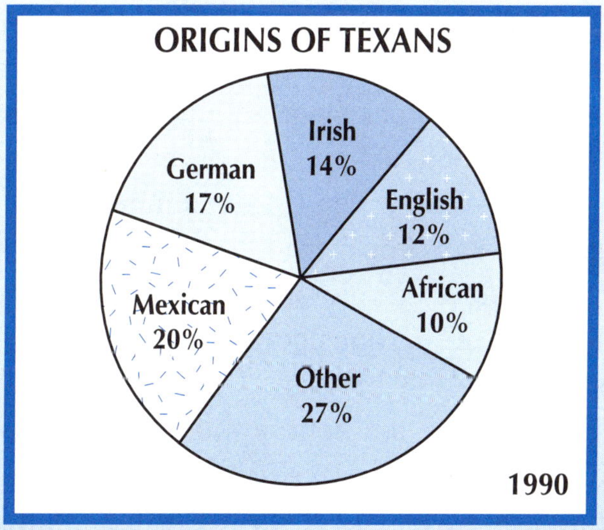

★ CHECKING YOUR UNDERSTANDING ★

Name three ethnic foods popular in the United States.

Food (dish)

☆ ______________ ? ______________

☆ ______________ ? ______________

☆ ______________ ? ______________

This food comes from ...

☆ ______________ ? ______________

☆ ______________ ? ______________

☆ ______________ ? ______________

An old fashioned barbeque.
What kinds of foods are popular with members of your ethnic group?

RELIGION

Another way people often group themselves is by religion. There is no exact definition ★ of **religion,** but religions usually have:

a belief in a God or several gods	a set of customs and practices	an organization, such as a church, which sets rules for its members

One example of a religion is **Judaism.** In ancient times, the first people known to have believed in a single God were the Jewish people. **Judaism,** the religion of the Jewish people, is based on the belief that God is the creator of the universe and is all-powerful and just. Jews also believe that God made a special promise to protect them, so long as they obeyed the Ten Commandments. Much of their religion is based on following the Ten Commandments and leading righteous and proper lives.

A Catholic Church in Castroville.
What other Christian groups are there besides Roman Catholics?

Another example of a religion is **Christianity.** Like Jews, Christians believe in one God. They take their name, "Christians," from Jesus Christ of Nazareth, who they believe was the son of God. Christians believe Jesus sacrificed himself for the sins of humanity. After his death, Christians believe Jesus returned and rose to heaven. They see this as proof that God opens the gates of heaven to all those who have faith in Jesus and lead righteous lives. Roman Catholics and Protestants are two groups of Christians, each with their own church organization.

Muslims follow the religion of **Islam.** They live mainly in the Middle East, Asia and Africa. Muslims, like Christians and Jews, believe in one all-powerful God. They believe that God has complete control over each person's future and that some day all people will be held responsible for their actions. They base their religious beliefs on the teachings of Mohammed, who they believe was the last of God's great messengers. These teachings form the basis of their holy book, the Qu'ran (*Koran*).

San Jose Mission, San Antonio.
Why did the Spanish build missions?

Many people came to America because they were not allowed to practice their religion in their home country. As a result, the United States became a nation with a variety of religious groups, allowing religious freedom for all.

The Old Rock Church, Cransfills Gap, Texas.
About how many churches are there in Texas?

People of many religions live in Texas. There are almost 17,000 churches in the state. In fact, Texas leads the nation in the number of churches and church members. The first organized settlement in Texas was a mission built by Spanish priests to convert Native Americans to Catholicism. Today, Roman Catholics make up the largest religious group in Texas. Most Mexican Americans are Roman Catholics. In addition, many Texans with Irish, French, Polish and German ancestors are members of the Catholic Church.

Southern Baptists are the second largest religious group in Texas. Other religious groups include Methodists, Episcopalians, members of the United Church of Christ, Jews and Muslims. The first Protestant church in Texas was built in 1815 by Methodists at Jonesborough. By 1854, the Jewish population of Houston had grown large enough to build the first **synagogue** (*Jewish house of prayer*). Texans are very proud of their **religious diversity** (*variety of differences*).

Religious diversity is also found in the rest of the Western Hemisphere. Most people in **Latin America** (*Mexico, Central America, the West Indies and South America*) are Roman Catholics. The Catholic Church has been a force for unity throughout Latin American history. However, there are also significant Protestant and Jewish communities in many Latin American cities. Canada, our neighbor to the north, also has a diversity of religions. Their largest single group is Roman Catholic. The next largest group is Protestant.

U.S. RELIGIOUS GROUPS, 1990

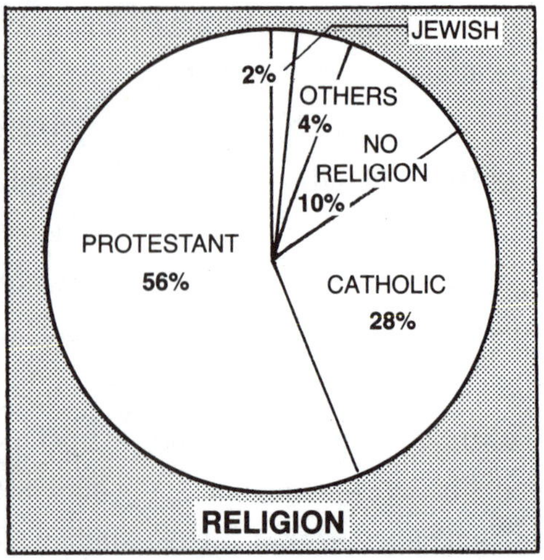

★ CHECKING YOUR UNDERSTANDING ★

Name two major religious groups in Texas. Try to identify the countries where each religious group first came from. Also, list some of the main religious beliefs of each religion.

Religion

☆ _______________ ? _______________

☆ _______________ ? _______________

Came to Texas from:

☆ _______________ ? _______________

☆ _______________ ? _______________

Major religious beliefs:

☆ _______________ ? _______________

☆ _______________ ? _______________

A Lutheran Church in New Sweden.
What other religions are found in Texas?

At the start of this activity you filled in a chart to "group" yourself. Look back at page 184 to remind yourself what you wrote. How would you now group yourself?

☆ What is your race?	☆ What is your ethnic group?
☆ What is your nationality?	☆ What is your religion?

LEARNING ABOUT OTHER PEOPLE

Now that you have learned about yourself, let's learn about someone else. Find someone in your class who belongs to a different race, ethnic group or religion. Compare your families' traditions and customs.

1. Do you celebrate any different holidays? If so, what are they?
2. Do you eat different kinds of foods? If so, what are they?
3. Do you both celebrate any of the same holidays or share any other traditions or customs? If so, what are they?

A Thai restaurant in Houston
Do you have a friend from a different racial, ethnic or religious group?

HISPANICS IN THE UNITED STATES

EXTENDING THE ACTIVITY

Every ten years the Census Bureau, an agency of the U.S. Government, conducts a census of the U.S. population. A **census** is a count of every person in our country. The last census was done in 1990. The next census will take place in the year 2000.

In the last census, people in the United States were asked if they were Hispanic. About 1 of every 11 persons said yes. The Census Bureau also asked Hispanics to group themselves into categories based on national origin. The following chart shows what these Hispanic people told the Census Bureau:

HISPANICS BY NATIONAL ORIGIN: 1990

Mexican	60%	South American	5%
Puerto Rican	12%	Dominican	3%
Central American	6%	Spaniard	3%
Cuban	5%	Others	7%

As you can see, about 6 out of every 10 Hispanics (60%) said they were of Mexican origin. This makes Mexican-Americans the largest Hispanic group in the United States.

Often, people convert a table of information into a pie chart. This helps make the information clearer. Let's change this information into a pie chart. Copy the circle below. Then take each item from the table and fill in its section. Use the markings around the circle to help you to divide the "pie." Each space between the marks represents 3% of the whole "pie." The pie chart has already been started for you.

Mexican-Americans celebrating Cinco De Mayo.
What other Hispanic groups live in Texas?

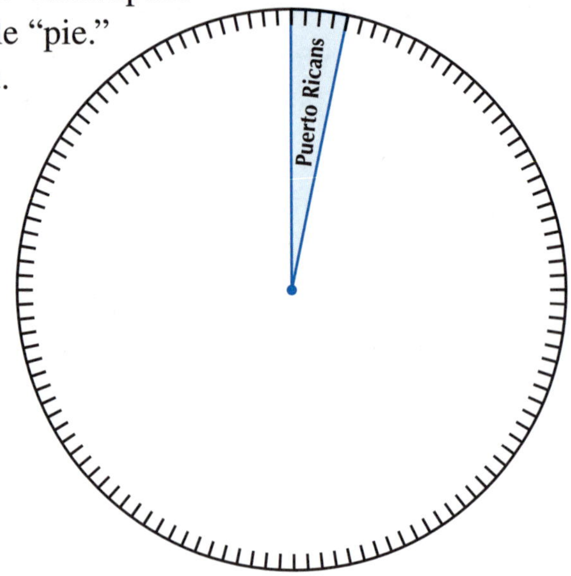

REVIEWING YOUR UNDERSTANDING

Directions: Fill in your Vocabulary Cards. Then complete the exercise that follows.

Race

Define the term:

Give an example of a racial group:

Ethnicity

Define the term:

Give an example of an ethnic group:

Finding Out About More Groups

Now that you have studied the way people have identified themselves in the United States, let's find out how people identify themselves around the world:

- ☆ What is the largest racial group in the world?
- ☆ What country has the largest population?
- ☆ What language is most commonly used around the world?
- ☆ What is the largest religious group in the world?

This information can be found in an almanac or a current yearbook of an encyclopedia.

4B HOW DOES AMERICAN SOCIETY MEET ITS BASIC NEEDS?

In this activity, you will learn about basic institutions that all societies have. Look for the following important words:

★ Tradition ★ Folklore ★ Customs ★ Institution

People are social creatures—they like and need to be with other people. Because of this need, people organize themselves into groups known as societies. Each society has its own unique way of doing things. **Sociologists** (*people who study society*) refer to the way people do things as culture. **Culture** is everything a person must learn in order to live in a particular society. Culture includes language, traditions, folklore, customs, folkways and institutions.

- ☆ **Language** is the system of sounds and symbols that people in a society use to communicate with one another and to express their ideas.
- ☆ **Traditions** are ways of doing things, based on how they were done in the past. ★ Traditions are usually passed from parents to their children by examples and direct instruction.
- ☆ **Folklore** are stories about a society's past. They explain why a society does ★ things the way it does.
- ☆ **Customs** and **folkways** are also long-established ways of doing things that are ★ accepted by members of a society.
- ☆ **Institutions** are organizations that establish ways of doing things to help the ★ members of a society meet their basic needs.

KEY SOCIAL INSTITUTIONS OF A SOCIETY

Every human society has similar basic needs. These needs are based on our physical needs as individuals as well as on the special needs each society faces as a group.

THINK ABOUT IT

What do you think are the most important needs of a society?

Most sociologists would answer that the most important needs for a society are to:

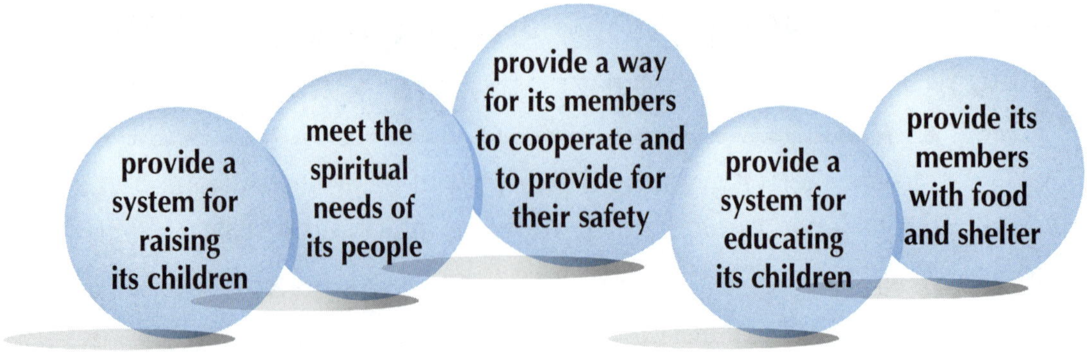

To meet these essential needs every society develops institutions. As you just learned, institutions are the organizations created by a society to take charge of doing things to meet its basic needs.

THINK ABOUT IT

What do you think are the most important institutions of a society?

Let us take a closer look at some of the institutions our society has developed to meet some of its basic needs.

THE FAMILY

The family is the most basic institution in any society. A **family** is a group of individuals who are related to one another by bloodline or by marriage. A **nuclear family** consists of parents and their children. An **extended family** includes grandparents and other relatives.

A family takes care of its members and the upbringing of its children. It establishes how to speak to others in society, how to dress and eat, and how to act in general.

A Chinese family enjoys a meal in a Houston restaurant.
Is this a nuclear or extended family?

Each family also has its own division of authority and responsibility. For example, in some societies the role of women is to take care of the home, while the men work outside the home. In other societies, tasks are shared more equally. **Roles** are social rules for the behavior of individuals in certain positions and situations. Once we are given a role in society, we know how we are supposed to act.

THINK ABOUT IT

In our society a mother is given a particular "role." How is a mother expected to behave toward her children?

RELIGION

All societies have some form of religious belief. Religions often have a tremendous impact on the way people think and behave. They help meet people's need to understand the purpose of life. Because most religions have an organization, such as a church, they are institutions. People often look to their religion to guide them in leading a good life. Religions often have specific rules, such as the Ten Commandments, to spell out good and bad behavior.

Baptisms are an important part of some religions.
What are some of the beliefs of your religion?

THINK ABOUT IT

Why do you think people are often influenced by their religious beliefs?

GOVERNMENT

Communities need rules to settle disagreements among their members. They must also protect themselves from individuals who break the rules. The institution set up for these purposes is known as **government.** Governments are created by citizens to make laws to help and protect the people in their society. Those who break the law are usually punished by the government. The government also protects the members of a society from outsiders who may be hostile.

Austin is the center of government in Texas.
What is the center of your national government?

THINK ABOUT IT

Can you think of a law that was passed by thc government of Texas that either helps or protects you and the other members of your community?

EDUCATIONAL SYSTEM

Education is another important institution in most societies. Some education takes place informally within the family. In addition, most societies have schools. Schools teach young people about their history, their responsibilities as members of society, their culture and their other institutions. Another important job of schools is to prepare young people for the responsibilities of adulthood. This is done by teaching young people the skills they will need for working and living as adults.

In Texas, the educational system is a very important institution. Texas has a tradition of providing a fine education for its students. There are nearly four million students in Texas attending elementary and secondary schools. Much of the tax money that the state of Texas collects is spent on schools.

THINK ABOUT IT

Can you think of skills you learned in school that will help you as an adult?

ECONOMIC SYSTEM

All societies must have some kind of system to allow their members to meet their needs for food, shelter, clothing and other goods and services. This is called an **economic system.** In America, the economic system we use is called the **free enterprise system.** In this system, people are free to work and to run their own businesses with very little government interference. Most workplaces also have their own set of rules, which affect lifestyles.

A shopper in Gainesville.
What makes our economic system unique?

THINK ABOUT IT

Do you know someone who has started a business? Who is that person, and what kind of business is it?

In this activity, you were asked what you thought were the most important institutions in our society. After reading this activity, would you now change your answer?

READING ABOUT OUR MULTICULTURAL SOCIETY

As you can see, a society's institutions—its families, religious organizations, governments, schools and economic system—greatly affect the way its members live. In the United States, many people are also influenced by their identification with various racial and ethnic groups. These groups also have their own unique traditions, customs and beliefs. The institutions of family, religion and education often help these groups to preserve and pass down their own traditions, customs and beliefs.

Wouldn't it be interesting if you could learn about the culture of another group? You might become a part of a group for a long time and see how they do things. Often, this is not practical. Books, however, let you experience another group's customs and institutions without leaving your own family and community. By using your imagination, books let you "taste" their unique foods and share in the excitement of their holidays.

A group of Texans playing Greek music.
What other cultures do you come in contact with?

Let's look at some books available to you. Starting on page 198 is a list of books about different cultural groups in Texas. Select **one** book from the list. Also, feel free to select a book that is not on the list. After reading the book, complete the Book Evaluation Form:

Book Evaluation Form

Title of the book: ______?______

Author's name: ______?______

Publisher: ______?______ Date published: ______?______

Cultural group described in the book: ______?______

Briefly summarize some of the information you learned about the cultural group you read about: ______?______

What institutions help the members of this group maintain their culture? ___?___

How does this group's culture help meet its member's basic needs? ___?___

Here are some suggested books you may wish to choose from:

The Ethnic Heritage Series

(Institute of Texan Cultures)

This series describes the many ethnic groups of Texas. Each book in the series provides a general survey of the first settlers in Texas from each ethnic group. It also describes their major settlements and looks at several of their best known individuals.

The Mexican Americans

Julie Catalano *(Chelsea House)*

This is a story about the history, culture and religion of the Mexican people. The book looks at the reasons why many Mexicans decided to make the United States their home.

Our Mexican Ancestors

Jeanne D. Callihan and Samuel Nesmith *(Institute of Texan Cultures)*

This book deals with the Mexican influence on almost every part of Texan life. The book will help you appreciate the importance that Mexican culture has had on Texas. In addition, you will learn about many Mexican contributions to American society.

Texans: A Story of Texan Cultures for Young People

Barbara Stanush *(Institute of Texan Cultures)*

This book gives details about fifteen different cultures in Texas. The book looks at each culture's crafts, activities, and history. It also contains accounts of notable people from each of these cultures.

Deep in the Heart: The Lives & Legends of Texas Jews
Ruth Winegarten and Cathy Schecter
(Eakin Press)

This is a visual history of Texan Jews. Five hundred and fifty photographs provide a window into the lives and legends of Jewish Texans in the past. The book also deals with the issue of prejudice against Jews and others.

Portrait Series
(Hendrick Long)

This is a series of separate books about African Americans, Asian-Pacific Americans, Mexican Americans and Native Americans. Each book in the series is designed to acquaint students with a particular ethnic group.

CREATING AN ETHNIC COOKBOOK

EXTENDING THE ACTIVITY

British Americans love fish and chips; Chinese Americans like Szechuan pork; Greek Americans savor roast lamb. One of the best ways to make the study of different cultures more exciting is by learning about some of the unique foods of each culture. Recipes often reflect the traditions of a cultural group as well as the main crops and livestock that were available to it.

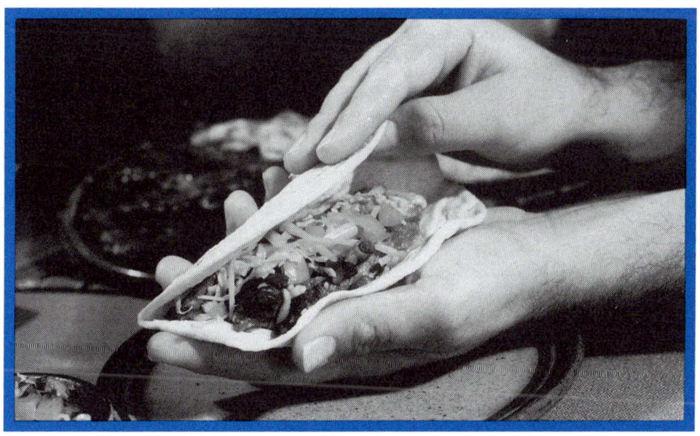

A fajita.
What foods do members of your ethnic or cultural group most enjoy?

Each student in the class is a member of some ethnic or cultural group. In this part of the activity, your class will create an "ethnic" cookbook. To help put together the cookbook, each student will bring to school a recipe for **one** ethnic dish. Students may want to ask their parents or other adults in their ethnic group to help suggest a recipe popular with their group. Students can also bring in recipes from different groups.

Let's look at a recipe popular with one of the largest cultural groups in Texas—Mexican-Americans. Mexican cooking is known for its wide variety of dishes, reflecting a Native American as well as a Spanish heritage. Corn, rice and beans are very popular ingredients in the Mexican diet. These foods are used in a variety of ways to make different dishes.

Tortillas are an item popular with many Mexican Americans. You can use the format of this recipe as your guide for writing other recipes. Note how a recipe usually starts with a list of ingredients, and then describes the steps for preparing the dish:

TORTILLAS

Ingredients: 1 cup masa harina (tortilla flour)
1 1/4 cups warm water

Steps:
1. Put the masa harina (tortilla flour) into a medium sized bowl.
2. Mix in the warm water to form a soft dough.
3. Shape the dough into egg-sized balls.
4. Flatten the dough into pancakes 4 inches wide on a tortilla press or floured board.
5. Heat an ungreased griddle over medium heat.
6. Cook tortillas for about 1 minute or until browned.
7. Fill tortillas with ingredients such as beef, or serve plain.

Servings: This will make 6 to 8 tortillas.

A woman preparing tortillas.
Have you ever eaten a tortilla?

REVIEWING YOUR UNDERSTANDING

Directions: Fill your Vocabulary Cards. Then complete the exercise that follows.

Traditions
Define the term:
Give two examples:

Institutions
Define the term:
Give two examples:

Reading a Specialized Map

Use this map to answer the questions that follow:

LARGEST ANCESTRY GROUP IN EACH STATE: 1990

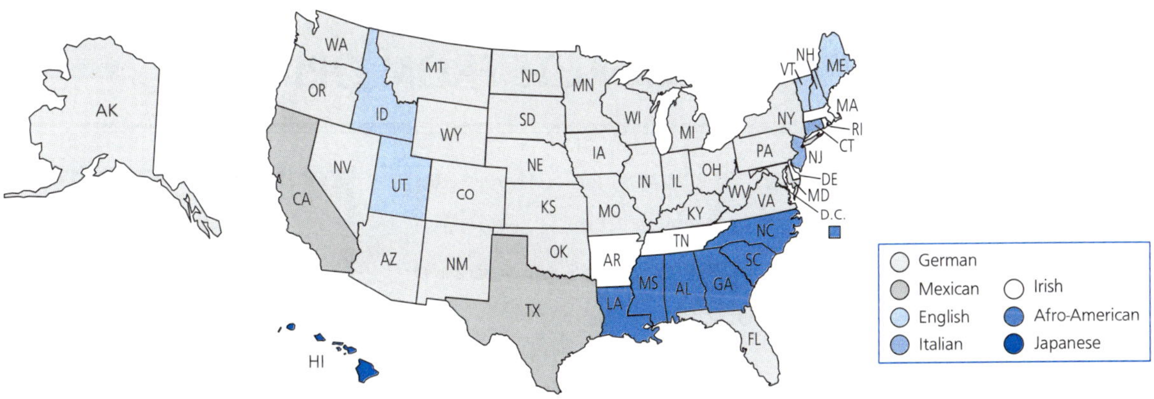

1. Can you identify the largest ancestry group in the nation?
2. Which is the largest ancestry group in Texas?
3. What other states, besides Texas, have this as their largest single ancestry group?
4. In which state would you find Japanese Americans as the largest ancestry group?
5. In which state do Italian Americans make up the largest ancestry group?
6. In which states are African Americans the largest ancestry group?
7. In which two Southern states would you find the most Irish Americans?
8. In which states do English Americans make up the largest ancestry group?

4C IS THERE SUCH A THING AS A "TYPICAL" TEXAN?

In this activity, you will learn about the different ethnic groups that have settled in Texas and their impact on the state. Look for the following important words:

- ★ Factual Statement
- ★ Opinion Statement
- ★ Tejanos
- ★ Vaqueros
- ★ Oktoberfest
- ★ Buffalo Soldiers

Imagine your school will soon print its yearly magazine. This year's magazine will focus on the various immigrant, religious and cultural groups that have settled in Texas.

You have been given your first assignment by the Chief Editor—the person who puts the magazine together. "Here is an article to read," the editor says. "It was written by one of your classmates. One of the things I need you to do is to make sure it contains only facts. I don't want personal opinions in this article. Before you begin, please read this summary about facts and opinions."

DISTINGUISHING FACTS FROM OPINIONS

★ A statement of **fact** (*factual statement*) is information that can be checked for accuracy. You check something for accuracy by looking at other sources to see if the information is correct or incorrect.

Correct	***Incorrect***
Austin is the capital of Texas.	San Antonio is the capital of Texas.

★ An **opinion** is a statement of someone's personal beliefs. It is not a statement that is true or false. An opinion *cannot* be checked for accuracy. There are two main types of opinion statements:

Opinions of personal taste express a person's feelings. For example, "Texas is the best state to live in."

Opinions about the future make a prediction. For example, "When I grow up, I am going to attend the University of Texas."

I love food prepared in a cook-out.
What type of opinion statement is this?

"Distinguishing between fact and opinion is only part of your assignment," the editor continues. "I also need you to check some facts and to look for errors in punctuation, spelling and grammar. Finally, the writer never wrote a conclusion to the article. As you read, decide what you think a 'typical Texan' is." Here is the article you are asked to read.

EDITOR'S INSTRUCTIONS: Read the first two paragraphs and identify all opinion statements. In addition, identify one factual statement.

SEARCHING FOR THE TYPICAL TEXAN

THE NATIVE AMERICANS

(1) The first people to settle in the area we now call Texas were the Native Americans. (2) The chief tribes in this region were the Caddo, Jumano, Karankawa, Tonkawa, Kiowa, Comanche, Apache and Witchita. (3) Later, Cherokee, Tigua and Alabama-Coushatta tribes arrived. (4) Many Native Americans died from exposure to new diseases brought by the Europeans. (5) Others were pushed onto reservations outside the state. (6) Today, only the Tigua and Alabama-Coushatta have reservations in Texas.

(7) These Native Americans were the most important people ever to settle in Texas. (8) Although their number in Texas is now small, their influence survives in the names of many places in Texas, in some of the foods of Texas and in the legends of Texas past. (9) For example they were the first to grow tomatoes, potatoes, yams, corn and squash.

Tigua Reservation in El Paso.
Which Native American groups live on reservations in Texas?

★ YOUR NOTES ★

1. List the sentence numbers of all the opinion statements.
2. List the sentence number of **one** factual statement.
3. What source might you check to see that the factual statement you identified is accurate?

EDITOR'S INSTRUCTIONS:
Continue to identify all opinion statements and find one factual statement. In addition, find answers to certain questions.

HISPANIC AMERICANS

(1) Many Spanish-speaking people have come to Texas. **(2)** In colonial times, the Spanish established missions and ranches in Texas. **(3)** By 1836, Spanish-speaking colonists and **tejanos** (*those born in Texas*) lived mainly in San Antonio, Laredo, El Paso and Brownsville. **(4)** Some tejanos, like **Juan Seguin,** played an important role in Texas' struggle for independence. **(5)** Seguin commanded a small number of tejanos at the Alamo. **(6)** He was sent from the Alamo with messages seeking reinforcements, so his life was spared. **(7)** Later, Seguin was a member of the Texas Congress and Mayor of San Antonio. **(8)** He was the greatest tejano who ever lived in Texas.

(9) When Texas became independent, wealthy tejanos lost most of their lands and influence. **(10)** Spanish-speaking **vaqueros** (*cowboys*) and sheepherders continued to play an important role in the Texas economy. **(11)** The tejanos often suffered unfair treatment because of their Spanish language, Catholic religion and different customs.

A tejana woman and an Anglo-American man in front of Mission San Jose.
What is a tejanos?

★ YOUR NOTES ★

1. List the sentence numbers of all the opinion statements.

2. List the sentence number of **one** factual statement.

3. What source might you check to see if the factual statement you identified is accurate?

4. Who were the Tejanos?

5. What role did Juan Seguin play in the struggle for Texas' independence?

EDITOR'S INSTRUCTIONS: Continue to identify all opinion statements and one factual statement. You will also need to check certain punctuation, especially the use of periods and question marks.

- Periods (.) are used when you wish to end a sentence.
- Question marks (?) are used at the end of a question.

(1) In the late 1800s, new immigrants began arriving in Texas from Mexico. **(2)** Why did they come to Texas [./?] **(3)** They came to find better jobs and a new way of life. **(4)** Mexican immigrants cleared land, dug irrigation ditches, picked cotton, and herded sheep and cattle. **(5)** Others found jobs building railroads or working in factories [./?] **(6)** Some became farmers, while others were forced to live in barracks or work camps without their families. **(7)** Others lived in their own neighborhoods, or **barrios** [./?] **(8)** In the barrios, they could feel comfortable speaking Spanish and carrying on their own customs and traditions. **(9)** They also benefited from associations called **mutualistas,** which helped those members who had special difficulties. **(10)** Despite these hardships, the immigrants were happy.

Mexicans often worked at harvesting crops.
What other contributions did Mexican workers make to the development of Texas?

(11) Mexican immigration increased greatly after the Mexican Revolution in 1910. **(12)** Thousands of Mexicans crossed the border to escape violence and economic hardship [./?] **(13)** They continued to face poor treatment and prejudice in their new land. **(14)** Their children often attended segregated, all-Mexican schools. **(15)** The men could not join labor unions and took low paying jobs. **(16)** The women often worked as maids, cooks and waitresses.

☆ YOUR NOTES ☆

1. List the sentence numbers of all the opinion statements.

2. List the sentence number of **one** factual statement.

3. Which is the correct punctuation for sentence:

☆ **2:** [period/question mark] ☆ **7:** [period/question mark]
☆ **5:** [period/question mark] ☆ **12:** [period/question mark]

(1) For a number of reasons, Hispanic Americans are happier today than at any other time in their history. **(2)** The Civil Rights Movement of the 1950s and 1960s greatly improved conditions for Mexican Americans and other ethnic groups [?/.] **(3)** The old system of segregation was eliminated. **(4)** More money was spent on schools [?/.] **(5)** Hispanic Americans formed their own political groups. **(6)** Some Mexican Americans, like Henry Cisneros, were elected to public office [./?]

(7) The Spanish heritage has deeply affected the way of life in Texas in many ways—including its architecture, foods, language, ranching methods, music and clothing. **(8)** Chili, for example, was chosen as the Texas State dish in 1977. **(9)** Spanish cathedrals, missions and forts have influenced building styles throughout the Southwest. **(10)** Thus, we can truly say that Spanish-speaking Texans are typical Texans [./?]

EDITOR'S INSTRUCTIONS:
Continue to identify all opinion statements and identify one factual statement. Continue to look for incorrect punctuation and answer certain questions

Concepcion Mission, San Antonio.
What other evidence shows the strong Spanish influence in Texas?

☆ YOUR NOTES ☆

1. List the sentence numbers of all the opinion statements.

2. List the sentence number of **one** factual statement.

3. Which is the correct punctuation for sentence:

☆ **2:** [period/question mark] ☆ **6:** [period/question mark]
☆ **4:** [period/question mark] ☆ **10:** [period/question mark]

4. What were some of the reasons why Mexicans migrated to Texas?

5. How has Texas been influenced by its Spanish heritage?

EDITOR'S INSTRUCTIONS:
Identify all opinion statements and one factual statement. Editors also need to check spelling. In this section, use a dictionary to find the correct spelling for those words in blue print.

THE ANGLO-AMERICANS

(1) The term **Anglo-American** refers to English-speaking people. **(2)** In 1822, Stephen F. Austin started the first colony of Anglo-Americans in Texas. **(3)** Most of the early Anglo-American **[setlers/settlers]** came from other parts of the United States, but their ancestors came from Great Britain or Ireland. **(4)** After Austin, other **empresarios** (*land agents*) established more colonies for Anglo-American **[pioneers/pieoneers]**. **(5)** Most Anglo-Americans came to Texas in search of cheap land and the chance to work for a better way of life. **(6)** They turned forests and prairies into the best ranches and farms in the world. **(7)** They built cities, criss-crossed the state with railroads, roads and telephone lines, and tapped the state's enormous mineral resources.

Anglo settlers braved many harsh conditions. *What contributions did Anglo-American settlers make to the development of Texas?*

(8) For most of Texas history, Anglo-Americans have been in positions of political and economic leadership. **(9)** They absorbed ideas from other cultures, but contributed their own methods of government, work ethic, laws, system of education, religious ideas, technology and language. **(10)** In particular, the Anglo-Americans in Texas were shaped by **[frontier/frontear]** conditions and a spirit of independence. **(11)** Anglo-Americans have left a lasting impression on Texas' system of government, food, art, literature, **[architecture/arckitecture]**, music, business methods, technology and way of life.

☆ YOUR NOTES ☆

1. List the sentence numbers of all the opinion statements.

2. List the sentence number of **one** factual statement.

3. Which word is spelled correctly in sentence:

☆ **3:** [setlers/settlers] ☆ **10:** [frontier/frontear]
☆ **4:** [pioneers/pieoneers] ☆ **11:** [architecture/arckitecture]

EDITOR'S INSTRUCTIONS: Identify all opinion statements. Editors also check a writer's grammar. One error is using the wrong verb forms: "He (singular) do (should be does) what he wants." A similiar mistake is to use a plural noun with a singular verb: "They (plural) eats (should be eat) their dinner early." In this section look for problems in the use of nouns with verbs.

Plaza and Courthouse in New Braunfels
Where else did German-Americans settle in Texas?

THE EUROPEAN AMERICANS

(1) Immigrants from other countries in Europe also came to Texas. **(2)** For instance, many Texans can trace their ancestors to Germany. **(3)** Early German settlers went to central Texas. **(4)** In 1842, a group of German noblemen **[sets/set]** up a special society to send immigrants from Germany to Texas. **(5)** As more German immigrants came to Texas, they settled in Galveston, San Antonio, Houston, New Braunfels, Fredericksburg and Castroville. **(6)** Many of these German pioneers continued to speak German, their native language.

An early German pioneer family.
What do you know about early German pioneers in Texas?

(7) In 1847, John Meusebach bought land and began a German settlement at Fredericksburg. **(8)** The land **[were/was]** a Comanche hunting area. **(9)** However, Meusebach persuaded the Comanches to sign an agreement not to attack the settlers.

(10) The German immigrants built colorful houses of timber and stone, and celebrated ★ traditional festivals like the **Oktoberfest** (*October festival*). **(11)** A large number of German immigrants farmed their own land and improved it by putting up fences and buying farm equipment. **(12)** The German immigrants did not like the use of slaves. **(13)** Many so opposed slavery that they tried to escape to Mexico when the Civil War broke out. **(14)** Today, the German heritage in Texas **[live/lives]** on. **(15)** German-style beer halls can still be found in many parts of central Texas. Fredericksburg and New Braunfels celebrate traditional **wurstfests** (*sausage festivals*). **(16)** German sausages **[is/are]** now the best in the world.

☆ YOUR NOTES ☆

1. List the sentence numbers of all the opinion statements.

2. Which is the correct use of the verb in sentence:

☆ **4:** [sets/set] ☆ **14:** [live/lives]

☆ **8:** [were/was] ☆ **16:** [is/are]

EDITOR'S INSTRUCTIONS: *Identify all opinion statements and also continue checking for agreement of nouns and verbs.*

The Germans **[was/were]** not the only group to arrive from Europe. French, Norwegians, Czechs, Poles, Swedes, Danes and Jews from Eastern Europe also immigrated and started communities in Texas.

French settlers first arrived in Texas in the late 1600s. In 1842, a French empresario established a colony of French families close to San Antonio. French-speaking Cajuns from Louisiana came to Texas in the early 1900s, after the discovery of oil at Beaumont. The "Golden Triangle" area of Port Arthur-Beaumont-Orange **[is/are]** now a major center in East Texas for Cajun music and food. Most Texans love to eat Cajun-style foods such as gumbo, jambalaya and red beans and rice.

Our Sorrows Lutheran Church, Norse.

Where else in Texas did Norwegians settle?

The first Norwegian settler, Johannes Nordboe, arrived in Dallas in 1841. Soon after, other Norwegian settlements in Texas **[was/were]** begun in Henderson County. Norwegians continued to emigrate to Texas, settling in Cranfils, Gap, Norse and Clinton. They built dry-laid rock fences. These fences, made without mortar, rely on gravity and the skill of the builder to protect land from wild-roaming cattle. One of the most famous women in sports, Babe Didrickson Zaharias, was of Norwegian ancestry.

Many Czechs came to Texas in the 1850s, fleeing a revolution taking place in their homeland. They settled in the towns of Praha, Fayetteville and Halletsville. The Texas dance-hall **[was/were]** first introduced by Czechs. The Czech language ranks third in household use in Texas. Only English and Spanish are spoken more frequently. The newspaper "Vestnik," begun in 1879, was the first Czech newspaper in Texas.

CONTINUED

Polish settlers also first arrived in Texas in the 19th century. The first large group, about 150 Poles, crossed the Atlantic Ocean on the ship *Weser*. They started the small town of Panna Maria (meaning Virgin Mary) in 1854. Its Polish church and school **[is/are]** still standing today. St. Hedwig is one of the largest and best Polish settlements in Texas. It was begun in 1855, when about a dozen Polish families moved there from San Antonio.

Czech dancers.
Where else did many Czechs settle when coming to Texas?

Immigrants from Ireland, Sweden, Denmark and Eastern Europe began arriving in greater numbers at the end of the 1800s. Many of these later immigrants were Catholic or Jewish. All of these immigrants **[was/were]** part of a great wave of people coming from Europe to the United States. They helped develop the farmlands of Texas, and also worked in cities and factories. They came to escape poverty and persecution and to find new opportunities. These immigrants contributed more to the growth of Texas than any other group.

Wagon train of Polish settlers in White Deer.
Where else did Polish settlers move in Texas?

☆ YOUR NOTES ☆

1. Write out all sentences that are opinion statements.

2. Which is the correct use of the verb in paragraph:

☆ **1:** [is / are]
☆ **2:** [love/loves]
☆ **3:** [was/were]
☆ **4:** [is/are]
☆ **5:** [is/are]
☆ **6:** [was/were]

EDITOR'S INSTRUCTIONS:
Identify all opinion statements and resolve any problems in spelling, punctuation, or noun/verb agreement.

THE AFRICAN AMERICANS

African Americans have played a very important role in Texas history. In 1528 a black slave named **Esteban** was sailing with Cabeza de Vaca, when they were shipwrecked [./?] They traveled throughout Texas for six years before arriving in Mexico City. Esteban was among the very first foreigners to explore the interior of Texas.

Early in Texas history, African Americans were [forcibley/forcibly] brought as slaves to work on the plantations of East Texas. They endured many hardships, working from early morning until sunset. The slaves were treated like pieces of property. They could be bought and sold, separated from their families or even whipped for no reason. Their hard work helped to develop cotton as the leading agricultural crop in Texas.

William Goyens.
What do you know about the life of William Goyens?

Before the Civil War, a small number of African Americans entered Texas as free men and women. The most famous African American to ever live was probably **William Goyens.** He [was/were] the son of an ex-slave and made a fortune as a blacksmith, wagon builder and gunsmith. During the Texas Revolution, Goyens acted as an interpreter with the Native Americans for Sam Houston. Afterwards, he operated a sawmill and gristmill (*mill for grinding grain into flour*). When he [died/dyed] in 1856, he owned a large mansion and 12,000 acres of land.

The slaves of Texas were freed on "Juneteenth"—June 19, 1865. Following the Civil War, the freed slaves faced many problems but continued to contribute to Texas. The Freedman's Bureau helped them face the challenges of freedom.

CONTINUED

During Reconstruction, several African Americans **[played/plaid]** major roles in government. For example, **Richard Allen,** a former slave, became chairman of an important committee in the Texas legislature. Allen helped rebuild Texas' transportation system. Despite these contributions, African-American Texans were terrorized and discriminated against when Reconstruction ended.

In spite of many hardships, African-Americans helped tame the frontier in Texas. The 10th Cavalry of the U.S. Army, composed of African-American troops on horseback, was sent to the southwest of Texas. These brave troops became known as the **buffalo soldiers** among the Native Americans.

The first African Americans to serve in Congress.
Can you name an African American who served in Texas government?

Other African Americans rode in the cattle drives on the open range. One out of every four cowboys on the **Chisholm Trail** was an African American. African American Bill Pickett became famous in rodeos and wild west shows. The Bill Pickett Invitational Rodeo is now held each year in Beaumont. It provides an opportunity for black cowboys to display their skills.

At the end of the 19th century, black Texans began moving from farms to cities. During the years of the Civil Rights Movement, they won more political and legal rights. Their courage provided an inspiration to other minority groups. African Americans **[have/has]** contributed to the development of Texas throughout its history. They helped pick its cotton, drive its cattle and tame its frontier. They have had a special influence in politics and music. Many foods enjoyed in Texas today are contributions of African Americans—black-eyed peas, collard greens, sweet potato pie and hush puppies, to name just a few.

African American cowboy at a Juneteenth Parade.
What contributions have African Americans made to Texas?

☆ **YOUR NOTES** ☆

1. Write out all sentences that are opinion statements.

2. Which is the correct form to use in paragraph:

☆ **1:** [period/question mark]	☆ **3:** [was/were]	☆ **4:** [played/plaid]
☆ **2:** [forcibley/forcibly]	☆ **3:** [died/dyed]	☆ **7:** [have/has]

EDITOR'S INSTRUCTIONS: *Identify all opinion statements and find any problems in spelling, punctuation, or noun/verb agreement.*

THE ASIAN AMERICANS

People whose ancestors come from Asia also contributed to the growth of Texas. In the 1860s, many men from China emigrated to California to earn money to send back to their families in China. They **[was/were]** hired to lay tracks for the railroads, to work in mines, to run laundries and to perform manual labor. From California, some of these Chinese workers moved to Texas to help build the railroad line from Calvert to Dallas. Throughout the United States, Chinese immigrants faced **[prejudice/prejudise]** and discrimination because of their unique appearance, clothes, language and customs. Because they were willing to work for very low wages, they were often disliked by other workers.

Japanese farm workers (1905). *What contributions have Asian Americans made to Texas and the world?*

In the 20th century, emigration from Asia to the United States has again increased. I think they will soon be the largest immigrant group in the United States. Large numbers of Asian immigrants, especially from Vietnam, have found homes in Houston, Port Arthur and Beaumont. These people **[brings/bring]** with them a tradition of hard work, a desire for learning and respect for others. Their presence adds greatly to the diversity and excitement of life in Texas. For example, I. M. Pei, a Chinese immigrant to America, designed the Morton H. Meyerson Symphony Center and the City Hall in Dallas.

CONTINUED

Asian culture **[has/have]** also influenced Texas indirectly. The Chinese invented paper, printing, silk, gunpowder, **[porcelain/porselin]** and the compass. These inventions spread to Europe and were later brought by Europeans to Texas.

It is easy to see why people of many different backgrounds have found they can live and work together in Texas **[./?]** The blend of Native American, Hispanic, African American and Anglo-American cultures, and the arrival of other immigrant groups, have created a unique Texas culture. Indeed, it would seem that a "typical Texan" is…

Interior of Myerson Symphony Center in Dallas.
Who was the architect that designed this building?

☆ ✎ YOUR NOTES ✍ ☆

1. Write out all sentences that are opinion statements.

2. Which is the correct form to use in paragraph:

☆ **1:** [was/were]	☆ **2:** [bring/brings]	☆ **3:** [porcelain/porselin]
☆ **1:** [prejudice/prejudise]	☆ **3:** [has/have]	☆ **4:** [period/question mark]

REVIEWING AND CHECKING THE ARTICLE

You have now finished reviewing the article. It's time to write your Chief Editor. You must inform her of how would you define what a "typical" Texan is.

Dear Chief Editor,

I have reviewed the article. I found that the article contained (*some/many*) opinions. To conclude the article I would write that a "typical Texan" is…

Sincerely,

(your signature)

Two days later you meet the Chief Editor in the hall. She thanks you and asks you to do one more task—to check the **accuracy** of the information in the article. Remember, a factual statement is accurate if you can show that it is true and error-free.

Since it would take too long to check all of the facts in the article, she suggests you choose any **two** factual statements. You can refer to either a textbook, an encyclopedia or an almanac to check the accuracy of these two factual statements.

Statements You Selected To Check	Source Used	The Statement is:
(1) ?	?	? ❐ Accurate ❐ Not Accurate
(2) ?	?	? ❐ Accurate ❐ Not Accurate

COMPARING AND CONTRASTING AFRICAN CULTURES IN THE WESTERN HEMISPHERE

EXTENDING THE ACTIVITY

In this activity, you learned about different groups of people in Texas. Members of related groups are also found in other parts of the Western Hemisphere. For example, people of African heritage are found throughout the United States and Latin America.

People of African descent played a major role in the history of Texas, the Caribbean and Brazil. Read the following passages about people of African heritage living in the islands of the Caribbean and the country of Brazil. As you will learn, there were differences, as well as similarities, between each of these communities.

THE AFRO-CARIBBEAN COMMUNITY

The Caribbean (*or West Indies*) consists of a large number of islands in the Caribbean Sea. The four largest islands are Cuba, Jamaica, Trinidad and Hispaniola. (The island of Hispaniola is divided into Haiti and the Dominican Republic).

At one time, these islands were occupied by Native Americans. However, after the Spaniards conquered these islands, the local population began to die from European diseases. To supply a workforce, the Spaniards began buying slaves from Africa. Slaves were forced to work on plantations, planting and cutting sugar cane. In the severe tropical climate, slaves were often not given enough to eat and drink, and many died.

CONTINUED

In the late 1600s, France, England and Holland took over several of the islands from Spain. They brought even more African slaves to the Caribbean. By 1800, Africans out numbered whites by ten to one on most of these islands.

In addition to the slaves, people of mixed ancestry, known as **mulattoes,** lived on these islands. There was also a large number of **freedmen**—people of African heritage who had been freed by their owners. Some of these freedmen became landowners and even had slaves of their own.

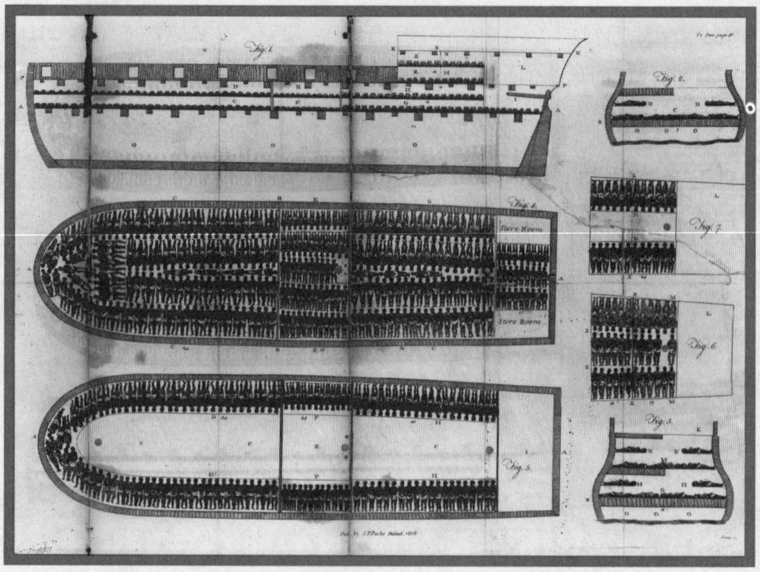

Upper and lower deck of a slave ship.
Why did the Spanish start importing slaves from Africa?

Haiti. In 1791, the slaves of Haiti rose up in rebellion, defeating the French army and declaring independence. Haiti came under the control of its blacks and mulattoes. Soon after independence, social divisions began to emerge. Haitian mulattoes generally controlled the government. They usually spoke French and were Roman Catholics. Haitian peasant farmers spoke a local language called Creole. They practiced their own religion, known as voodoo.

Former President Jean Bertrand Aristide
Today, Haiti is moving toward democracy.
Why is such a move by Haitians necessary?

From 1957 to 1986, Haiti was ruled by two different dictators. They favored the middle class and did little to help the peasants. Haiti remained the poorest nation in the Western Hemisphere. Today, Haitians of all classes are trying to cooperate in rebuilding their country.

CONTINUED

Cuba. In Cuba, slavery increased when restrictions on the slave trade were lifted in 1791. Over the following decades, hundreds of thousands of slaves were brought to Cuba. The island became the largest producer of sugar in the Caribbean. Slavery did not end in Cuba until 1868. Former slaves continued to plant and cut sugar cane. Black workers from Haiti and Jamaica also moved to Cuba in the early 1900s to work in the fields. Today, a large part of the Cuban population is mulatto or black. Most Cubans speak Spanish. About 85% of the people are Roman Catholics.

Jamaica. Slavery was abolished in the British colonies, such as Jamaica, in 1834. On some islands, the end of slavery resulted in the growth of a new class of Afro-Caribbean farmers. In Jamaica, former slaves took their own small plots of land and grew food. Today, three-fourths of Jamaicans are of African heritage. The official language on Jamaica is English, but many people speak Jamaican Creole. Over half of the people are Protestants.

Trinidad. In Trinidad, laborers from India were brought over to work on the sugar plantations in place of the former slaves. People of African heritage are the largest ethnic group on the island and control the government and army. Blacks make up 43% of the population. The group that faces the most prejudice are the descendants of the Indian workers, who make up 40% of the population. English is the official language of Trinidad. Over 60% of the population are either Roman Catholic or Protestant. One out of every four people is Hindu.

Dominican Republic. In the Dominican Republic, the majority of people are mulatto. Yet Dominicans identify more with their Spanish than with their African roots. Almost 95% of the people are Roman Catholics. The main language spoken is Spanish.

You have just read about some people of African descent living in the Caribbean. Do you see any similarities between them and the people of African descent in Texas? Do you see any differences? Now read the following passage about another community with African ties.

BRAZIL

Brazil is the largest country in South America. Unlike the rest of South America, Brazil was once a Portuguese colony. As a result, Portuguese is the official language of Brazil. In the Americas, the system of sugar plantations was first developed in Brazil. Because the Portuguese controlled the West coast of Africa, their ships could supply Brazil and the Spanish colonies with African slaves. In Brazil, slaves were not only used to plant and harvest sugar cane, but also for gold mining, fishing, herding cattle, farming grains and growing cotton and coffee.

By 1800, Brazil had nearly a million slaves of African heritage—more than any other nation. Brazil also had a large group of mulattoes. As in the Caribbean, Portuguese slave owners sometimes freed their slaves. This created a large class of freed blacks even before the official end of slavery.

After slavery officially ended in 1888, many former slaves moved to the frontiers of Brazil or to the cities. In southern Brazil they faced competition from large numbers of Italian and Spanish immigrants, who took many jobs.

Today, over half of all Brazilians have some African roots. Race in Brazil, as in the Caribbean, is not simply black or white. There are many racial categories, from white to light-skinned, to brown, to black. Brazilians pride themselves on being a "racial democracy"—free from racial prejudice. The influence of African culture in the country is seen in the Brazilian samba and annual Carnival.

Some Brazilians do not believe Brazil is a true racial democracy. They say white Brazilians are better off than others. They say non-whites earn less and are less able to get an education. In the 1970s, some Afro-Brazilians began a movement to fight against racial inequality in Brazil.

As you just learned, there were both similarities and differences between each of these communities. Did you catch these similarities and differences? Let's see. Make a copy of the following chart. In each box of the chart, write **one** sentence about Africans in Caribbean countries and Brazil that shows whether they were similar or different from African Americans in Texas. The first set of boxes has been done for you as a model.

TEXAS	THE CARIBBEAN	BRAZIL
1. Africans were brought to Texas as slaves.	*The Spaniards brought Africans to the Caribbean as slaves. The English, Dutch and French also owned slaves.*	*The Portuguese brought Africans to Brazil as slaves.*
2. Slaves were forced to work hard growing and picking cotton.	**?**	**?**
3. Very few slave owners in Texas freed their slaves.	**?**	**?**
4. Slavery in Texas ended in 1865 after the Civil War.	**?**	**?**
5. African Americans suffered discrimination in Texas.	**?**	**?**
6. Through their hard work and many contributions, African Americans helped develop the State of Texas.	**?**	**?**
7. African Americans speak English.	**?**	**?**

After you have completed the chart, write a compare and contrast essay. Your essay should compare and contrast the different groups of African descent in Texas, the Caribbean and Brazil.

REVIEWING YOUR UNDERSTANDING

Directions: Fill in your Vocabulary Cards. Then complete the exercise that follows.

Factual Statement
Define it:
Provide an example:

Opinion Statement
Define it:
Provide an example:

Applying Generalizations

One generalization you might have made in **Activity 3G** was that Native Americans were made up of different groups, speaking different languages and following different customs. Is this same generalization also true for people of African descent living in different parts of the Western Hemisphere? Do you agree with this generalization? Explain your answer.

Mapping Immigration to the United States

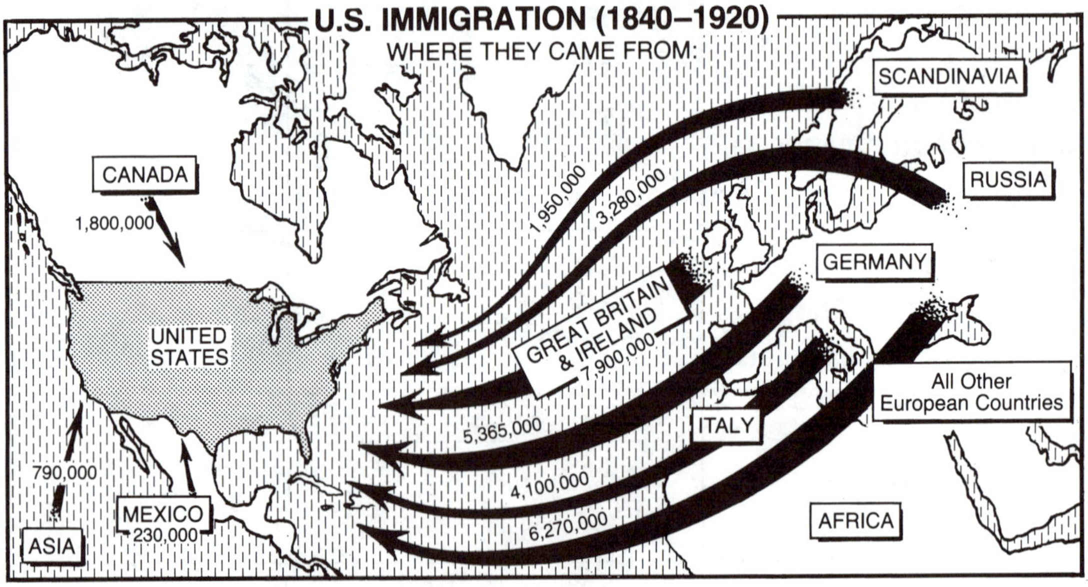

1. Which time period is covered by this map?

2. How many immigrants came to the United States from Germany?

3. Which country in **North America** sent the most immigrants to the United States?

4D WHO WOULD YOU NOMINATE TO THE TEXAS HALL OF FAME?

In this activity, you will learn about some of the diverse groups of people who have contributed to the greatness of Texas. Look for the following:

- ★ Biography
- ★ Autobiography

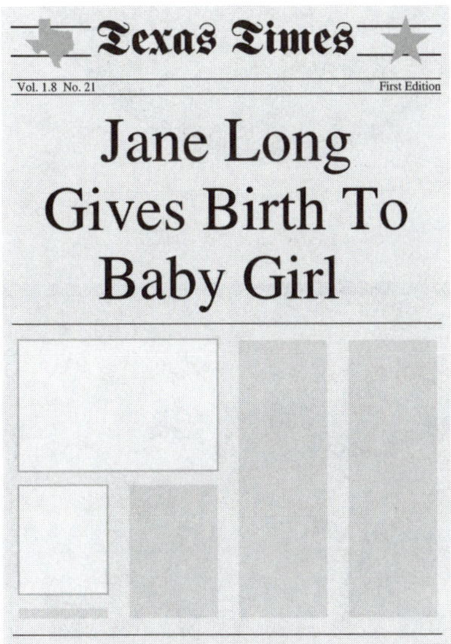

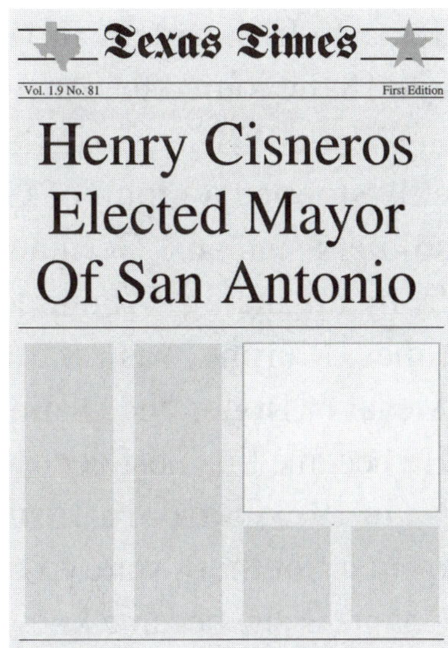

THINK ABOUT IT

What do you think all of these headlines have in common?

Let's look briefly behind each headline.

Jane Long first came to Texas in 1819. She is the first Anglo-American woman known to have given birth in Texas.

Jane Long.
What is she known for?

Jose Antonio Navarro was born in San Antonio in 1795. A delegate to the Convention of 1845, Navarro voted for the annexation of Texas to the United States. He also helped to write the state's first constitution.

Gail Borden, Jr., was a pioneer and the editor of the state's first newspaper in Galveston. Born in New York, Borden moved to Texas and then later to Connecticut. Borden was awarded a patent for his creation of condensed milk. Borden made a fortune selling condensed milk to the army during the Civil War. When the war ended, he returned to Texas. Texans named Borden county after him and also named the county seat "Gail" in his honor.

U.S. soldiers fighting in World War II.
Why is Audie Murphy famous?

Audie Murphy was born in Texas to Irish parents in 1924. At age 18, he joined the Army. During World War II, he single-handedly stopped a group of German soldiers and six German tanks from advancing. Wounded eight times, Murphy was awarded the Medal of Honor, the Distinguished Service Cross and the Purple Heart for his bravery. He became the most decorated American soldier in World War II.

In 1973, **Barbara Jordan** of Houston became the first African-American woman from a Southern state to be elected to the U.S. House of Representatives. While in Congress she became known as a distinguished and well-spoken leader.

Born in San Antonio, **Henry G. Cisneros** has established himself as a national Hispanic leader. Cisneros was the first Hispanic elected Mayor of San Antonio in 1981. Later, he served in the Cabinet of President Bill Clinton as Secretary of Housing and Urban Development.

These individuals represent different races, religions and ethnic backgrounds. However, they all have one thing in common—all are Texans who have made a lasting contribution to the development of our state.

Many sports honor their best players by setting up a Hall of Fame. In this activity, you will be asked to nominate **two** persons to be included in an imaginary Texas Hall of Fame. Who would be your candidate for the Texas Hall of Fame? You may wish to look through the other chapters of this book as well as other sources for the names of possible nominees, or you may look through other books written about Texas. Here are the necessary qualifications for your nominees:

QUALIFICATIONS FOR THE TEXAS HALL OF FAME

- Each nominee must have been born in or have lived in Texas.
- One nominee must be **like** yourself. This nominee must be of either the **same** race, religion, nationality or ethnicity as you.
- One nominee must be **unlike** yourself. He or she must be of a **different** race, religion, nationality or ethnic group than you.

President Johnson meets with his advisors. *Will he be one of your nominees?*

- A nominee can come from any field—for example, a sports figure, scientist, inventor, politician, president or corporate executive.
- A nominee can still be living, or may be a historical figure who has died.

RESEARCHING YOUR NOMINEE

Your first task will be to research your **two** nominees. You can find information about them in a number of sources:

ENCYCLOPEDIA

Encyclopedias have articles about many well-known people. These articles are arranged in alphabetical order. An encyclopedia has guide words or letters on the spine of each volume. They will help you to locate the name of the person you are looking up.

BIOGRAPHY

A **biography** is a book about a person's life. It can be an excellent source of detailed ★ information about that person. Some well-known people have had several biographies written about them by different authors.

★ CHECKING YOUR UNDERSTANDING ★

A biography will have facts about why a person became famous. It will also contain other important information about the person's life. On a separate sheet of paper, write **three** things that you might expect to find about a person in a biography.

AUTOBIOGRAPHY

Sometimes a person will write a book about his or her own life. This kind of book is ★ called an **autobiography.** In an autobiography, the writer will often build up the good things about his or her life and play down the bad things.

★ CHECKING YOUR UNDERSTANDING ★

1. Why do you think a person might exaggerate the good things and play down the bad things when writing an autobiography?
2. Imagine that you were going to write your own autobiography. On a separate sheet of paper, list **three** events in your life that you might include in your autobiography. Explain why you selected each event.

Most libraries have entire sections devoted to biographies and autobiographies. They are not arranged on the library shelf by the name of the author. Biographies and autobiographies are listed in alphabetical order by the **last name of the person** the book is about. For example, a biography about Gail Borden by Mary Wade would be under the letter **"B"** and not under the letter "W."

★ CHECKING YOUR UNDERSTANDING ★

Where would you find …?

1. Under which letter would you look to find information in an encyclopedia about **Cabeza de Vaca?**
2. Under which letter of the alphabet would you look in the library to find a book about the life of **Quannah Parker** by Len Hills?
3. Under which letter of the alphabet would you look in the library to find an autobiography by **Barbara Jordan?**

Now you are ready to go to the library to start your research. On a separate piece of paper, complete the research guide that follows:

Name of Nominee: ___?___ (from the same group as you)
How is this person the same as you?
Why is this person famous?
Source Used: Identify one source of information—the title of a book, the name of an article, or the section of an encyclopedia you read.
Brief summary of the person's life.
Some of the person's major accomplishments.
Reasons why the person should be in the Hall of Fame.

Name of Nominee: ___?___ (from a different group than you)
How is this person different from you?
Why is this person famous?
Source Used: Identify one source of information—the title of a book, the name of an article, or the section of an encyclopedia you read.
Brief summary of the person's life.
Some of the person's major accomplishments.
Reasons why the person should be in the Hall of Fame.

LEARNING ABOUT A BOOK FROM ITS TITLE

EXTENDING THE ACTIVITY

One way to learn more about people or past events is to read about them in a book. Often, you can learn a great deal about a book from its **title.** Each of the following four books has some information about Texas history. However, the specific information in each book is different. Match each description on the following page to the book on the right:

- ☆ This book has some information about Texas, but probably not a great deal. It also covers the history of the other 49 states and the history of America as a whole. Which book is it?
- ☆ This book provides you with information about the entire history of Texas. It even covers the time before Texas became a state. It has a great deal of information about Texas. Which book is it?
- ☆ The information in this book focuses mainly on Texas from 1861 to 1865. Which book is it?
- ☆ This book focuses on the life of an important activist in the Texas Revolution. He was a Mexican who upheld the cause of Texas independence from Mexico. He signed the Texas Declaration of Independence and served as Vice-President of the Texas Republic. Which book is about him?

Study the following book titles. **One** title in each group has more information about the listed topic than the others. Identify the book title in each group that you think has the most information about that topic (*shown in capital letters*).

1. THE RIO GRANDE
America's Waterways
The Mighty Rio Grande
Rivers of America

2. TEXAS COURT SYSTEM
The U.S. Legal System
The Justice System in Texas
Texas State Government

3. TEXAS STATE GOVERNMENT
A History of Government in America
America's Greatest Governors
The Government of Texas

4. ESTEBAN
A History of Slavery in America
Slavery in Texas
Esteban: An Explorer in Slavery

REVIEWING YOUR UNDERSTANDING

Directions: Fill in your Vocabulary Cards. Then complete the exercise that follows.

Biography
What is a biography?
What information will you find in a biography?

Autobiography
What is an autobiography?
What information will you find in an autobiography?

Writing A Persuasive Essay About A Famous Texan

Each year the U.S. Postal Service receives letters requesting that a famous American be honored on a stamp. In this section, you will be asked to write a letter about **one** famous Texan from this activity that you would like to see honored on a stamp. Your letter should persuade the reader that your view on the subject should be honored.

☆ **1. Start Writing.** Your introduction should state the purpose of your letter—to offer the name of a person for commemoration on a stamp.

☆ **2. Body of Your Letter.** Think of as many reasons as you can to convince the Stamp Advisory Panel to support the person you select. Organize your persuasive letter so that it follows a clear and logical order. Discuss the person's accomplishments and importance to Texas and American society. Mention specific facts to support your nominee. For example, if you were writing about Thomas Edison, you would mention his work in developing the light bulb and other inventions. Then you would explain the importance of these inventions to modern-day society. Finally, you would explain to the panel that it is important to honor inventors to encourage others to follow their example.

☆ **3. Closing The Letter.** End by summarizing your main points. Impress your reader by concluding with some words spoken by the person or a memorable quote about the person. Suggest a date for issuing the stamp. For example, the day the person was born or the date of a significant event occurred in that person's life. Also try to think of a city from which the stamp should be issued.

☆ **4. Mail Your Letter.** If you think you have written a strong persuasive letter, send it to the Stamp Advisory Panel at the following address: U.S. Postal Service Headquarters, 475 L'Enfant Plaza S.W., Washington, D.C. 20260

4E

WHAT DOES THE CONCEPT OF CULTURAL DIFFUSION MEAN?

In this activity, you will examine some examples from different cultures. Look for the following important words:

★ Concept ★ Cultural Diffusion

★ In Activity 4A, you learned a definition for the word concept. Recall that a **concept** gives a name to things that, although different, have something in common. For example, a person who helps you to learn new things in school is called a "teacher." The term "teacher" is a concept.

The concept "teacher" does not refer to any particular one of your teachers. Instead, it refers to all of your teachers. All of your teachers have certain characteristics in common. Each of your teachers works in a school. Each of your teachers helps you to learn new things. Each of your teachers is in charge of a class. All of these characteristics help us to define the concept of "teacher." In this activity, you will practice looking at several examples for common characteristics to identify an important concept.

CULTURAL DIFFUSION: A COMPLEX PROCESS

Centuries ago, traveling was very difficult. Mountains, oceans and deserts were barriers that often prevented people in one area from meeting people in other areas. However, as time went on, people eventually came into contact with other groups. Sometimes this contact was brought about by trade. Other times, contact was created by war. Often, ★ when these contacts took place, a process known as **cultural diffusion** occurred.

In this activity, you will read about five examples of cultural diffusion. After each example, try to figure out what characteristics the example has in common with the other examples. At the end of this activity, you will be asked to define cultural diffusion on the basis of what you have learned from the specific examples.

Example 1: Cultural Diffusion FROM THE MIDDLE EAST TO EUROPE AND ASIA

The wheel was invented more than 5,000 years ago in the area we now call the Middle East. The wheel made it easier to carry heavy loads by using carts. Over the next thousand years, the use of the wheel spread westward into Europe. It had also traveled eastward across the center of Asia. Meanwhile, people in the Middle East improved the wheel to make it lighter and faster. This allowed them to build horse-drawn chariots.

Within 400 years, use of the wheel had spread as far east as India. Each new group that started making wheels changed them slightly to suit its own purposes.

★ CHECKING YOUR UNDERSTANDING ★

In this example of cultural diffusion, what happened to the invention of the wheel?

Example 2: Cultural Diffusion FROM CHINA TO EUROPE

In the early 1200s, few Europeans had ever heard of China. In 1271, Marco Polo traveled to China in search of wealth. After 20 years in China, he returned to Italy. He told of China's foods and inventions such as gunpowder. The use of gunpowder was later adopted by Europeans. Polo also described China's copper coins, paper money and postal service. He spoke of magical black stones (coal) that, when burned, would provide heat. These black stones, commonly found in Europe, were soon heating homes all over Europe.

Marco Polo arrives at Cathay (China).
Why were Marco Polo's travels important to Europeans?

★ CHECKING YOUR UNDERSTANDING ★

In this example, how did contact with China affect the people of Europe?

Example 3: Cultural Diffusion FROM EUROPE TO AFRICA

In most parts of Africa, Christianity did not exist until the 1800s. At that time, European nations were busy gaining control over Africa. Protestant and Roman Catholic missionaries followed Dutch, French, Belgian and British merchants into Africa. Today, the number of Africans that follow the Christian religion is estimated to be about 160 million.

★ CHECKING YOUR UNDERSTANDING ★

Which European religions were adopted by people in Africa?

Example 4: Cultural Diffusion FROM THE AMERICAS TO EUROPE AND FROM EUROPE TO THE AMERICAS

Five hundred years ago, Native Americans grew tomatoes and potatoes. People in Europe had never seen these foods. In the early 1500s, Europeans first began exploring the Americas. They brought some of the foods they had eaten in the Americas back to Europe. Soon, Europeans were eating tomatoes and potatoes. In the meantime, Europeans brought horses, sheep, goats, cattle and cats to the Americas. Rats, mice, and honey bees were unknown in the Americas. These animals were introduced to the Americas by the Europeans. The Europeans also brought new germs to the Americas. Before the Europeans came, Native Americans had never suffered from smallpox, measles, chickenpox, influenza or yellow fever.

The Europeans used horses when going into battle in the Americas. *What other items did the Europeans introduce to the Americas?*

★ CHECKING YOUR UNDERSTANDING ★

In this example, what exchanges took place between the Europeans and Native Americans?

Example 5: Cultural Diffusion FROM MEXICANS TO ANGLO-AMERICANS IN TEXAS

In the 1500s, the Spaniards introduced cattle and horses to their colony in Mexico. Mexicans brought these cattle and horses with them when they first settled in Texas. Mexican cowboys, or *vaqueros,* introduced their language and customs to Texas. Later, these words and customs were adopted by the Anglo-Americans who settled there. For example, the words *corral, bronco, loco* and *sombrero* are all words taken from the Spanish language. Other Spanish words, slightly altered, were also adopted by the Anglo-Americans in Texas.

The Spanish introduced their religion to the people of Mexico. *What other items did they introduce?*

The word "ranch" is taken from the Spanish *rancho,* rodeo from *rodear* and stampede from *estampida.* The traditional broad-brimmed hat, cotton bandanna and Western-style saddle of the cowboy are all items first introduced into Texas by the *vaqueros.*

★ CHECKING YOUR UNDERSTANDING ★

In this example, how did contact with Mexicans affect the Anglo-Americans in Texas?

CREATING A DEFINITION

Now that you have read five examples of cultural diffusion, how would you define this concept?

REVIEWING YOUR UNDERSTANDING

Directions: Fill in your Vocabulary Cards. Then complete the exercise that follows.

Concept

What is a concept?

Provide an example of a concept:

Cultural Diffusion

What is cultural diffusion?

Provide an example of cultural diffusion:

Cultural Diffusion Today

In this activity you learned about the concept of cultural diffusion. Cultural diffusion is not limited to the past. In fact, cultural diffusion occurs every day throughout the world. For example, when young Japanese students wear Western-style clothing, that is cultural diffusion. When a Disneyland theme park opens in France, or a McDonalds in Mexico, that too is cultural diffusion.

What other examples of cultural diffusion can you point to?

4F WHAT DO YOU KNOW ABOUT THE DIVERSE CULTURES OF TEXAS?

Diversity refers to the differences among people. In this activity, you will learn about the many diverse cultures of Texas by participating in a Cultural Fair. Look for the following important words:

- ★ Texas State Fair
- ★ Multicultural
- ★ Tex-Mex foods
- ★ Piñata
- ★ Fandango
- ★ Rosh Hashanah

True to tradition, Texans often do things in a big way—even when it comes to having a good time! There are about five hundred fairs and festivals held each year in Texas. Ever since 1886, the biggest fair in Texas has been the ★ State Fair held in Dallas each year. The **Texas State Fair** is the most widely attended annual event held anywhere in the United States, drawing about three million people each year.

Texas State Fair (1995).
What fairs exist in your part of Texas?

★ CHECKING YOUR UNDERSTANDING ★

Have you ever attended the Texas State Fair? If so, what was it like? Describe what you enjoyed the most.

In Brownsville, the city celebrates a **Charro Day Festival** to honor Mexican cowboys. New Braunfels holds a German festival known as the **Wurstfest.** Each May in Fort Bend, there is a **Czech Fest** featuring Czech foods, music and dances. In San Antonio, even though a large part of the city is Hispanic, everyone pretends to be Irish on **St. Patrick's Day.** Even the San Antonio River is dyed green. These are just some of the many cultural fairs and festivals held each year throughout Texas. At these events, people parade, listen to ethnic music, wear traditional costumes and eat a variety of ethnic foods.

Charro Day Festival in Brownsville.
Have you ever attended a cultural fair or festival in your area?

Coming into contact with and meeting people from different cultures at these events is often an exciting experience. It also allows us to learn about the culture, music, holidays and dances of the many peoples of Texas. These fairs and festivals help us experience some of Texas' rich **multicultural** (*many cultures*) heritage. ★

Wouldn't it be exciting if your class had an opportunity to "visit" a fair that had the different cultures of Texas on display? In this activity, you and your classmates will do just that. Your class will hold a **"Cultural Fair."** Your teacher will divide your class into six groups. Each group will select a different cultural group in Texas to learn about. Your teacher may ask you to pick a cultural group different from your own.

Here are a few ethnic groups from which to choose. Feel free to add to this list.

- ☆ Mexican Americans
- ☆ German Americans
- ☆ Vietnamese Americans
- ☆ African Americans
- ☆ Irish Americans
- ☆ English Americans
- ☆ Jewish Americans
- ☆ *You Select One*

Each group will be assigned a section of the classroom. Each section will be used to create a booth for the Cultural Fair. Each booth should represent a different cultural group in Texas. Booths will be decorated to reflect the cultures they represent. On the day of the fair, students will take turns visiting the other booths.

DECORATING YOUR BOOTH

To decorate the booths, each team should collect or make the items listed below. Teams will be awarded points for each item they can find, make or create:

ART (10 Points)

Students may display pictures or photographs of artwork (*paintings, murals, statues, textiles*) done by members of their cultural group. For example, if your group represents German Americans, you might show some of the works of German-American sculptress **Elisabet Ney.** She immigrated to Texas in the 1870s, and her works became famous throughout the world.

FOODS (10 Points)

Students may display recipes and pictures of typical ethnic food dishes. These foods should be ones for which their cultural group is well known. For example, a German-American group might bring bratwurst (*a type of sausage*), sauerkraut or sauerbraten (*a meat dish*). A Mexican-American group might bring in pictures or recipes for tortillas, burritos or enchiladas. They might also display some **Tex-Mex** foods, which are foods based on Mexican-style cooking.

> **BONUS:** For each student who cooks food from his or her selected culture for other students to sample, his or her team will receive a bonus of 10 points.

A Mexican-American restaurant.
What type of foods can you order in a Mexican restaurant?

CUSTOMS AND TRADITIONS (10 Points)

Students may display posters or pictures showing some of the interesting and unique customs or practices of their cultural group. For example, the piñata is an interesting tradition in Mexican culture. A **piñata** is a candy-filled paper decoration often found at birthday parties, Christmas or other special events. Children, while blindfolded, try to break open the piñata with a stick. Another tradition followed by Mexicans is placing a **lazo** or rope over the heads of the bride and groom at a wedding. The lazo has two loops, one that goes over the head of the bride, the other over the head of the groom. The rope is knotted in the middle symbolizing the unity of their marriage.

MUSIC (10 Points)

Students may bring in tapes of music popular among members of their cultural group. For example, **Scott Joplin** was a famous African-American musician. Born in Texarkana in 1868, he is considered the "Father of Ragtime Music." Ragtime music is a style of jazz written mainly for the piano. During his lifetime, Joplin wrote more than five hundred pieces of music, including a ballet and two operas.

DANCE (10 Points)

Students may perform traditional dances popular with members of their cultural group. For example, the Coushatta Indians of East Texas often perform tribal dances. The Irish do a jig. If your group was representing Mexican Americans, they might perform the **fandango.** This Spanish dance was popular with Mexican-American settlers in Texas.

Early settlers in Texas dancing the "Fandango."
What dances are popular with your cultural group?

LITERATURE AND FOLKLORE (10 Points)

Students may display books, stories or poetry from noted members of their cultural group. For example, an Anglo-American group might display the writings of **J. Frank Robie** on Texas folklore, or the Pulitzer-prize winning novelist **Larry McMurtry.** Several of McMurtry's novels have been made into movies, including the *The Last Picture Show* and *Terms of Endearment.* Students may also write up and display some of the well-known legends, tales or folklore of their group.

ARCHITECTURE (10 Points)

Students may display pictures, drawings or photographs of buildings representative of members of their cultural group. For example, one interesting form of architecture used by Native Americans on the Great Plains was the **tepee.** An Anglo-American group might show pictures of buildings designed by architect **Philip Johnson,** including Pennzoil Place in Houston and the Amon Carter Museum of Western Art in Fort Worth.

The Amon Carter Museum, Ft. Worth.
What other buildings did Philip Johnson design in Texas?

LANGUAGE (10 Points)

Students may display any words from the language of their cultural group that have become part of the English language. For example, the techniques of the Texan cowboy were borrowed from the Mexican *vaquero.* Along with these techniques, many Spanish words were introduced into our language—including corral, lariat, rodeo, lasso, sombrero and mesquite.

HOLIDAYS (10 Points)

Students may display items, articles or signs showing which holidays their cultural group celebrates. For example, most people celebrate New Year's Eve on December 31st. This holiday is marked by late-night parties and dancing. However, Jewish Americans observe their own special New Year, called **Rosh Hashanah,** in late September or early October. This holiday is usually observed with quiet prayers and thinking about one's actions in the year just ending.

COSTUMES (10 Points)

Students may display pictures, drawings or photographs of people dressed in the traditional costumes of their cultural group.

BONUS: For each student who wears a traditional costume representative of his or her selected culture on the day of the fair, the team will receive a bonus of 10 points.

A Comanche in traditional dress.
What traditional clothing is worn by members of the ethnic group you represent?

REPORTING ON YOUR CULTURAL GROUP

The members of each team will also be expected to make a brief report about their cultural group to the rest of the class. On the day following the Cultural Fair, members of each group will make an oral report to the class. The report will be about the cultural group they have represented at the Cultural Fair. The report can consist of some or all of the following:

- what they have learned about their cultural group
- some of the interesting and unusual customs of their cultural group
- how their cultural group adds to Texas' multicultural society
- the contributions of their group to American society

CULTURAL GROUPS IN OTHER PARTS OF THE WESTERN HEMISPHERE

EXTENDING THE ACTIVITY

In this activity you learned about the different cultural groups of Texas. However, cultural groups are not unique to Texas alone. In fact, many different types of cultural groups exist throughout the Western Hemisphere. What are they like? What are their customs, traditions, folkways and religious beliefs?

YOUR TASK

Choose one cultural group to investigate that exists in the Western Hemisphere outside of the United States. Complete the following research guide for that cultural group. Then, use the information to write a short essay describing that group.

Research Guide

Name of Cultural Group:

- ☆ What are some of the group's traditions, customs and folkways?
- ☆ What are the religious beliefs of the cultural group?
- ☆ Describe some of its art, music and dance.
- ☆ Describe some of the homes, buildings and churches.
- ☆ Describe some of the group's folklore and works of literature.

GATHERING INFORMATION

Find information about the group you have chosen to investigate, by using:

- ☆ **Encyclopedias:** look for articles that are listed under the group's name.
- ☆ **History Books:** check the index for information about the group.

REVIEWING YOUR UNDERSTANDING

Directions: Fill in your Vocabulary Cards. Then complete the project that follows.

Texas State Fair

What is it?

Where is it held?

Multicultural

Define the term:

Name three ethnic groups in Texas.

Recent Immigrant Groups to Texas

Throughout its history, Texas has attracted ethnic groups from all over the world. Today, immigrants to Texas continue to come from many different countries. Each group brings to Texas its own unique traditions, customs, folkways and religious beliefs. The following information table shows where most recent immigrants to Texas have come from:

IMMIGRANTS SETTLING IN TEXAS (1993)

Mexico	China	Philippines	Vietnam	Russia
31,733	3,606	2,031	5,173	808

Use an **atlas** and find where these countries are located. Then, write in the names of the countries on a copy of the map below. Draw a line from each country to Texas.

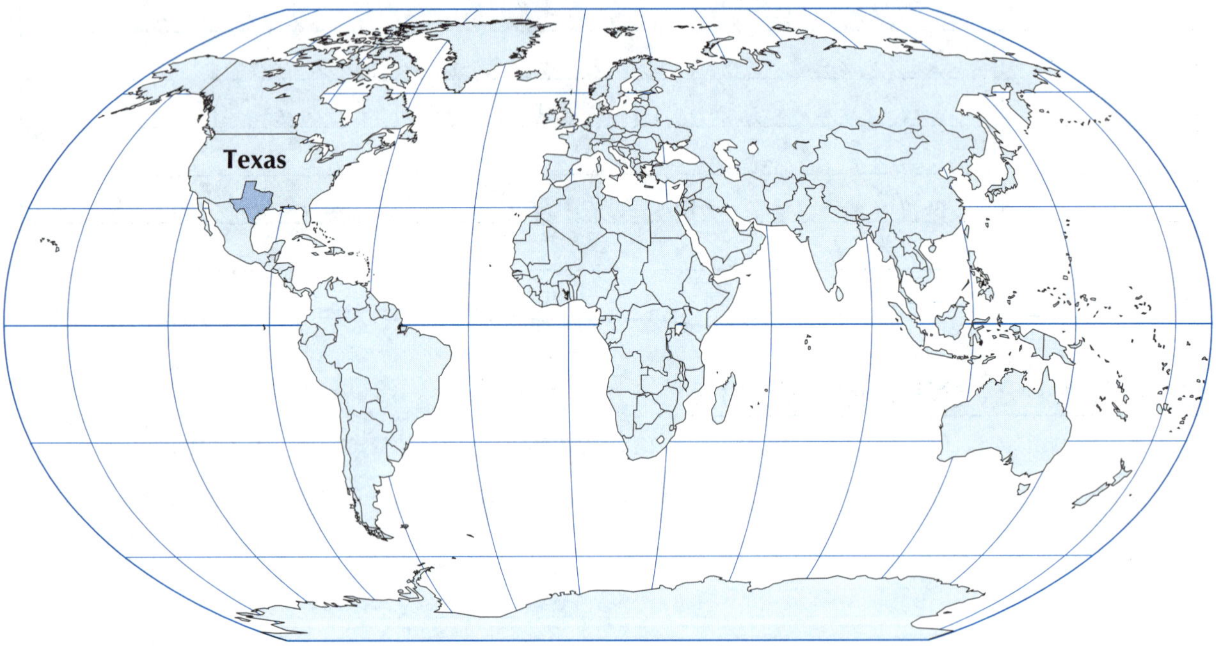

THINK ABOUT IT

Do you have any friends who are immigrants to the United States?

- From which country did they come?
- If their former countries are not listed on the chart, find their location in an atlas and add them to your map.
- Ask your friends why their families came to the United States. Write down some of their reasons.
- Do your friends remember life in the countries they came from?
- What are some of the things your friends remember most about life in their previous homeland?

SUMMARIZING YOUR UNDERSTANDING

Directions: Use your knowledge to complete the following graphic organizers.

WAYS THAT GROUPS OF PEOPLE CAN BE CLASSIFIED

1.

2.

3.

4.

IMMIGRANT GROUPS AND WHY THEY CAME TO TEXAS

1. Group:
   Reason:

2. Group:
   Reason:

3. Group:
   Reason:

4. Group:
   Reason:

BASIC INSTITUTIONS IN SOCIETY

1.

2.

3.

4.

5.

FACT AND OPINION STATEMENTS

Use this reading passage to answer the questions that follow:

(1) Sandra Day O'Connor was born on March 26, 1930, in El Paso, Texas. **(2)** After graduating from college, she began her career as a judge in Arizona. **(3)** She served as a county judge in Arizona. **(4)** In 1979, she was appointed to the Arizona Court of Appeals. **(5)** Everyone believes she was the smartest judge in Arizona. **(6)** In 1981, President Ronald Reagan nominated her to the U.S. Supreme Court. **(7)** When she took her seat on the high court, she became the first female Associate Justice in the history of the Supreme Court. **(8)** Since her appointment, she has done a far better job than most other Justices of the Supreme Court.

Sandra Day O'Connor.
What do you know about this remarkable woman from Texas?

Distinguishing Fact from Opinion

1. What are the numbers of two factual statements?
2. What are the numbers of two opinion statements?

READING A CHART

The U.S. Census Bureau asked if people spoke a language other than English at home. For those who answered yes, here are the languages they reported speaking:

LANGUAGES OTHER THAN ENGLISH SPOKEN AT HOME: 1990 AND 1980

LANGUAGE	NUMBER (in thousands) 1990	1980
Spanish	17,345	11,116
French	1,930	1,609
German	1,548	1,587
Chinese	1,319	631
Italian	1,309	1,618
Tagalog (*Filipino*)	843	452
Polish	723	821
Korean	626	266
Vietnamese	507	195
Portuguese	431	352

Use the information in the chart to answer the following questions:

1. Which was the most common language, other than English, spoken in American homes in 1990?
2. Which European languages declined in use in the decade from 1980 to 1990?
3. Which language spoken at home had the largest numerical increase from 1980 to 1990?
4. Where do you think people who speak Tagalog come from?
5. Which Asian language is spoken most in American homes?
6. Which languages spoken at home more than doubled from 1980 to 1990?

FACTS AND FIGURES ABOUT THE PEOPLE OF TEXAS

DID YOU KNOW THAT ...

Gender: In Texas there are 8,620,547 females (1990 Census).
There are 8,365,963 males in Texas (1990 Census).

Age: About 28% of the people in Texas are under 18 years of age.
About 10% of the population are 65 or older.

JUNETEENTH TEXAS STYLE

The Emancipation Proclamation was issued by President Lincoln on January 1, 1863. News of the Proclamation did not reach Texas until June 19, 1865. As a result, June 19th or "Juneteenth," is now celebrated by African Americans in Texas. On January 1, 1980 the Texas legislature made "Juneteenth" a state holiday. Texas was the first state in the Union to so honor emancipation.

THE POLES COME TO TEXAS

Late in 1854, about 150 Poles set sail for Texas. They landed in Galveston. On foot, they marched inland and established a community east of San Antonio at Panna Maria. This community was the first Polish settlement in North America.

CAN YOU HELP ME READ THAT STREET SIGN?

In Southwest Houston, the Chinese-American community has grown over the years. The "New Chinatown" community is now quite large. This has prompted the city of Houston to add some street signs written in Chinese characters.

MEXICAN AMERICANS IN TEXAS

In the United States today, over half of the Hispanic population lives in just two states—California and Texas. Texas also boasts four of the ten largest Hispanic cities: San Antonio (4th), Houston (5th), El Paso (6th) and Dallas (9th).

AFRICAN AMERICANS IN TEXAS

Three states had African American populations of over 2 million in 1990: New York, California and Texas. However, Texas had only one of the nation's ten cities with the largest number of African Americans—Houston (7th).

TEXAS: A MIX OF RESIDENTS

In the census of 1990, Texas had the largest number of persons who reported their general ancestry category as "American." At the same time 6 of every 10 foreign born residents in Texas were not U.S. citizens.

CHAPTER 5

ECONOMICS

Peanut harvesting in Pearsall

Oil drilling in the Gulf of Mexico

Cattle ranching in the Panhandle

Economics concerns itself with how people earn money and what they buy. It also concerns itself with banks, factories, stores and farms, and how they work. In this chapter you will learn about the things that are needed to make goods and to provide services—natural resources, labor, capital goods and knowledge. You will also learn about the risks of starting your own business, about conserving natural resources, and about the factors influencing international trade.

5A HOW WOULD YOU SPEND YOUR MONEY?

In this activity, you will make some decisions about how to spend your money. This activity introduces you to two ideas in economics —scarcity and opportunity cost. Look for the following important words:

★ Economics
★ Scarcity
★ Opportunity Cost
★ Production
★ Consumer
★ Consumption

To help you find these terms, the ★ symbol will appear in the margin where the term is first explained.

Today must be your lucky day. You have opened the mail and found a birthday card from your favorite aunt and uncle. Inside the card is a gift of one hundred dollars. Excitedly, you ask your mother, "What do you think I should do with this money?" She says there are many things you could do it. She suggests you make a list of different ways of using the money. On a separate sheet of paper, list the things you might like to do with the hundred dollars:

I Want:	It Would Cost:
1.	$
2.	$
3.	$

If you are like most people, the items you want will cost more that $100. So you have to make a choice. You look over the items on your list. How would you spend the money?

You may not have realized it, but you were just involved in economics. In fact, whenever you make choices about how to use your money, you are involved with economics.

THE PROBLEM OF SCARCITY

★ **Economics** is the study of how nations, businesses and individuals make things, buy things, spend money and save money. People who study economics are known as **economists.** Economists state that the basic problem of economics is the problem of scarcity.

Scarcity involves two basic economic ideas: ★

1. People usually have unlimited wants. For example, with your aunt and uncle's birthday gift of $100, you probably want more things than $100 could buy.
2. A society can produce only a limited number of things at one time. There is only a certain amount of available goods (video games, cars, clothes). There is only a certain amount of available services (car-washing, banking services, restaurants) people can obtain at any one time.

The problem of scarcity exists because (1) most people don't have enough money to buy all the things they want, and (2) a society can't produce an unlimited amount of goods and services.

★ CHECKING YOUR UNDERSTANDING ★

Suppose every person were given $5 million dollars a year. Do you think this would end the problem of scarcity? If yes, explain how. If not, explain why not.

As the problem of scarcity shows, there is an **opportunity cost** involved in every economic activity. This is the opportunity one gives up to do other things. For instance, assume you have saved enough to buy either a radio or a book. You decide to buy the radio. The "opportunity cost" of your radio was the book you might have bought. ★

LEARNING ABOUT PRODUCTION AND CONSUMPTION

EXTENDING THE ACTIVITY

Because of the problem of scarcity, every society must decide (1) what to produce (*make*) and (2) who will be allowed to consume (*use up*) these products. Most economies are based on the actions of two groups: businesses and consumers. Businesses are involved in production. **Production** is the act of making and producing goods and services. ★

THINK ABOUT IT

List some items that are produced by businesses.

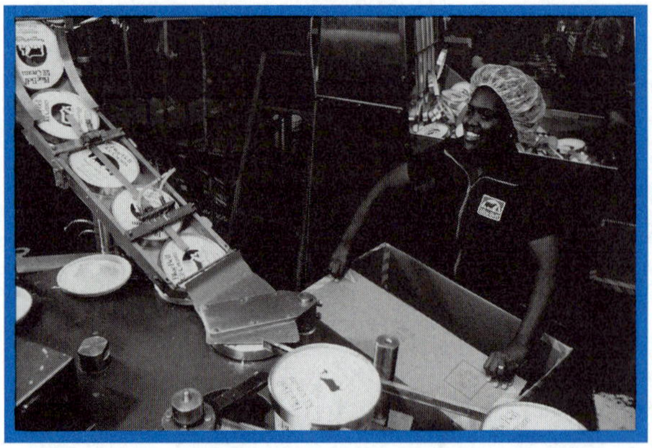

An ice cream making plant in Brenham.
How can you tell that this is a modern factory?

The Farmer's Market in Austin.
What items do you consume?

★ The **consumer** is the final person who buys and uses the goods and services made by businesses. Food, for example, is **consumed**—eaten up by the consumer. Other examples are buying a radio or using a barber's services by having a haircut. The final buying and using of goods and ★ services is called **consumption.**

THINK ABOUT IT

List some items you have consumed.

★ CHECKING YOUR UNDERSTANDING ★

Do you now understand the difference between production and consumption? Make a copy of this chart. Then place a check mark (✔) in the correct column, showing if the action involves production or consumption.

ACTION	PRODUCTION?	CONSUMPTION?
Drinking milk		
Building a house		
Reading a book		
Eating in a restaurant		
Growing corn		
Riding a roller coaster		
Driving a taxi		
Making steel		
Buying groceries		
Listening to a CD		
Making a wristwatch		
Teaching a class		

REVIEWING YOUR UNDERSTANDING

Directions: Fill in your Vocabulary Cards and complete the exercises that follow.

Production
What is production?
Give an example of production:

Consumption
What is consumption?
Give an example of consumption:

Dealing With The Problem of Scarcity

In this activity you learned about the problem of scarcity. Let us see how this problem might have an effect on your school. The following is a list of problems facing your school and the amounts of money needed to fix or repair the problem:

Problems	Amount Needed
The basketball team needs new uniforms	$3,000
New instruments are needed for the band	$4,000
The school wants to replace certain computers	$6,000
The school needs a new roof	$4,000
The school needs to be painted	$3,000

You have only $9,000 in your budget to spend. How would you spend the money? Assume you are writing a letter to your school newspaper. In a persuasive essay, explain your position.

Items That Can Be Consumed

In this activity, you learned about consumption. On a separate sheet of paper:

1. List **four** goods or services that you and your friends buy and consume.
2. List **two** goods or services that teenagers buy and consume.
3. List **two** goods or services that adults buy and consume.

5B WHAT ARE THE FUNCTIONS OF MONEY?

One way people exchange the goods and services they produce for other goods and services is through the use of money. In this activity, you will learn about money and some of its functions. Look for the following important words;

★ Barter ★ Medium of Exchange ★ Unit of Value ★ Storer of Value

A group of people may have goods that fill some but not all of their needs. Another group of people may have the resources to help the first group. For example, the people of Kuwait have oil, but need computers. The people of Japan have computers, but need oil. How do you think these two groups could help each other out?

DOES ANYONE WANT TO TRADE?

In this activity you will have the chance to learn first-hand how different groups help each other by trading goods and services. You will play a game called "Does Anyone Want To Trade?" Let's look at how it's played.

OBJECT OF THE GAME

The object of the game is to obtain items that you want from other students in your class. You should make as many trades as you can with other players to get those items.

GETTING STARTED

Your teacher will select six students to act as traders. The other students in the class will be observers.

HOW THE GAME IS PLAYED

The game will have two rounds.

ROUND ONE: BARTERING

Traders will **only** be allowed to exchange with other students items that they possess. ★ Direct trading of goods for other goods is known as **"barter."** For example, you might have a chicken to eat, but want to eat a fish. You would have to find someone to trade with who had a fish and wanted to eat chicken.

The table on page 249 shows:

1. what each trader has for exchange.

2. what each trader wants.

TRADERS	What They Have To Exchange*	What They Want
Trader A	5 pencils 	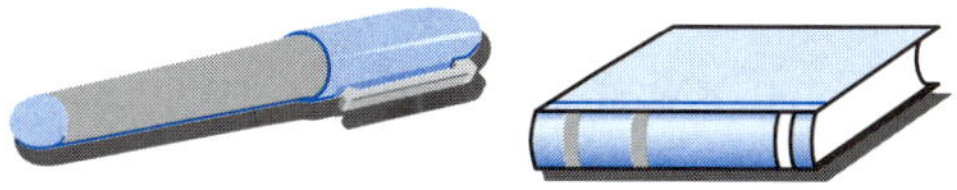
Trader B	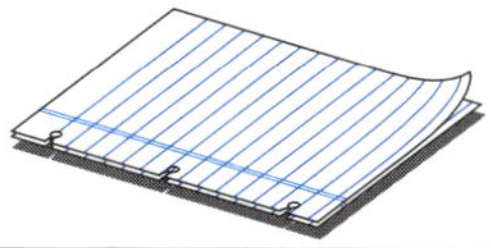 10 sheets of paper	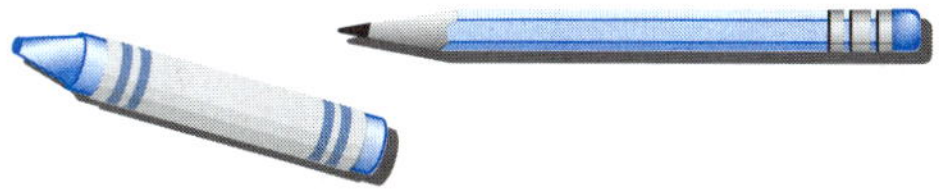
Trader C	 6 crayons	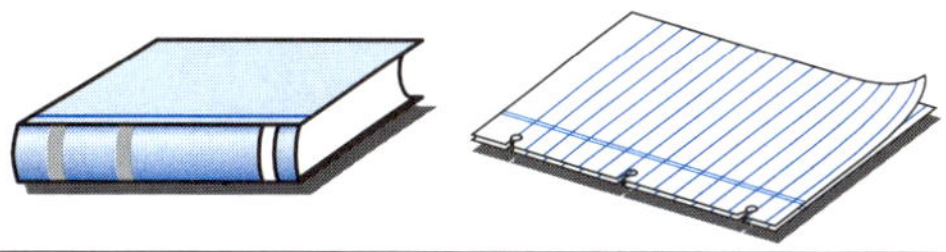
Trader D	 2 school books	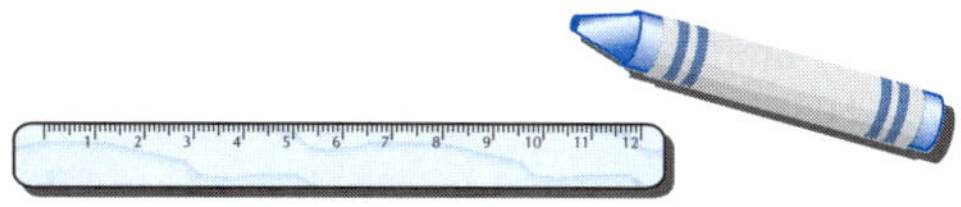
Trader E	4 rulers 	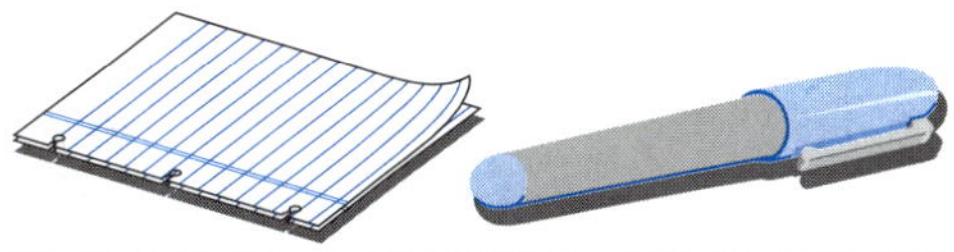
Trader F	5 pens 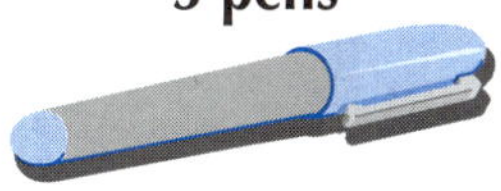	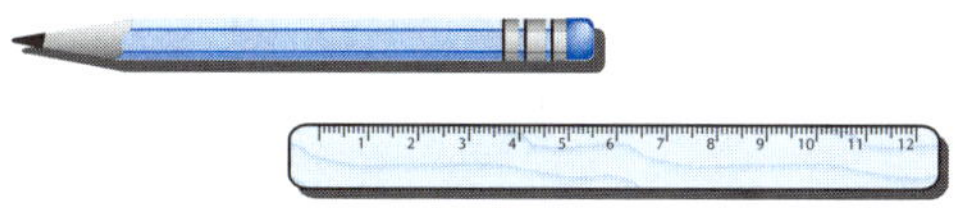

**All items for trade will be supplied by your teacher.*

Each trader must barter for the items he or she wants by using some or all of the items he or she has.

Round One of the game will take about 5 to 8 minutes. Afterwards, observers (*the rest of the class*) will answer the questions in the box to the right.

> ***DEBRIEFING SHEET***
>
> **1.** Describe what is happening among the traders.
>
> **2.** Do you see any problems developing among the traders?
>
> **3.** What steps would you suggest to make trading easier?

ROUND TWO: USING MONEY

Students who were traders will now become observers. Six different students are chosen to be traders. Each new trader will be given 25 paper clips in addition to the items mentioned in the above table. Paper clips are the **only** accepted form of payment for other goods during the game. In other words, a trader can no longer trade crayons for paper or rulers for books. Instead, a trader must pay for books, crayons, paper or rulers with paper clips. All traders will decide for themselves how many paper clips they want to give up for the items they want.

Trading now begins again for about 5 to 8 minutes. Observers will describe what is happening during Round Two.

> ***DEBRIEFING SHEET***
>
> **1.** Describe what is happening between the traders.
>
> **2.** Was trading any easier in this round?
>
> **3.** If so, explain what made trading easier in this round.

REVIEWING WHAT YOU HAVE LEARNED

In this activity, the paper clips acted or functioned as something known as **"money."** ★ Let's examine this concept more closely. Money is a **medium of exchange**—something that is accepted by everyone for all goods and services. Without money, Trader A, who wanted pens, had to find a pen owner who wanted pencils. With money, Trader A can sell pencils to anyone. The money (*paper clips*) he or she receives in payment for pencils will then be accepted by other traders. Money can thus be exchanged for any goods and services the trader wants. In this way, money serves as a medium of exchange—it is used **in exchange** for other goods and services.

WHAT OTHER THINGS DOES MONEY DO?

Money does other things besides acting as a medium of exchange. See if you can figure out another function (*use*) of money based on the following story:

> **Story #1: GOING TO THE SUPERMARKET**
>
> One day you go to the supermarket. You see that milk is selling for $2.00 a gallon, bread is selling for $1.00 a loaf and butter is selling for $1.50 a pound.
>
> Based on this information, what other purpose does money perform in this case?

★ If you said that a second function of money is to act as a **unit of value,** you would be correct. This means that money is used to tell us the prices of different things. In the United States, we use *dollars* and *cents* as money.

In Story #1, the price of a pound of butter is one dollar and fifty cents. Stating prices in this way makes it easy for anyone to quickly see the value of different items. For example, in the supermarket, we can see that a gallon of milk is twice as valuable as a loaf of bread. We know this because $2.00 is twice as much as $1.00

Now let's see if you can figure out a third important function of money:

Story #2: SAVING MONEY FOR A PAIR OF BOOTS

You decide that you want a new pair of boots. Each week, you save some money from your allowance. You put this money in the bank. After a year, you have saved $100.00. You go to the bank to take out the money to buy the boots.

Can you now figure out this third function of money?

A bootmaker in Nocona.
Do you own a pair of boots?

If you said that another function of money is to store value, you would be correct. To serve as a **storer of value,** money has to last a long time. We would not use apples, ★ for example, as money. Apples would spoil after a time, and people would not accept spoiled apples. That is why we use long-lasting objects like metal coins and expensive paper for money.

★ CHECKING YOUR UNDERSTANDING ★

What other objects do you think would be good to use as money? Explain why you picked those objects.

ASIDE: TYPES OF MONEY

When we think of money today, we usually think of metal coins, paper bills and checks. However, the idea of money is not new. Money has a long and fascinating history.

We do not know when money was first used. However, we do know its history reaches back in time to humankind's earliest written records. Money has taken many strange and different forms. Some societies have used feathers, stones, beads, shells and rock salt as money.

Yap is a small island in the Pacific Ocean. The people of Yap once used stone disks as money. Some were only the size of a small plate. However, some stones measured up to 12 feet across. Try putting these stone disks in your pocket!!!

CONTINUED

The Admiralty Islands are a small group of islands in the South Pacific. The people of these islands used dog's teeth as money. Some were traded one tooth at a time. Others were strung together to form a necklace.

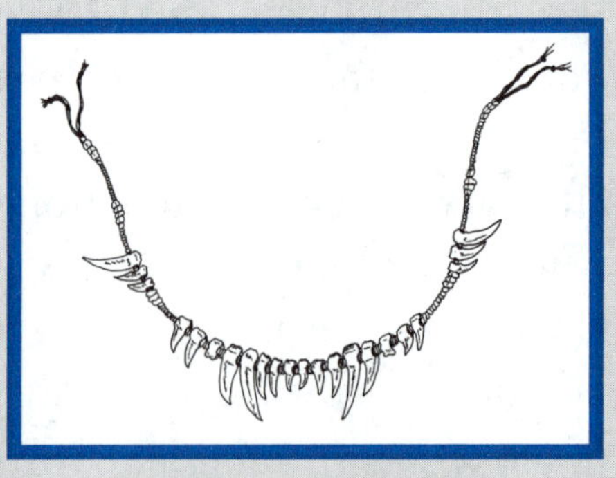

The Pacific islanders of Santa Cruz used tiny red feathers as money. The brighter the feather, the more value it was given by the people of this island community. The feathers were glued together and tied into a fancy coil. Some of these coils reached 30 feet in length. The feathers would be used during marriage ceremonies or to buy objects, like canoes.

Societies in the Middle East began developing coins with a standard value several thousands of years ago. With such standard coins, people could put a value on things as different as elephants, books, pottery and olive oil. Coins were most often made of precious metals, like gold and silver. Indeed, even into the early twentieth century, the international monetary system was based on gold.

WHAT DOES $1,000,000 LOOK LIKE?

EXTENDING THE ACTIVITY

Many people dream of becoming a millionaire one day. But have you given much thought to what $1,000,000 might look like? Let's see.

There are four quarters in $1. How many quarters would there be in $1,000,000?

Answer: Multiply $1,000,000 by 4 (*the number of quarters in $1*). Four times 1,000,000 equals 4,000,000. So there are 4,000,000 quarters in $1,000,000.

Let's look at some other interesting situations involving $1,000,000.

HOW MANY OF THESE *"MILLION DOLLAR"* QUESTIONS CAN YOU ANSWER?

1. A million one-dollar bills, stacked one on top of another, would form a pile about 625 feet high. Each floor of an office building is 10 feet tall. How many floors would an office building have in order to be as tall as a pile of a million dollar bills?
2. A dollar bill is about 6 inches long. Two dollar bills placed end to end would be one foot long. A mile is 5,280 feet long. How many dollar bills, placed end to end, would it take to reach a mile? How many miles would 1,000,000 dollar bills extend, if placed end to end?
3. It's not easy carrying around $1,000,000. If you had $1,000,000 in pennies, it would weigh over 57 tons. An elephant generally weighs 3 tons. How many elephants weigh the same as $1,000,000 in pennies?

REVIEWING YOUR UNDERSTANDING

Directions: Fill in your Vocabulary Cards and complete the organizer that follows.

Barter
Define barter:
Give an example of barter:

Money
What is money?
Give an example of money:

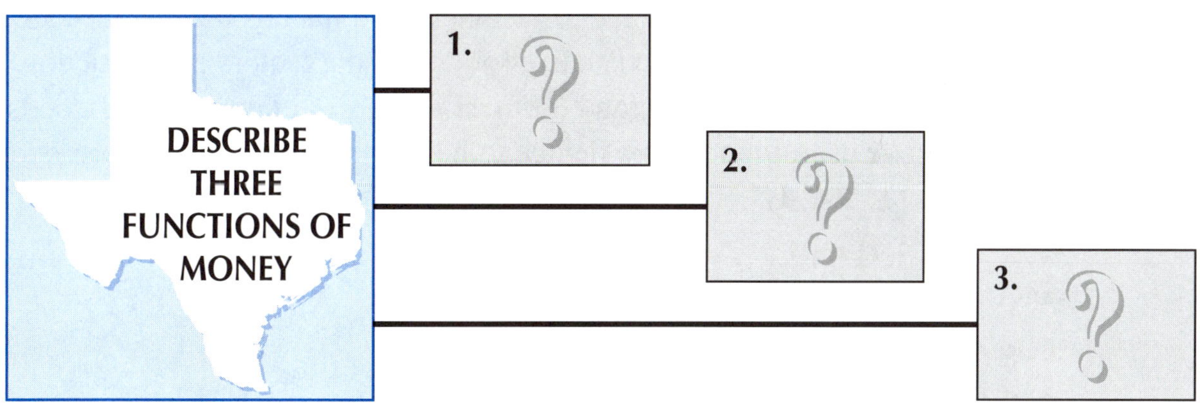

5C HOW WOULD YOU ILLUSTRATE THE FACTORS OF PRODUCTION?

In this activity, you will learn about the things that go into the making of a product. These items are called the factors of production. Look for the following important words:

★ Goods and Services	★ Land	★ Capital Goods
★ Factors of Production	★ Labor	★ Entrepreneurs

In the first activity of this chapter, you learned about the "production" and "consumption" of goods and services. Let's take a closer look at goods and services.

WHAT ARE GOODS AND SERVICES?

★ ☆ **Goods.** Goods are things that people make. For example toys, clothes, cars and houses are goods. Department stores, shoe stores, bakeries and restaurants all sell goods.

> **★ CHECKING YOUR UNDERSTANDING ★**
>
> Name two other "goods" that people make.

★ ☆ **Services.** Services are things that people do for others. People who provide services include electricians, plumbers, barbers and auto mechanics.

> **★ CHECKING YOUR UNDERSTANDING ★**
>
> Name two other "services" that people supply to others.

THE FACTORS OF PRODUCTION

★ The **factors of production** are all the things needed to produce goods and services. Think of a can of soda: what materials, labor, machinery and management skills came together to produce it? To find out, let's visualize (or "see") the factors of production.

There are four factors of production: land (*natural resources*), labor, capital goods, and entrepreneurship. A useful mnemonic device to help you remember the factors of production would be C-E-L-L.

LAND (NATURAL RESOURCES)

Economists use the term "land" to mean the resources found in nature. These include metals, minerals, water, plants, soil and animals. For example, steel is needed to make a car. Iron and coal are needed to make steel. These resources—iron and coal—are taken from the Earth. Natural resources are the starting point for producing goods. No matter how advanced a society is or how skilled its workers are, it cannot make goods without natural resources.

Canoeing on the Brazos River. *Identify a natural resource in this picture.*

★ CHECKING YOUR UNDERSTANDING ★

List some of the natural resources that would be needed to build a house.

LABOR

Labor is the work that people do to make goods or provide services. Labor includes the talents, training, skills and knowledge of the people who contribute to making things and providing services.

Labor involves many kinds of workers. These include plumbers, bus drivers, welders, police officers, fire fighters, nurses, teachers, bankers and singers. All goods and services include some human labor. For example, even a completely **automated** (*machine-run*) factory needs workers to design, build and run the machinery.

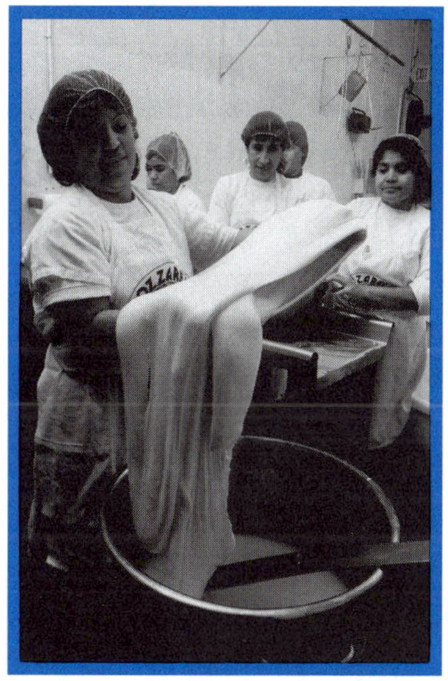

A cheese factory in Dallas producing mozzarella cheese. *Identify a factor of production in this picture.*

★ CHECKING YOUR UNDERSTANDING ★

List some of the workers whose labor would be needed to build a house.

CAPITAL GOODS

Capital goods are goods created to make other goods and services. For example, machines and tools are capital goods. They are used to make other goods or to help perform other services. Buildings, railroads and trucks may also be capital goods if they are used to produce other goods or services.

★ CHECKING YOUR UNDERSTANDING ★

List some of the capital goods you would need to build a house.

★ ENTREPRENEURSHIP

Land, labor and capital goods must be combined and organized to make something. People who bring these factors of production together are called **entrepreneurs.**

Entrepreneurs are the owners of businesses. They combine, coordinate and organize the other three factors of production. What makes an entrepreneur do this? An entrepreneur risks his or her money in the hope of making a **profit.** A profit is the amount of money left over after the expenses of the business have been paid.

Often a business grows too large and complex for one person alone to do everything. Then the business is run by people called **managers.** The managers work for the entrepreneur.

★ CHECKING YOUR UNDERSTANDING ★

What is the person called who risks his or her money to make a profit?

Making fruitcake in Corsicana.
Can you identify a capital good in this picture?

A house under construction.
Who combines and organizes the factors of production to build this house?

"SEEING" THE FACTORS OF PRODUCTION

"Seeing" or "visualizing" is one of the best ways to understand something. The idea is to connect a concrete picture with an abstract idea. You have just learned about the four factors of production. Now tie a picture to these factors. The picture makes the idea easier to understand. Let's look at these factors of production together. This photograph shows three of the four factors of production. The fourth factor was responsible for bringing these three factors together.

★ CHECKING YOUR UNDERSTANDING ★

Look carefully at the details in the photograph. Then explain which items in the photograph illustrate each factor of production. Remember, only three of the four factors are directly shown.

Now, let's see how well you can find on your own, pictures of the factors of production. Look through some newspapers or magazines. Find a photograph or illustration to show each factor of production. You may use one photograph or illustration to show more than one of the four factors of production.

Generally, all four of the factors of production are needed to produce a good or a service. For instance, a farmer needs soil and water (*land*) to grow a crop. In addition, fuel and machinery are necessary (*capital goods*). The farmer must also work hard at plowing, planting, fertilizing and harvesting (*labor*). Finally, the farmer must be able to put all three of these factors of production together in a reasonable way to ensure a good harvest (*entrepreneurship*).

THINK ABOUT IT

Can you think of any goods or services that require only three out of the four factors of production? Explain your answer.

IDENTIFYING RESOURCES IN THE WESTERN HEMISPHERE

EXTENDING THE ACTIVITY

In this activity you learned about the four factors of production. Among the types of resources are land (natural resources), labor (human resources) and capital goods.

Let's take a look at some of the natural resources found in the Western Hemisphere. For each country in the chart on page 258, list some of its natural resources. Where the chart asks for a Caribbean nation, select one country located in the Caribbean Sea. Then select one country in South America.

Shoppers in Quebec, Canada.
What natural resources do you think you might find in Canada?

THINK ABOUT IT

What do you think are the three most important natural resources a country could have?

COUNTRY	MAJOR NATURAL RESOURCES
United States	
Canada	
Mexico	
Caribbean Nation	
South American Nation	

You can find the information called for in the chart above in a **reference book.** In earlier chapters, you learned about using an almanac, atlas, encyclopedia and dictionary. These reference books are usually found in the reference section of your library.

REVIEWING YOUR UNDERSTANDING

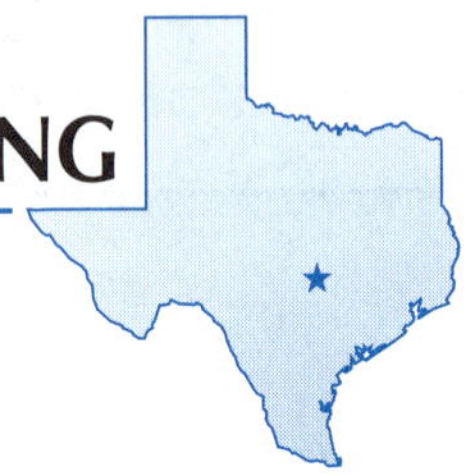

Directions: Fill in your Vocabulary Cards and complete the project that follows.

Goods

What are goods?

Give two examples of goods:

Services

What is a service?

Give two examples of a service:

The Factors of Production

The factors of production are used to make different goods and services. Any factor of production can be used in many different ways. For example, aluminum (*land/natural resource*) may be used to make a soda can, a bracelet or an automobile part.

1. What other things can be made of aluminum?
2. A carpenter (*labor*) may build furniture or a house with his or her labor. What other things can a carpenter build?
3. A truck (*capital good*) may haul bricks or carry furniture. In what other ways can a truck be used?
4. A business person (*entrepreneur*) may decide to invest his or her money in starting a farm or a shoe store. What else can an entrepreneur invest in?

5D WOULD YOU START YOUR OWN BUSINESS?

In this activity, you will learn about the free enterprise system by imagining what it is like to start your own business. Look for the following important words:

★ Free Enterprise System ★ Capitalism ★ Occupation ★ Livestock

We live in a society that makes it possible for anyone, with hard work, to own a business. It's possible because Americans live under a way of life known as the **free enterprise system.** ★ Under this system (*sometimes called* ***capitalism***), anyone is free to start a business.

Individuals who want to start a business invest their money in the hope of making a profit. A profit is the amount of money left over after a business pays its expenses. A business can survive only if it continues to make a profit.

Consumers play an important role in the free enterprise system. Consumers (*buyers*) are the people who ultimately determine what will and what will not be produced. Consumers buy from businesses that sell the best products or services at the lowest prices. If consumers refuse to buy a product, the business that makes that product will stop producing. It may even go out of business.

A class visiting a sugar packaging factory.
Are there any factories in your area? If so, what do they produce?

If enough consumers buy a product, a business can make a great deal of money. No wonder that in 1995 almost nine million new businesses were started in the United States. How would it feel to start your own business? What's it like to be a young entrepreneur? In this activity, you will have an opportunity to imagine what it might be like to start your own business.

STARTING A BUSINESS

Every business begins with an idea. To start, you must choose some kind of work that you enjoy and you think you would be good at. Here are some suggestions:

- **Pet Care:** Caring for household pets: feeding, walking and washing pets.
- **Book Covers:** Making book covers with your own designs on them.
- **Lawn Service:** Mowing lawns.
- **Other (Your Idea):** ___?___

Now it's time for you to make a choice. Which business would you like to try?

> My business will be ___?___ because I like ___?___ .

GETTING INFORMATION AND ADVICE

Before starting a business, it is a very good idea to get advice from other people. Speak to your parent or guardian. Explain that you would like to know some of the advantages and disadvantages of starting a business like the one you are imagining. On a separate sheet of paper make a list of their suggestions.

Advantages	Disadvantages
1.	1.
2.	2.
3.	3.

THE FACTORS OF PRODUCTION

Earlier in this chapter you learned about the **factors of production.** On a separate sheet of paper list the factors of production you would need for your business:

Land (Natural Resources):
Labor:
Capital Goods:
Entrepreneurship:

FINDING OUT IF THERE WILL BE A PROFIT

Starting a business takes money. You may need money to buy raw materials (*land*) and for tools and equipment (*capital goods*). Sometimes you may also need money to hire other workers (*labor*). About how much money would you need to start your new business? With the following chart, first estimate what the costs might be in your first month of business (*left side of chart*). Then on the right hand side of the chart try to figure out how much money you might earn from selling your product or service.

My First Month of Business

A. Cost of Materials:	?	Selling price of the item or service:	?
B. Cost of Advertising:	?		
C. Other:	?		
(add A, B, C, for monthly costs)		Number of items or services you can sell each month: ?	
		Multiply selling price by number of items sold. This is your	
Monthly Costs:	?	Monthly Income:	?

Subtract your monthly costs (column 1) from your monthly income (column 2):

Total Monthly Income: \$?
− (minus) Monthly Costs: \$?

Monthly Profit or Loss: \$?

★ CHECKING YOUR UNDERSTANDING ★

You now have some idea of the requirements and the risk of starting your own business. If your monthly costs amount to more than your monthly income, you will have a loss. Based on what you have learned in this activity, do you think you would like to start your own business?

❒ Yes ❒ No Explain your answer.

LEARNING ABOUT DIFFERENT OCCUPATIONS

EXTENDING THE ACTIVITY

You have just learned about some of the things to consider in starting a business. Now ★ let's look at some of the other types of businesses and **occupations** (*jobs*) from which you might choose when you get older. There are three general types of occupations:

- Using the land
- Making things
- Providing services

USING THE LAND: FARMING, FISHING AND MINING

Farming, fishing and mining are three occupations that use the land and its natural resources. **Farmers** are involved in **agriculture** (*growing crops*). Texas farmers grow cotton, sorghum, rice, wheat, corn, rye, oats and barley. To grow crops, farmers may use **fertilizers** that add minerals and other nutrients to the soil. Farmers also use **pesticides** to kill insects that attack their crops.

★ **Ranchers** are people who raise **livestock** such as cattle, chickens and pigs. The livestock are then sold for meat. Some farmers raise cows for their milk and for cheese products that can be made from milk. Many Texas farmers and ranchers enter their best crops and livestock in contests at the State Fair of Texas, held each year in Dallas.

A worker sorts peaches in Weatherford.
What agricultural items are grown in your area?

Fishermen and miners also earn their living from the land. **Fishermen** in Texas make their living by catching fish primarily in the Gulf of Mexico. Texas is the only state with five major ports—Houston, Beaumont, Port Arthur, Corpus Christi and Texas City—all on the Gulf of Mexico.

★ CHECKING YOUR UNDERSTANDING ★

1. Name two crops that Texas farmers grow.
2. What factors of production go into the operation of running a shrimp boat in the Gulf of Mexico?

Ranchers at work at the King Ranch.
What skills do ranchers need?

Workers drilling for oil.
What products do miners find when they dig deep below the ground?

Miners dig or drill deep holes in the ground to try to find minerals such as coal. Mining is of great importance to Texas. There are many miners in Texas who drill into the Earth looking for oil or natural gas. Coal, oil and gas can be burned to make energy for heat, or to produce electricity. Oil is used to make other products, like gasoline, fertilizers and artificial rubber. If Texas were an independent nation, it would be the world's fifth-largest oil producer.

★ CHECKING YOUR UNDERSTANDING ★

Name two other jobs that use the land.

MAKING THINGS: MANUFACTURING AND INDUSTRY

Other people work at making things. Economists call this **manufacturing** or **industry.** About 15% of Texas workers have manufacturing jobs. Construction is the fastest-growing major industry in Texas.

Most people with jobs in industry work in factories. **Factories** are buildings in which a product is produced. In Texas, some factory workers make steel and rubber products—such as cars, washing machines or tires. Still other factory workers make products out of clay or glass, such as bricks, roof tiles, windows and dishes. Some work in high-tech industries, making computers, aircraft or medical instruments.

The Comanche Peak Power Plant.
What skills are needed by workers at a high-tech power plant?

★ CHECKING YOUR UNDERSTANDING ★

Name two other jobs where a product is made.

SERVICES: TRANSPORTATION, SALES, BANKING, EDUCATION, ENTERTAINMENT

Today, most people do not actually make things. They work in **service industries** instead. These workers provide a **service** for other people.

Some workers serve others by moving people or goods from one place to another. This work is known as **transportation.** The transportation system in Texas is excellent. The state has the largest system of roads and highways in the United States. There are over 275,000 miles of highways in Texas.

A highway leading to the McDonald Observatory on Davis Mountain. *Which highways do you live near?*

Other people buy goods in large amounts and resell them locally. This is what a department store or grocery store does. Still others serve us by giving us information, entertaining us, teaching us, cleaning our clothes, cooking and serving our food, and investing our money. Doctors, bankers, lawyers, grocery store cashiers, teachers, nurses, telephone operators, waiters and hair dressers all provide a service.

★ CHECKING YOUR UNDERSTANDING ★

Name two other service industry jobs.

REVIEWING YOUR UNDERSTANDING

Directions: Fill in your Vocabulary Cards and complete the exercise that follows.

Free Enterprise System
What is the free enterprise system?
What are some of the features of the free enterprise system?

Occupations
What does the term "occupations" mean?
List some occupations that are open to people in society.

Occupations in Texas

Texas Non-Farm Occupations (1994)

★ CHECKING YOUR UNDERSTANDING ★

Use the information in the pie chart to answer the following questions.

1. What is the title of the pie chart?
2. What occupations are being compared?
3. What percentage of people are government workers?
4. In what occupation are the largest number of Texans employed?
5. In what occupation are the lowest number of Texans employed?
6. How many more people work in service occupations than in manufacturing?

Texas State Capitol at Austin.
Do you know anyone who works for the government of Texas?

5E HOW CAN WE HELP CONSERVE OUR NATURAL RESOURCES?

In this activity, you will learn more about the natural resources of Texas and think about ways to conserve them. Look for the following important words:

- ★ Minerals
- ★ Brainstorming
- ★ Conservation
- ★ Non-renewable Resources

Natural resources are the materials that are found in nature and are available for use. These include both the food we grow to eat and the materials we use to make products. Texas is a state that has many natural resources. It has large areas of fertile farmland for planting crops, grasslands for grazing cattle, forests for lumber and water for irrigation. In addition, Texas has many valuable minerals.

THE NATURAL RESOURCES OF TEXAS

Throughout its history, Texas has been rich in oil and gas. Up through the 1800s, coal was the main energy source in Texas. Coal was mined in the eastern part of the state. However, in the early 1900s, oil and gas became the preferred source of energy.

The first major discovery of oil occurred in 1894. While drilling a water well in Corsicana, workers struck oil. However, it was not until a huge oil field at Beaumont was discovered in 1901 that the future of Texas as an oil state was assured. Soon, other areas in Texas were discovered to have oil. Oil and gas fields are located in most counties of Texas. Texas is one of the nation's leading producers of oil and natural gas. Oil can also be used to make petroleum products, especially petrochemicals. The *petrochemical* industry has developed into one of Texas' biggest industries. This industry makes nylon, plastics and other products from oil.

An oil well in Beaumont.
Name two products made from oil.

★ CHECKING YOUR UNDERSTANDING ★

What other kinds of minerals can you think of?

Texas is also rich in other minerals. A ★ **mineral** is something found in the Earth, but is not a plant. Oil, natural gas and cement materials are the largest mineral industries in Texas. Stone, asphalt, magnesium, sulphur and gypsum are other important minerals found in Texas.

Producing lumber and other wood products is another major industry. Texas has many trees, especially in the Piney Woods area of East Texas. These trees are cut down and used to make paper products, lumber and plywood.

A sulphur mine in Texas.
What do you think sulphur is used for?

The Gulf Coast is Texas' center of commercial fishing. Fishermen haul in millions of gallons of fish each year. Texas is a major supplier of shrimp for the nation.

Texas is also known for its agriculture. It is one of the most important occupations in Texas. Texas has more fertile land than any other state. Much of this land is used for farming and ranching. About 3% of the state's workforce is employed in agriculture. Texas farmers grow cotton, sorghum grain, wheat, rice and peanuts. Farmers also raise cattle, sheep, poultry, hogs and turkeys. The number of farms in Texas have been decreasing. However, the average value of farm production has been increasing due to better farming practices and equipment.

Preparing apples for market in Turtle Creek.
What agricultural products are grown in Texas?

★ CHECKING YOUR UNDERSTANDING ★

Name two other farm crops that are grown in Texas.

THE NEED FOR CONSERVATION

Although Texas has many resources, we now realize that these resources will not last forever. People have therefore become very aware of the need for conservation. **Conservation** means the protection of natural resources to keep them from being ★ wasted or used up. In this activity, you and your classmates will be asked to think of ways to help conserve the natural resources of Texas.

Sometimes it is hard to come up with new ideas. One technique for thinking in new ways is known as brainstorming.

★ BRAINSTORMING

Through brainstorming, people in a group communicate their thoughts on a problem and propose new ideas to solve it. The excitement of hearing other people's ideas often helps the members of a brainstorming group think of new ideas of their own. People in business and government often use brainstorming to help solve difficult problems. In this activity, you and your classmates will use the brainstorming technique to see what ideas you can come up with to help conserve the natural resources of Texas.

Before you begin your brainstorming session, you should have some understanding of why most people think conservation of natural resources is important. Read the following selection written by a conservationist.

When people first settled in Texas, it seemed as if the land and resources would last forever. In the past fifty years, this view has begun to change. Texas is still rich in resources, but its supply is not endless.

The natural resources of Texas allow many of its people to enjoy a high standard of living. But Texans must learn to conserve their resources. This will enable future generations of Texans to live well and to preserve the beauty of their recreational areas. Preservation of local wildlife is also important to scientists who study plants and animals to find new uses for them. Finally, preserving clean water and air is important for the survival of our planet.

Bosque River in Waco—part of Texas' many beautiful recreational areas.
What areas in Texas do you like to visit?

There are many ways Texans can help to preserve their resources. Some natural areas, like Big Thicket and Big Bend, have been set aside as parks to protect them. Farmers can use different crops to avoid **erosion** (*washing or wearing away of the soil*). This will permit future generations to farm the same lands for a long time to come. It is equally important not to cut down too many trees. Forests should not be cut faster than new trees can grow to replace those cut down. In this way, Texans can preserve the forests and provide new lumber for the future.

CONTINUED

Water is another valuable natural resource. While rainfall is plentiful in East Texas, the western half of the state is dry. Farmers rely on irrigation to provide enough water to their crops. For this reason, it is important not to pollute water or waste it needlessly.

Non-renewable resources, like oil and natural gas, cannot be replaced. There is no way to use these resources and also preserve them. It is therefore important to put these resources to the best possible use and to avoid wasting them. In the past, each Texan with land used to drill his or her own well to recover oil. This led to producing more oil than could be used efficiently. It also reduced the underground pressure in the oil fields, making it harder for more oil to be taken out.

To make sure oil resources are not wasted, the state legislature passed new laws preventing oil wells from being drilled too close to one another. Landowners were forced to bring their plots of land together and to share the oil from a smaller number of wells. This allows the oil supply to last longer and made it possible to bring more oil out of the ground.

YOUR BRAINSTORMING SESSION BEGINS

Your teacher will divide the class into several small brainstorming groups. The members of each group should make a list of ways to help conserve the natural resources of Texas. Try to be as creative as possible. Members of each group should begin by stating any ideas they can think of to conserve natural resources.

Group ideas should be about preventing the waste of energy, stopping pollution of the environment or slowing the use of non-renewable resources. To the right is a short list of ideas to get you started.

After each group has listed its ideas, the whole class should meet. The whole class should then create a master list of good ideas for promoting conservation.

PROMOTING CONSERVATION IN TEXAS

- ☆ Turn electric lights off when you are not in a room.
- ☆ Recycle paper, glass and plastic.
- ☆ Do not run the tap water while brushing your teeth.
- ☆
- ☆
- ☆
- ☆

INTERPRETING A PRODUCT MAP OF TEXAS

EXTENDING THE ACTIVITY

As you have learned in Chapter 2, maps come in all different sizes and shapes. They can be also provide different kinds of information. The following map is called a **product map.** Look at the product map and then read the Skill Builder on page 271, to help you interpret the map.

SKILL BUILDER: INTERPRETING A PRODUCT MAP

On the product map, picture symbols are used to represent the agricultural and mineral products of Texas.

Questions: List **three** crops found in Texas.
Name **two** animals raised in Texas.
Name **two** minerals found in Texas.

The legend explains what each symbol represents. For example, each area in Texas that grows cotton is shown on the map with a small ball of cotton.

Questions: What does the symbol represent?
What does the symbol stand for?
What symbol is used for corn?
Which city is located near to where oil is produced?
Name **two** cities are located near manufacturing centers?

REVIEWING YOUR UNDERSTANDING

Directions: Fill in your Vocabulary Cards and complete the project that follows.

Natural Resources

What are natural resources?

Give two examples:

Non-Renewable Resources

What is a non-renewable resource?

Give two examples:

The Natural Resources of Texas

The list below contains the natural resources found in Texas and some of the products made from those resources. On a separate sheet of paper, copy the list. If the item is:

☆ a **natural resource** write **NR** ☆ a **product** write a **P**

1. forests
2. natural gas
3. oil
4. chairs
5. coal
6. lumber
7. chemicals
8. cars
9. plywood
10. shrimp
11. rice
12. books
13. calculators
14. cattle
15. clothing

5F HOW WOULD YOU PROMOTE THE ECONOMY OF TEXAS?

In this activity, you will look at many important resources of Texas. Then you will design a campaign to help convince foreign businesses to locate in Texas. Look for the following important words:

★ Investments ★ Governor

Texas Times
Vol. 1.4 No. 7 First Edition
Governor Meets With Foreign Officials In An Attempt To Attract Business To Texas

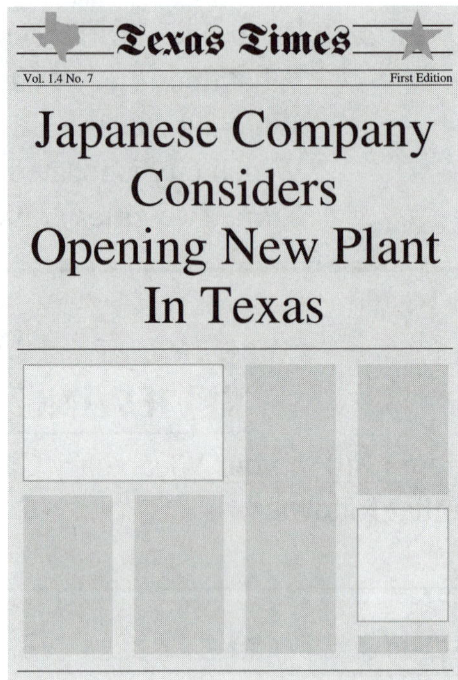
Texas Times
Vol. 1.4 No. 7 First Edition
Japanese Company Considers Opening New Plant In Texas

You may have noticed similar headlines in your local newspaper. Texas, like other states, tries to attract companies to build factories and locate their businesses in Texas. ★ These **investments** can mean more tax dollars for the state treasury and more jobs for state residents.

CREATING AN ECONOMIC PROFILE OF TEXAS

★ The **Governor** of Texas has many economic duties. One of the most important is to help the state's economy. Imagine that the Governor has asked your help to design an advertisement to attract companies to Texas. Before you can do this, you will need some information about the economy and resources of Texas. Use an almanac or encyclopedia to do your research. On a separate sheet of paper, complete the following information:

AN ECONOMIC PROFILE OF TEXAS

I. Information about the Geography and People of Texas

Total Area: ______________________
Acres of Forest Land: ______________________
Climate: ______________________
Major Geographic Features: ______________________
Population: ______________________
Rank in Population: ______________________

II. Information about the State's Economy

Major Natural Resources: ______________________
Major Industries: ______________________
Major Goods Manufactured: ______________________
Chief Agricultural Crops: ______________________
Chief Agricultural Products: ______________________
Chief Ports: ______________________
Unemployment Rate: ______________________

III. Other Information about the State

Major Tourist Attractions: ______________________
Texas State Motto: ______________________
Famous People Born In Texas: ______________________
Other Information About Texas: ______________________

A ship at the Port of Beaumont. *What are some of the state's other important ports?*

DESIGNING YOUR AD CAMPAIGN FOR TEXAS

On a separate piece of paper, create your advertisement to run in foreign countries. Ask yourself which features in the above economic profile you should focus on in trying to attract foreign businesses to Texas. Remember:

- ☆ artistic skill is **not** important
- ☆ creating an interesting and lively ad is essential
- ☆ search magazines and newspapers for pictures to use in your advertisement
- ☆ you may want to ask your parents for help in taking photographs for use in your advertisement

REVIEWING YOUR UNDERSTANDING

Directions: Fill in your Vocabulary Cards and complete the project that follows.

Foreign Investments

What are foreign investments?
How can they help the state of Texas?

Governor

Who is the current Governor of Texas?
What are some economic concerns of the Governor?

Creating An Economic Profile of Your Community

In this activity you created an economic profile of Texas. What about the community where you live? What is your community best known for? What are its chief crops or major industries? Its most important businesses?

Visit your school or local library. Ask the librarian for help in finding economic information about your community. Also, talk to your parents and other adults. On a separate piece of paper, copy the following chart. Ask them for help in completing the chart:

Economic Profile of My Community: ?

Climate:
Geographic Features:
Natural Resources:
Industries:
Manufactured Goods:
Agricultural Crops:
Agricultural Products:
Ports:
Tourist Attractions:

The Mission San Juan Capistrano in San Antonio attracts many visitors each year. *What attractions exist in your community?*

5G HOW INTERDEPENDENT ARE WE WITH FOREIGN COUNTRIES?

In this activity, you will learn how people in different countries have become economically interdependent (*dependent on each other*). Look for the following important words:

★ Interdependent ★ Imports ★ Exports ★ Hypothesis

Technologies like the telephone, fax, television, airplane and computer are said to be "shrinking" our world. Of course, the world isn't actually getting smaller; it just seems that way. Because of these new technologies, people have more contact with distant places than they had a long time ago.

THE WORLD'S GROWING INTERDEPENDENCE

This increased contact has made people around the world highly interdependent. Nations are **interdependent** when they depend on each other for goods and services. We **import** goods and services from foreign countries. Imported goods are those goods brought into the United States from other countries. Other countries equally depend on products from the United States.

The "Global Highway" carrying autos to Texas. *What other products are imported into Texas?*

> The leading foreign imports into Texas are cars, petroleum and petroleum products, iron, steel and chemicals. Japan and Germany are two of Texas' largest foreign trading partners.

Many American jobs depend on selling **exports.** Exports are goods sold from the United States to other countries.

> Texas exports oil-related and non-electrical machinery, electric and electronic equipment, lumber and wood products, stone, clay and glass products. Texas ranks second in the nation in the number of workers involved in producing goods and services for other countries.

THINK ABOUT IT

How many goods in your house do you think come from foreign countries?

❑ less than half ❑ about half ❑ more than half

★ At this point, your answer above is only a hypothesis. A **hypothesis** is an educated guess that may or may not turn out to be correct. In this activity, you will try to find out if your "guess" is correct. One way to do this is to conduct an inventory of the items in your home.

DOING AN INVENTORY IN YOUR HOME

Let's begin by looking at the contents of any **two** rooms of your home. Examine some of the items found there. Consider furniture, lamps and only smaller objects that you can easily move.

- ☆ You will find that many goods have the name of the **country of origin** (*country where they came from*) stamped or printed somewhere on them. For example, in the kitchen you might find a can of coffee. Look closely at its label. You will see that it probably came from Brazil or Colombia. If you cannot identify where an object came from, move on to another item.
- ☆ If an object is made in the United States, include it on your list. You are not just looking for items made in foreign countries, but also things made in the United States. If an item has been partly made in two countries, list the names of both countries. (Example: USA/Spain)

Japanese women harvesting tea leaves.
What products in your home come from Japan?

HOME SURVEY: Room #1: _______

Item	Country From Where the Item Came
1.	
2.	
3.	
4.	
5.	
6.	
7.	
8.	
9.	
10.	

HOME SURVEY: Room #2: _______

Item	Country From Where the Item Came
11.	
12.	
13.	
14.	
15.	
16.	
17.	
18.	
19.	
20.	

FIGURING THE PERCENTAGE OF IMPORTED PRODUCTS

Make a separate list of all the countries on your chart. Next to each country, write the number of items you found from that country in your two rooms. Using a calculator, turn that number into a fraction by dividing the number of items from each country by the total number of all the items in your survey. For example, if you found

$$\frac{\text{2 items from Brazil}}{\text{20 is the total number of items}} = \frac{2}{20} = \frac{1}{10}$$

In this case, one out of every ten (one-tenth) of the items in the two rooms came from Brazil.

You may have studied **percentages** in your math lessons. They make it easier to compare different quantities. Turn each fraction into a percent by using a calculator. This method will allow you to see the percentage of products in the two rooms that came from the United States and from other countries. Use the chart on the following page to help you keep track of your calculations.

Country	Number of Products	Fraction	Percent
1.			
2.			
3.			
4.			
5.			
6.			

THINK ABOUT IT

1. Was the percentage of products from the United States more than half (*over 50%*)?

2. Which country, other than the United States, supplied the most products in your survey?

MAPPING THE COUNTRIES OF ORIGIN

Use an atlas to find the location of each country on your chart. The countries on your chart are those you listed from your home inventory. Make a copy of the map below. Then list the items around the outside margin of the map. Finally, draw a line from each item to the location of its country of origin.

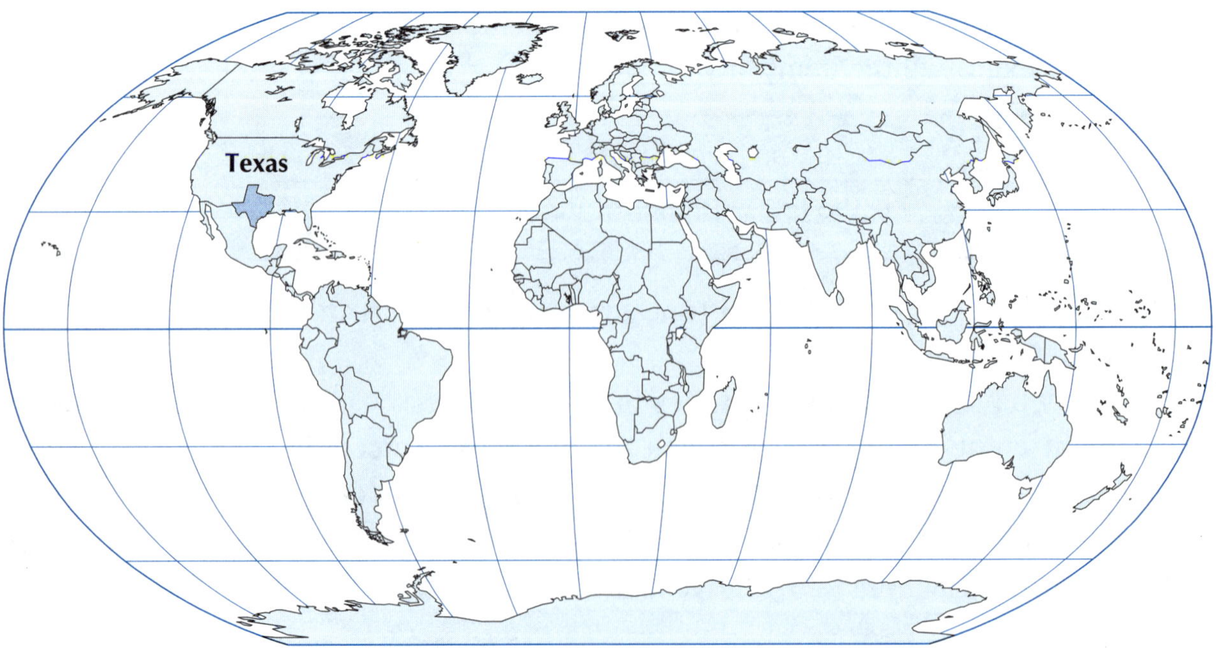

★ Checking Your Understanding ★

1. How many items in your inventory came from foreign countries?
2. How accurate was your original hypothesis when you started this activity?
3. Were you surprised by the results of your inventory? ❑ Yes ❑ No
   If so, how? If not, why not?
4. What conclusions about global interdependence can you draw from the results of your inventory and those of your classmates?

REVIEWING YOUR UNDERSTANDING

Directions: Fill in your Vocabulary Cards and complete the project that follows.

Exports

What is an export?

Name an example of an export:

Imports

What is an import?

Name an example of an import:

Major Trading Partners of the United States

In this activity, you learned about the interdependence of the United States with foreign nations. Which particular foreign nations do we trade with the most? What goods do we most often export? What do we most often buy from other countries? In activity 2C, you learned about an almanac. Let's get some practice in using this important reference tool.

1. To which **three** nations do we export the most goods?
2. From which **three** nations do we import the most goods?
3. Name **three** kinds of products that we sell the most to other nations.
4. Name **three** kinds of products that we buy the most from other nations.

SUMMARIZING YOUR UNDERSTANDING

Directions: Use your knowledge to fill in the blanks in the following graphic organizers.

DESCRIBE EACH FACTOR OF PRODUCTION

LAND

LABOR

CAPITAL GOODS

ENTREPRENEURSHIP

THE NATURAL RESOURCES OF TEXAS

1.

2.

3.

4.

5.

6.

7.

8.

DIFFERENT KINDS OF OCCUPATIONS

Occupations that use the land

1.
2.
3.

Occupations that make things

1.
2.
3.

Occupations that provide a service

1.
2.
3.

THE DIFFERENCE BETWEEN A GOOD AND A SERVICE

Directions: Copy the chart below. Then write whether the person involved in each occupation sells a good ***or*** performs a service:

Does this Person Sell a Good or Provide a Service?			
Barber		*Teacher*	
Auto Mechanic		*Pharmacist*	
Doctor		*Electrician*	
Baker		*Police Officer*	
Grocer		*Tailor*	
Lawyer		*Carpenter*	

IDENTIFYING THE FACTORS OF PRODUCTION

Directions: Copy the following chart. Then mark which factor of production each item represents by placing a check mark (✔) in the appropriate column.

Item	Natural Resource	Human Resource	Capital Good	Entrepreneur
Bus Driver				
Vegetables				
Plumber				
Computers				
Welding Machine				
Cash Registers				
Corporate Owner				
Sledge Hammer				
Water				
Office Building				
Farm Tractor				
Truck				
Nails				

FACTS AND FIGURES ABOUT TEXAS ECONOMY

DID YOU KNOW THAT …

OIL AND TEXAS

Oil has had many nicknames—such as "Texas tea" and "black gold." Its uses are sometimes even stranger than its names. In the 1860s, oil was used on Texas roads to keep the dust down. In 1878, Martin Meinsinger was selling oil as a lubricant, but he found that he could make more money by selling oil as a medicine. People paid him 25¢ for a 4-ounce bottle. Cattlemen also used oil in the early days. They would dip their cattle in oil to rid them of ticks.

WOULD YOU LIKE SOMETHING TO DRINK?

During the Great Depression, oil prices in the United States fell. By mid-1931, oil prices had dropped to about 10¢ a barrel. A barrel of oil has 42 gallons in it. At the same time, drinking water was selling in some parts of Texas for 10¢ a gallon!

A HOME GROWN BUSINESS

Soon after the first oil well was discovered in Corsicana, Joseph S. Cullinan built the first oil refinery in Texas. He also built an oil pipeline to transport crude oil to his refinery. In 1902, Cullinan and some of his partners formed a company—the Texas Fuel Company. Later on, this company became Texaco.

DID YOU SAY YOU WERE FIRST?

Many "firsts" have occurred in Texas. The city of Jefferson used the first natural gas lamps. Galveston built the state's first electrical power plant, first electric street lights, first private bank and first medical school. The first city in Texas to issue traffic tickets was Houston. T. Brady was caught speeding and fined $10.

"GOLDEN" MILK

At first, all of Gail Borden, Jr.'s business ideas—a wind-powered wagon, a portable bathhouse for women and a meat biscuit sandwich—failed. In 1856, he received a patent for condensed milk. Early sales of condensed milk were poor. However, when the Civil War broke out, Union troops needed a milk that wouldn't spoil. Borden made a fortune selling his condensed milk. After his death, Texans named a county after Borden. They also named the county seat "Gail" in his honor.

CHAPTER 6

GOVERNMENT

Texas State Capital

President Clinton

Texas Constitutional Convention, 1974

Every society has some form of government. A government helps to regulate society by providing a system of authority. People must obey the laws of the government or face some punishment. The government also provides an opportunity for cooperation. People are able to work together through the government to make changes in the rules of society. In this chapter, you will examine the ways in which governments can be organized. You will also learn some of the main features of our local, state and national governments.

6A WHAT RULES WOULD YOU MAKE FOR YOUR CLASS?

In this activity, you will learn how governments make rules by helping write a set of rules for your own class. Like laws, rules will tell students how to behave and what they can expect if they break the rules. Look for the following important words:

★ Rules ★ Penalties ★ Government

To help you find these terms, the ★ symbol will appear in the margin where the term first appears.

★ A **rule** tells people to do something or not to do something. Once a rule is made, ★ there are usually **penalties** for breaking it. For example, one common rule states that cars must stop if a traffic light is red. If a driver does not stop at a red light, the driver has broken the rule. The driver is penalized for breaking the rule, usually by having to pay a fine.

★ Checking Your Understanding ★

Can you list another "rule" in our society that tells us what to do? What is the penalty for breaking that rule?

Can you list a "rule" in our society that tells us what we **cannot** do? What is the penalty for breaking that rule?

CREATING RULES

Imagine that it is the first day of school. Your teacher begins by talking about the class rules. Your teacher says that certain rules will be made by the class itself. These rules must protect the rights of students and allow class members to do their work without distractions. The rules must be accepted by your teacher and the principal. As an example, your teacher suggests the following rule about class tests:

☆ Graded papers should be returned no later than one week after the test.

Now it's your turn. Let's see how good you are at making rules and penalties for your class. What rules and penalties would you suggest? Some topics for rules are listed in the following box:

YOUR RULES FOR THE CLASS

Tests
Rule:
Reason:
Penalty for breaking the rule:

Classroom Behavior
Rule:
Reason:
Penalty for breaking the rule:

Homework
Rule:
Reason:
Penalty for breaking the rule:

Grades
Rule:
Reason:
Penalty for breaking the rule:

Absence Notes
Rule:
Reason:
Penalty for breaking the rule:

Other Areas
Rule:
Reason:
Penalty for breaking the rule:

CREATING RULES FOR YOUR CLASS

Is your list of rules and penalties similar to those of the other students? Compare yours with those of your classmates. Come to some **consensus** (*agreement*) about a common set of class rules. List them below:

Class Rules:

Tests	Grades
Rule:	Rule:
Reason:	Reason:
Penalty for breaking the rule:	Penalty for breaking the rule:
Classroom Behavior	**Absence Notes**
Rule:	Rule:
Reason:	Reason:
Penalty for breaking the rule:	Penalty for breaking the rule:
Homework	**Other Areas**
Rule:	Rule:
Reason:	Reason:
Penalty for breaking the rule:	Penalty for breaking the rule:

THE NEED FOR GOVERNMENT

People have a need to live with others in groups or communities. By cooperating, people are able to make a living, exchange ideas, raise a family and enjoy themselves. When people live together they usually need rules to settle their disagreements.

Can you imagine what disorder would result if we were allowed to do anything we pleased, without regard for other people? Each community needs to protect its members against the forces of nature and possible attacks by other groups.

Among animals, the strongest usually rules over the rest of the herd. The earliest human societies possibly may have operated in much the same manner. However, as human societies grew more advanced, members learned to better cooperate with each other and to set up rules that the whole society could support.

The organization that people set up to protect their community and make rules for themselves is called a ★ **government.** By enforcing the rules, the government keeps order, protects people's lives and safeguards property.

Rules are an important part of our lives.
What rules do you come in contact with on a typical day?

REVIEWING YOUR UNDERSTANDING

Directions: Fill in your Vocabulary Cards and complete the exercise that follows.

Rules
What are rules?
Give an example of a rule:

Penalty
What is a penalty?
Give an example of a penalty:

Comparing Your School and Community

In a short essay, describe some of the ways that rules in your school are similar to rules in your community.

6B WHICH TYPE OF GOVERNMENT DO YOU THINK IS BEST?

In this activity, you will learn about three types of government. You will also listen to a debate about the advantages and disadvantages of each type. Look for the following important words:

★ Monarchy ★ Absolute Monarchy ★ Dictatorship ★ Democracy

All governments have powers to carry out their authority. These powers include:

- a **legislative power** to make the laws
- an **executive power** to carry out the laws
- a **judicial power** to interpret the laws

TYPES OF GOVERNMENT

There are various ways of organizing a government. Throughout history, three main types of government have been monarchy, dictatorship and democracy.

MONARCHY

A **monarchy** is a type of government in which a king or queen holds power. When the king or queen dies, all power passes to one of the monarch's children—usually the oldest son. There are two kinds of monarchies. In an **absolute monarchy,** the monarch has total control. In **constitutional monarchies,** the monarch's power is limited by a constitution. In these nations, some of the power is often held by a legislature elected by the people.

Peter the Great of Russia was an absolute monarch.
Are there any absolute monarchs still in power today?

DICTATORSHIP

A **dictatorship** is a type of government where power is in the hands of one person or a small group. The ruler or group does not answer to the people, and is not limited by them. With power concentrated in the hands of a single person or group, people's rights are not guaranteed.

DEMOCRACY

★ In a **democracy,** the people hold the real power of government. The government's power comes from the permission of the people it governs. In a **direct democracy,** the people decide directly on every important issue. However, this is usually possible only in a small community. In a nation as large as the United States, a direct democracy is just not practical.

An African woman votes.
Who holds the real power in a democracy?

The United States has a **representative democracy.** The will of the people is carried out by elected officials, known as **representatives.** In both kinds of democracy, the government and the people are under the rule of law. In addition, the basic rights and liberties of the people are guaranteed.

★ CHECKING YOUR UNDERSTANDING ★

Does your school have a student government? If so, how are its representatives chosen? How well do they represent you? The class? The school?

WHICH TYPE OF GOVERNMENT IS BEST?

Thomas Jefferson

Joseph Stalin

What if you could listen to some former government leaders who actually led these types of governments? Just imagine what it would be like to overhear them discussing types of government:

☆ **Thomas Jefferson.** Jefferson was the principal author of the Declaration of Independence and served as the third U.S. President. He is recognized by many people as a leading supporter of **democracy.**

☆ **Joseph Stalin.** Stalin was the leader of a nation once known as the Soviet Union. He ruled from 1924 to 1953. His policies made the Soviet Union one of the most powerful dictatorships in the world. Stalin was a feared **dictator.**

☆ **Louis XIV.** Louis XIV was king of France in the late 17th century. He was known as the "Sun King" because of his absolute power and luxurious style of living. He built up the power, wealth and authority of the French **monarchy.** Louis XIV believed that he ruled by "Divine Right"—by the will of God.

Louis XIV

Note: The following conversation is not real. These leaders did not live at the same time, so this imaginary discussion could never have taken place. However, each leader expresses views that he is known to have held during his lifetime.

THE DEBATE BEGINS

Jefferson: Gentlemen, a democracy is certainly the best type of government. Only a democracy protects its citizens' rights and freedoms. In a dictatorship or monarchy, people who speak out against the government are often arrested. Both dictatorship and monarchy are based on the wishes of the ruler. No one else has any rights. But in a democracy, people do not live in constant fear of the government. They are free to vote and to speak out. With this power, if they think someone in government is not protecting their rights and interests, they can vote that person out of power in the next election.

Stalin: Comrade Jefferson, I agree with you that the purpose of government is to protect the rights of the people. This was always my aim as ruler. The problem is that the people do not always know what is best for them. A smart ruler can do much more than a bunch of arguing politicians unable to make up their minds. In the Soviet Union, I was able to increase our nation's power in a shorter period than it could have been done in a democracy. I loved my people and did everything to improve my nation. I did make mistakes sometimes, but in a democracy even more mistakes are made.

Louis XIV: Sirs, I agree with Mr. Stalin. In a democracy, the people are supposed to protect their own rights. What kind of government is that? It leads to chaos, fighting and disorder. Nobody benefits. However, in a monarchy, the monarch has only the people's welfare at heart. What better protection could there be for the people? As King of France, I was carrying out God's will for the good of my people.

★ CHECKING YOUR UNDERSTANDING ★

Why does Thomas Jefferson think democracy protects its citizen's freedom better than dictatorship or monarchy? Do you agree? Explain.

Stalin: A dictator is not chosen by birth like a king, but on the basis of talent. A dictator struggles to get to the top. Once in power, he brings together all of society to achieve a single goal. I think a dictator can do more in two years than a democracy can in twenty. In a democracy, listening to everybody's opinion takes too much time, and forces people to compromise. Whenever people compromise, nobody gets everything they want. A dictatorship can get things done quickly, with no quarrels. Look at my country. For centuries, it was ruled by monarchs and fell far behind the industrial West. When I came to power, I changed all that. We built factories, produced cement and steel, and manufactured tractors. Some people who disagreed with me were put into prison or executed, but that is not so important. In the long run, the Soviet Union became powerful.

Louis XIV: I agree with you in part, Mr. Stalin. The will of one person can achieve wonderful things when it is given total control. Society moves towards one goal—building the economy or defeating an enemy in war. In a democracy, as soon as the government starts to accomplish something, a new group may be voted into power and changes direction. Dictatorships also have a weakness. The dictator is not born to rule, like a king. So a dictator never knows when another person might try to overthrow him. Your own career is proof of this, Mr. Stalin. You murdered millions of people to keep control. No monarch would ever wage such a war on his own people.

★ Checking Your Understanding ★

What does Stalin see as the main advantages of dictatorship? Do you agree? Explain.

Jefferson: Both of you say that a ruler has the interests of the people at heart. How can anyone believe that? Mr. Stalin, you killed millions in your struggle to keep power. King Louis, you dragged France into debt and senseless wars to increase your power. This proves that only when people rule themselves are they protected from abuse. True, democracy is slow. There are often disagreements and government leaders change frequently. All this is good, because democratic leaders know their power is temporary. No one dares to do anything that will be harmful to others without just cause. It is good that most of the citizens have to agree with government decisions, because over-active governments rob the people of their freedoms.

Louis XIV: Throughout most of history, gentlemen, monarchy has been the main form of government. The advantages are easy to see. Monarchy promotes the well-being of the community. A monarch acts as a referee who stands above society. Because the monarch has no interest in who wins, he or she can be an impartial judge. Since the monarch inherits power by royal birth, he or she does not need to struggle to keep it. Monarchy gives a society unity and stability. Important decisions are made by the monarch. Monarchs act firmly and consistently. Unlike a democracy, the leader does not often change. Foreign countries can depend on a consistent foreign policy.

Stalin: Your two over simplify. Comrade Jefferson says democracy protects the people from over-active governments, but what about other dangers—such as not acting quickly to pass laws or responding to attacks from hostile nations? By the time a democracy acts, it is often too late. With total power, my country can respond quickly to threats. A dictatorship is also better than a monarchy because inheriting power by birth is a weakness. However brilliant a monarch is, his or her heir may not be. That would destroy all of his or her achievements. Or suppose a monarch has no children. When he or she dies, the country faces chaos and civil war. I have to laugh when Louis claims monarchy is a stable form of government. History says otherwise.

★ CHECKING YOUR UNDERSTANDING ★

What does Louis XIV see as the main strengths of monarchy? Do you agree? Explain.

Jefferson: Gentlemen, no system of government is perfect. At times there may have been a good dictator or monarch, but most dictators and monarchs have proven short-sighted and selfish. The people can only rely on themselves to create a government that looks after their interests. Besides, of the three forms of government, only democracy recognizes the worth and dignity of each person. Other governments use secret police and terror to keep the people in check. I believe in democracy. That is why I have always put my trust in the people.

COMPARING EACH FORM OF GOVERNMENT

Now that you have read this conversation, let's compare each form of government. Copy the chart below onto a separate piece of paper. Then,

- ☆ place a check mark (✔) in one or more of the columns if these types of governments accomplish the named characteristic.
- ☆ Then rank the characteristics in their order of importance. (**1** = most important, **5** = least important)

Characteristic	Democracy	Monarchy	Dictatorship	Rank
Protects liberties of the people	?	?	?	?
Takes quick and strong action				
Assures stability and little change	?	?	?	?
Promotes the peoples' well-being				

Suppose one of the speakers invited you to participate in the discussion. How would you reply if you were asked: Which form of government do you think is best? Write a **one** page essay explaining your reasons.

REVIEWING YOUR UNDERSTANDING

Directions: Fill in your Vocabulary Cards and complete the exercises that follow.

Monarchy
What is a monarchy?
What are the two types of monarchy?

Dictatorship
What is a dictatorship?
Name one advantage and one disadvantage:

Identifying Characteristics of Types of Governments

Read each of the items listed below. Then, for each item indicate:

- ☆ **MY** if the item is a main characteristic of a **monarchy**
- ☆ **DI** if the item is a main characteristic of a **dictatorship**
- ☆ **DE** if the item is a main characteristic of a **democracy**

1. In the "direct" form of this system, people vote directly on important issues.

2. People who disagree with the leader are often punished.

3. Leaders are chosen in elections by the people.

4. Rights, such as free speech, are guaranteed to the people.

5. The ruler claims to hold power by God's favor.

Defining Democracy

A dictionary defines "democracy" as a government in which power is in the hands of the people. However, democracy can mean different things to different people. To better understand this, ask two adults how they would define "democracy" and what they think is the most important characteristic of a democracy.

Person #1

Definition: ____?____

Main Characteristic: ____?____

Person #2

Definition: ____?____

Main Characteristic: ____?____

Researching Rulers

As a research project, look up Thomas Jefferson, Joseph Stalin and King Louis XIV in an encyclopedia or history book. Do their accomplishments as rulers support the arguments they raised in the debate you have just read?

Do the accomplishments of other rulers support their arguments? Select **one** ruler from **one** of the following groups. Research that ruler and compare him or her to Jefferson, Stalin or King Louis XIV.

MONARCHY	DICTATORSHIP	DEMOCRACY
Henry VIII *of England*	Adolf Hitler *of Germany*	George Washington
Charles I *of England*	Benito Mussolini *of Italy*	Andrew Jackson
Peter the Great *of Russia*	Francisco Franco *of Spain*	Abraham Lincoln
Catherine the Great *of Russia*	Fidel Castro *of Cuba*	Konrad Adenauer *of Germany*
Philip II *of Spain*	Saddam Hussein *of Iraq*	Charles de Gaulle *of France*

6C WHO GOVERNS YOU?

In this activity, you will learn about the different levels of government—national, state, county and city. Look for the following important words:

- ★ Federalism
- ★ Local Government
- ★ Texas Legislature
- ★ County Government
- ★ Commissioners
- ★ Constituents

Texas Times
Vol. 1.4 No. 7 First Edition
President Asks Congress To Lower Age For Serving In Military

Texas Times
Vol. 1.7 No. 12 First Edition
Governor Asks For Law To Ban Smoking In Schools

Texas Times
Vol. 1.9 No. 12 First Edition
Mayor Orders City Swimming Pool To Be Closed

These newspaper headlines show the different levels of government that affect us. The U.S. Constitution created a system of government in which power is shared between the **national** (**federal**) government and the state governments. This division of government powers is called **federalism.** Our national government deals with things that affect the whole country, such as the defense of the United States. State governments handle their own affairs, such as making state laws, issuing licenses to drivers and supervising the state police. There are also **local governments** that deal with county, city and town matters. Local governments get their governing power from the state.

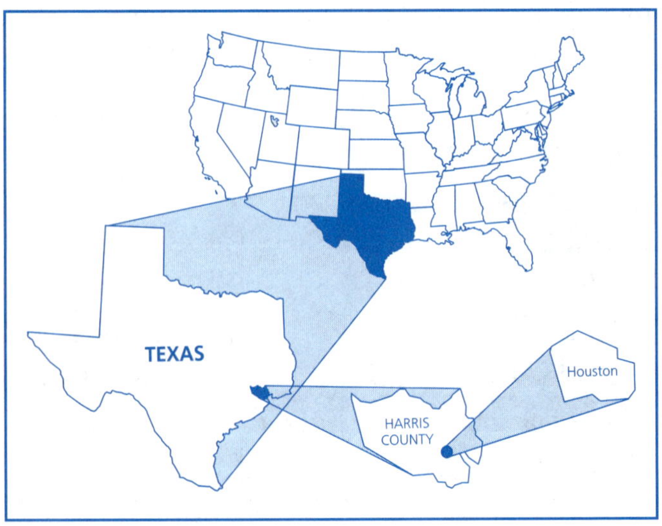

Look back at the headlines at the top of page 294. Notice that key words give us clues about which level of government each one is written about:

- "**President** asks **Congress** ..." has to do with the *national* government
- "**Governor** asks for ...." has to do with the *state* government
- "**Mayor** orders City ..." has to do with *local* government

DIFFERENT LEVELS OF GOVERNMENT

Each level of government—local, state and national—is divided into three branches: a legislative branch, an executive branch and a judicial branch. The following chart shows these different levels of government with their particular branches.

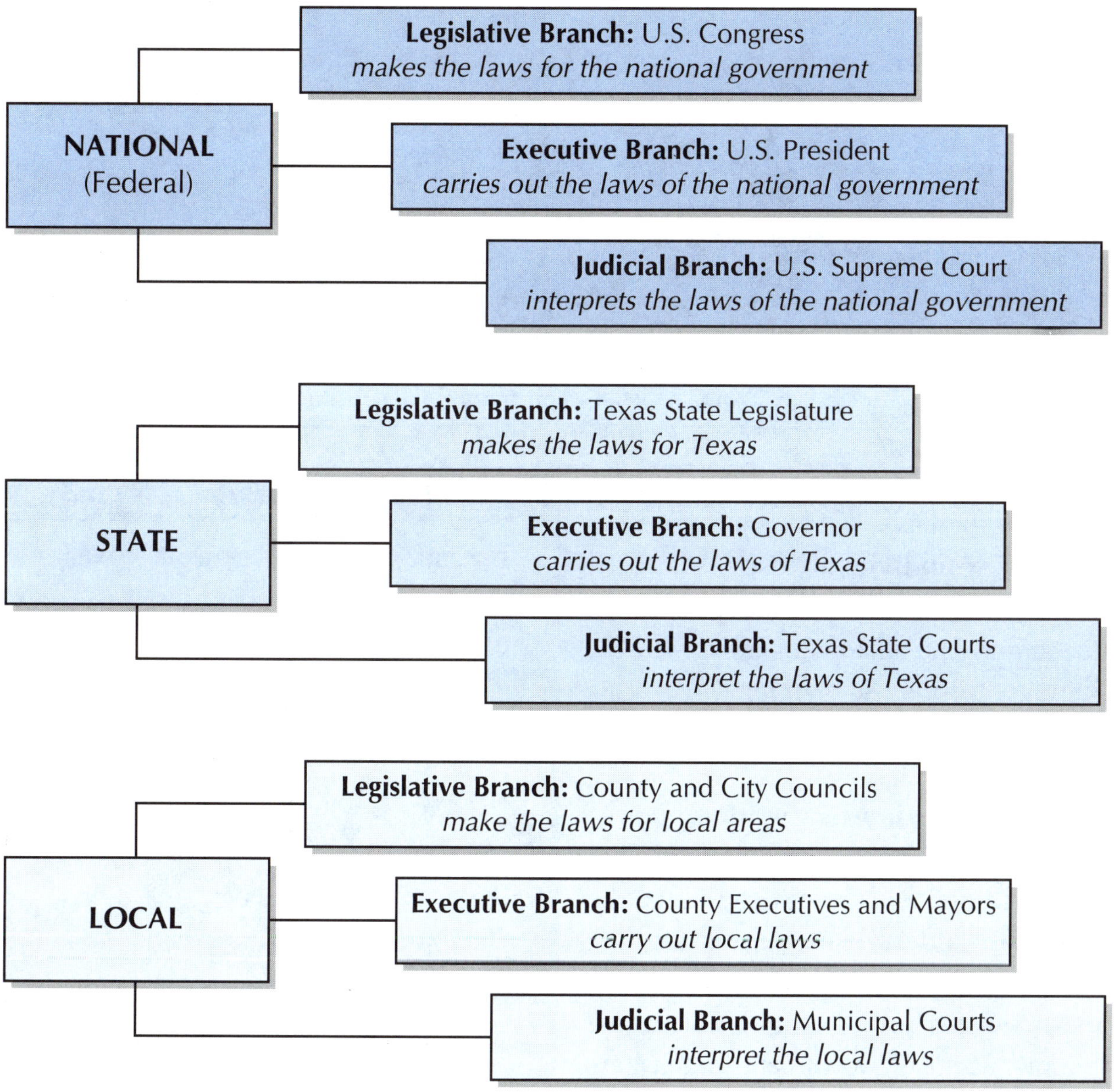

Let's take a closer look at each level of government.

THE NATIONAL GOVERNMENT

The national government is located in Washington, D.C. The legislative branch is called **Congress.** Its main job is to make laws. Congress consists of two houses or parts: the **Senate** and the **House of Representatives.** There are 100 Senators in the U.S. Senate. Each of the 50 states, including Texas, has two members in the U.S. Senate. Each state also has members in the U.S. House of Representatives. The number of representatives a state has in Congress depends upon the size of its population. Out of the 435 members in the U.S. House of Representatives, Texas has 30 representatives, (as of 1995).

The main job of the executive branch is to carry out or enforce the laws. The nation's chief executive is the **President of the United States.** The President is elected for 4 years.

The U.S. Capitol building where the U.S. Congress meets.
Why do you think it is called the capitol?

The role of the judicial branch is to interpret the laws. This means applying the laws to individual cases. The **U.S. Supreme Court** is the highest court in the nation. The nine members of the U.S. Supreme Court base their legal decisions on our national laws and on the U.S. Constitution.

A **constitution** is a written plan of government. It spells out how a government will make, carry out and judge the laws. The federal constitution we live under is called the **U.S. Constitution.** It spells out the relationship between the federal and state governments. Each state also has its own constitution.

★ CHECKING YOUR UNDERSTANDING ★

How many people represent Texas in the U.S. Congress?

The National Archives where the U.S. Constitution is on exhibit.
What is a constitution?

FOCUS ON DOCUMENTS: THE TEXAS CONSTITUTION

Texas has existed under several constitutions. After Texas became an independent republic in 1836, it adopted its first constitution. This was modeled after the U.S. Constitution. The Republic of Texas had a President, a two-house Congress and a Supreme Court.

Delegates voting on the Constitution of 1836.
Why do you think the delegates modeled it after the U.S. Constitution?

In 1845, Texas entered the United States as the 28th state. It adopted a new state constitution. Another state constitution was adopted in 1861 when Texas became a part of the Confederate States of America during the Civil War. After the war, Texas had to adopt yet another new state constitution to be readmitted back into the United States. This new constitution was written in 1869 by a special convention.

After the end of Reconstruction, many Texans were unhappy with the Constitution of 1869. A new constitutional convention wrote yet another document that became the **Constitution of 1876.** This is the basic document that governs Texas today.

Many of the provisions of the Texas Constitution are similar to the U.S. Constitution. The state government is divided into three branches: legislative, executive and judicial. The specific powers of each branch are spelled out. Each branch has some ability to **check** (*stop*) the actions of the other two branches.

One of the features of the Constitution of 1876 is the ease with which it can be **amended** (*changed*). Of almost 500 proposed amendments, 352 amendments were adopted (*approved*) between 1876 and November 1995. In 1995, voters in Texas decided on 14 new amendments.

The Constitution of 1876 contains the **Texas Bill of Rights,** which gives political power to the people. All citizens enjoy equal rights. These rights include freedom of religion, speech and press, the right to a trial by jury and the right to carry firearms. The Texas Constitution also provides for free public schools.

STATE GOVERNMENT IN TEXAS

The **state government** of Texas handles matters that affect citizens throughout the state. The state government provides money for schools, builds and maintains state roads and provides a system of justice. The state government also protects the safety and health of its citizens.

In 1837 Houston was the capital of Texas.
Where is the capital of Texas located today?

BRANCHES OF GOVERNMENT

Like the federal government, the Texas state government is divided into legislative, executive and judicial branches. It is located in Austin, the state capital.

Texas Legislators taking their Oath of Office
Do you know who represents you in the Texas Legislature?

The legislative (*law-making*) branch of ★ Texas state government is called the **Texas State Legislature.** The legislature meets for no more than 140 days in every odd-numbered year (1995, 1997, 1999, etc.). Special sessions may be called by the governor. The legislature is made up of two houses or parts. One part is called the **House of Representatives.** The other part is called the **Senate.** The people of Texas elect their senators and representatives, who make the state's laws.

Each member of the Texas legislature is elected from a single district. In the Texas House of Representatives, there are 150 members. Each member of the Texas House of Representatives is elected for a term of two years.

In the Texas Senate, there are 31 members. They are elected by voters in 31 separate districts. Each member of the Texas Senate is elected for a term of four years.

The chief executive of the Texas state government is called the **Governor.** The Governor's job is to enforce the laws that have been passed by the Texas State Legislature.

James P. Henderson,
first Governor of Texas.
What is the name of the current Governor of Texas?

The Governor also runs the state government, prepares the state budget and commands the state's National Guard. The Governor is elected for a term of four years.

The judicial branch of the state government is headed by the **Supreme Court of Texas** and the **State Court of Criminal Appeals.** These are the two highest courts in the state. The State Court of Criminal Appeals handles criminal cases, while the Supreme Court handles all other matters (*known as civil cases*). There are nine judges on each court. Each judge is elected for a six-year term. There are other state courts also, such as the Court of Appeals.

★ What House District Do You Live In? ★

This map shows the 150 districts that make up the House of Representatives in Texas. In which district do you live?

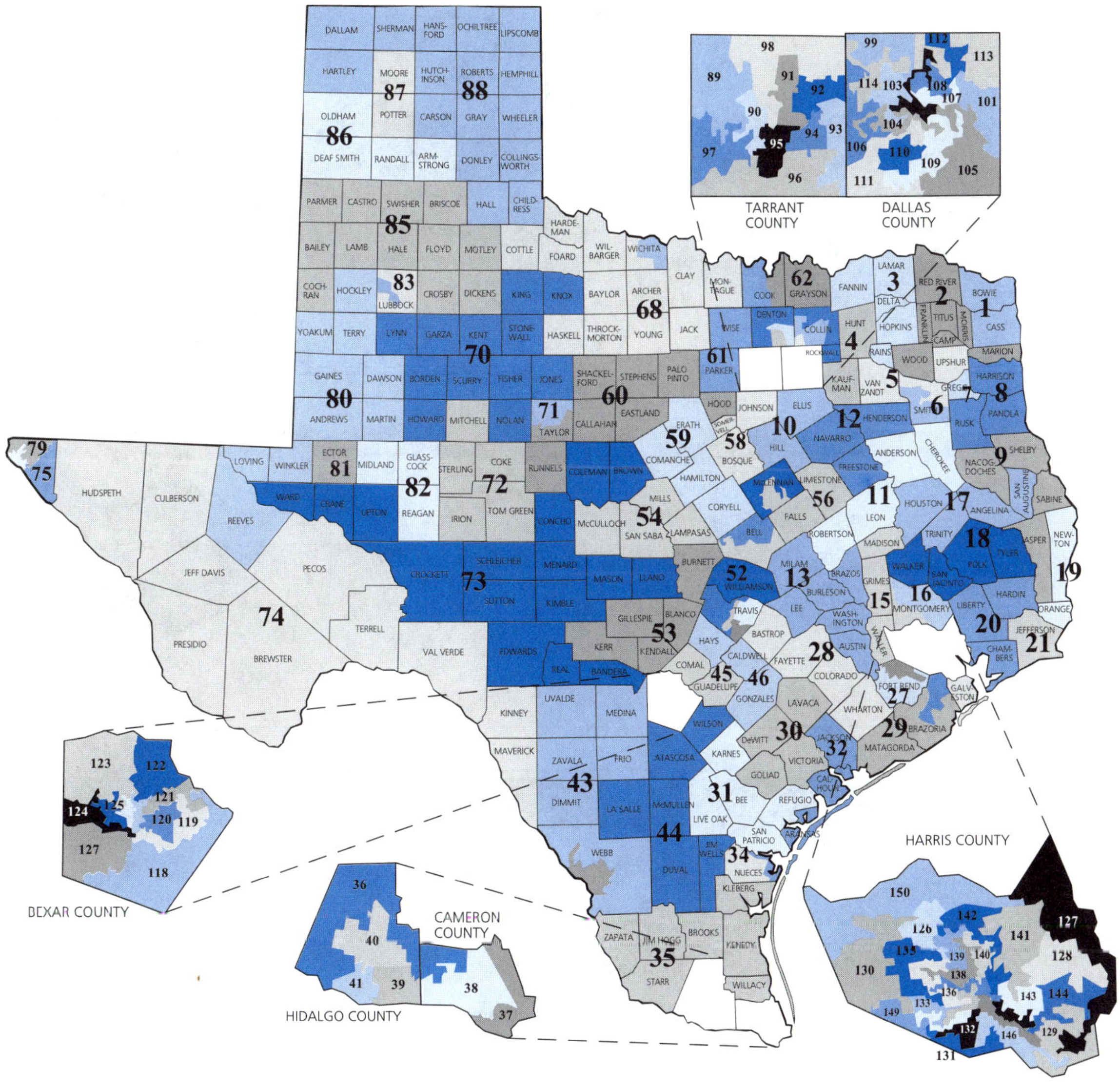

★ What Senate District Do You Live In? ★

This map shows Texas' 31 Senate districts. In which district do you live?

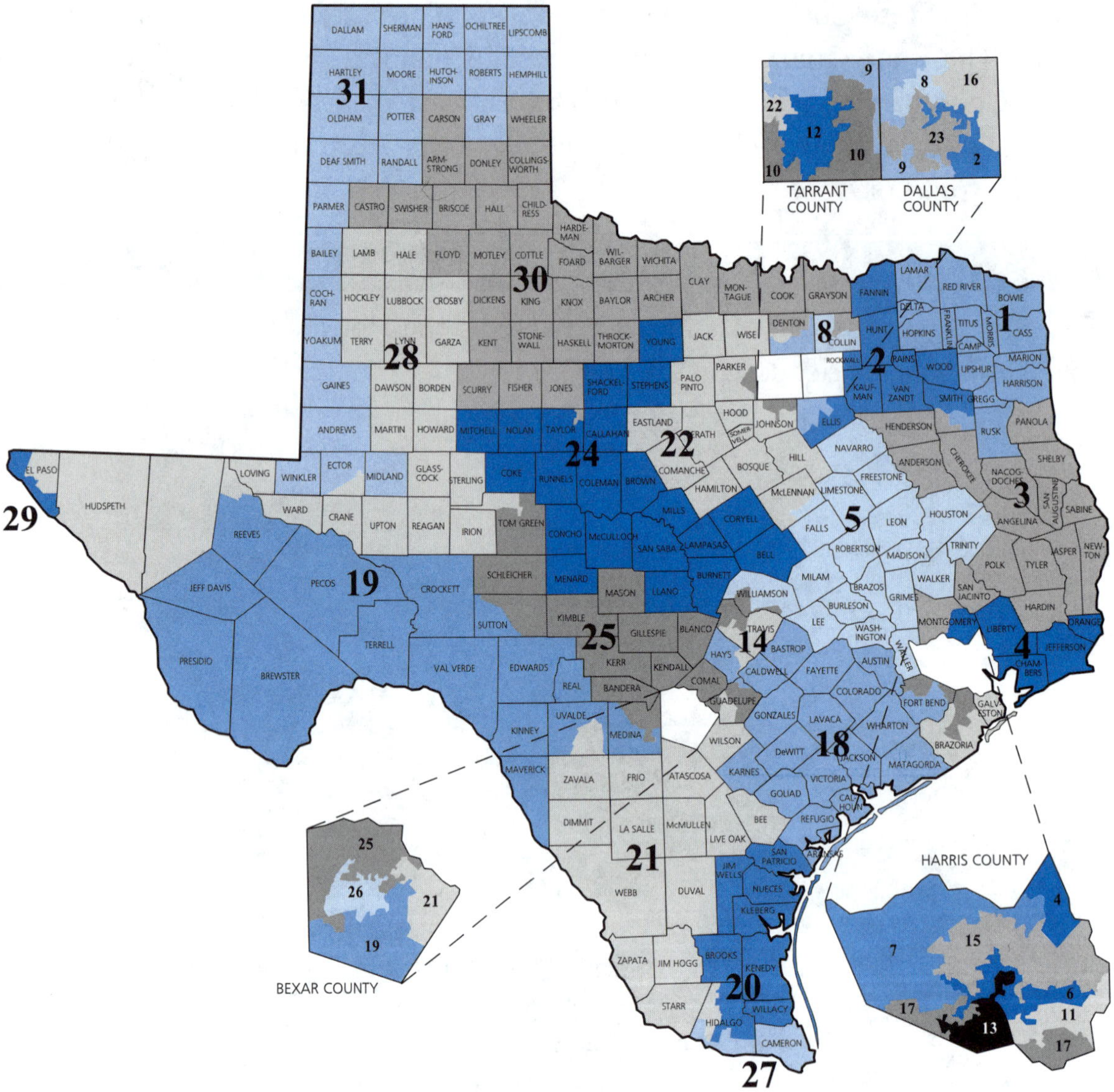

★ Checking Your Understanding ★

On a separate sheet of paper, answer the following questions:

1. Name the districts that border your district.

2. Why do you think some districts are larger that others?

TEXAS LOCAL GOVERNMENTS

In addition to the state government, there are several types and levels of local government in Texas—including **counties, municipalities** (*cities*) and **special districts.** These local governments get their power from the state government.

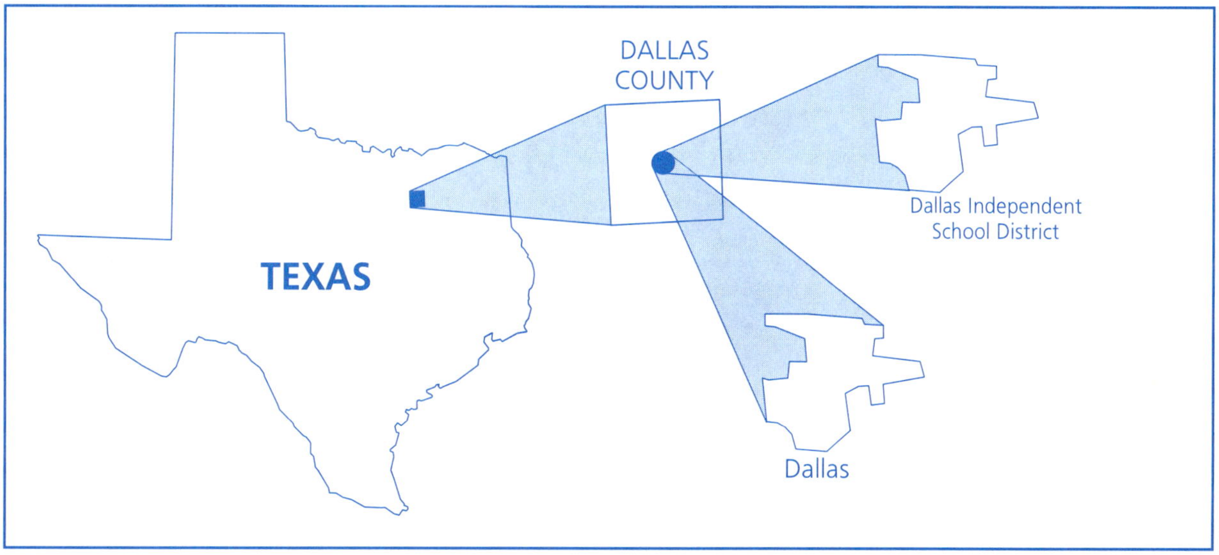

The local level of government involves passing and enforcing local rules and laws. For example, local governments deal with setting local tax rates, local school budgets and establishing fines for local crimes such as speeding. They also decide on the types of buildings that can be built and where they may be built.

COUNTY GOVERNMENT

Just as the United States is divided into 50 states, Texas is divided into 254 counties. Counties conduct elections, register voters, collect state and county taxes, operate courts and provide some health care. Counties are governed by a group of five elected officials. This group is called a **commissioners court.** They serve as a governing group rather than a judicial court. One of the commission members is elected as the chief executive of the county.

The old Dallas County Criminal Courts.
Do you know what the new Dallas Criminal Courts building is called?

★ What County Do You Live In? ★

This map shows Texas' 254 counties. In which county do you live?

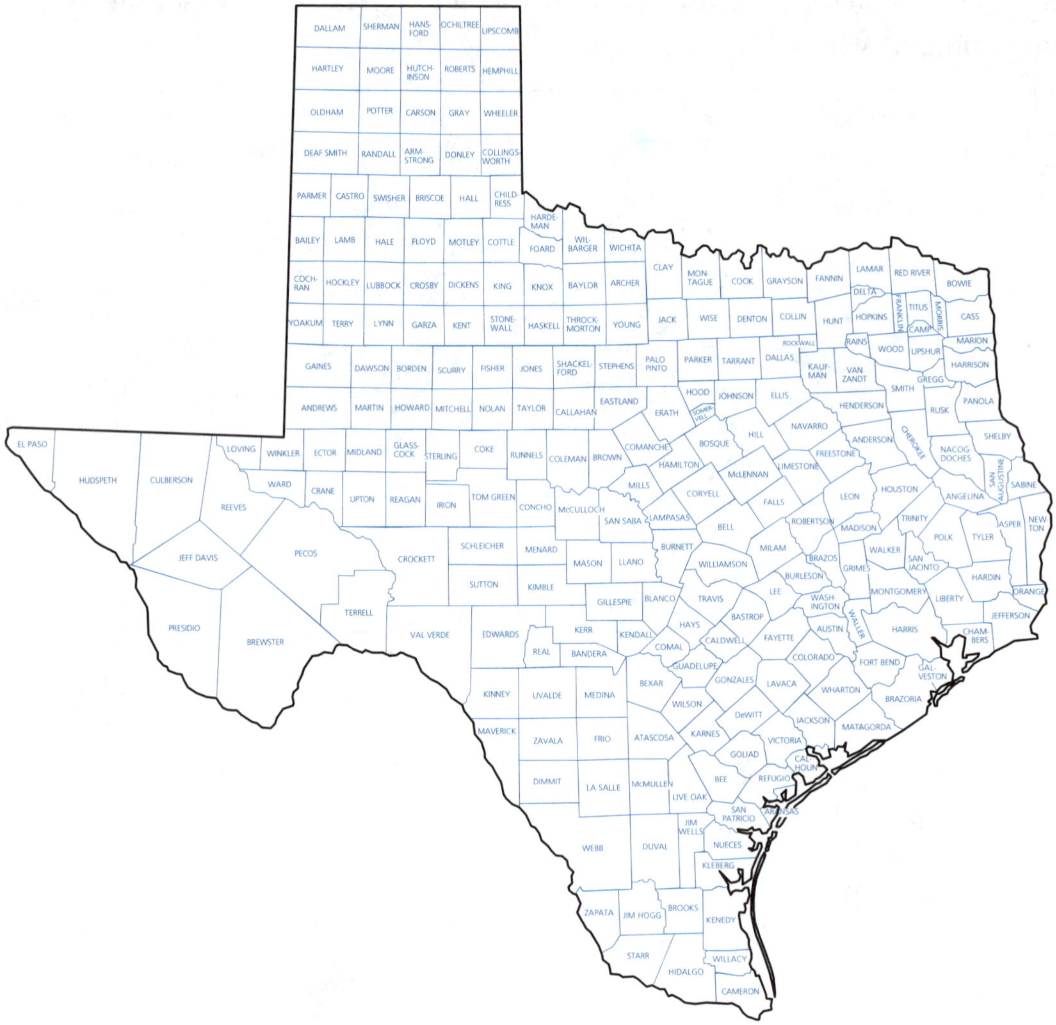

★ Checking Your Understanding ★

On a separate sheet of paper, answer the following questions:

1. Name the counties that border your county.

2. Why do you think some counties are larger that others?

MUNICIPAL GOVERNMENT

Within counties, there exist political governing units called **cities.** Over 80% of the people of Texas live in cities. Cities in Texas are governed by **municipal governments.** Most municipal governments have a **city council.** The city council makes laws that protect the health and safety of the city. City governments also provide police and fire protection. They maintain local parks and libraries, and pass zoning laws to control how land is used. They also control the delivery of water, electricity and sewers.

A city will often have a **mayor** or **city manager** as its chief executive. Usually the mayor or city manager is responsible for running the city government. Some cities are managed by people called **commissioners,** who act together as the city's chief executive.

Municipal governments often have their own local court systems. There are 853 Municipal Courts in Texas and 884 Justices of the Peace Courts (1995).

★ CHECKING YOUR UNDERSTANDING ★

1. Which of the levels of government that you live under is the largest: the state, county or local government?
2. Which of the levels of government that you live under is the smallest: the state, county or local government?

DISTRICT GOVERNMENT

In Texas, the fastest growing form of local government is the **special district.** Special districts are created to provide a specific service. They include road districts, health districts, water districts, mosquito control districts and fire prevention districts. In addition to the special districts, there are public school districts. Each of these is established to run a school system in a specific area. In 1994, there were 1,051 independent school districts in Texas.

IDENTIFYING WHO REPRESENTS YOU IN GOVERNMENT

EXTENDING THE ACTIVITY

You live in a **representative democracy.** This means that citizens' wishes are carried out by officials whom they elect. Elected officials represent you and your family in local, state and national government. These representatives play a large role in your life.

How many of these elected government officials can you identify? You will be given points for each elected official you can name and provide a copy of his or her photograph. If you can identify who the official is, fill in the space. Otherwise, leave the space blank. The following sources of information will help you in your hunt:

1. Visit or call your local office of the League of Women Voters.
2. Look in your phone book's *Blue Pages* for information.
3. Check local newspapers for stories and pictures about your elected officials.

FEDERAL GOVERNMENT: 33 Points

A. President of the United States

(name) 2 points: (photo) 3 points

B. U.S. Senators from Texas

1. (name) 4 points: (photo) 5 points **2.** (name) 4 points: (photo) 5 points

C. Texas Members of U.S. House of Representatives

(name) 4 points: (photo) 6 points

STATE GOVERNMENT: 33 Points

A. Governor of Texas

(name) 3 points: (photo) 4 points

B. State Senator from Your State Senate District

(name) 5 points: (photo) 8 points

C. State Representatives in the State Legislature

(name) 5 points: (photo) 8 points

LOCAL GOVERNMENT: 34 Points

A. Mayor or City Manager

(name) 5 points: (photo) 6 points

B. County Legislator or Commissioner

(name) 5 points: (photo) 6 points

C. County or City Judge

(name) 4 points: (photo) 8 points

BONUS: 10 Points

★ Most elected officials like to hear from their constituents. **Constituents** are the people who live in an official's home district. Write a letter to one of your elected officials mentioned in this activity. You may ask the official any number of questions. For example, you may want to know

- ☆ why did he or she want to become an elected official
- ☆ what he or she finds most interesting about the job
- ☆ what he or she thinks is most important about the job
- ☆ what advice he or she would give to young people about being a good citizen

How many points did you score? Which level of government gave you the most trouble in trying to locate information? Explain.

REVIEWING YOUR UNDERSTANDING

Directions: Fill in your Vocabulary Cards and complete the exercises that follow.

Texas Legislature

What is the job of the Texas Legislature?

What two houses make up the Texas Legislature?

Local Government

Define local government:

What things are local governments responsible for?

The Governments of Texas

Number of Governments in Texas (1992)

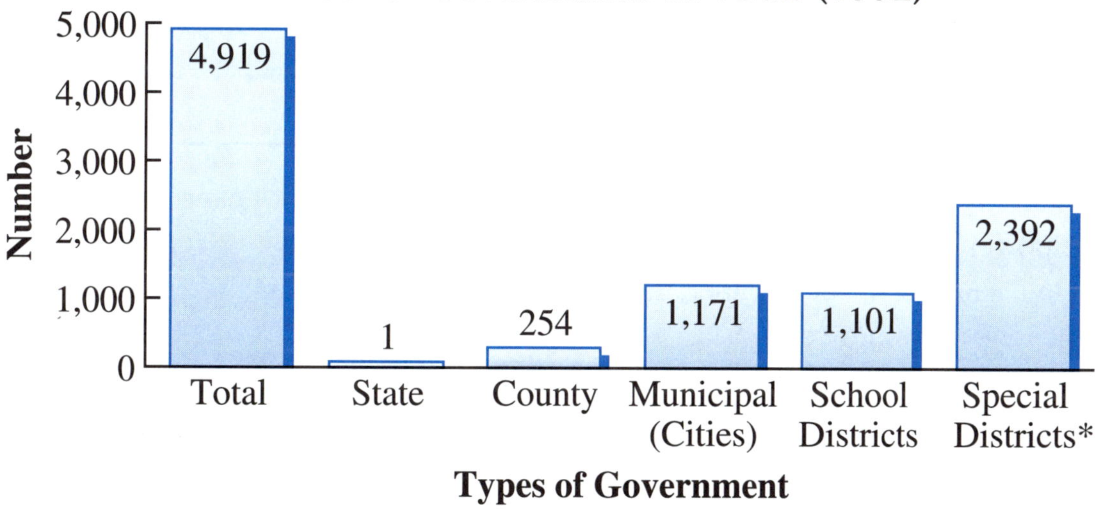

(*fire, housing, wealth, health, etc.)

To help you better understand this graph, read the following Skill Builder.

SKILL BUILDER: BAR GRAPHS

What Is A Bar Graph?

A bar graph is a chart that shows parallel bars of different lengths. Its main job is to compare several items.

Question: What items are being compared in this bar graph?

CONTINUED

Keys To Understanding A Bar Graph

Bar graphs are made up of a vertical axis, which runs from top to bottom. Bar graphs also have a horizontal axis, which runs from left to right.

Questions: In this graph, what does the vertical axis show?
What does the horizontal axis show?

Interpreting A Bar Graph

Start by looking at the title. It will give you an overall idea of the information presented in the bar graph.

Question: What is the title of this bar graph?

To find specific information, look at each bar in the graph. For example, how many school districts were there in Texas in 1992? Slide your finger along the horizontal axis until you reach the bar marked "School Districts." Next, run your finger up to the top of the school district bar. If you look at the number scale along the vertical axis, you will see where the bar ends.

Questions: About how many school districts were there in Texas in 1992?
What is the total number of governments in Texas?
What is the name of your school district?

The Powers of Government

In this activity you have learned about the three main powers of government—the legislative power, the executive power and the judicial power.

1. On a separate sheet of paper, describe each of these powers:
   A. Legislative Power
   B. Executive Power
   C. Judicial Power

2. Of the three powers of government, which do you think is the most important? Explain your answer.

Levels of Government

In this activity you learned about the various levels of government—national, state and local. Each of these has important responsibilities. Which level of government do you think has the greatest impact on your life? Explain your answer.

WHAT DO STATE AND LOCAL GOVERNMENTS DO?

In this activity, you will learn more about what your state and local governments do. Look for the following important words:

★ Government Powers ★ Purposes of Government

Do you know the saying: "a picture is worth a thousand words"? It states that it is often easier to understand something when you change a description of something into a diagram. A diagram is a picture that shows how something is organized or how it works. In this activity, you will put this saying to the test. Read the following description.

ORGANIZATION OF MY SCHOOL

My school is headed by the principal. The principal has two assistant principals, who help to run the school. Each assistant principal is in charge of three teachers. Each teacher is responsible for a class of students.

Let's see what it would be like to turn this description into a diagram:

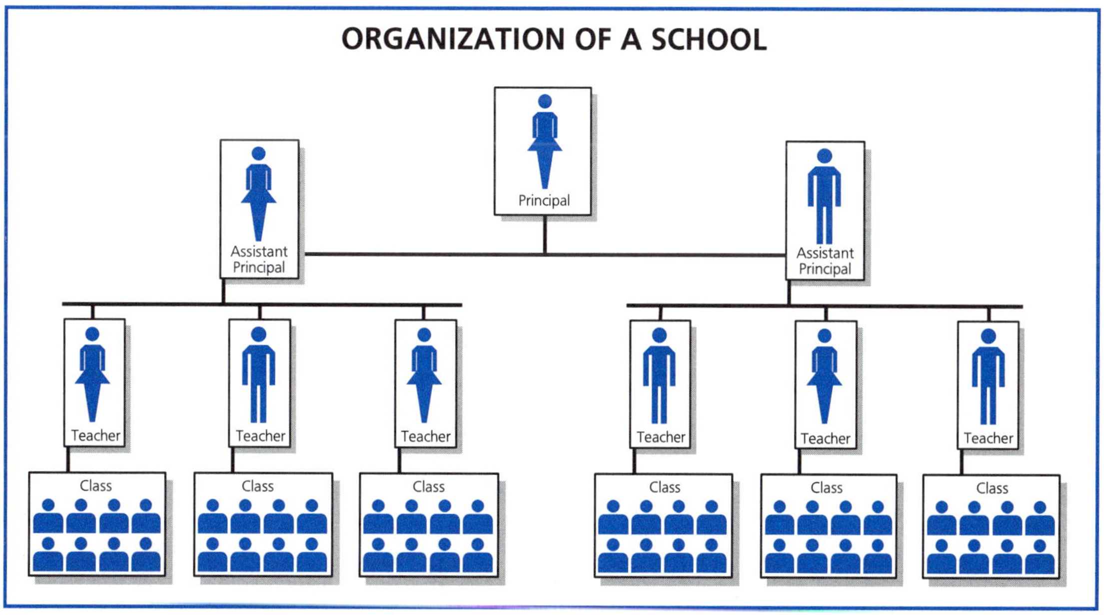

★ CHECKING YOUR UNDERSTANDING ★

Which do you think was easier to understand—the word description or the diagram? Explain.

THE POWERS OF GOVERNMENT

Let's test two other examples. First, let's look at how governments are organized and see how they work. Read the following description of the powers of government.

★ **GOVERNMENT POWERS**

Governments have three basic powers. First, they have a **legislative** power. This means that a government can *make* laws. Second, governments have an **executive** power. This means that a government *carries out* and *enforces* its laws. Third, governments have a **judicial** power. This means that a government can set up courts, with judges who *interpret* and *apply* the laws.

An engraving of the interior of the Senate chamber in Austin in 1880.
Which power of government does the State's Senate perform?

Now, let's turn the description into a diagram. To help you get started, we have given you a few clues. Make a copy of this diagram and fill in where the question marks appear.

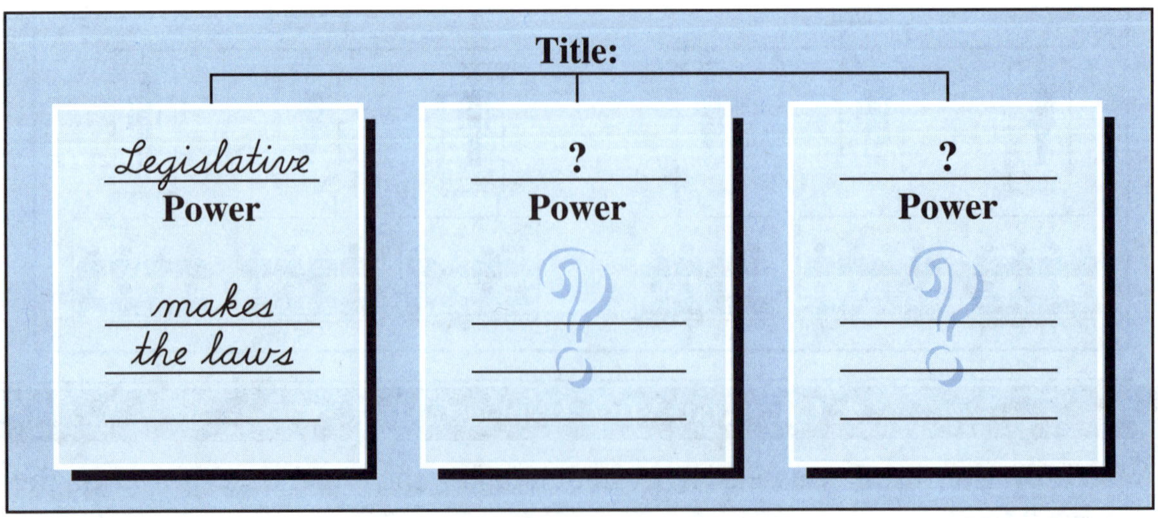

Which was easier to understand: the written description or the diagram? Explain.

PURPOSES OF STATE AND LOCAL GOVERNMENT

Now, let's reverse the order of what we've been doing by making a written description from a diagram. Study this diagram. It shows some of the main purposes of state and local government in Texas.

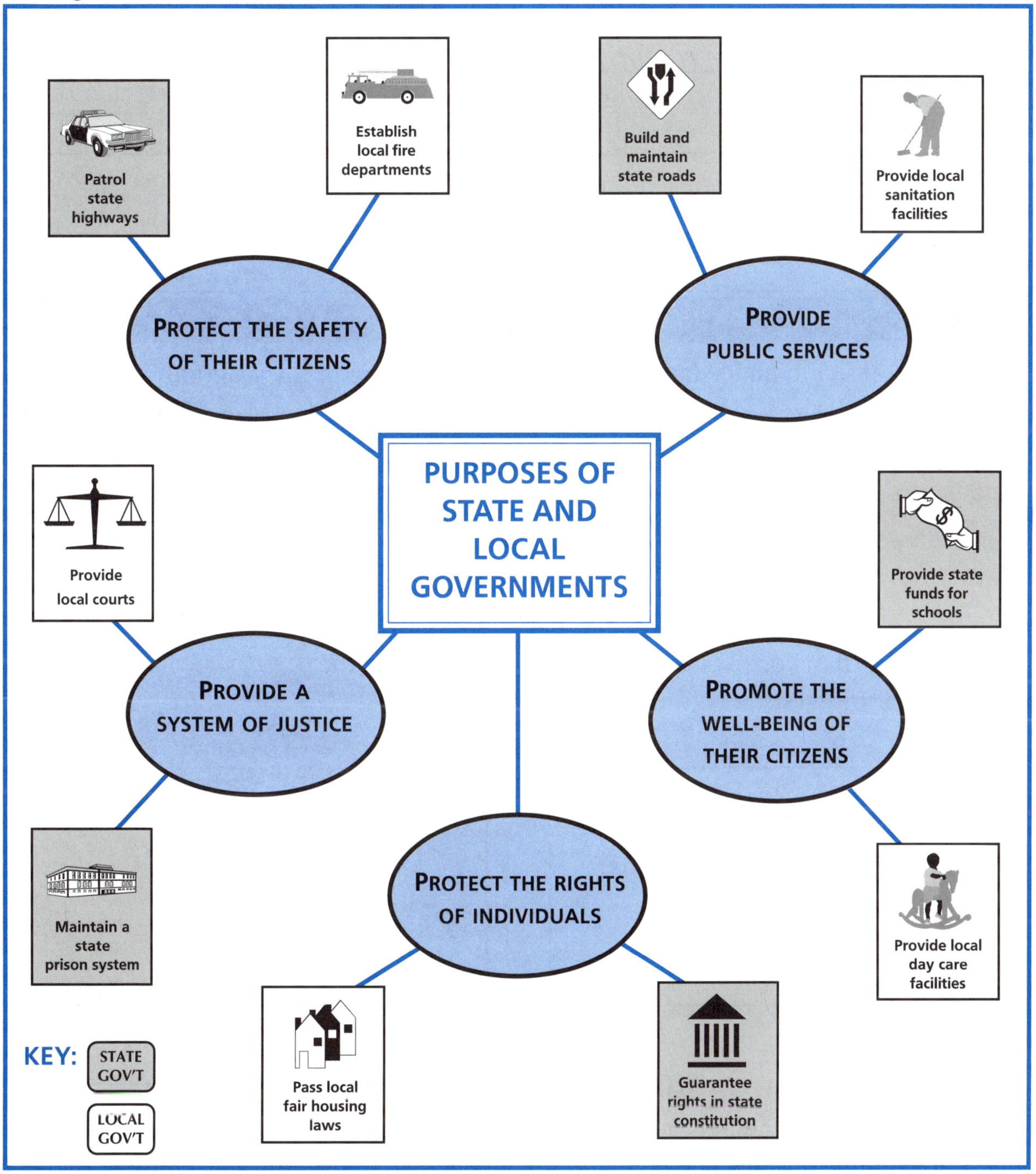

As you might notice from this chart, sometimes state and local governments have overlapping or parallel functions. For example, local governments build and patrol local streets, while the state government builds and patrols state highways.

On a separate sheet of paper, describe some of the things that state and local governments do. Use the diagram on the previous page to get this information.

Some of the Things That State and Local Governments Do

State	Local

★ Checking Your Understanding ★

Which is easier to understand, your written description or the diagram? Explain.

Now that you have looked at three examples, do you think "a picture is worth a thousand words?" Explain.

REVIEWING YOUR UNDERSTANDING

Directions: Fill in your Vocabulary Cards and complete the exercise that follows.

Government Functions

What are the three functions of government?

Define each function:

Purposes of Government

List two purposes of:

state government

local government

Describing How You Are Affected By Government

State and local governments are responsible for many rules that affect your every day life. For example, the bus you take to school must obey traffic rules established by your state and local governments. In a one page essay, describe your typical day. In your essay, show **three** ways in which you are affected by state and/or local government.

6E WHAT IS YOUR PLAN FOR HANDLING A MAJOR EMERGENCY?

In this activity, you will learn about some of the benefits that result when national, state and local government agencies cooperate with one another. Look for the following important words:

★ Hurricane ★ United Nations ★ Cooperation ★ OAS

A **hurricane** is a large tropical storm. Hurricanes have severe winds—over 74 miles per hour—and bring heavy rains and flooding. ★

The Gulf Coast of Texas is subject to hurricanes. These occur because the weather in Texas is influenced by the Gulf of Mexico. The Gulf of Mexico provides cooling sea breezes and humid weather. It also provides a path for hurricanes to strike Texas.

Hurricanes can be very dangerous. The following newspaper article describes one of the worst hurricanes ever to strike Texas. Look at the date.

THINK ABOUT IT

Have you ever experienced a hurricane? ❐ Yes ❐ No If you have, describe what it was like. If not, what do you think it might be like?

Galveston Times

First Edition — September 8, 1900

HURRICANE BRINGS DEATH AND DESTRUCTION

Yesterday the worst natural disaster in U.S. history struck Texas. A killer-hurricane smashed into Galveston Island. The hurricane's winds were clocked at up to 120 miles per hour. Storm tides reached 15 feet as the massive hurricane hit. Few structures escaped the force of the hurricane. Huge mountains of rubble, some five stories high, were left in the path of the storm. Many residents fled just before the hurricane hit. Despite this, the Great Galveston Storm, as it is now being called, has killed as many as 8,000 people.

Galveston residents struggling for life during the hurricane.

It is not possible to stop a hurricane. However, many things can be done to prepare for a hurricane and limit the damage when it strikes. Imagine that the mayor of your city has asked **you** to be part of a special group. This group will be revising (*changing*) a plan to help deal with hurricanes and other natural disasters when they strike.

DEALING WITH A HURRICANE

At your first meeting, the mayor's aide hands you a list of some problems you and your group must consider when a hurricane is coming:

- evacuating people from the path of the hurricane
- providing weather information before and during the storm
- opening and staffing shelters during and after the storm
- feeding people made homeless by the storm
- draining flooded streets and highways
- cleaning up damage from the hurricane
- preventing looting and stealing
- counseling frightened people
- assisting people caught in boats or trapped in their homes by the storm

THINK ABOUT IT

What other necessary actions can you think of?

WHERE TO TURN FOR HELP

The mayor's aide then gives you a chart showing certain groups and agencies that might be helpful in a hurricane or natural disaster.

LOCAL GOVERNMENT AGENCIES

Fire, Rescue and Emergency Services. These agencies put out fires and provide emergency services. They handle such things as people trapped in a fallen building or people who need to be evacuated from rising flood waters.

Police Department. This agency directs traffic, provides protection and prevents looting of abandoned homes and buildings.

Boards of Education. This group makes schools available as shelters during a hurricane or other disaster.

Destruction left after the Galveston hurricane.
Have you ever experienced a natural disaster?

STATE GOVERNMENT AGENCIES

Office of the Governor. The Governor's office provides overall assistance in carrying out an emergency plan.

Texas Department of Public Safety. This agency assists local police departments in handling natural disasters.

Texas Department of Health. This agency oversees emergency medical services in the state.

Texas Department of Transportation. This agency makes sure that roads and highways continue to stay open during a storm.

FEDERAL GOVERNMENT AGENCIES

Federal Emergency Management Agency. FEMA provides people to oversee the handling of a natural disaster.

U.S. Coast Guard. The Coast Guard is a branch of the U.S. Armed Forces. It patrols the nation's coastline and provides rescue operations for people trapped on boats or in danger of drowning.

National Guard. This is a well-equipped and highly trained military force used to restore order and protect property in times of war or national emergencies.

National Weather Service. This agency provides information about approaching hurricanes, 12 to 24 hours before they strike. The service issues a "Hurricane Watch" when a hurricane threatens a coastal area. A "Hurricane Warning" is issued when the storm is expected to hit an area within 24 hours.

> In addition to local, state and federal government agencies, there are some important private organizations that offer help during a disaster.

PRIVATE AGENCIES

Red Cross. This organization provides volunteers to run shelters for the homeless and feed people during a disaster or other emergency.

Salvation Army. This is a religious organization that provides free food and clothing during a disaster or other emergency.

Utility Companies. Utility companies provide electric power, gas and telephone services to the people of Texas. In an emergency they work to maintain and restore service.

Area Hospitals. These hospitals provide emergency care and beds for those injured in an emergency.

CREATING A DISASTER PLAN

It's now time for you to come up with a plan of action that can be used during a hurricane or other natural disaster. Your teacher will divide the class into groups. Each group must create its own disaster plan. One person from each group will be asked to present the group's plan to the rest of the class. You may use diagrams, pictures and other material when presenting your plan to the class.

The following chart will help organize your thoughts on what must be done during a hurricane or other natural disaster. The first problem in the chart has already been addressed.

PROBLEM	PLAN of ACTION
1. Evacuating people who are old or sick from the path of the hurricane	*Send police officers to area nursing homes and hospitals to help evacuate people to shelters. The Governor's Office might provide radio and TV announcements. These would request old or sick people to call a special number for assistance.*
2. Providing weather information before and during the storm	?
3. Opening and staffing shelters during and after the hurricane	?
4. Feeding people made homeless by the storm	?
5. Draining flooded streets and highways	?
6. Cleaning up damage from the hurricane	?
7. Preventing looting and stealing	?
8. Counseling frightened people	?
9. Assisting people caught in boats or trapped in their homes by the storm	?

THINK ABOUT IT

1. Do you think an emergency like a hurricane could best be handled by just your local government? ❒ Yes ❒ No Explain your answer.
2. ★ **Cooperation** means working together toward a common purpose. Do you think the proposals in this activity would require cooperation among the different governments and agencies? ❒ Yes ❒ No Explain your answer.

CREATING A DIRECTORY OF EMERGENCY TELEPHONE NUMBERS

Unlike a hurricane, some emergencies strike without advance warning. The best way to be ready for an emergency is to prepare ahead of time. In this section, you will make a list of emergency telephone numbers. You can find such information:

1. by speaking to your parents.

2. by consulting a local telephone directory.

On a separate sheet of paper, copy down the following chart. Then, in the spaces provided, list the emergency telephone numbers you have gathered:

Emergency Telephone Numbers

Police Department:	*Phone number:*
Fire Department:	*Phone number:*
Doctor's Office:	*Phone number:*
Ambulance Service:	*Phone number:*
Local Hospital:	*Phone number:*
Poison Control Center:	*Phone number:*
Gas and Electric Co.:	*Phone number:*
Other:	*Phone number:*
Other:	*Phone number:*
Other:	*Phone number:*

COOPERATION AMONG NATIONAL GOVERNMENTS

EXTENDING THE ACTIVITY

In this activity, you saw the benefits of cooperation between national, state and local governments. Because cooperation is so helpful, countries also sometimes come together to solve problems. Let's take a closer look at an organization created to solve problems among countries of the world.

INFORMATION SHEET

★ **Name of Organization:** United Nations (UN)

When Formed: The United Nations was created in San Francisco in 1945.

Membership: Most nations in the world are members. In 1994, there were 184 countries in the United Nations.

Purpose: The member countries of the United Nations cooperate with each other in order to achieve international peace and security. Through cooperation among its members, the UN tries to solve many of the economic, social and humanitarian problems in the world.

United Nations headquarters in N.Y.C.
What is the main purpose of the UN?

In this exercise, you will be asked to find out about **one** regional organization. You may select either the:

★
- ☆ **Organization of American States** (OAS)
- ☆ **European Economic Community** (EEC)
- ☆ **Caribbean Community and Common Market** (CARICOM)

For the organization you choose, you will complete an Information Sheet. Use the Information Sheet on the United Nations as a guide. You can locate this information in:

- **Almanacs.** Refer to an almanac, checking under *Major International Organizations.*
- **Encyclopedias.** Check an encyclopedia for an article about the organization.
- **Books.** Find a book in the library that has information about the organization.

Information Sheet

Name of Organization:

When Formed:

Membership:

Purpose:

REVIEWING YOUR UNDERSTANDING

Directions: Fill in your Vocabulary Cards. Then complete the project that follows.

Cooperation

Define cooperation.

Give an example that shows cooperation between governments:

OAS

What do the letters OAS mean?

Describe how this organization shows cooperation among nations:

Looking At Community Organizations and Agencies

How might a real organization or agency plan for an emergency? The class should write a letter to one of the agencies or organizations mentioned in this activity. Ask the officials of that agency or organization to explain how they would cooperate with other organizations and agencies to solve a community crisis such as a hurricane or other natural disaster.

SUMMARIZING YOUR UNDERSTANDING

Directions: Use your knowledge to complete the following graphic organizer.

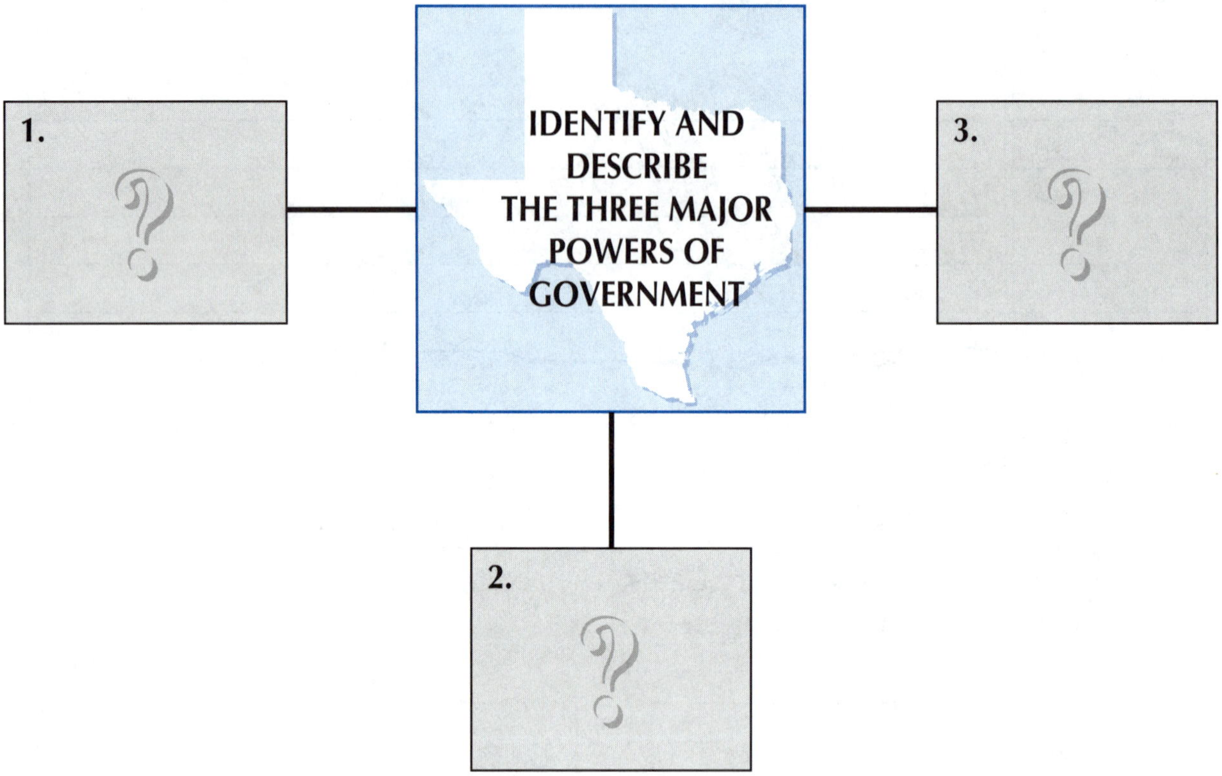

Directions: Use your knowledge about Texas state government to complete the following chart.

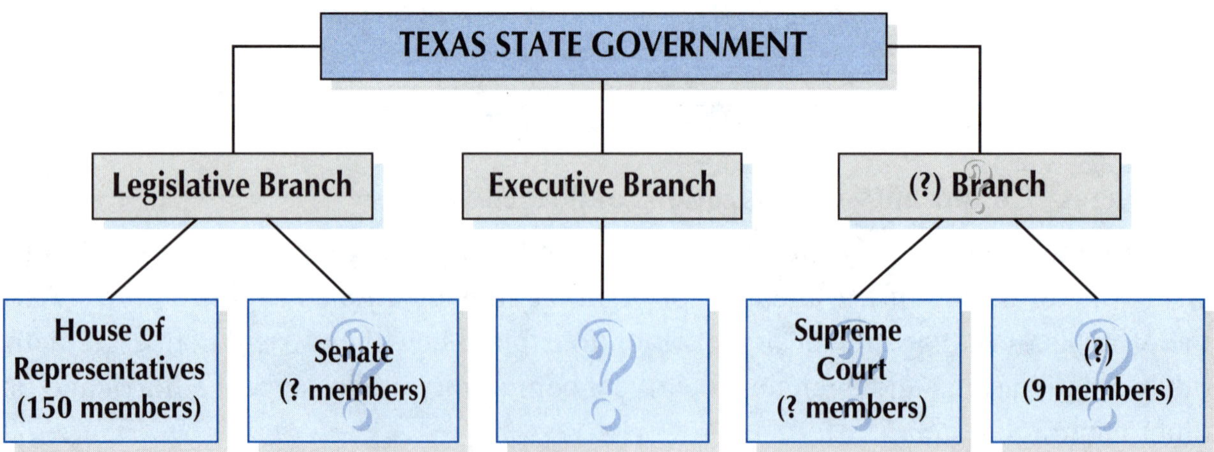

PURPOSES OF STATE AND LOCAL GOVERNMENTS

PURPOSE	STATE GOVERNMENT	LOCAL GOVERNMENT
Protect health and safety of citizens	Patrol the state highways; control use of the Texas National Guard; pass safety laws for work, homes and schools.	Establish local fire and police departments; remove snow; pass local traffic laws; zone property to insure proper use.
Provide and maintain public services	Collect taxes; borrow money; build and maintain roads; preserve wildlife	Collect taxes; borrow money; provide libraries and public records offices; provide sanitation facilities; provide public schools.
Provide a system of justice	Provide state criminal and civil courts; provide state prisons.	Provide local criminal and civil courts, provide local jails.
Protect the rights of individual citizens	Guarantee individual rights in the state constitution and state laws; for example, state laws prohibit unfair discrimination.	Pass fair housing ordinances; zone property.
Promote the common welfare (well-being)	Provide funds for schools; send trade missions to other nations to promote trade with Texas.	Provide local day care facilities; provide public parking; zone property.

Directions: Copy the chart on a separate sheet of paper. Examine items 1 to 10. Then, place a check mark (✔) in the proper column if the item is (1) provided by the state government; (2) provided by the local government; or (3) provided by both governments.

	STATE	LOCAL	BOTH
1. Provides fire protection			
2. Gives permits to build factories			
3. Collects taxes			
4. Makes traffic laws			
5. Prohibits crime in the state			
6. Prohibits citizens from carrying weapons			
7. Provides civil and criminal courts			
8. Maintains roads in a local area			
9. Provides funds for schools in the state			
10. Operates the libraries in a community			

COMPARING DIFFERENT TYPES OF GOVERNMENT

Directions: On a separate sheet of paper, create a chart of what you think are the possible advantages and disadvantages of each type of government:

Government	Advantages	Disadvantages
Monarchy	?	?
Dictatorship		
Democracy		

COMPARING CHIEF EXECUTIVES

Directions: The chief executive is in charge of the executive branch of a government. There is a chief executive officer at each of the national, state, and local levels. On a separate sheet of paper, complete the blanks in the chart for each level of government:

Government	Example	Example
National	?	President
State	Texas	?
City	Houston	?

A FUNCTION OF GOVERNMENT

Directions: Base your answer to the next question on the information in the box to the right:

The photograph illustrates a function of which level of government?

FACTS AND FIGURES ABOUT TEXAS GOVERNMENT

CAN YOU IMAGINE FIVE TEXASES?

The Constitution of 1845 has a provision giving Texas the right to divide its lands to create four additional states. Although this has not occurred, the legal right to divide the state still remains on the books.

FINALLY A GOVERNOR BORN IN TEXAS

After becoming a state, Texas began electing its governors. James P. Henderson was the first governor of Texas, although he was born in North Carolina. It took 45 years before a native-born Texan was first elected governor. In 1891, James S. Hogg became the first elected governor born in Texas.

DO YOU WANT TO TRADE?

During the battle at the Alamo, in 1836, Mexican soldiers captured the flag of Texas—a Lone Star flag. Later in that same year, General Santa Anna was defeated at the Battle of San Jacinto. During that battle, three Mexican flags were captured. Each nation has held the captured flags of the other ever since. In 1991, the North American Free Trade Agreement (NAFTA) was signed by Mexico, Canada, and the United States. Talks went so well that U.S. and Mexican officials opened discussions on trading back their captured flags.

HOW MUCH SHOULD A CAPITOL BUILDING COST?

In 1882, the state wanted to build a new capitol building, but lacked money to begin construction. In an unusual deal, the legislature gave 3 million acres of land to a Chicago company in exchange for building a new capitol. The deal created the XIT Ranch—a 30-mile-wide strip of land measuring 200 miles long, on the Texas-New Mexico border. This deal involved more land than the states of Delaware and Rhode Island combined.

OTHER CALAMITIES TO BEFALL TEXAS

The 1900 Galveston hurricane was not the only tragedy to hit Texas. In the past 25 years, Texas was hit by Hurricane Allen (August 1980), which killed 272 people. During Hurricane Alicia (August 1983), 17 people lost their lives. That same year a tornado killed 12 people in Texas. In May 1987, a tornado ripped through Sargasso, killing 29 people.

CHAPTER 7

CITIZENSHIP

Governor's Mansion, Austin—1990s

Saluting the America flag—1950s

A political demonstration—1980s

Citizens hold political power in a democratic society like the United States. American citizens should therefore be well-informed and be willing to express their opinions. In this chapter, you will learn what it means to be a citizen in a democracy. You will explore the ways in which citizens express their views. You will also examine the steps that citizens take to reach their own conclusions about public issues. After you have completed the activities in this chapter, you will understand some of your rights and responsibilities and how you can better participate in our society as a good citizen.

7A

HOW WOULD YOU DEFINE A "GOOD" CITIZEN?

You will begin your study of citizenship by examining a definition of citizenship. In this activity, you will conduct a survey of people in your community to find out what they think makes a "good citizen." Look for the following important words:

★ U.S. Constitution	★ Naturalized Citizen	★ Duty
★ Citizenship	★ Rights	★ Responsibility

To help you find these terms, the ★ symbol will appear in the margin where the term first appears.

In 1987, a survey was taken on the 200th birthday of the **U.S. Constitution** (*the written plan of government for America*). ★ Several people were asked what it means to be a citizen of the United States. Here is one person's answer:

> I was not born here. I have become a citizen of the United States. I did this because this country does not ask you whether you are the right race, color or religion. This country was built by immigrants like myself. I came here because I value the freedoms protected by the Constitution.
>
> —*a foreign-born medical doctor*

WHAT IS A CITIZEN?

In some ways, **citizenship** can be compared to a membership card. Citizenship means ★ that a person is a member of a particular country. This concept of citizenship goes back to ancient Greece and Rome. In modern times, every country has developed its own rules to define citizenship.

In our country, you are an American citizen if you were born here or if your parents are American citizens. People who were not born in the United States and whose parents are not American citizens can also become citizens. These people are called **naturalized citizens.** To become naturalized, a person has to live in the United States ★ for a specific period of time and pass a citizenship test.

In the United States, all citizens enjoy certain rights. They also have specific duties and responsibilities. Let's look more closely at these three concepts—rights, duties and responsibilities.

★ A **right** is something that everyone in society is entitled to. For example, in America everyone has the right to practice his or her religion. This right is protected by the U.S. Constitution and cannot be taken away by the government.

★ **Duties** include those actions that are the "musts" of citizenship—things that you are legally obligated to do. If you refuse to perform your duties, you can be punished by the government. You may pay a fine or even go to jail.

People who break laws are often sent to jail. *What are some other functions of the police?*

DUTIES

- ☆ Obey the laws of your local, state and federal government
- ☆ Serve on a jury if called upon
- ☆ Help to defend the nation by serving in the armed forces if called upon
- ☆ Pay taxes to help support the government
- ☆ Testify in court if called upon to present evidence
- ☆ Attend school in order to receive an education

Besides the duties required of a citizen, there are also responsibilities that come with citizenship. There is no punishment for failing to meet these responsibilities. However, the success of our democratic system depends on people being responsible citizens.

★ **Responsibilities** include all those things that a citizen should do. Often they require time and effort, but democracy depends on people's active participation.

RESPONSIBILITIES

- ☆ Vote in local, state and national elections
- ☆ Inform your elected representatives about issues that concern you
- ☆ Stay informed about the activities of local, state and federal government
- ☆ Serve in government if elected or appointed
- ☆ Join a political party or work as an independent voter
- ☆ Help enforce laws by cooperating with the police

However, simply being a citizen does not make someone a "good" citizen. How, then, would you define a "good" citizen? Let's find out what you think.

> **THINK ABOUT IT**
>
> I think a "good citizen" is someone who ...

How does your answer compare with those of others? Compare your answer with those of your classmates.

How would adults in your community answer this question? In this activity you will interview **two** adults to find out how they define a "good" citizen.

CONDUCTING A SURVEY

In the interviews you are about to conduct, there are no right or wrong answers. The purpose of the survey is to find out how adults in your community define a "good" citizen. To carry out your survey, follow these steps:

- ☆ Ask your parent or guardian to suggest **two** adults who would be willing to participate in your project. One volunteer might even be your parent or guardian. If someone refuses to participate, thank him or her and move on to the next person.
- ☆ After you have finished your questions, thank your volunteer for his or her help with your survey.
- ☆ Begin your survey by reading the following statement to each adult:

> As part of a school project, I am surveying two adults to find their answers to the question:
>
> *How would you define a "good" citizen?*
>
> This will only take a moment of your time.

Use a tally sheet like the following one to record the answers of your volunteers:

> *How would you define a "good" citizen?*
>
> ☆ What did your first volunteer say?
>
> ☆ What did you second volunteer say?

After your survey is complete, bring your answers to class. Share your answers with your classmates. The class should then select the responses that they feel best define what a "good" citizen is.

A "good" citizen is someone who …

HOW DO EXPERTS DEFINE A "GOOD" CITIZEN?

How does your class definition of a "good" citizen compare with those of the experts? Following are qualities that many experts think a "good" citizen should have.

A ***"good"*** *citizen is someone who is...*

- ☆ **Respectful.** Good citizens treat others with respect, even when they disagree with other people's opinions.
- ☆ **Responsible.** Good citizens are responsible for their actions. They keep their promises and are willing to pay the penalty when they do something wrong.
- ☆ **Self-Disciplined.** Good citizens use self-control and follow the rules.
- ☆ **Civic-Minded.** Good citizens sometimes give their own time and donate money for the good of the community.
- ☆ **Open-Minded.** Good citizens are willing to listen to others. Sometimes, after listening to other people, a good citizen will change his or her opinion. Good citizens will compromise to solve problems in a way that is acceptable to others.
- ☆ **Willing To Accept Differences.** Good citizens accept and support others with different traditions, customs and ways of living.

Now that you have read the views of the experts, would you change your definition of a "good" citizen? If so, how would you now define a "good" citizen.

THINK ABOUT IT

1. As a citizen, what do you think is your most important:
   ☆ Right ☆ Duty ☆ Responsibility
2. Now that you have examined the qualities of being a "good" citizen, would you call yourself a "good" citizen? Explain why or why not.

THE DIFFERENCE BETWEEN RIGHTS AND DUTIES

EXTENDING THE ACTIVITY

As stated in the beginning of this activity, a **right** is something to which everyone is entitled. A right cannot be taken away by the government. For example, you have a right to free speech in our society. A **duty** is an obligation of a citizen. For example, each of us has a duty to respect the rights of others. Do you see a connection between rights and duties? If yes, what do you think that connection is? If not, why do you think there is no connection?

REVIEWING YOUR UNDERSTANDING

Directions: Fill in your Vocabulary Cards. Then answer the questions that follow.

Duties

What is a duty?

What are some of the duties of a citizen?

Rights

What is a right?

What are some rights that American citizens have?

Questions about Rights, Duties and Responsibilities

1. List five characteristics of a good citizen.

2. What are the items in the box examples of?

- Everyone must be on time for class.
- Once the lesson begins, there is no talking.
- If you have been absent, you must bring in an absence note.

3. A citizen's responsibility can best be defined as ____?____

4. Students in the United States have both rights and duties:

☆ What rights do you enjoy as a student?

☆ What duties do you have as a student?

7B WHAT CHARACTERISTICS MAKE A PERSON A GOOD LEADER?

Citizens depend upon their leaders to help them solve problems and to guide them through good and bad times. Democratic society especially depends upon some of its citizens stepping forward to fill positions of leadership. In this activity, you will identify some of the characteristics that make a person a leader. Look for the following important words:

★ Leader ★ Characteristics ★ Dictionary ★ Social Reformer

Throughout history, there have been certain people who had an especially important ★ effect on the lives of others. These people are often called leaders. A **leader** is a person whom others are willing to follow. What makes a person a leader? Most experts say that a leader must meet three requirements. A leader has to:

THINK ABOUT IT

Identify a person who you think is a leader. What qualities make him or her a leader?

- have a vision for the future
- be able to communicate his or her vision to others
- have the ability to motivate others to act

CHARACTERISTICS OF A LEADER

★ A **characteristic** is a special trait or distinguishing feature. What personal characteristics do leaders need to meet the requirements above? Which characteristics from the following list do you think would help someone to become a leader?

PERSONAL QUALITIES

☆ fair	☆ unselfish	☆ compassionate	☆ courageous
☆ ruthless	☆ expressive	☆ honest	☆ popular
☆ humane	☆ intelligent	☆ devious	☆ ethical
☆ charismatic	☆ cunning	☆ caring	☆ diligent
☆ skillful	☆ benevolent	☆ spirited	☆ unscrupulous

Note: You may not know the meanings of some of the words on this list. Use a dictionary to look up any words you do not understand.

DICTIONARY

A **dictionary** is a reference book with many thousands of words in alphabetical order. Dictionaries explain how to say each word correctly. This is done by dividing the word into parts (*syllables*) and showing which syllables in the word get accented. Some dictionaries tell you the origin of the word. Dictionaries show the different parts of speech (*noun, verb. etc*) that the word can take. Finally, a dictionary will list the meaning of the word for each part of speech. Sometimes a dictionary gives a sample sentence to make clearer the meaning of the word. ★

fair (fĕr). [Old English "foeger"] *Noun.* Gathering for sale of goods or display of goods or farm products, as in "state fair."
Adjective. **1.** Beautiful, pleasing. **2.** Clear and sunny, as in "fair weather." **3.** With blond hair and light complexion. **4.** Just, unbiased, impartial, with equal treatment for all, as in "he received a fair trial."

There are often several meanings for a word. You have to pick the one that makes the most sense in the sentence you are reading. For the characteristics of a leader, the proper definition of "fair" would be #4: "Just, unbiased, impartial, with equal treatment for all."

Copy the following chart onto a separate sheet of paper. After you find the meaning of any words you did not know, write them down. This will help you to build your vocabulary while learning about the characteristics of leadership.

	New Word	Definition of the Word
1.		
2.		
3.		
4.		
5.		
6.		
7.		
8.		

Now that you understand all the words, what personal characteristics do you think help to make someone a good leader?

LOOKING AT TWO IMPORTANT LEADERS

Let's test your answer above about the personal characteristics of a good leader. We can begin by looking at two people considered by many to have been good leaders. Let's see what leadership characteristics they possessed.

- **Stephen F. Austin** was a political leader in Texas. A **political leader** is someone who is involved in government—at the local, state or national level.
- **Dr. Martin Luther King, Jr.,** was a social reformer. Unlike political leaders, **social reformers** do not usually hold political office. Instead, they try to make changes in society by working in or creating private organizations.

Read the following account of Austin's career to find out which leadership characteristics he had.

STEPHEN F. AUSTIN (1793-1836)

Stephen F. Austin was a quiet and hard-working man. He was known for his patience, honesty and dedication.

In 1821, the Spanish government allowed Austin's father to bring American settlers into Texas. When his father died, Austin carried out his father's plan. Austin chose the area between the Colorado and Brazos Rivers as the place for his colony. The Mexican government also appointed Austin as the chief government official in that area. Between 1822 and 1827, Austin brought about 300 families to the colony. These families became known as the "Old Three Hundred."

Stephen Austin
Why do you think Stephen Austin is known as the "Father of Texas?"

Austin made sure that each new family received both farming and grazing land, and some land along the river. At first, the colonists faced such problems as harvest failures and attacks from Native Americans. Later, the settlers had difficulties with the Mexican government.

Austin held the colony together with his courage and determination. He published rules to govern the colony, and organized groups to fight off Native American attacks. Austin thought of the colonists as his

CONTINUED

"family." He spent his time caring for their needs. He was so busy helping the colonists that he never had time to marry and raise a family of his own. The success of Austin's colony led thousands of other Americans to move to Texas.

Later, when the settlers had disagreements with the government of Mexico, Austin presented their complaints. Austin was elected President of the Texas Convention of 1832. At this convention, Texans asked for their own state government in Mexico. In 1833, Austin was sent to Mexico City to discuss Texan's demands. When Austin wrote home that the Texans should form their own government, he was sent to prison by the Mexican authorities. Austin's one-and-a-half year imprisonment permanently damaged his health.

Austin, the capital of Texas, as it looked in 1840.
Why do you think the Texas state capital was named Austin?

Austin played a crucial role in the Texas Revolution. Sam Houston chose Austin as his Secretary of State in 1836. Austin spent the last year of his life attempting to obtain U.S. recognition of the new Republic of Texas. He died at the early age of 43. Because of his efforts, Austin is known as the "Father of Texas." In 1839, the capital of Texas was renamed Austin, in his honor.

QUESTIONS ABOUT STEPHEN F. AUSTIN

1. What personal characteristics do you think made Stephen F. Austin a leader?

2. Are these the same characteristics that you selected for a good leader?

MARTIN LUTHER KING, JR. (1929-1968)

Dr. King, a Baptist minister, emerged in the late 1950s as the main organizer and leader of the Civil Rights Movement. The Civil Rights Movement was started in response to the harsh treatment suffered by African Americans.

After the Civil War, the rights of most African Americans were limited by the laws and practices of many states. For example, African Americans in the South were legally **segregated** (*separated by race*) in schools and forced to use separate public places such as restaurants, drinking fountains and buses.

CONTINUED

In addition, groups like the **Klu Klux Klan** committed acts of violence against African Americans.

Dr. Martin Luther King, Jr.

In the 1950s and 1960s, the Civil Rights Movement attempted to end racial segregation. Dr. Martin Luther King, Jr., became one of the leaders of that movement. King believed in non-violence. If the government passed an unjust law, he believed people should oppose that law with non-violent action. He felt that peaceful resistance would eventually change most people's attitudes. King was very effective in using non-violent demonstrations and boycotts (*refusing to buy certain products*) against segregation.

Dr. King leading the March on Washington. *What other methods did Dr. King use in the battle to win equality?*

One of King's most effective demonstrations involved bringing hundreds of thousands of people together for a **March on Washington** in 1963. King was a gifted speaker who communicated his vision of future justice. It was during this demonstration that he delivered his "I Have A Dream" speech. In this speech, he told Americans of his dream of a nation free of prejudice and discrimination. His personal courage in the face of violence inspired his followers. His methods put pressure on the U.S. Congress and the President to act.

Dr. King and his followers brought public segregation to an end. King was successful in getting a new law passed that stopped discrimination in public transportation, hotels and restaurants. King also successfully fought for an end to literacy tests as a requirement for voting.

King was a great social reformer who was able to get people to act. He organized African Americans and supporters of Civil Rights from all races into a powerful group. Once organized, this group accomplished major social changes in America.

QUESTIONS ABOUT MARTIN LUTHER KING JR.

1. What personal characteristics do you think made Dr. King a good leader?

2. Are these the same characteristics that you selected for a good leader?

You just read about two people who many consider to have been good leaders. Would you now change your definition of characteristics that you think a good leader must have?

LEADERS FROM THE PAST AND PRESENT

EXTENDING THE ACTIVITY

Do the characteristics you identified for Stephen F. Austin and Dr. Martin Luther King, Jr., also hold true for other leaders?

YOUR TASK On page 334 is a list of other leaders from Texas, the United States and the Western Hemisphere. Select **one** political leader and **one** social reformer or business leader from the list. For each leader that you select, prepare a **one** page summary of his or her life and accomplishments.

WHERE TO FIND INFORMATION To research your subject, use the following sources:

- ☆ **Encyclopedias:** Look for articles listed under the person's name.
- ☆ **History books:** Check the index for information about the person.
- ☆ **Biographies:** Find books written about the leader by other people.
- ☆ **Autobiographies:** See if the leader has written a book about himself or herself.

PRESENTING YOUR INFORMATION Before you write your one-page summary, you should organize the information you find. Use the following Research Guide to help you:

Research Guide: (?) Name of leader
Summary of the life of the leader:
Major accomplishments:
What characteristics made this person a leader?

POLITICAL LEADERS

☆ **Simon Bolivar** (1783-1840) was known as the "Liberator." Many historians called him the greatest figure of the independence movements in South America. Between 1819 and 1825, he helped to free Venezuela, Colombia, Ecuador, Peru and Bolivia from Spanish rule.

President Johnson meeting Dr. King

☆ **George Bush, Sr.** (1924-present) was born in Massachusetts. He settled in Texas in 1948. He earned a fortune when he helped to form an oil company. He was the 41st President of the United States (1988-1992). He also served as a U.S. Congressman (1967-1971), Director of the Central Intelligence Agency and Vice-President under Ronald Reagan (1981-1988).

☆ **Dwight D. Eisenhower** (1890-1969) was born in Denison, Texas, but raised in Kansas. He served as 34th President of the United States (1953-1961). He also served as Supreme Commander of the allied invasion of Europe during World War II (1943-1945).

President Anson Jones

☆ **Henry B. Gonzalez** (1916-present) was born in San Antonio. He became the first Mexican-American Texas state senator in 110 years. In 1960, he was elected to Congress, making him the first Texan of Mexican descent to serve in the U.S. House of Representatives.

☆ **Lyndon B. Johnson** (1908-1973) was born near Stonewall, Texas. He was the 36th President of the United States (1963-1969). He also served Texas as a U.S. Congressman (1937-1949), U.S. Senator (1949-1961), and Vice-President under John F. Kennedy (1961-1963).

☆ **Anson Jones** (1798-1858) served as the Secretary of State for the Republic of Texas (1841). He was the fifth and last President of the Republic of Texas (1844-1846). He laid the groundwork for the annexation of Texas by the United States.

☆ **John A. MacDonald** (1815-1891) MacDonald became Canada's first Prime Minister. He worked to bring the British territories west and north of Ontario under the control of the Canadian government.

☆ **Ann W. Richards** (1933-present) After raising a family, she entered politics as a county commissioner in 1976. She was the first woman elected as the State Treasurer (1982). In 1990, she was elected Governor of Texas.

☆ **Carlos Salinas** (1948–present) President of Mexico from 1988 to 1994; he helped put Mexico on the road to economic health. He also helped create the North American Free Trade Agreement (NAFTA).

☆ **José San de Martin** (1778–1850) led troops over the Andes mountains in South America. This helped to liberate Argentina, Chile and Peru from Spanish rule during the independence movements between 1816 and 1818.

REFORMERS AND BUSINESS LEADERS

☆ **Susan B. Anthony** (1820–1906) was a leader in the movement to abolish slavery and to achieve equal rights for women. She helped found the National American Woman Suffrage Association.

☆ **Mary Kay Ash** (1923–present) In 1963, this divorced housewife invested $5,000 to buy a cosmetics formula. The Dallas-based Mary Kay Cosmetics company now has over one billion dollars in sales each year. Mary Kay Cosmetics sell in the United States and 15 other countries.

☆ **Dorothea Dix** (1802–1887) was a social reformer who campaigned to improve conditions in prisons. She also started a revolution in mental health care.

☆ **James Farmer** (1920–present) was born in Marshall, Texas. He became a civil rights leader and founder of the Congress of Racial Equality (CORE). He served as National Director of the organization from 1961 to 1966.

☆ **Howard R. Hughes** (1905–1976) was born in Houston, Texas. He was a business leader, film producer and aviation pioneer.

☆ **Richard King** (1825–1885) was the founder of the most famous ranch in Texas, the million-acre King Ranch.

Susan B. Anthony (*standing*) and Elizabeth C. Stanton. *Can you name any female political leaders today?*

☆ **M.E.Y. Moore.** M.E.Y. Moore was an African American woman. In 1905, she organized the Texas Association of Colored Women's Clubs in Gainesville. The group was successful in getting the state legislature to recognize and later to fund a home for delinquent African American girls.

☆ **H. Ross Perot** (1930–present) was a business leader. He helped to reform Texas schools. He also ran as an independent candidate for President in 1992.

REVIEWING YOUR UNDERSTANDING

Directions: Fill in your Vocabulary Cards. Then complete the exercises that follow.

Leader
What is a leader?
What are some of the characteristics of a good leader?

Social Reformer
What is a social reformer?
Name two social reformers:

Practice Using a Dictionary

Read the following definition and answer the questions that follow.

> **Cit·i·zen** (sit´i zen), *noun* **1.** a native or naturalized member of a state or nation who who owes loyalty to its government and is entitled to its protection. **2.** an inhabitant of a city or town, especially one entitled to its privileges. **3.** an inhabitant: *The deer is a citizen of our woods.* **4.** a civilian, rather than a soldier or police officer.

- ☆ What is the word being defined?
- ☆ What part of speech is the word?
- ☆ How is the word pronounced?
- ☆ How many definitions are given for the word?
- ☆ Which definition of the word are you most familiar with?

Identifying A Person With Leadership Qualities

In this activity, you learned about some of the characteristics and qualities that identify someone as a leader. In addition, you researched some important people who are commonly accepted as leaders. However, leaders need not be in the national spotlight. In fact, a leader does not even have to be famous. People with leadership qualities exist everywhere. Select one person that you know who you think has leadership qualities. Then answer the following questions about that person:

1. What is the name of that person?
2. How has that person displayed leadership qualities?
3. What qualities make that person a leader?

7C HOW WOULD YOU REDUCE POLLUTION?

In the next three activities, you will examine how good citizens solve problems and make decisions on public issues. Informed decision-making is one of the most important parts of being a good citizen. In this activity, you will look more closely at environmental pollution and use a problem-solving approach to help resolve this problem. Look for the following important words:

- Environment
- Pollution
- Problem-Solving
- Acid Rain
- Ozone Layer
- Global Warming

The pollution of the environment is one of the greatest dangers facing our society. It is no wonder that protecting the environment has become a major concern for Americans.

DANGERS TO OUR ENVIRONMENT

Our **environment** refers to the Earth and the natural resources that surround us. People ★ used to think that because the world was so large, the actions of humans could not damage the environment. People made fires or put their garbage in rivers without thinking much about it. However, the rise of industry and the growth of the world's population over the last 200 years has greatly changed our thinking.

Today, a major danger to our environment comes from pollution. **Pollution** is ★ made up of dirt, fumes and chemicals that make our environment unclean. Pollution is in the air we breathe and the water we drink. Some people with allergies or lung diseases are already wearing masks outdoors. Many people fear that if pollution is not controlled, it could eventually make our planet unlivable.

New York City skyline with its air heavily polluted. *Why is pollution of the environment such a danger to people?*

Pollution has a number of causes. For example, chemicals are used by farmers to kill insects. However, these chemicals can also be harmful to people. The rain washes these chemicals into our rivers and streams. Another source of pollution is from the millions of cars that pour harmful exhaust fumes into the air. Some cities burn garbage. Some factories dump chemical **toxins** (*poisons*) into our rivers, lakes and oceans. Accidents involving oil tankers result in **oil spills.**

Such spills often cover hundreds of miles of ocean. These spills have made some seashores unusable and killed plants and wildlife.

★ Another type of pollution is **acid rain.** Factory smokestacks and automobile exhaust fumes rise high into the air. These fumes form acid chemicals in the atmosphere that return to the Earth in the form of rain or snow. Acid rain is poisonous. It causes damage to forests, lakes, fish and even to people.

A Pennsylvania steel factory.
In what way is this factory contributing to environmental pollution?

A LOOK AT LOCAL ENVIRONMENTAL PROBLEMS

Pollution is not somebody else's problem. It is a problem every community faces. That means even the community you live in faces environmental problems.

> What do you think is the greatest environmental danger to your community?

Are you correct? Compare your answer with those of your classmates. The class as a whole should decide which are the most serious dangers to the local environment.

> List some of the dangers to the local environment.

AN APPROACH TO PROBLEM-SOLVING

What can be done about local environmental pollution? To help solve this problem, your teacher will break the class into groups. Each group should select a different danger facing your local environment and try to figure out possible solutions for it. First, consider the appropriate steps to follow when ★ **solving a problem.**

1. DESCRIBE THE PROBLEM

Begin by describing the problem. For example, as our population continues to grow, a problem has developed over where to put the billions of tons of garbage produced each day. A helpful hint: go through a mental checklist—*who, what, where, when*—to describe or define the problem.

> **THINK ABOUT IT**
>
> **Describe** the local environmental problem chosen by your group.

2. IDENTIFY THE CAUSES

Next, you will need to explain why or how the problem came about. "Causes" are the different things that led to the problem. By understanding how the problem developed, it is often easier to think of solutions. For example, many products we buy come wrapped in elaborate packaging. All this packaging is thrown away. This adds to the mountains of garbage we must burn or bury every day.

> **THINK ABOUT IT**
>
> **Identify** the causes of the local environmental problem chosen by your group.

3. EXPLAIN THE EFFECTS

You also need to explain the effects or impact that the problem has on society. This helps you to decide how much effort should be spent in solving the problem. For example, what is the impact of rising amounts of garbage? To get rid of the rising amounts of garbage, some communities tow the garbage out to sea and dump it. Other communities burn the garbage. Burning garbage releases harmful toxins into the air we breathe.

> **THINK ABOUT IT**
>
> **Explain** the effects of the local environmental problem chosen by your group.

4. SUGGEST SOME POSSIBLE SOLUTIONS

Finally, you will need to discuss some actions that citizens, the government or private groups can take to **solve** the problem. For example, one partial solution to the garbage problem is **recycling**—creating new products from garbage in the form of bottles, paper and plastic. When thinking about solutions, some people only consider the costs involved. Are the benefits worth what it would cost?

> **THINK ABOUT IT**
>
> Provide some **solutions** to the local environmental problem chosen by your group.

Garbage dumped along a street.
Is this another part of the pollution problem?

A barge tows garbage out to sea to be dumped.
Why is this a danger to the environment?

REPORTING TO THE CLASS

One member from each group should report the group's findings to the class. The report should follow the problem-solving model in this activity. Members of the class should make a copy of the following Information Sheet to take notes:

INFORMATION SHEET ON ENVIRONMENTAL PROBLEMS

	Problem #1	Problem #2	Problem #3
1. Describe the problem:			
2. Identify the causes:			
3. Explain the effects:			
4. Provide solutions:			
5. Which solution do you most favor?			

CHANGES IN THE EARTH'S ENVIRONMENT

EXTENDING THE ACTIVITY

For thousands of years, people have tried to influence the weather without much success. However, certain changes over the last 100 years are now changing the Earth's atmosphere at a rapid rate.

★ There is great concern that we are destroying the Earth's **ozone layer.** This layer is a band of gas that surrounds the Earth. The ozone layer acts as an umbrella or shield that prevents the harmful rays of the sun from reaching us. The harmful rays of the sun can cause skin cancer and damage other parts of the body. Scientists have discovered a huge hole, as large as the United States, in the ozone layer over the Antarctica.

Pollution in the air and rising amounts of gases such as carbon dioxide also block heat from escaping into space. Some environmentalists fear this is leading to global ★ warming. **Global warming** is a general rise in the Earth's temperature. Eventually, temperatures may rise enough to cause farmlands to become deserts, rivers to dry up and polar ice to melt—raising the level of the oceans and causing terrible floods

Many scientists believe the Earth will be much warmer in the following ten years than at any time over the last 100,000 years. In the 1980s, scientists have recorded four of the warmest years of this century.

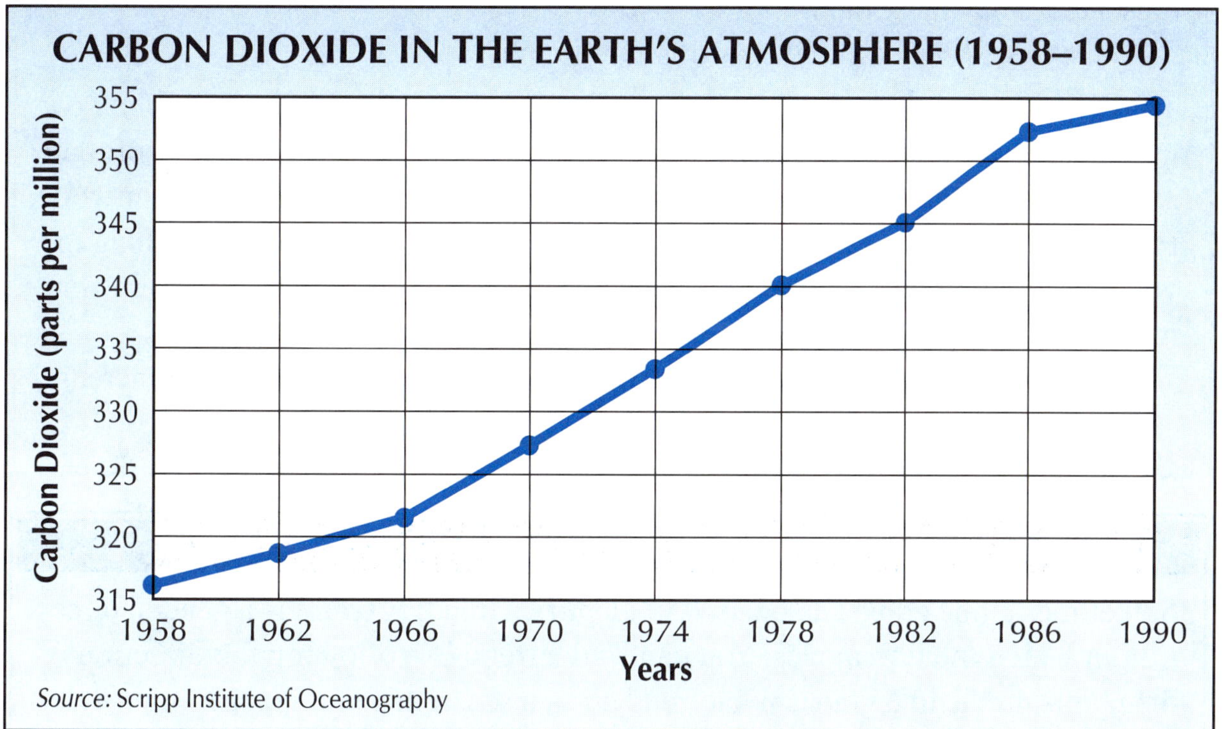

To help you to better interpret the information in this line graph, read the following Skill Builder.

SKILL BUILDER: LINE GRAPHS

What Is A Line Graph?

A line graph is a chart made up of a series of points connected by lines. It is used to show how something has increased, decreased or remained the same over a period of time.

Question: What items are shown in this line graph?

Keys To Understanding A Line Graph

Line graphs have a vertical axis, which runs from top to bottom. They also have a horizontal axis, which runs from left to right.

Questions: In this graph, what does the vertical axis show?
What does the horizontal axis show?

Parts per million means that out of every million parts of air this number of parts are carbon dioxide.

CONTINUED

Interpreting A Line Graph

Start by looking at the title. It will give you an overall idea of the information being presented in the line graph.

Question: What is the title of this line graph?

To find specific information look at each point in the graph. For example, how much carbon dioxide was in the Earth's atmosphere in 1982? Slide you finger along the horizontal axis until you reach the line marked 1982. Next, run your finger up until you reach the line graph. If you look at the number scale along the vertical axis you will see the numbers at this point. You will see that for every million parts of air in 1982, there were 345 parts of carbon dioxide.

Question: How much did carbon dioxide in the Earth's atmosphere increase from 1958 to 1990?

★ CHECKING YOUR UNDERSTANDING ★

Sometimes a line graph can be used to identify a trend. A **trend** is a general direction in which the line moves. You can find a trend by following the direction of the points on the line graph. What trend do you see in this line graph?

REVIEWING YOUR UNDERSTANDING

Directions: Fill in your Vocabulary Cards. Then answer the questions that follow.

Acid Rain

What is acid rain?

What causes acid rain?

Global Warming

What is global warming?

What causes global warming?

Questions

1. List four factors that are causing damage to the Earth's environment.

2. What steps should you follow when attempting to solve a problem?

7D WHERE DO YOU STAND ON THIS ISSUE?

Sometimes citizens disagree about the laws their government should pass or the actions their society should take. In a democracy, people discuss these issues and settle them by majority rule. In this activity, you will learn how to make a decision about a public issue. Look for the following important words:

★ Issues ★ Rain Forest ★ Point of View

In a democracy, people are free to have different points of view. An **issue** is something ★ that people have opposing opinions about. Just as Americans often disagree about how to solve a problem, they sometimes disagree over what activities should be allowed or prohibited. The following is a list of issues that many Americans have disagreed about. Where do you stand on each of them?

☆ WHERE DO YOU STAND ☆			
• Should penalties for minors convicted of a crime be the same as for adults?	❐ Yes	❐ No	❐ Not Sure
• Should the government provide health care for all Americans?	❐ Yes	❐ No	❐ Not Sure
• Should the United States send soldiers to fight in foreign wars?	❐ Yes	❐ No	❐ Not Sure

HOW TO LOOK AT AN ISSUE

As a citizen in a democratic society, you will frequently be asked to take a stand on public issues such as these. In this activity, you will learn how to examine an issue. When you take a stand on a public issue, you should follow these steps:

DEFINE THE ISSUE

First, you must know what the issue is about. For example, the central point in the first issue is whether minors should be given special treatment because of their age.

LOOK AT BOTH VIEWPOINTS

Next, you must look at both sides of the issue. What are the arguments that supporters on each side of the issue make? See how well each side supports its case with facts.

For example, someone might say that harsher penalties will reduce crime. You should ask for some proof of this statement. Do states with harsher penalties really have less crime than states where penalties are not so harsh? In deciding on a public issue, be sure to weigh the advantages and disadvantages of each argument.

DECIDE WHERE YOU STAND

Lastly, after looking at both sides of the issue, you must decide what you think should be done to solve the problem or answer the question.

LOOKING AT AN ISSUE

How good are you at looking at an issue? Let's find out. First, read the following passage on an important issue:

SHOULD WE HELP PAY TO SAVE THE RAIN FORESTS?

For many years, Americans have worried about the destruction of the world's tropical **rain forests.** These forests produce a large part of the world's oxygen. They also have many unique plants and animals. Finally, tropical rain forests are home to thousands of native peoples. Most people would agree that cutting down the trees in the rain forests is wrong—but what should be done about it?

One major problem is that most rain forests are located in the world's poorest regions. Countries like Brazil, Malaysia, Ghana and Burma need the money they get from cutting and selling valuable wood from the rain forest. Also, their people are eager to have more land cleared for farming.

The World's Tropical Rain Forests

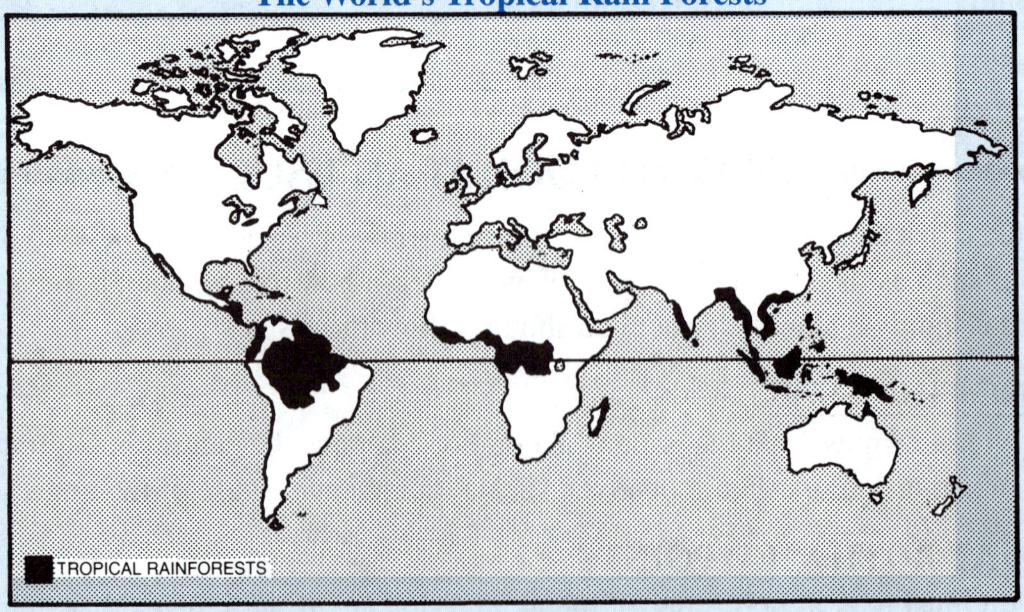

CONTINUED

The leaders of these countries argue that their citizens should not have to pay the price of protecting the environment for the rest of the world. They point out that much of Europe and North America was once forest land. No one complained when pioneers cut down the trees in these areas and farmed the land.

Recently, a new idea has been suggested. Costa Rica, Brazil and other Latin American countries have offered to stop cutting down their rain forests. In exchange, they want financial help from richer countries like the United States.

Some Americans call this idea blackmail. After all, Costa Ricans and Brazilians do not help the United States pay for its environmental clean-up. Others ask, "Why should we care?" However, many people see some justice in the Latin American idea. Why shouldn't Americans, who will share the benefits of rain forest conservation, also share some of the cost? The real question is, do we share in the cost of saving the rain forests? Or are we only willing to tell others what sacrifices they should make, while we are not willing to make sacrifices ourselves?

Part of a rain forest being cleared for a highway
Why do we need the rain forests in the world?

THINK ABOUT IT

Now that you have read about this issue, let's analyze what was stated:

1. Define the issue in the reading selection: ________ ? ________

2. Describe the two opposing points of view: ____ ? ____ ____ ? ____

3. Where do you stand on this issue? ________ ? ________

4. Explain why you took this stand: ________ ? ________

USING PRIMARY SOURCES TO EVALUATE DIFFERENT VIEWPOINTS ON AN ISSUE

EXTENDING THE ACTIVITY

Christopher Columbus claims land in the New World for Spain.
Do you think Columbus was a hero or a villain?

In this activity, you learned to examine an issue. Keep in mind that some people may view the same issue very differently. For one thing, a person's background, experiences and interests help to shape his or her viewpoint. By examining several different **points of view,** you can often reach a better understanding of the issue. This will help you to form your own opinion.

The importance of looking at different points of view is illustrated by the debate that took place about Christopher Columbus. The year 1992 marked the 500th anniversary of Columbus' first voyage across the Atlantic Ocean. Many places celebrated with exhibitions and festivities. However, the anniversary also awakened a debate about Columbus—was his voyage really a cause for celebration? Was Columbus himself a hero or a villain?

THINK ABOUT IT

Where do you stand on this issue?

Based on what you know about Christopher Columbus, do you think he was: ❐ a hero or ❐ a villain? Explain the reasons for your viewpoint.

Imagine you could go back in time and hear from some of the people who actually knew Columbus. Reports from eyewitnesses to past events are known as primary sources. They serve as a key means by which historians try to understand the past. Often different eyewitness accounts provide contrasting viewpoints of the same event. Here is what five eyewitnesses might have reported about Columbus.

Columbus came to us in 1486 with a plan to sail west to the Indies. He promised us wealth and power. After six years, we finally gave him the ships and supplies he needed. We agreed to give him part of all the riches if he kept his word. Columbus did obtain new lands for Spain. His discovery made us the richest nation in the world. We ate new foods and used new products because of him. Columbus widened our horizons. Because of him, we now realize the world is a larger place than we ever imagined.

King Ferdinand and Queen Isabella of Spain

Columbus was feared and respected by our crew. We left Spain on August 3, 1492, sailing west. We had no idea what we would find or even if we would return. Many of the crew believed the world was flat. If you sailed far enough out on the ocean, you would fall off the edge. When we lost sight of land, many of the men cried, fearing they might not live to see land again. By early October, most of the crew were ready to kill Columbus and turn the ship back. Luckily for Columbus, land was sighted just in time.

Peralonsa Niño, member of Columbus' crew

Columbus was probably the greatest man who ever lived. His wisdom and courage allowed him to reach land by sailing west. His discovery of the Western Hemisphere introduced its native peoples to our Christian teachings. These people were not believers in our Christian faith. They now have a chance to save their souls and enter the heavenly gates. Columbus' discovery led to riches and power for our country. We have been able to teach the natives to grow new crops, to speak new languages and to lead lives as good Christians.

Father Marchena, a Spanish priest

Columbus was a man without feelings for us. The arrival of Columbus was a horrible event for our people. He claimed our homeland for his masters. When he returned to Spain, he left many of his men on our island. They bullied our people. I finally led an attack of our warriors against them. We killed them all and burned down their settlement. But the next year, Columbus returned with 17 ships. He sent many of our people to Spain as slaves. His soldiers and cannons defeated us in battle. Soon we were all slaves. Meanwhile, thousands of my people died from mysterious diseases these invaders brought with them.

Chief Caonabo of the Taino Native Americans

THINK ABOUT IT

Answer the following questions:

1. How **reliable** (*trustworthy, dependable*) do you think each view of Columbus is?

- ☆ the rulers of Spain: __?__ ☆ the Spanish priest: __?__
- ☆ the crew member: __?__ ☆ the Taino Chief: __?__

2. Were any of these speakers affected by their situations?

- ☆ Did being the rulers of Spain affect the point of view of King Ferdinand and Queen Isabella? Explain.
- ☆ Did being a crew member on Columbus' ship affect Niño's point of view? Explain.
- ☆ Did being a Spanish priest influence Father Marchena's point of view? Explain.
- ☆ Did being a Taino Chief affect Caonabo's point of view about Columbus? Explain.

3. Based on these different points of view, do you now think Christopher Columbus was: ❐ a **hero** or ❐ a **villain?** Explain your answer.

REVIEWING YOUR UNDERSTANDING

Directions: Fill in your Vocabulary Cards. Then complete the project that follows.

Issue

What is an issue?

How is an issue different from a problem?

Point of View

Define "point of view."

How is it often affected by a person's position or background?

Conducting Research With Primary and Secondary Sources

In this activity, you looked at the issue of saving the rain forests. Assume your teacher assigned the class a research project on this topic. List **three** primary and **three** secondary sources you could use to find information about your topic.

The Case of the Spotted Owl

Read the following passage and answer the questions that follow.

A few years ago, the fate of the northern spotted owl became a national issue. The small bird was close to becoming **extinct** (*no more of its kind would exist*). At this point, the national government stepped in to protect the northern spotted owl.

There already was a law for saving wildlife threatened by human development. Animal **species** (*types*) in danger of extinction were placed on a special list. The law made it a crime to harm these listed species in any way or to destroy the areas where they lived. Environmentalists proudly pointed out that this approach had already saved the bald eagle and the gray whale. The government added the northern spotted owl to the endangered species list.

A **logger** is a person who earns his or her living by cutting down trees for lumber. Loggers and their families saw the situation very differently. To them, the new law seemed to value the survival of rare birds over their jobs and families. Since the government began protecting the spotted owl, millions of acres of woodland in Oregon and Washington, mostly in national forests, were no longer available for cutting down trees.

Loggers earn their living by cutting trees for lumber. *Should they be prevented from cutting trees down when this threatens the homes of rare birds?*

The timber industry predicted that 300,000 jobs and millions of dollars in timber sales would be lost as a result of the law. The loggers and their families took their case to the U.S. Supreme Court. They hoped to get some of the new rules relaxed. However, the Supreme Court supported the government's power to protect wildlife. A large part of the spotted owl's living area was saved, even though the cost fell mainly on one industry.

1. What was the issue in this story?
2. Do you think the government should be able to limit the use of land in order to protect certain species?
3. Which side of the debate would you have supported? Explain your answer.

7E SHOULD WE LIMIT THE AMOUNT OF VIOLENCE SHOWN ON TELEVISION?

This activity again looks at the role of the citizen in discussing and resolving public issues. In this activity, you will examine a public issue by reading different sources. Then you will form your own conclusions and write a letter explaining your views. Look for the following important words:

✦ Informed Decision ✦ Editorials ✦ News Articles

Should the President send soldiers to other countries to protect U.S. citizens there?

Should your town spend money to build a new library?

Should your county raise taxes to build a homeless shelter?

These are the kinds of public issues that citizens often think about and discuss. When you are 18 years old you will be able to take a stand on these and other issues by voting. To be an informed voter, you must learn to make decisions on public issues. In this activity, you will have a chance to practice this important skill.

STEPS TO MAKING AN INFORMED DECISION

★ In making **informed decisions** on public issues, you will need to:

1. Identify the problem or issue	For example, you might be concerned that watching violence on television often leads people to become violent in real life.
2. Get information from several sources	The more sources you look at, the more information you will find. You will also get the benefit of different points of view.
3. Evaluate the information	You should compare what each of your sources of information has to say about the problem or issue. Be sure to separate facts from opinions.
4. Identify and compare possible solutions	You should think of all the possible ways of dealing with the problem or issue. Then you will list the advantages and disadvantages of each way and compare them.
5. Make your own decision	Finally, after comparing different solutions, you will choose the solution you think is best. You may be able to come up with a compromise of several views. A **compromise** is a solution in which each side gives up something, but also gets something in return.

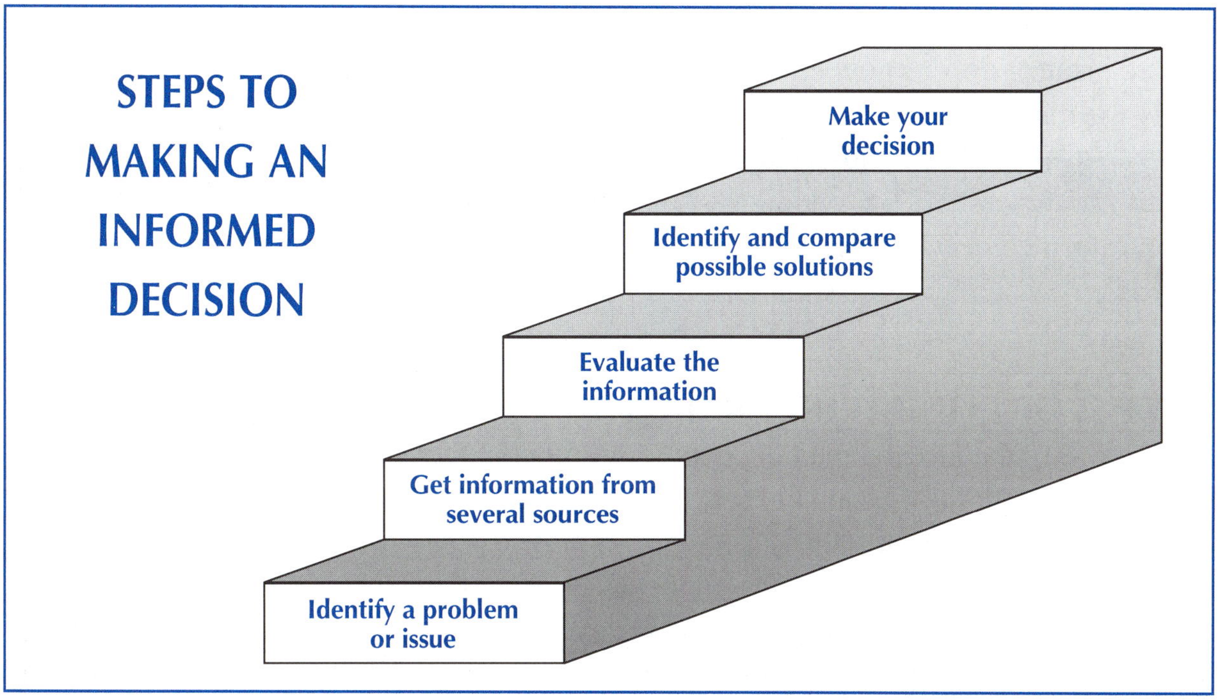

To better understand these steps and how they can help you make an informed decision, let's take a look at a real-life example in which you are asked to make an informed decision.

WOULD YOU SIGN A PETITION TO LIMIT TELEVISION VIOLENCE?

One evening at dinner, you are telling your parent what you learned in school about making informed decisions. Just then, someone rings your doorbell. It is one of your neighbors. He is holding some pamphlets and a **petition** (*a request for some action sent to a person or group in authority*).

STEP 1: IDENTIFYING THE PROBLEM OR ISSUE

Your neighbor reads the petition to both of you. It is addressed to your representative in Congress. The petition states that violence shown on television is one of the major reasons for increasing violence throughout our nation.

> The petition asks Congress to pass a new law limiting the amount of violence shown on television.

Your neighbor asks your parent to sign the petition. Signing the petition would mean that your parent agrees that such a law is needed. Before signing, your parent would like to think more about it.

After your neighbor leaves, your parent turns to you and says: "This is an important public issue. I don't know enough about it yet to make up my mind. Why don't we apply the method you learned in school today about making an informed decision?"

★ CHECKING YOUR UNDERSTANDING ★

An informed decision begins by identifying the problem or issue. What is the problem raised by your neighbor?

STEP 2: OBTAINING INFORMATION FROM SEVERAL SOURCES

In order to make an informed decision, you must gather information about the problem or issue from different sources. Using reference books is a good place to begin. They give you information about the problem or issue. Also, they can tell you where to find other information, such as articles written by experts.

★ CHECKING YOUR UNDERSTANDING ★

Encyclopedias and almanacs are good starting points for any investigation. Some topics you may want to look up are:

Encyclopedia:	***Almanac:***
1. Television	**1.** Number of violent crimes last year

How is television controlled? Who decides what is shown?
What other topics do you think might help you on this issue?

More information about an issue or problem can be found in newspapers, books, magazines and TV news reports. As you learned earlier, be careful to separate **facts** from **opinions.**

Your parent suggests that you visit the library together. After speaking with the librarian, you find these four sources of information:

1. An article from *The Encyclopedia of Science* about television.

2. A newspaper story from the *Texas Times* on teenage violence.

3. An editorial from the magazine, *The Texas News and World Report.*

4. A page from a book about how to raise children.

STEP 3: EVALUATING THE INFORMATION

Bringing together different sources of information is an important step in making an informed decision. Next, you have to read and compare the different sources. Let's take a look at the first of the sources you found in the library.

Source: THE ENCYCLOPEDIA OF SCIENCE

Television. The first television broadcasts began in the 1930s. The introduction of television raised an important question: Should television stations be run by the government or by private companies? In some countries, the government runs all the television channels and controls what shows will appear. In the United States, private companies run the television channels. We have a tradition of free speech and free press. As a result, the government usually cannot tell TV companies what to show. However, the government does not let the private television stations do just anything they want. The government still has the power to refuse to allow some shows to be aired. It rarely uses this right, but it always can.

Now you have read some background information about the history of television.

★ Checking Your Understanding ★

1. What question did the introduction of television raise?

2. How was this question answered in the United States?

3. What powers does the government have in the United States when it comes to television?

See whether the following statements are facts or opinions. If you can't recall the difference between a fact and an opinion, you may want to look back at Activity 4C. For **opinions only,** decide whether you agree or disagree.

In some countries, the government controls television.
Is this a fact or an opinion? (❒ Agree ❒ Disagree)

Television shows always influence what people do in real life.
Is this a fact or an opinion? (❒ Agree ❒ Disagree)

Now that you have learned something about the background of television, let's look at the second source of information you found—a newspaper article.

Source: THE TEXAS TIMES

Texas Times

First Edition — Friday

TWO TEENS DIE IN HIGHWAY "DARE"

It all began as a joke. On Thursday night, Channel 3 was showing the latest action-adventure picture. In the movie, several teenagers lie down on the center divider line of a highway to show their friends they are not afraid.

After watching the movie, teenagers from Dallas began daring each other to lie down on the center line of the highway, just as the teenagers in the movie had done. Two teenagers took the dare, and now they are dead—run over by a driver who could not see them in the dark.

This is part of a growing number of violent, senseless deaths in America. Movies and television shows often influence us. Sometimes, we imitate what we see, as these teenagers did. Other times, we are influenced without even knowing it.

Parents, teachers and doctors across the nation are becoming alarmed at the growing amount of violence shown on television. Children watching television see thousands of acts of violence before they are old enough to go to school. Even cartoons often show violence between the cartoon characters. Some experts believe television violence may be partly responsible for the increasing violence in America.

★ CHECKING YOUR UNDERSTANDING ★

1. What did this newspaper story have to say about violence on television?

2. Why are some people alarmed about the growing amount of violence on television?

See whether the following statements are facts or opinions. For **opinions only,** decide whether you agree or disagree.

Children see many acts of violence on television.
Is this a fact or an opinion? (❒ Agree ❒ Disagree)

Violence on television often causes violence in real life.
Is this a fact or an opinion? (❒ Agree ❒ Disagree)

Next, let's look at the third source of information you found—a newspaper editorial.

NEWSPAPER EDITORIAL

Editorials are opinions written in newspapers and magazines. They are not **news articles,** which report facts. Editorials represent the opinions of the editors. This allows them to speak out on topics that concern them. When trying to make an informed decision, you should read editorials in several different newspapers and magazines. This allows you to learn about the various opinions that people have on the topic. ★

Source: THE TEXAS NEWS AND WORLD REPORT, EDITORIAL

A growing number of people are seeking a new law to limit the violence shown on television. Have these people carefully thought about the issue? They think that violence on television is the main cause of violence in America. They are wrong. Poverty and the large number of guns are the main causes of violence.

Have the people in favor of this new law thought about the dangers of government control? Who in the government will decide which television programs are violent and which are not? Will the government also prevent stations from reporting violent stories on the news? Once the government can control some subjects on television, it may try to control other subjects. Soon, the government might control everything we see. This violates our rights of free speech and a free press.

We believe it is better to let private television stations show what they want. Parents should decide what their children can watch. If parents don't want their children to watch a television show because it is too violent, there is a simple remedy. All they need to do is to change the channel or turn off the set. Once we allow the government to control what we watch, who can say where government controls will end?

★ CHECKING YOUR UNDERSTANDING ★

What does this editorial tell you about allowing the government to control what private television stations can show?

See whether the following statements are facts or opinions. For **opinions only,** decide whether you agree or disagree.

Parents, not the government, should decide what their children watch on television.
Is this a fact or opinion? (❐ Agree ❐ Disagree)

Some people are asking for a new law to limit the violence on television.
Is this a fact or opinion? (❐ Agree ❐ Disagree)

Your last source of information is a book about bringing up children.

Source: "HOW TO RAISE CHILDREN: ADVICE FOR PARENTS"

Page 231

Nightmares. As we all know, nightmares are terrifying. They are dreams in which the dreamer feels helpless, afraid or sad. Tests show children are the ones most likely to suffer from nightmares. Children may seem to enjoy television programs that show violence. However, once the children are asleep, they often suffer from terrible nightmares caused by these programs.

Educational Television. Since the 1960s, there have been many attempts to create interesting television programs. There are many shows that are both educational and fun for children to watch. The most successful of these has been "Sesame Street." Tests show that three-year olds watching Sesame Street regularly do better in learning some skills than those who do not watch the program.

★ CHECKING YOUR UNDERSTANDING ★

1. What does the book say about nightmares?
2. What does the book say about how television can shape our behavior?

See whether the following statements are facts or opinions. For **opinions only,** decide whether you agree or disagree.

Some children who see violence on television have nightmares.
Is this a fact or an opinion? (❒ Agree ❒ Disagree)

There are many shows that are fun to watch.
Is this a fact or an opinion? (❒ Agree ❒ Disagree)

STEP 4: IDENTIFYING AND COMPARING POSSIBLE SOLUTIONS

You have just completed reading several sources. Now go back to the original issue: **Should the government limit the amount of violence shown on television?** Think of all the possible ways of dealing with this issue. For example, if the problem is not very serious, it may be best to do nothing. If the problem is very serious, maybe the government should stop all violence shown on television.

The next page has a list of possible solutions. Copy the chart on a separate sheet of paper. For each solution, write its advantages and disadvantages. Then compare the advantages and disadvantages of each solution with those of the other solutions.

Possible Solutions— The government should:	Advantages	Disadvantages
☆ make no changes	?	?
☆ rate television shows like movies, based on the amount of violence they show	?	?
☆ ban all violent television shows before 10 o'clock at night	?	?
☆ ban all violent shows	?	?
☆ *(you fill in)* ____________	?	?

STEP 5: MAKING YOUR DECISION

Now that you have compared the advantages and disadvantages of each solution, it is time to make an informed decision. There is usually no "correct" answer; all solutions have some advantages and disadvantages. Based on your own analysis, number the solutions in order, from the best solution (#1) to the worst solution (#5).

Possible Solutions— The Government Should:	Number
☆ make no changes	?
☆ rate television shows like movies, based on the violence they show	?
☆ ban all violent television shows before 10 o'clock at night	?
☆ ban all violent shows	?
☆ (you fill in)	?

Remember your neighbor's petition? Now that you have made an informed decision, would you recommend that your parent sign it? ❐ Yes ❐ No

WRITING TO YOUR REPRESENTATIVE IN CONGRESS

EXTENDING THE ACTIVITY

Maybe you should try to convince others that you have made the best possible decision. Make a copy and then complete the following letter, based on what you have decided.

(your address)
(your city and state)
(date)

The Honorable *(name of representative)*
U.S. House of Representatives
Washington, D.C. 20515

Dear *(name of representative)* :

My name is ______. I live in *(your city or town)* . You are my representative in the United States Congress. I believe that violence on television *(should/should not)* be limited by Congress. I have taken this position because of the following reasons ______ .

How do you feel about this issue? I would appreciate your letting me know your views on this issue.

Sincerely,
(your signature)

MAILING YOUR LETTER

You should consider actually mailing your letter to your Congressperson in Washington, D.C. Your representatives like to hear from the citizens they represent. After you have written your letter, put it in an envelope addressed to your representative.

Your Name
Address
City, Texas Zip Code

The Honorable *(name of representative)*
c/o The United States House of Representatives
House Office Building
Washington, D.C. 20515

REVIEWING YOUR UNDERSTANDING

Directions: Fill in your Vocabulary Cards. Then answer the question that follows.

Editorial
What is an editorial?
How are editorials helpful in
making an informed decision?

News Article
What is a news article ?
How is a news article different
from an editorial?

Steps in Making an Informed Decision

In the following graphic organizer, fill in the steps a person must take to make an informed decision:

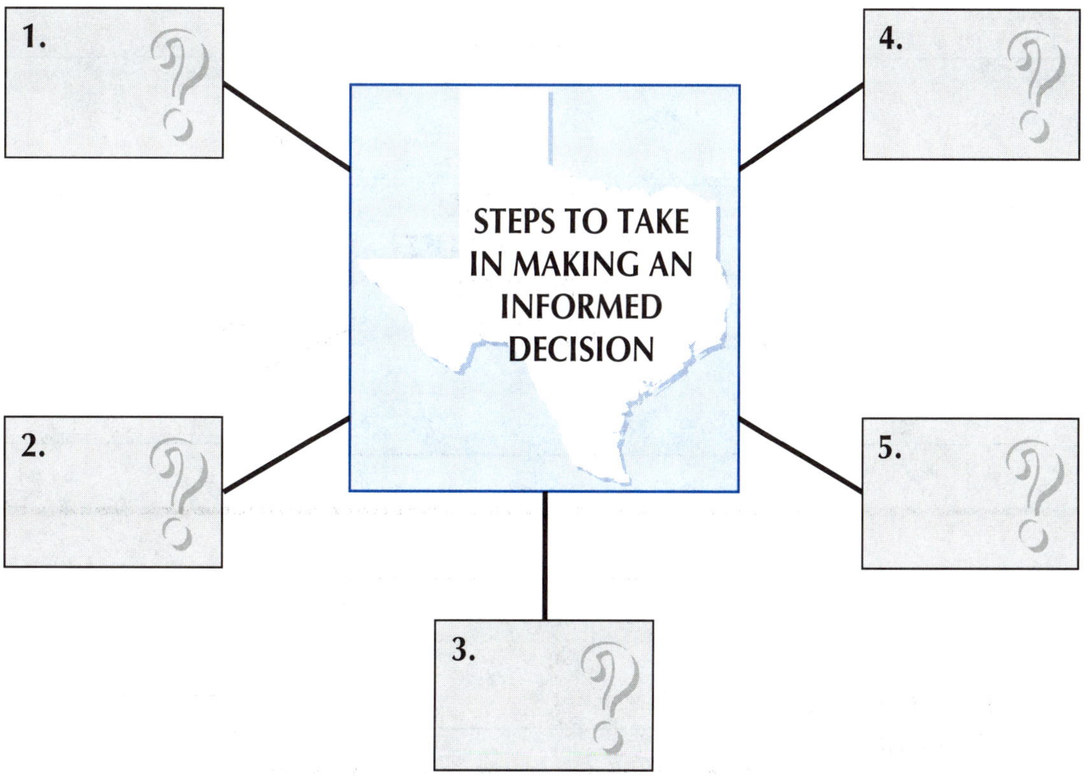

SUMMARIZING YOUR UNDERSTANDING

Directions: Use your knowledge to complete the following graphic organizers.

CHARACTERISTICS OF A "GOOD" CITIZEN

1.

2.

3.

4.

DESCRIBE THE APPROACH TO USE IN PROBLEM SOLVING

1.

2.

3.

4.

STEPS TO TAKE WHEN TAKING A STAND ON AN ISSUE

1.

2.

3.

FACTS AND FIGURES ABOUT TEXAS CITIZENS

DID YOU KNOW THAT …

THAT'S SOME LOAD OF DOCUMENTS

In 1997, the George Bush Presidential Library will open on the campus of Texas A&M University in College Station. This will be the second Presidential Library in Texas (the Lyndon Johnson Presidential Library in Austin is the first). The new library will house 36 million pages of documents. Each will tell about a small part of the Bush Presidency.

WHAT'S IN A NAME?

Nogalus is a small town in Trinity County. It got its name under strange circumstances. When the town was first settled, it lacked enough money to build its own gallows to hang horse thieves and other desperadoes. Instead, criminals were hanged from a tree limb. At first, the town was called Nogallows—literally meaning "no gallows." However, when a post office was built in 1858, they made it Nogallis Prairie. In 1894, the name was changed to what it is called today—Nogalus.

RUBBING SHOULDERS WITH THE PRESIDENT

In 1935, Sarah T. Hughes was the first woman chosen as a district judge in Texas. Ms. Hughes was re-elected seven times. She caught the attention of President John F. Kennedy, who appointed her the state's first female federal judge in 1961. Her name was further noted in the history books when, following President Kennedy's assassination in 1963, she was chosen to swear in Lyndon Johnson as the 36th President of the United States.

A MUSEUM THAT PEOPLE ARE DYING TO SEE

Texas has many unique museums. Did you know it even has a museum to honor the funeral parlour industry? In Houston, the Funeral Service Museum houses the largest collection of funeral memorabilia. You can find on display many funeral-related items—horse-drawn hearses, a funeral sleigh and cast-iron caskets.

CLOSING ACTIVITY

THE IMAGE I NOW HAVE OF TEXAS IS ___?___

At the beginning of this book, you were invited to take a journey through Texas—its land and its people. When you started out, you wrote what Texas meant to you. Your trip through Texas has covered its geography, history, people, economy and government. It has been a long journey, but you have learned a great deal.

WHAT DOES "TEXAS" MEAN TO YOU NOW?

Your journey is about to come to an end. We want you to think once again about what Texas means to you. One way to do this is to create an "ABC" book about Texas. Your "ABC" book about Texas should have the following:

- ☆ Each page should feature a different letter of the alphabet. Each letter should appear on a separate page.
- ☆ Each page should describe something different that you have learned about Texas' geography, history, people, economy or government.
- ☆ Each page should have a different illustration. These illustrations could be drawings you make yourself or pictures you cut-out or photocopy from a newspaper, magazine or book. Each illustration must have a description or explanation.

Here is a sample of how one page dealing with the letter "A" might look:

Aa

Austin

Located on the north bank of the Colorado River, Austin became the capital of Texas in 1839. The city was named after Stephen F. Austin, the "Father of Texas." Austin serves as the center of Texas state government and the northeast gateway to the Texas Hill Country.

To help you organize your ABC book about Texas, copy the following chart:

LETTER	ACTION	DESCRIPTION	ILLUSTRATION
A			
B			
C			
D			
E			
F			
G			
H			
I			
J			
K			
L			
M			
N			
O			
P			
Q			
R			
S			
T			
U			
V			
W			
X			
Y			
Z			

CANADA
ATLANTIC OCEAN
GULF OF MEXICO
PACIFIC OCEAN
MEXICO
CUBA
BAHAMAS
Scale of Miles
0 250 500
MAINE
Augusta
N.H.
Concord
VT.
Montpelier
MASS.
Boston
Providence
RHODE I.
Hartford
NEW YORK
Albany
Syracuse
Buffalo
New York
Trenton
NEW JERSEY
DEL.
Dover
Annapolis
MD.
WASH. D.C.
PENNSYLVANIA
Allentown
Harrisburg
Pittsburgh
VIRGINIA
Richmond
Roanoke
WEST VA.
Charleston
N. CAROLINA
Raleigh
Charlotte
S. CAROLINA
Columbia
Charleston
GEORGIA
Savannah
Atlanta
Columbus
FLORIDA
Jacksonville
Orlando
Tampa
Miami
Tallahassee
OHIO
Cleveland
Columbus
Cincinnati
MICH.
Detroit
Lansing
Grand Rapids
Lake Huron
Lake Michigan
Lake Superior
INDIANA
South Bend
Indianapolis
KENTUCKY
Frankfort
Lexington
Louisville
Ohio R.
TENNESSEE
Knoxville
Nashville
Memphis
Tenness R.
ALABAMA
Birmingham
Montgomery
Mobile
MISSISSIPPI
Jackson
LOUISIANA
New Orleans
Baton Rouge
Shreveport
Mississippi R.
ILLINOIS
Chicago
Peoria
Springfield
WISCONSIN
Milwaukee
Madison
MINNESOTA
Duluth
St. Paul
Minneapolis
Mississippi R.
Cedar Rapids
Des Moines
Sioux City
MISSOURI
St. Louis
Jefferson City
Springfield
Kansas City
Missouri R.
ARKANSAS
Little Rock
Arkansas R.
OKLAHOMA
Tulsa
Oklahoma City
Red R.
TEXAS
Dallas
Fort Worth
Houston
Austin
San Antonio
Corpus Christi
Amarillo
Lubbock
El Paso
Brazos R.
Colorado R.
Rio Grande R.
Pecos R.
Canadian R.
KANSAS
Topeka
Wichita
Arkansas R.
NEBRASKA
Omaha
Lincoln
Platte R.
Missouri R.
SOUTH DAKOTA
Sioux Falls
Pierre
NORTH DAKOTA
Bismarck
Fargo
COLORADO
Denver
Colorado Springs
Grand Junction
Colorado R.
NEW MEXICO
Santa Fe
Albuquerque
WYOMING
Cheyenne
Sheridan
Bighorn R.
Powder R.
MONTANA
Billings
Helena
Missoula
Missouri R.
Yellowstone R.
Milk R.
IDAHO
Boise
Pocatello
Snake R.
UTAH
Salt Lake City
Provo
Green R.
ARIZONA
Flagstaff
Phoenix
Tucson
Gila R.
NEVADA
Las Vegas
Reno
Carson City
CALIFORNIA
Sacramento
San Francisco
Fresno
Bakersfield
Los Angeles
San Diego
OREGON
Portland
Salem
Eugene
Pendleton
Klamath Falls
WASHINGTON
Seattle
Olympia
Spokane
Columbia R.
HAWAII
Honolulu
Hilo
PACIFIC OCEAN
0 Miles 200
ALASKA
CANADA
RUSSIA
Juneau
Fairbanks
Anchorage
Barrow
Nome
Yukon R.
Kuskokwim R.
Beaufort Sea
Gulf of Alaska
Bering Sea
0 Miles 500

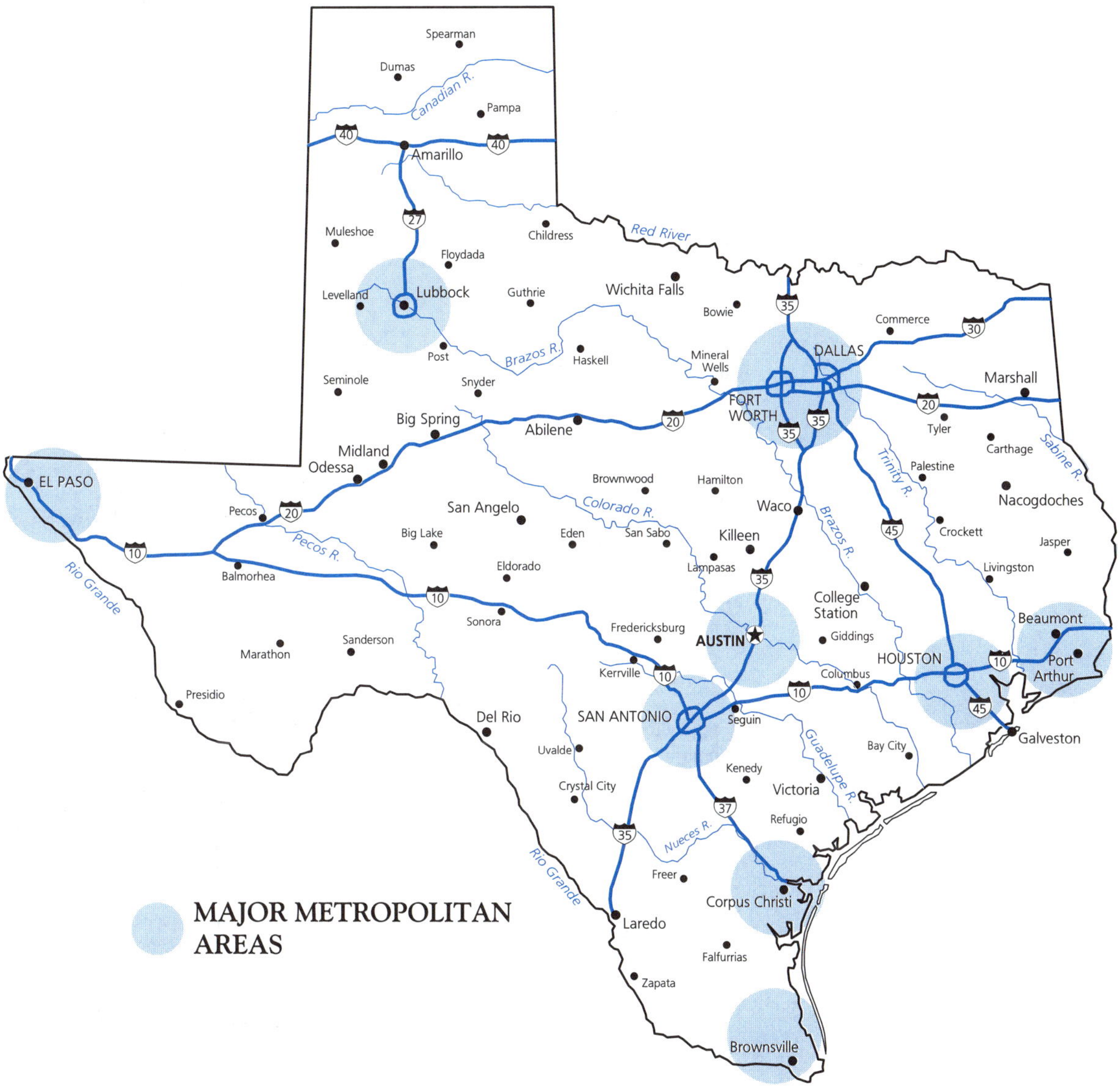
Spearman
Dumas
Canadian R.
Pampa
40
40
Amarillo
27
Muleshoe
Childress
Red River
Floydada
Levelland
Lubbock
Guthrie
Wichita Falls
Bowie
35
Commerce
30
Post
Brazos R.
Haskell
Mineral Wells
DALLAS
Marshall
Seminole
Snyder
FORT WORTH
20
Big Spring
20
Abilene
35
35
Tyler
Carthage
Sabine R.
Midland
Odessa
Trinity R.
Palestine
EL PASO
Brownwood
Hamilton
Nacogdoches
Pecos
20
San Angelo
Colorado R.
Waco
Brazos R.
10
Pecos R.
Big Lake
Eden
San Saba
Killeen
45
Crockett
Jasper
Balmorhea
Eldorado
Lampasas
Livingston
Rio Grande
10
35
College Station
Beaumont
Sonora
Fredericksburg
AUSTIN
Giddings
Marathon
Sanderson
HOUSTON
10
Port Arthur
Kerrville
10
Columbus
10
Presidio
Del Rio
SAN ANTONIO
Seguin
45
Galveston
Uvalde
Bay City
Guadalupe R.
Kenedy
Crystal City
Victoria
37
Refugio
35
Nueces R.
Rio Grande
Freer
Corpus Christi
MAJOR METROPOLITAN AREAS
Laredo
Falfurrias
Zapata
Brownsville

INDEX